I0754368

I remain your's &c.

John McMillan

P.S. Duval & Co. steam lith. press, Phila.

OLD REDSTONE;

OR,

Historical Sketches

OF

WESTERN PRESBYTERIANISM,

ITS

EARLY MINISTERS, ITS PERILOUS TIMES,

AND

ITS FIRST RECORDS.

BY

JOSEPH SMITH, D.D.

"Remember the days of old; consider the years of many generations: ask thy father, and he will show thee: thy elders, and they will tell thee."—DEUT. xxxii. 7.

PHILADELPHIA:
LIPPINCOTT, GRAMBO & CO.
1854.

TO THE

REV. WILLIAM WYLIE, D.D.,

THE

REV. FRANCIS HERRON, D.D.,

AND THE

REV. ROBERT JOHNSTON,

THIS HUMBLE ATTEMPT

TO ERECT A MONUMENT

TO

THE MEMORY OF OUR PIOUS FOREFATHERS,

IS,

WITH FILIAL AFFECTION AND VENERATION,

INSCRIBED.

J. S.

JULY 30, 1854.

TO THE READER.

In the preparation of the work, now submitted to your inspection, we have availed ourselves of every source of information, to which we could obtain access. The "History of Western Pennsylvania," (the author of which is not given in the title page,)—the "History of Pittsburg" and the "Olden Time," both from the able pen of Neville B. Craig, Esq.—"Day's Historical Collections of Pennsylvania"—"Howe's Historical Collections of Virginia," and also of "Ohio"—"Foote's Ecclesiastical Sketches of North Carolina and of Virginia"—"Davidson's Ecclesiastical History of Kentucky"—the printed "Records of the Synod of New York and Philadelphia"—"Alexander's 'Log College'"—"Miller's Life of Dr. Rogers"—"Miller's (J. P.) Sketches and Sermons"—the "Western Missionary Magazine"—"The American Pioneer,"—"Brackenridges's, Findley's, and Carnahan's 'Western Insurrection'"—"Colonial Records of Pennsylvania," and "Hazard's Pennsylvania Archives," and numerous other works, have been carefully consulted. We are also greatly indebted to the Rev. Dr. Elliott, William Darby, Esq., N. B. Craig, Esq., the Rev. Lemuel F. Leake, the Rev. Dr. Jacob Lindley and the Rev. Dr. William Wylie, for essential aid in a great variety of particulars. We might indeed greatly extend this list of kind friends who have rendered us special service. But perhaps it is unnecessary to parade the names of all in a matter of this kind. We cannot forbear to mention that Wilson Shannon, Esq., Ex-Governor of Ohio, has given us much assistance in procuring some valuable sources of information from Washington City. To the Rev. Dr. Carnahan, of Princeton, and the Rev. Dr. Van Renselaer, of Philadelphia, we are under special obligations also. We have not deemed it necessary to crowd our pages with references to our authorities, knowing that but few readers would thank us for that trouble, and that those who are concerned to be accurately informed in any particular, will have no difficulty, in most instances, in referring to many of the sources to which we have thus in general referred.

The celebrated Scottish geologist, Hugh Miller, has written a book about the "Old Red Sandstone." To the scientific world, it has been a rare treat. We cannot spread before you such a repast, if your taste inclines you to revel upon "Ichthyosauri," "Glyptolepes," "Diplopteri," "Chondropterygii," and other such euphonious sounds in the science of Palaeontology. But we offer you a book about "Old Redstone"—its Presbytery, its men, and its times. To the mere geologist, such a work can have few attractions. But we doubt not that such a a Christian geologist as Professor Miller would not disdain to turn from "Old Red Sandstone," to "Old Redstone."

Fire was perhaps the agent in the present condition of the former. The fires of many sore trials and sorrows conspired to reform and fit for Heaven, the men of the latter. When the final conflagration shall have melted down, and consumed forever the former, Old Redstone Christians shall shine as the stars in the firmament of Heaven. Let us tell you of those times and of the leaders of the sacramental host. Much is irretrievably lost that ought to be told. No pains have been spared to gather up the fragments that have been left; and here are some of them, gentle reader, at your service. More are at hand, should they ever be called for.

The Biographical Sketches which appear in this volume, were prepared for publication in the form of "notes" to the "Records of Presbytery." After the work had been placed in the hands of the Stereotyper, this plan was changed, but by a misunderstanding on the part of the Printer, the sketches of the Rev. Messrs. Brice and Hughes were left in the form of "notes." Although this circumstance cannot affect the value of those sketches, and much less the character of those eminent men, we have thought this statement due to all concerned, lest any misapprehension might arise.

ELIZABETH, July, 1854.

CONTENTS.

PAGE

INTRODUCTION.—Reasons why the Reminiscences of Early Western Presbyterianism should be collected and preserved . . . PAGE 11

CHAPTER I.—An Historical Sketch of the Western Country, from its first settlement 21

Life and Times of the Rev. Joseph Smith, and some notices of Mrs. E. Smith 51

CHAPTER II.—Manners, Customs, Usages, and Domestic Circumstances of the Country, prior to, and during the existence of the old Redstone Presbytery 93

CHAPTER III.—History of the early Efforts to introduce the Gospel; including some account of the Rev. Charles Beatty, one of the first Missionaries 111

CHAPTER IV.—General Facts and Circumstances, respecting the Old Presbytery and its members 128

A Sketch of the Life of the Rev. Thaddeus Dod 139

CHAPTER V.—Houses of Worship, Sacramental Scenes, Stoves in Churches, Baptisms, Catechising, Privations, &c. 152

A Sketch of the Life of the Rev. Dr. John M'Millan 166

CHAPTER VI.—The Rural State of Presbyterianism in the West seventy years ago; Religious Conversation then prevalent . 216

PAGE

A Biographical Sketch of the Rev. Dr. James Power, with some account of the Burning of Hanna's-town, which occurred in one of his Congregations 225

CHAPTER VII. — Temperance, and the Whiskey Insurrection 250

CHAPTER VIII.—The Bright Side of the Picture — the Sources of support, comfort and joy which our fathers experienced . 269

A Biographical Sketch of the Rev. James Finley 279

CHAPTER IX.—The Views and Practice of our forefathers on the subject of Psalmody 290

A Biographical Sketch of the Rev. John Clark 297

A Biographical Sketch of the Rev. James Dunlap, D.D. 301

CHAPTER X.—Early Troubles of our Ministers and People about State Boundaries 304

CHAPTER XI.—Other Evangelical Bodies in the West 307

RECORDS OF THE PRESBYTERY OF REDSTONE — from 1781 to 1793, with copious Notes, &c. 311

NOTE 1. Redstone — Origin of the Name 311

" 2. First Meeting of the Presbytery of Redstone, one month before the Surrender of Cornwallis, at Yorktown 312

" 3. Pigeon Creek Congregation, History of 312

" 4. 1781-2, Years of Trial and Sorrow 314

" 5. Dunlap's Creek Congregation, History of 315

" 6. Mr. Dod's Absence from Presbytery: Why? 316

" 7. James Edgar, Judge, Sketch of his Life 316

" 8. Ohio Court-house 318

" 9. Westminster Directory, about Marriage 318

" 10. Pennsylvania Law about Marriage 321

" 11. Congregational Settlements, their Remarkable Origin ... 322

" 12. Mount Pleasant Congregation, History of 323

" 13. Buffalo Congregation, History of 326

" 14. Pittsburg, singular History of 327

" 15. Chartiers Congregation, History of 329

PAGE

NOTE 16. Dr. Ewing, the Boundary Line, and the Bibles 331
" 17. Rehoboth and Roundhill Congregations 332
" 18. Strange Circumstance about Mr. Finley's Dismission from New Castle Presbytery 334
" 19. Mr. Hughey, Hughy, or Huey, his Slippery Name and Character 336
" 20. Fast-day, Reference to previous Revivals 336
" 21. The action of Presbytery about the lax Administration of Baptism 338
" 22. Mr. Addison: Why not received...................... 339
" 23. Mr. Addison turned Lawyer, and became a Judge 340
" 24. John Brice, Sketch of his Life 343
" 25. James Hughes, Sketch of his Life 344
" 26. Waite Cornwell, Some Account of 348
" 27. Lebanon Congregation, History of 351
" 28. 1787, Why a Remarkable Year 351
" 29. Bethel Congregation, History of...................... 353
" 30. The New England Emigrants 355
" 31. John Coleman, His Singular Case 356
" 32. James M'Gready, Sketch of the Life of 359
" 33. The Presbytery requiring Promises of Parents 359
" 34. John M'Pherrin, Sketch of the Life of 367
" 35. Samuel Porter, A Brief Memoir of 368
" 36. First Commissioners to the General Assembly 374
" 37. Pittsburg Congregation, History of 375
" 38. Laurel Hill Congregation, History of 383
" 39. Raccoon Congregation, History of, and of the Rev. Joseph Patterson 384
" 40. Short Creek Congregation, History of 411
" 41. George Hill, Sketch of his Life 414
" 42. Mr. Hanna, Some Account of, and of Morris County Presbytery 419
" 43. William Swan, Sketch of his Life 421
" 44. Canonsburg Presbyterial Academy: What became of it. 429

PAGE

NOTE 45. Jacob Jennings, Sketch of the Life of 429
" 46. Disasters of 1790–1—Fast-day: Why 428
" 47. Thomas Marquis, Sketch of the Life of 432
" 48. Robert Marshall, Sketch of the Life of 439
" 49. Fairfield Congregation, History of 441
" 50. David Smith, Sketch of the Life of 443
" 51. Long Run and Sewickly Churches 450

Appendix 456

INTRODUCTION.

The Lord commanded his people, in ancient times, to stand in the ways, and see and ask for the old paths, where is the good way, and walk therein; promising them that thus they should find rest for their souls. In the right performance of this duty, essential aid has often been obtained from well-directed inquiries into the history of God's methods of providence and grace, with his people, in earlier times. The history of the trials and conflicts of the church, while engaged in the discharge of her great mission — "to display her banner, because of the truth" — is fraught with lessons "profitable for doctrine, for reproof, for correction, for instruction in righteousness." But every portion of the church has not equal claims upon all, in regard to the earlier periods of her life. Nor can the story of such times be invested with a like *interest* to every portion of the Christian world. New England Christians must always read with absorbing interest the narratives of the adventures, trials, and sorrows of their pilgrim fathers. Methodists must feel a peculiar interest in the life and character of their great founder. Western Baptists cannot soon forget the thrilling story of their noble pioneer, *John Corbley*. Can Western Presbyterians cease to cherish a grateful remembrance of those who were instrumental in laying the foundations of our western Zion? But does the early history of Trans-Allegheny Presbyterianism possess any special claims to attention, apart from an affectionate interest in the history of our own ancestors? Does this section of our church that was first organized west of the mountains, challenge inquiry into its early times, on any other grounds? We think it does. We will suggest two or three reasons additional, why such inquiry may be made, without being subjected to the charge of vanity or arrogance.

1. In the first place, extensive portions of the West are deeply indebted, so far as Presbyterianism is concerned, to that part of our church which was once included in the bounds of the *Presbytery of Redstone*. It will be borne in mind that these bounds included not only all Western Pennsylvania, but a considerable section of Western Virginia. Now, from this region, vast numbers of Presbyterians, from almost the beginning of this century, began to emigrate into the North-western Territory, and to disperse themselves widely over Ohio, Indiana and Illinois. There, in numberless places, they formed the materials out of which the first Presbyterian churches, now spread over the bounds of at least four of our largest western synods, were formed. It is remarkable what great numbers thus removed from almost all the first churches in the bounds of the Redstone Presbytery. This was, perhaps, in part, owing to the very imperfect Scotch-Irish system of farming which generally prevailed; answering well enough, so long as a virgin soil would yield its plentiful returns of crops. But it was a system that soon exhausted the lands. And our ancestors did not understand, or had not the patience to adopt, the methods of the "Pennsylvania Dutch," as they were called, for recuperating exhausted lands. At any rate, the prospect of cheap fresh lands, and of larger farms across the "big river," as they called the Ohio, presented too inviting a lure to be resisted. But, though they went to the West too often, perhaps, from mere selfish motives, God had his own purposes to accomplish by them. If they did not carry the gospel with them, and sometimes settled where, for a season, they seldom heard it, they soon contributed largely to invite ministers and build churches all over the West. The influence which Presbyterians from the old Redstone Presbytery thus

exerted, is incalculable. Does not this view of the case justify an inquiry into "the old paths" of our fathers?

2. But, in connexion with this point, let us widen the range of our vision upon the past and future. There was a race of Protestants that originated in the north of Ireland, whose history, in their successive generations, is as remarkable as any that the world contains. *Dr. Foote*, in his valuable works on North Carolina and Virginia, has shown how, in the wonderful providence of God, this race entered and spread through those States; some of them, immediately from the land of their fathers—some of them, after a brief sojourn in the Middle States: how they formed the largest portion of the materials out of which were formed the Southern Presbyterian Church: how, commingling with some contributions from the land of the Huguenots, with some from the Highlands and Lowlands of Scotland, and with a few from England, they unitedly laid the foundations of our Southern Zion. And he has, in view of the sublimity of their glorious mission, in both works, but especially in the latter, led us back to the earlier history of the Irish Presbyterian Church, and shown us the remote influences that were employed in preparing such a race, and propelling them forward in their course and entrance upon the new world. *Dr. Davidson*, not overlooking their remarkable origin, but briefly tracing the strange fortunes of the province of Ulster, in Ireland, has given us an account of a portion of this race, and of the results of their labors in Kentucky, and of the rise and progress of Presbyterianism in the mighty Valley of the Mississippi. And he has very properly begun with an account of the Presbyterian Church in Virginia, especially in the valley of Virginia, the principal hive of Presbyterian emigration to Kentucky. Neither of these works is complete without some account of the rise and progress of the *Presbyterian Church*, west of the Allegheny mountains, in Western Pennsylvania and Western Virginia—that noble, prolific mother of churches throughout the Western States.

There is something singular in the course of events, in regard to this race, whence our Church has mainly derived its materials and its strength. Dr. Foote has noticed how many of our first Presbyterian settlers that eventually reached Virginia and the Carolinas, had tarried for a while in Eastern Pennsylvania and Maryland. It was so, too, in regard to those who found their way toward the West. While many of our forefathers had come immediately from Scotland and Ireland, a large proportion were of those who had sojourned, for a season, east of the mountains, or of their children. The truth is, the stream divided. Part went south, and part west. Even families divided. Some of the *Edgars*, *Gilkesons*, *M'Millans*, &c., went south—some, to the West. And these streams united again in Kentucky, and elsewhere in the great Valley, and *are still uniting*. But why was this sojourn in the Middle States? We may say, indeed, that their western and southern homes were not yet open for them. But was there not another reason in the divine purpose, though employing secondary causes as the immediate instruments of its will? A sublime mission for them and their children was intended, though altogether concealed from their view. They were not yet prepared for that mission. They must receive that preparation through the great revivals under Whitefield, the Tenants, the Blairs, and a host of others, whom God raised up in the earlier part of the last century, to be instruments in his hands of spreading a new life through the Church. From 1740 to 1760, there was a mighty baptism of the Church of God in this land; and then were prepared the noble spirits that afterwards were called to so glorious a work in Virginia, North Carolina, and Western Pennsylvania. And these again trained and marshalled those who, in after years, were to spread the gospel through all the West. If Virginia sent her Rices, and her Blythes, and her Carys, to Kentucky; Western Pennsylvania trained and sent forth her M'Greadys and her Marshals. And if Ohio received from Kentucky and Virginia her Hoges and her Wilsons, she got from Pennsylvania her Reas, her Hughes's, her Welches, and her Andersons. Now, in looking back from our present stand-point upon these great general features of our Zion's history, can we fail to see the wonder-working hand of God, amidst a thousand other immediate, blessed results, working for the eventual evangelization of this vast Valley of the Mississippi, where every decennial period counts its increase of population, not by thousands, but by millions!

We doubt whether our early fathers, M'Millan, Smith, Power, Dod, and others, had the least conception of the grandeur of their mission, in its bearings upon the future church militant. Dear servants of God! they thought, perhaps, mainly, of saving souls around them, and of peopling heaven with those who would be their future "crowns of rejoicing." Little did they dream, at least in the earlier part of their toils, of the vast tide of human beings that were soon to fill the West, and that these were to receive the gospel mainly through instruments and agencies which they first prepared and directed. It is from views of the above character that we are led to think that we do not overrate the interest which belongs to our early history.

3. A very few years have passed since the whole Presbyterian Church was convulsed, from its centre to its circumference, with a mighty conflict, involving great constitutional principles and doctrines of vital importance. There was a time, never to be forgotten, when men's hearts almost failed them in view of the alarming invasion from without and the extensive defection from within.

But the vessel of the Church, though tempest-tossed and often dashed against the breakers, weathered the storm, and was safely guided into a peaceful haven. The vessel was lightened; a part of her crew was dismissed, and many, sympathizing with them, voluntarily forsook her. They all rallied in a new vessel, which they call the "American Presbyterian Church;"* and perhaps they would have likewise

* Many of them, it is said, labor under a pleasing illusion that it is the same old vessel in which their fathers sailed.

assumed the name of "Bible Christians," had not that expression been already monopolized.

Now, what portion of the Church proved most faithful in those trying times? Comparisons here, perhaps, are invidious. We would not disparage the claims which other portions of our Zion may have to the character of firmness and integrity in that hour of her agony; but we verily believe that if any are entitled to the precedence in this case, it is that portion of the Church within the limits of the original Presbytery of the West. Do not the scenes of 1835–6–7 throw an interest around the early history of this part of the Church? Perhaps we are more indebted, under God, to the early impulse given to the cause of sound Presbyterianism by the ministerial Pioneers of Western Pennsylvania and Virginia, than we have ever duly appreciated. The only man of all the "first set," as he called them, of our ministers who lived on till our stormy times began, and who was called home just before they reached their height, was Dr. M'Millan; and we know that till his last breath he gave his noble testimony to the cause of Old School Presbyterianism and its distinctive theology. A sermon of Dr. M'Millan, published in the "Western Presbyterian Preacher," abundantly attests this statement. Now, we have ever regarded him as truly representing the views and sentiments of his cotemporaries. He was, ecclesiastically, the "Charles Carroll, of Carrollton; the last surviving signer of the Declaration of Independence;"—yes, of true Presbyterian independence, when the old Presbytery of Redstone spread its banner to the breeze in 1781. Now with such reminiscences of a period within the memory of even the young of the Presbyterian Church, can we fail to regard with some interest the times when, amidst multiplied trials, and dangers, and sorrows, the walls of our Western Zion began to rise?

4. The Presbyterian Church, from the first day of her American organization, recognised her missionary character. The printed Records of the Presbytery of Philadelphia, and

of the Synod of New York and Philadelphia, prove beyond all question, that through a period of more than *eighty* years, the Presbyterian Church adhered firmly to the principle and duty of conducting missions at home and abroad through her *ecclesiastical organizations.* She had a mighty mission to perform, and nobly did she gird herself to the work.

It was by this means that the Gospel was first preached west of the Alleghany Mountains. Missionaries sent out by the Synod of New York and Philadelphia first penetrated the howling wilderness, and proclaimed the glad news of salvation alike to the *emigrant*, the *hunter*, the *trader*, and the *Indian.* This part of our past history is perhaps little known, and will deserve and shall receive special notice hereafter. But though our Church always, through her early days, and even for more than *thirty* years after the General Assembly, in 1789, was called into existence, acted upon the principle that "the Church of Christ, in her organized capacity, is a missionary society for the conversion of the world,"* there came a period when, through an amiable weakness that "leaned to virtue's side," she was seduced from her old propriety. Congregationalists of New England had carried on their missionary operations, not by Ecclesiastical Boards—of which their peculiar form of church organization did not, in the nature of the case, admit—but by voluntary associations. They were doing a noble work in their own way — the best

* If the claims to Scriptural and Apostolic sanction, made alike by Episcopalians, Independents, and Presbyterians, for their respective forms of church organization, be tested by this principle, will it not set in a clear light the stronger claims of Presbyterianism? If one grand design of the great Head of the Church in setting up and maintaining a visible Christian church in the world be the propagation of the gospel and the conversion of the world, — and who will question this? — then that *form of church government* which affords the greatest facilities for carrying on the work of *missions* must be most in accordance with the mind of Christ. Now, cannot prejudice itself discern the superior advantages of Presbyterian organization for carrying out and accomplishing this grand mission of the visible Church of God?

way of which they were capable with their defective form of church government. They persuaded us, and many among us who had come originally from them united with them, in coaxing us to adopt *their way* of doing this great work. They were truly eloquent, and profoundly philosophical in their arguments to convince us that we ought to fall in with them, and not only to carry on missions in the same way, but to take their defective and irresponsible organizations as the channels of our work. These good brethren assured us we would get along much better by adopting their more free and easy system, without *Committees* or *Boards*, under ecclesiastical supervision. They succeeded in their object for a time. We do not mean to question their motives. We verily believe they were generally honest. Nay, more; we have no doubt they thought sincerely they would do us great good, and not evil. It was thought that by a combined movement, under the guidance of the Home Missionary Society, and the American Board of Commissioners for Foreign Missions, a mightier work for the conversion of the world could be effected. Our Church, in a season when she received a fresh baptism of the Spirit of Missions, constituting her "mollia tempora fandi," yielded her assent. Now during this season of almost universal abandonment of the old Presbyterian principle on the subject of missions through church organization, what portion of our Zion held most firmly to the old paths of our fathers? We have no hesitation in saying it was the portion within the original bounds of the Redstone Presbytery. And here was first revived the good old principle of conducting missions by the Church in her organized capacity. Measures were adopted by the Synod of Pittsburg, and the work of foreign missions was set on foot and carried on for several years by the Synod. Let it never be forgotten that when our *present Board of Foreign Missions* was organized, it was by a transfer of this whole concern from the Synod of Pittsburg to the General Assembly in 1835. And when in 1836, with a New School majority, the Assembly undid and nullified this work of the previous year, that *bold stroke of their policy* led more than all other things put together to the *momentous transactions* of the General Assembly of 1837! Now, have we not a right to enquire about the early history of this portion of the Church, that aided directly and indirectly to recover her from her former defections, and to reinstate her on the ground ever held by our Zion from the beginning, and on the principles to which she owed, under God, her earliest life? What does the Presbyterian Church owe to this section of her now wide-spread territory?

Let us briefly recapitulate, not in the order we have just indicated, but in a somewhat transposed, but equally available order, the above particulars. We hope they are worth summing up.

We remark, then, that that portion of the Presbyterian Church which, in these latter days, made the first effectual movement, through ecclesiastical organization, in the cause of foreign missions, was located in the bounds of the old Redstone Presbytery. The synod of Pittsburg, amongst her sister synods, may be entitled to the same honor, ecclesiastically, which has been assigned, politically, to the State in which it is mainly situated—"the keystone of the federal arch." Perhaps the phrase, "the back-bone of the Presbyterian Church," is more significant. We cheerfully surrender both expressions, if they are thought to savor of ambitious pretension.

Again, this portion of the Church, during the period of its greatest conflict, near twenty years ago, for constitutional principles and rights, against alarming invasion, from without, and extensive defection from thorough Presbyterianism, from within, stood with more firmness and unanimity by her standards of doctrine and order, than almost any other part of our Zion.

Again, extensive portions of the West are deeply indebted

to that part of our Church which was once included in the bounds of Redstone Presbytery.

We might add a fourth particular, which ought to throw back a deep interest on our early history. The descendants of the Pilgrims remember with pride the efforts of their fathers in the cause of education, almost coeval with their landing on the Plymouth Rock, and are continually proclaiming to the world that, within less than twenty years after that event, Harvard University, (their *glory* and their *shame*,) was founded. Well, let it also be remembered that our early Christian fathers embarked in the cause of education, whilst yet their savage foes were prowling around them in their forests, and that *two colleges* were passing through *their infant state*, within less than *ten years* after the Presbytery of Redstone was formed.

We ask, then, cannot much of the *thorough orthodoxy*, the *evangelical and missionary spirit*, the *noble zeal for education*, and the *soundness in the faith*, propagated through the West, be all traced, under God, to the early state and character of the Western Presbyterian Church? Who were those men whom God employed in this great work? Under what circumstances of trial, of peril, and of self-sacrificing zeal, were the walls of our western Zion built? On all these accounts, it cannot be uninteresting to many, we think, to learn something about the *seven ministers* who composed the old Redstone Presbytery for many years, and about the early history of this section of our ecclesiastical territory.

OLD REDSTONE.

CHAPTER I.

THE EARLY STATE OF THE COUNTRY, AND ITS FIRST SETTLEMENTS.

An intelligent survey of our earlier history seems to require some general knowledge, at least, of the *secular history* of this portion of the United States. Without this knowledge, much that pertains to the organization and progress of our churches, to the domestic and social condition of our forefathers, and to the hardships and trials of our early ministers, must be involved in obscurity. There are many items in the early records of our first presbytery, that can be understood only by some acquaintance with the history, the laws, usages and customs of those times, and with the general state of society, and condition of the country. It will not, therefore, be deemed aside from the main design of this work, to attempt a comprehensive sketch of this character.

The territory embraced within the limits of the Presbytery of Redstone included all the south-western part of Pennsylvania, and that portion of Virginia which stretches along between the Ohio and the western border of Pennsylvania. This entire scope of country, larger than some of the smaller States of the Union, was, a hundred years ago, the hunting-ground of the Iroquois or Six Nations, the Delawares, and the Shawnees. The French, however, claimed it as theirs by right of discovery. This claim was wholly preposterous, resting upon no solid basis, and was mainly prompted by an ambitious desire to unite their Canadian with their Louisianian possessions, and to draw a cordon across the track of the advancing Anglo-Saxon race. Yet, as early as the beginning of the eighteenth century, Bancroft tells us that not a fountain bubbled on the west of the Allegheny, but was claimed as being within the French empire. Louisiana stretched to the head-springs of the Allegheny and the Monongahela, of the Kanawha and the Tennessee. But no subject of either France or England had, before the year 1700, trodden the shores of the Allegheny, the Monongahela, or the Youghiogheny. As early, however, as 1715 and 1720, occasionally a trader would venture west of the Allegheny mountains. And of these, says the historian of Western Pennsylvania, the first was James L. Fort, who resided, in 1700, east of the Susquehanna, but took up his residence west of it, at Le Fort Spring (Carlisle), in 1720. Peter Cleaver, John Evans, Henry Devay, Owen Nicholson, Alexander Magenty, Patrick Burns, John Evans, George Hutchinson, all of Cumberland county, (which then, indeed, included all the south-western part of the State) — also, Barnaby Currin, John M'Guire, a Mr. Frazer, the latter of whom had at an early day a trading-house at Venango (now Franklin), but afterwards on the Monongahela, at the mouth of Turtle creek — all these were traders among the Indians.*

But no attempt had been made by the whites at settlements in this entire region before 1748, when the Ohio Company was formed. The object of this company was to effect settlements on the wild lands west of the Allegheny mountains, through the agency of an association of gentlemen. Mr. Lee, one of the king's council in Virginia, was at the head of it. With the view of carrying his plan into operation, he associated himself with twelve other persons in Virginia and Maryland, and with Mr. Hanbury, a merchant in London, who formed what they called "The Ohio Company." Laurence Washington and his brother, Augustine Washington,

* History of Western Pennsylvania, p. 40.

(brothers of George Washington,) were among the first who engaged in this scheme. A petition was presented to the king, on behalf of the company, which was approved, and five hundred thousand acres of land were granted almost in the terms requested by the company. The object of the company was to settle the lands, and to carry on the Indian trade upon a large scale. Hitherto the trade with the western Indians had been mostly in the hands of the Pennsylvanians. The company conceived that they might derive an important advantage over their competitors in this trade, from the water communication of the Potomac, and the eastern branches of the Ohio, between the Monongahela and Kanawha rivers, and west of the Allegheny mountains. Though this was a most promising scheme, and met with much favor from the most influential quarters, yet, owing to the various troubles in which the country was involved, from French influence and Indian forays, comparatively little resulted from it. It, however, for some time, greatly promoted emigration into portions of Western Pennsylvania and Virginia.*

---

* One singular fact, connected with this subject, deserves notice. Mr. Lawrence Washington, upon whom fell the chief management of the affairs of this company, after the death of Mr. Lee, conceived the very plausible plan of inviting the "Pennsylvania Dutch," and their brethren from Germany to colonize this region. Their only objection was the *parish taxes* they would have to pay to support the Episcopal Church. Mr. Washington exerted himself to get this difficulty removed; but high church episcopacy was too strong for him; and so his scheme failed; and a large portion of Western Pennsylvania and Virginia was kept open for a different race—mainly for Scotch-Irish Presbyterians. Thus the intolerant Episcopal Establishment of Virginia was overruled by the purpose and providence of God, to contribute unwittingly to provide a home for many of our fathers; or rather *to keep open for them* such a home. Mr. Washington, in a letter to Mr. Hanbury of London, wrote, "I conversed with all the Pennsylvania Dutch whom I met—and much recommended their settling. The chief reason against it was the payment of an English clergyman, when few understood, and none made use of him. It has been my opinion, and I hope ever will be, that restraints on conscience are cruel, in regard to those on whom

This company sent out Christopher Gist, in 1750, to explore the country from the south branch of the Potomac, northward to the head of Juniata river. He explored this region accordingly, crossed the mountains and reached the Alleghany river by the Valley of the Kiskeminetas. He crossed the Alleghany about four miles above the forks, where Pittsburg now stands: thence went down the Ohio to some point below Beaver river; and thence over to the Muskingum valley. The first actual settlement made was within the limits of what is now Fayette Co., in 1752, by Mr. Gist himself, on a tract of land now well known there as Mount Braddock, west of

---

they are imposed, and injurious to the country imposing them. England, Holland, and Prussia I may quote as examples, and much more Pennsylvania, which has flourished under that delightful liberty, so as to become the admiration of every man who considers the short time it has been settled. As the ministry have thus far shown the true spirit of patriotism, by encouraging the extending of our dominions in America, I doubt not by an application, they would still go further, and complete what they have begun, by procuring some kind of charter to prevent the residents on the Ohio and its branches, from being subject to parish taxes. They all assured me that they might have from Germany any number of settlers, could they but obtain their favorite exemption. I have promised to endeavor for it, and now do my utmost by this letter. *I am well assured we shall never obtain it by law here.* This colony (Virginia), was greatly settled in the latter part of Charles the First's time, and during the usurpation by the zealous churchmen; and that spirit which was then brought in *has ever since continued*, so that, except a few Quakers, we have no dissenters. But what has been the consequence? We have increased by slow degrees, *except negroes and convicts;* whilst our neighboring colonies, 'whose natural advantages are greatly inferior to ours, have become populous.'" These sentiments do great honor both to the head and heart of Lawrence Washington. But he labored in vain. A proposition was made by several Germans in Pennsylvania, that if they would have the above exemption secured to them, they would take fifty thousand acres of the company's land and settle it with two hundred families. But nothing was done. Parliament was too busy with public affairs, and the ministry otherwise engaged. And Episcopacy in the colony was unyielding. Blessed be God, that he makes the wrath and even the *bigotry* of men to praise Him!

the Youghiogeny river. Mr. Gist induced eleven families to settle around him on lands supposed to be within the Ohio company's grant.

The more southern part of Western Pennsylvania (Greene, Washington, Fayette, and part of Somerset), which was supposed to be within the boundaries of Virginia, was visited by adventurers from Maryland, prior to 1754. Among these were Wendel Brown, and his two sons, and Frederick Waltzer, who lived four miles west of Uniontown. David Taggart had settled in the valley which still bears his name, in North-Western Virginia, where several other families came, a few years afterwards, and where the Redstone Presbytery appointed supplies for several years. These were the only settlements attempted prior to Braddock's defeat; and those made immediately afterwards—or prior to 1760, were repeatedly molested —families murdered—cabins burnt,—and for a time such settlements were broken up—alternately abandoned and again occupied.

In 1753, when Washington paid his visit to the French at Le Bœuf, he passed through this region going and returning. At that time, *Aliquippa*, queen of the Delawares, resided at the mouth of the Youghiogeny—now M'Keesport. Washington paid her a visit and made her a present of a watch-coat and a bottle of rum, "which latter was thought much the better present of the two." It is an incident worthy of a passing notice that *just one century* from that date, the present pastor of the Presbyterian church of that place, the Rev. Nathaniel West, D. D., was there installed in a new and beautiful house of worship. At the time of Washington's visit, king Shingis had his quarters near the mouth of Chartiers. Then not a single white man was found where Pittsburg now stands. He reached that point November 24th, 1753; and says in his journal, "As I got down before the canoe, I spent some time in viewing the rivers and the land in the fork, which I think extremely well situated for a fort, as it has the absolute command of both rivers. The land at the point is twenty-five feet above the common surface of the water; and a considerable bottom of flat, well-timbered land, all around it, very convenient for building." But the reign of solitude there was soon to be broken forever. A company commanded by Captain Trent, arrived there, February 17th, 1754—"a memorable day in our history." He was sent thither by the governor of Virginia, for the purpose of erecting a fort. We know not precisely when the work was begun; but it must have been prior to the 17th of April, 1754; for on that day, Monsieur Contrecœur with 60 batteaux, 300 canoes, 18 pieces of cannon, and 1000 men, Indians and Frenchmen, arrived from Venango, and summoned Ensign Ward, who commanded in the absence of Captain Trent, to surrender. Resistance, with about 40 men and even with the aid of an unfinished stockade, to some hundred French and Indians with several pieces of cannon, was out of the question. A capitulation, of course, followed; and Ward, with his men, ascended the Monongahela to Redstone, now Brownsville, where a stone house had previously been erected. This affair was the *commencement* of that *memorable war*, whose operations extended over continental Europe, Asia, Africa, and America—the *old French War*, which spread devastation, terror, and death, especially over the West—for eight entire years. And upon the successful termination of this war, the British government claiming some indemnity for their great losses and expenses, from the American Colonies, in the form of duties, taxes, &c., without their consent, and without any representation on their part in the British Parliament, were met with resistance from the colonies. And this, in turn, provoking to further encroachments on their rights—and to many insults and indignities—kindled the flames of the Revolutionary War—which terminated in the independence of the United States of America. *This greatest event of modern history*, in view of all its present and prospective bearings upon the destinies of the world, may be traced largely to the scenes in and around Pittsburg, just one hundred years ago. We shall not attempt the stories of the Great Meadows, of Fort Necessity, of

Braddock's defeat—and other incidents belonging to that period immediately succeeding the triumphant possession on the part of the French, of this point at the head of the Ohio, and of the surrounding region. Perhaps *the gloomiest period to the American colonies, to England*, and *to Protestant Europe*, that was ever experienced, either before or after, was that embraced in the two years immediately following Braddock's defeat. Lord Chesterfield, in England, exclaimed, "I never saw so dreadful a prospect." Horace Walpole in a letter said: "It is time for England to slip her cables and to float away into some unknown ocean." President Davies, in America, said, "I cannot help saying that our doom is dismally uncertain. I know not what a provoked God intends to do with us and our nation. I have my hopes, indeed; but they are balanced and sometimes overbalanced with fearful and gloomy apprehensions." * But it pleased the Mighty Sovereign of nations to raise to controlling political power, just when a universal gloom was settling upon the world, that great man, the immortal *Lord Chatham*,—under whose administration a new era began. And no part of the world felt its blessed influence more than Western Pennsylvania.

---

* The Rev. Aaron Burr, then President of Princeton College, in a sermon before the Synod of New York, September 30th, 1756, said—"It gives me no pleasure to be a messenger of evil tidings, nor would I make positive assertions about future events: yet I must say our public affairs wear a dark aspect. The nation we are engaged with in war is numerous, powerful, and politic. France abounds with men, and the king commands as many as he pleases into the field; on every occasion shows himself superior to our expectations; and his being an absolute monarch gives great advantage in point of secrecy and despatch."

"All our schemes hitherto prove unsuccessful: our enemies, small and contemptible as their numbers appeared to us, everywhere get the advantage."—"Braddock's mournful defeat last year, has been attended with a train of destructive consequences. It is not easy to conceive what we have suffered from the *barbarous natives*, under the influence and by the assistance of the French," &c.—*Burr's "Sermon," in Dr. C. C. Beatty's hands.*

A new spirit was infused into the utmost extremities of the realm. By a sort of instinctive wisdom, more than human, a new set of superior men were, everywhere, called into the service of the administration, inspired with dauntless energy and sleepless vigilance. The "Iron-headed" General Forbes was placed at the head of an army for the re-capture of Fort DuQuesne, and the recovery of the West. And Boquet, Lewis, Washington and Armstrong, were a part of his noble officers. The Rev. C. Beatty, a Presbyterian minister, was one of their Chaplains—a man of the spirit of Davies, in his peculiar talents for this service; of whom we shall have more to say in the sequel. The expedition was completely successful; and all the West was again recovered from the defeated and terrified French.* In a thanksgiving discourse, delivered on that cheering event, Davies broke forth in the following eloquent strain, "Fort DuQuesne, the den of those mongrel savages who have ravaged our frontiers, captured and butchered so many of our fellow-subjects, and ruined so many poor families — Fort DuQuesne — the object of Braddock's ever-tragical and unfortunate expedition, near which so many brave lives have been repeatedly thrown away in vain—Fort DuQuesne, the magazine which has furnished our Indian enemies with provisions, arms, and fury to make their barbarous inroads upon the British settlements, and prevented our growing country from extending its frontiers on the Ohio—

* "On the 25th of November, the youthful hero," (General Washington) " could point out to the army, the junction of the rivers; and entering the fortress, they planted the British flag on the deserted ruins. As the banners of England floated over the Ohio, the place was, with one voice, named *Pittsburg*. It is the most enduring trophy of the glory of *William Pitt*. America afterwards raised to his name statues, that have been wrongfully broken; and granite monuments, of which not one stone remains upon another; but, long as the Monongahela and the Alleghany shall flow to form the Ohio,—long as the English tongue shall be the language of freedom in the boundless valley which these waters traverse, his name shall stand inscribed on the gateway of the West."—*Bancroft's Hist. U. S., Vol. IV., p.* 313.

Fort DuQuesne is abandoned and demolished—demolished by those hands that built it, without the loss of a man on our side. The terror of the Lord fell upon them, and they fled at the approach of our army."

The treaty of 1762 brought quiet and repose to some extent, to the English colonies, and the first settlers on the frontiers returned to their abandoned farms. "The happy effects," says Smollet in his history of England, "of these measures were soon apparent—in the perfect security of about four thousand settlers who now returned to the quiet possession of their lands," and his authority was probably a passage in a letter dated at Pittsburg, March 21st, 1760, "The happy effects of our military operations are also felt by about 4000 poor inhabitants, who are now in quiet possession of their lands they were driven from on the frontiers of Pennsylvania, Virginia, and Maryland."

All things seemed now to promise peace and prosperity. But they were soon obliged again to leave their quiet homes and retire for safety to the more densely settled parts. Though Fort DuQuesne — thenceforward called Fort Pitt — never again fell into the hands of the French, their savage allies, treacherously instigated by the French, though professedly at peace with England, carried on a more furious and desolating war than ever against the frontier settlers. This was that horrible war, forever memorable under the name of *Pontiac's* war, of which we shall afterwards have occasion to speak. But it was soon brought to a successful issue by Colonel Boquet, in the fall of '63; and in '64, he compelled the turbulent and restless Kyashutha to sue for peace and bury the hatchet on the plains of Muskingum. He finally humbled the Delawares and Shawnees. Again the settlers returned to their cabins; and having resumed their labors, extended their improvements and cultivated their lands. From this time forth the prosperity of Western Pennsylvania advanced rapidly, and the tide of emigration, with the consequent settlements, rolled westward.

Previous to 1758, Westmoreland was a wilderness trodden by the wild beast and the savage, and, like other portions of Western Pennsylvania, by an occasional trader. No settlements of any account were attempted prior to this date, when Fort Pitt, having become an English military post, formed a nucleus for an English settlement. Two years afterwards, a small town was built near it, whose population, for several years, did not exceed two hundred. During *Pontiac's* war, indeed, it was for a short season quite abandoned; the villagers retiring into the fort, or fleeing elsewhere, and suffering the place to fall to decay. But in 1765, Pittsburg was, to a small extent, regularly laid out. In 1765 and 1766, settlements were made at Redstone and Turkey-Foot. Several of these were heads of Presbyterian families. The Indian titles had not yet been extinguished, and the governor warned them off. Some retired, but soon returned. Others paid no regard to the complaints of the Indians or the threats of the government. There was much trouble from this source about 1768; but it happily subsided, and the Indian claims were satisfied by treaties.

About this time, some emigrated from Berkley County, Virginia, and settled in what is now Fayette County, Pennsylvania, but then claimed by Virginia. In the summer of 1766, two Presbyterian missionaries visited Western Pennsyl vania, and spent two months among the settlers and Indians, of whom we will have occasion more fully to speak hereafter. During this period (from 1760 to 1770), settlements were rapidly made in various places, through all the region embraced by the Presbytery of Redstone. A considerable num ber of emigrants, soon after 1767, settled on the Youghiogeny, the Monongahela, and its several branches or tributaries, and in the year 1770–71, many of the Scotch-Irish from Bedford and York Counties, from the Kittatinny Valley, from Virginia, and some directly from the north of Ireland, commenced settlements in Washington County. These settlements soon extended from the Monongahela to the Ohio

River. The swelling tide of the Anglo-Saxon race spreading annually wider and wider, began to engage much attention. The forts at Redstone and at Wheeling were among the first and most conspicuous. The route the settlers pursued was the scarce practicable path called Braddock's Trail, which they travelled with no better means for their furniture and provisions than that afforded by pack-horses. The great object of most of these persons was to obtain possession of the lands, the titles to which cost little more than the office-fees. The Indian title was not then considered by the individual as presenting any obstacle; and Virginia, whose charter it was then supposed embraced this region of country, confirmed the titles of settlers with no other restrictions than such as were necessary to prevent the confusion of interfering claims. At an early period that State appointed three commissioners to give certificates of settlement rights, which were sent with the surveyor's plot to the land office, where they remained for six months, to give sufficient time to ascertain that there were no other claimants to the same tracts. If none appeared within that time, the patents were issued. There was an inferior kind of title, called a "Tomahawk right," which was made by deadening a few trees near a spring, and marking others by cutting in the bark, by the person who thus took possession. This ceremony conveyed no legal property; but was respected by the settlers as establishing a priority of claim, with which it was discreditable to interfere. These rights were therefore often bought and sold, because those who wished to secure favorite tracts of land chose to buy the Tomahawk improvements rather than quarrel with those who had made them. The Proprietary of Pennsylvania, in 1768, purchased the country from the Indians as far west as the Allegheny and Ohio Rivers, and opened the office for the sale of those lands. When the office was opened he made proclamation, and restricted the surveyors to respect the lands of actual settlers who had improved to the value of five pounds, and not to survey them, or warrants or locations of a date posterior to the settlements, except to those by whom the settlements were made. Favored by this indulgence,—which, however, was usual in both provinces,—few of those who lived adjacent to the Monongahela, and had already occupied the lands, applied to the office for locations or warrants. They were not certain to which state or province the soil belonged, and probably had a secret wish that it should belong to Virginia, because, in that case, it would cost them but about one-fourteenth part of the price for which lands were sold in Pennsylvania, and their wishes would be likely to govern their faith. In or about this year, Governor Lord Dunmore opened several offices for those within the bounds of what are now the four western counties of Pennsylvania; and the warrants were granted on paying two shillings and six-pence fees. The purchase money was trifling indeed, being only about ten shillings per hundred acres, and even that was not demanded. This was an effectual inducement to apply to Dunmore's agents in preference to the Pennsylvania land office. The land, being the property of the king, was at the disposal of the governor, who also procured a court of Virginia to be extended to the Ohio; and in a short time, two county courts were held south of the Monongahela, and one north of it, at Redstone Old Fort (Brownsville); all of them within the territory since ascertained to belong to Pennsylvania.

This course was afterwards changed—"The State of Virginia recognized, by a municipal regulation of May 3d, 1779, actual settlers" who had made a crop of corn, or resided on lands one year before January 1st, 1778, as "freeholders of that Commonwealth, and entitled to farms, not exceeding 400 acres."

In the year 1774, the peace of the western settlements was disturbed by alarms of Indian hostility, and a vexatious contest with the Governor of Virginia, in relation to the western boundary. Both of these, perhaps, sprang from a cunning policy, on the part of Lord Dunmore—aiming thereby to withhold or withdraw the attention of both Pennsylvania and Virginia from the subject of British aggressions on the liberties of the Colonies, by involving them in a war with the Indians, and in jealousies and quarrels among themselves about the disputed claims of these States. His subsequent conduct, in deserting the cause of American liberty, gave much plausibility to this construction of his motives. Though, after the *peace of Paris*, as it was called, first signed by the belligerent parties, November 3d, 1762—and the *Definitive Treaty*, February 3d, 1763—the close of the old *French War*—emigrants began to pour across the mountains, especially upon the close of *Pontiac's War*, in the fall of 1763-4; this stream was much enlarged, during the whole progress of the War of the Revolution.

This was from no unpatriotic desire to escape from their country's struggles for independence. They knew *that cause* was to be maintained, west as well as east of the mountains. The British government—at least its agents—sought the co-operation of the savages, every where through the western country, to humble and crush their colonies. It is believed that no portion of American citizens rendered more service to their country than the people of the West; by repelling the savage foe, and rendering abortive one of the principal means employed by Great Britain to crush our rising Republic.* And when peace at length was secured, by the Treaty of 1783, which secured forever our Independence, and staunched the bleeding wounds of a seven years' war—it brought no peace to the West. There was still little security for the twenty thousand Anglo-Americans in Western Pennsylvania, during the whole subsequent period, till 1794. The people suffered greatly from the Indians. Two armies sent out against them, in the Western part of Ohio, under General

* General Washington, in the gloomiest period of the Revolution, said to Colonel Reed, that, in the event of further reverses, he would retreat to Augusta County, Virginia; and driven from there, he would cross the Allegheny mountains, and take his stand in the West.—*Grimshaw's History U. S.*

Harmar and General St. Clair—the former in 1790, the latter in 1791—were both defeated, and shockingly cut to pieces; and not until General Anthony Wayne gave them a dreadful overthrow on the Miami-of-the-Lake, was there any thing like security or permanent peace established. Thus, during the entire period through which the Old Presbytery of Redstone existed, and was nobly performing its glorious mission, were there "fightings without."

In comparison with this never-ceasing source of anxiety to certain portions of the people, in the bounds of the Presbytery, other causes of trouble and peril were of small account. Yet, in themselves, they were often most harassing. The still conflicting claims of the two States—the impossibility, in many cases, of a faithful administration of law and justice—the uncertainty of land titles—the jealous heart-burnings between the two classes of emigrants, from Eastern Pennsylvania and from Virginia, which were not ended till the dividing line was finally fixed and settled in 1784 *—the exposure of many persons, especially women and children, to perilous adventures with the "feræ naturæ," howling beasts of prey—the want of bread, and danger of starvation at particular seasons—the scarcity of salt and iron—the absence of all roads across the mountains, except bridle paths—all these then, and many other things besides, rendered their condition hapless, and any thing but Eden-like. But whilst we will reserve for another place, an example or two, illustrative of their trials and dangers from the savages, we may, perhaps, as well here as elsewhere, give a sample of their trials from exposure to wild animals, and to want of food.

---

* "Civil authority is by no means properly established in this country; which, I doubt not, proceeds, in some degree, from inattention in the Executives of Virginia and Pennsylvania not running the boundary line—which is, at present, an excuse for neglect of duty of all kinds, for at least twenty miles on each side of the line. More evils will arise from this, than people are aware of." — *Extract of a Letter from Gen. Irwin to Gen. Washington, dated Fort Pitt, March 30th,* 1782.

About the year 1771 or 1772, Fergus Moorhead and James Kelly commenced improvements near where the town of Indiana now stands. The country around might well be termed a howling wilderness, for it was full of wolves. As soon as these adventurers had erected their cabins, each betook himself, at night, to his own castle. One morning, Mr. Moorhead paid a visit to his neighbor Kelly, and was surprised to find, near his cabin, traces of blood, and tufts of human hair. Kelly was not to be found. Moorhead, believing him to have been killed by the wolves, was cautiously looking out for his remains, when he discovered him sitting by a spring, washing the blood from his hair. He had lain down in his cabin at night, and fallen asleep; a wolf reached through a crack between the logs, and seized him by the head. This was repeated twice or thrice before he was sufficiently awakened to change his position. The smallness of the crack, and the size of his head, prevented the wolf from grasping it so far as to have a secure hold; and that saved his life. Some time after this, the two adventurers returned to Franklin county for their families, and, on their return, they were joined by others. They no doubt observed a prudent silence, especially with their wives, in regard to the wolf adventure.

Moses Chambers was another early settler. Having served several years on board of a British man-of-war, he was qualified for a life of danger and hardship. Moses continued to work on his improvements, till he was told one morning that the last johnnycake was at the fire! What was to be done? There was no possibility of a supply, short of Conegocheague. He caught his horse, and made ready. He broke the johnnycake in two pieces, and, giving one half to his wife, the partner of his perils and fortunes, he put up the other half in the lappet of his coat, with thorns, and turned his horse's head towards the east. There were no inns on the road, in those days—no habitation, west of the mountains, on his route, save, perhaps, a hut or two at Fort Ligonier. The

Kittanning path was used to Ligonier, and, from thence, the road made by General Forbes's army. Where good pasture could be had for his horse, Moses tarried and baited. To him, day was as night, and night as day. He slept only while his horse was feeding. Nor did he give rest to his body, or ease to his mind, until he returned, with his sack stored with corn. "How forcibly," adds the narrator, "would the affecting story of the patriarch Jacob apply itself to the condition of families thus circumstanced! 'Jacob said to his sons, "Why do ye look one upon another?" and he said, "Behold, I have heard that there is corn in Egypt: get you down thither, and buy for us from thence, that we may live and not die."' "

Moses Chambers was not the only one who had to encounter the fatigue and trouble of procuring supplies from Franklin county. But, as great as these difficulties were, the first settlers of Indiana had others to encounter, of a still more serious nature. The savage and hostile Indians gave them much trouble. Several of the inhabitants were killed and scalped; others were forced to leave their homes, and seek a place of safety on the eastern side of the mountains. Kelly and Moorhead had many narrow escapes from the Indians. But they finally caught Moorhead, together with a settler by the name of Simpson. Simpson was killed, and Moorhead was carried through the woods to Quebec, where he was confined eleven months. He was afterwards exchanged and sent to New York, and from thence made his way to his family. His wife and three children had fled to a place of safety, in a fort in Westmoreland county, and from thence to Franklin.

Settlements were gradually extended through the northwestern part of Pennsylvania, as far as Erie county, between 1790 and 1795. The Presbytery of Redstone sent out occasional supplies in that direction; but it was after it ceased to be the sole presbytery of the West.

The following article, written by the Hon. Judge Wilkeson, of Buffalo, N. Y., was furnished, some years ago, in several successive numbers, to the "American Pioneer," a monthly periodical published in Cincinnati, Ohio, 1842–3, by J. S. Williams, Esq., and now somewhat abridged, will be found to throw as much light upon the subject to which we have invited the attention of the reader, as anything which could be offered.

EARLY RECOLLECTIONS OF THE WEST.

INTRODUCTION—POVERTY CONSEQUENT UPON THE REVOLUTION—PIONEER MOTHERS—PIONEER MODE OF REMOVAL—GREAT DIFFICULTIES OF THE JOURNEY—FIRST EMPLOYMENTS OF THE PIONEER—MURDER OF AN INDIAN—PROGRESS OF THE FIRST SETTLERS.

The present happy population of our country, enjoying not only peace, but all the necessaries and conveniences of life, can form no just conception of the poverty and privations endured by the early settlers of the West.

The revolutionary war had withdrawn much of the labor of the country from agriculture and manufactures. There was no commerce, no money. The country at large could not furnish even necessary clothing. Hard as was the fate of the soldier while starving, freezing, and fighting for independence, still the prospective was cheering to him; he never doubted that his services would be rewarded, and be remembered with gratitude by his country. But, when discharged, he received his pay in continental money, worth but a few cents on the dollar, and, returning poor to his family, found them as destitute as himself. The pride and parade of the camp, which had excited and sustained him, were now gone — there was none to relieve or assist him. Some sank under their discouragements. Brave men, who never shrank from danger in their country's defence, and who cheerfully endured all the hardships incident to the soldier's life, had not the courage to contend with poverty, nor the resolution to exchange the excitements of war for that diligent pursuit of personal labor which was requisite for the support of their families. Many, however, resolved on crossing the mountains, and becoming farmers in the West. The difficulties to be encountered in effecting this resolution were many and great. The journey was full of peril, especially to women and children, poorly provided with even the most common necessaries.

It may interest some of your readers, who have never felt what privation or suffering is, to know by what expedients the pioneers of the West were enabled to remove their families across the mountains. I have often, when a boy, listened to the recital made by the mothers who were companions in these sufferings, and who, at every meeting in after life, would recur to them with tears.

My father's family was one of twenty that emigrated from Carlisle, and the neighboring country, to Western Pennsylvania, in the spring of 1784. Our arrangements for the journey would, with little variation, be descriptive of those of the whole caravan. Our family consisted of my father, mother, and three children, (the eldest one five, the youngest less than one year old,) and a bound boy of fourteen. The road to be travelled in crossing the mountains was scarcely, if at all, practicable for wagons. Pack-horses were the only means of transportation then, and for years after. We were provided with three horses, on one of which my mother rode, carrying her infant, with all the table furniture and cooking utensils. On another were packed the stores of provisions, the plough-irons, and other agricultural tools. The third horse was rigged out with a pack-saddle, and two large creels made of hickory withes, in the fashion of a crate, one over each side, in which were stowed the beds and bedding, and the wearing apparel of the family. In the centre of these creels there was an aperture prepared for myself and sister; and the top was well secured by lacing, to keep us in our places, so that only our heads appeared above. Each family was supplied with one or more cows, which was an indispensable provision for the journey. Their milk furnished the morning and evening meal for the children, and the surplus was carried in canteens for us during the day.

Thus equipped, the company set out on their journey. Many of the men being unacquainted with the management of horses, or the business of packing, little progress was made, the first day or two. When the caravan reached the mountains, the road was found to be hardly passable for loaded horses. In many places, the path lay along the edge of a precipice, where, if the horse had stumbled or lost his balance, he would have been precipitated several hundred feet below. The path was crossed by many streams, raised by the melting snow, and spring rains, and running with rapid current in deep ravines. Most of these had to be forded, as there were no bridges, and but few ferries. For many successive days, hair-breadth escapes were continually occurring; sometimes, horses falling; at other times, carried away by the current, and the women and children with difficulty saved from drowning. Sometimes, in ascending steep acclivities, the lashing of the creels would give way, and both children and creels tumble to the ground, and roll down the steep, until arrested by some traveller of the company. In crossing streams, or passing places of more than ordinary difficulty in the road, mothers were often separated from some of their children for many hours.

The journey was made in April, when the nights were cold. The men who had been inured to the hardships of war, could with cheerfulness endure the fatigues of the journey. It was the mothers who suffered; they could not, after the toils of the day, enjoy the rest they so much needed at night; the wants of their suffering children must be attended to. After preparing their simple meal, they lay down, with scanty covering, in a miserable cabin, or, as it sometimes happened, in the open air, and often, unrefreshed, were obliged to rise early, to encounter the fatigues and dangers of another day.

As the company approached the Monongahela, they began to separate. Some settled down near to friends and acquaintances who had preceded them. About half of the company crossed the Monongahela, and settled on Chartier's creek, a few miles south of Pittsburg, in a hilly country, well watered and well timbered. Settlers' rights to land were obtained on easy terms. My father exchanged one of his horses for a tract, (bounded by certain brooks and marked trees,) which was found, on being surveyed, several years after, to contain about 200 acres.

The new-comers aided each other in building cabins, which were made of round logs, with a slight covering of clapboards. The building of chimneys and laying of floors were postponed to a future day. As soon as the families were all under shelter, the timber was girdled, and the necessary clearing made for planting corn, potatoes, and a small patch of flax. Some of the party were despatched for seed. Corn was obtained at Pittsburg; but potatoes could not be procured short of Ligonier valley, distant three days' journey. The season was favorable for clearing; and, by unremitting labor, often continued through a part of the night, the women laboring with their husbands in burning brush and logs, their planting was seasonably secured. But, while families and neighbors were cheering each other on with the prospect of an abundant crop, one of the settlements was attacked by the Indians, and all of them were thrown into the greatest alarm. This was a calamity which had not been anticipated. It had been confidently believed that peace with Great Britain would secure peace with her Indian allies. The very name of Indian chilled the blood of the late emigrants; but there was no retreat. If they desired to recross the mountains, they had not the provisions or means, and had nothing but poverty and suffering to expect, should they regain their former homes. They resolved to stay.

The frontier settlements were kept in continual alarm. Murders were frequent, and many were taken prisoners. These were more generally children, who were taken to Detroit, (which, in violation of the treaty, continued to be occupied by the British,) where they were sold. The attacks of the Indians were not confined to the extreme frontier. They often penetrated the settlements several miles, especially when the stealing of horses was a part of their object. Their depredation effected, they retreated precipitately across the Ohio. The settlers for many miles from the Ohio, during six months of the year, lived in daily fear of the Indians. Block-houses were provided in several neighborhoods for the protection of the women and children, while the men carried on their farming operations, some standing guard while the others labored. The frequent calls on the settlers to pursue marauding parties, or perform tours of militia duty, greatly interrupted their attention to their crops and families, and increased the anxieties and sufferings of the women. The general government could grant no relief. They had neither money nor credit. Indeed, there was little but the name in the old confederation. The State of Pennsylvania was unable to keep up a military force for the defence of her frontier. She had generously exhausted her resources in the struggle for national independence. Her Legislature, however, passed an act granting a bounty of one hundred dollars on Indian scalps. But an incident occurred which led to the repeal of this law before the termination of the war.

A party of Indian spies, having entered a wigwam on French Creek, supposed to be untenanted, discovered, while breakfasting, an Indian extended on a piece of bark overhead. They took him prisoner; but reflecting that there was no bounty on prisoners, they shot him under circumstances which brought the party into disgrace, and the scalp bounty law into disrepute.

The settlement was guarded, and in fact preserved from utter dispersion, by a few brave men. *Brave* is a term not sufficiently expressive of the daring boldness of the Bradys, Sprouts, Poes, Lesnets, Wettzells, Caldwells, Crawfords, Williamsons, Pauls, Harrisons, and Zaneses, who for years encountered unheard-of privations in the defence of the border settlements, and often carried the war successfully into the Indian country.

GREAT DIFFICULTIES ENCOUNTERED BY EARLY SETTLERS—MORAL CONDITION OF THE SETTLERS—RELIGIOUS ZEAL AND POVERTY—CLOTHING AND EDUCATION—COMPARISON OF DIFFICULTIES BETWEEN SETTLING A NEW COUNTRY THEN AND NOW.

But to return to our emigrants. Besides their exposure to Indian depredations and massacres, they had other trials to endure, which, at the present day, cannot be appreciated. One of the most vexatious was, the running away of their horses. As soon as the fly season commenced, the horses seemed resolved on leaving the country, and re-crossing the mountains. The river was no barrier. They swam the Monongahela, and often proceeded 150 miles before they were taken up. During the husband's absence in pursuit of his horses, his wife was necessarily left alone with her children in their unfinished cabin, surrounded by forests, in which the howl of the wolf was heard from every hill. If want of provision, or other causes, made a visit to a neighbor's necessary, she must either take her children with her through the woods, or leave them unprotected, under the most fearful apprehension that some mischief might befal them before her return. As bread and meat were scarce, milk was the principal dependence for the support of the family. One cow of each family was provided with a bell, which, if good, could be heard from half a mile to a mile. The woman, left alone, on getting up in the morning, instead of lacing her corsets and adjusting her curls, placed herself in the most favorable position for listening to her cow-bell, which she knew, as well as she did the voice of her child, and considered it fortunate if she heard it even at a distance. By her nice and never-failing discrimination of sounds, she could detect her own, even among a clamor of many other bells; thus manifesting a nicety of ear which, with cultivation, might have been envied by the best musicians of the present day. If her children were small she tied them in bed, to prevent them from wandering, and to guard them from danger from fire and snakes; and guided by the tinkling of the bell, made her way through the tall meads, and across the ravines, until she found the object of her search. Happy on her return to find her children unharmed, and regardless of a thorough wetting from the dew, she hastened to prepare her breakfast of milk, boiled with a little meal or hominy; or in the protracted absence of her husband, it was often reduced to milk alone. Occasionally venison and turkeys were obtained from hunters. Those settlers, who were provided with rifles, could, with little loss of time, supply their families with fresh meat; but with the new settlers, rifles were scarce. They were more accustomed to the musket.

It may seem to some that these people, whose hardships and poverty we have been describing, must have been *a degraded race*, or they would have been better provided with the means of comfortable living. But they who would come to this conclusion, must be ignorant of the condition of our country at the close of the revolution. The poverty of the disbanded soldier was not the consequence of idleness, dissipation or vice. The times were in fault, not the men. The money which he had received for his services in the army, proved to be nearly worthless. But instead of brooding over this injustice, or seeking to redress his wrongs by means which would disturb the public peace, and demolish the temple of liberty, which he had labored to erect, he nobly resolved to bear his misfortunes, and brave the dangers and hardships of emigration.

A more intelligent, virtuous and resolute class of men never settled any country, than the first settlers of Western Pennsylvania: and the women who shared their sufferings and sacrifices were no less worthy. Very many of the settlers in what are now Washington and Allegheny Counties were professors of religion of the strictest sect of Seceders. I well remember hearing them, when a boy, railing at Watts' Psalms, and other like heresies. At a very early period of the settlement, a distinguished minister of that denomination, Mr. Henderson, was settled near Canonsburgh. It was common for families to ride from ten to fifteen miles to meeting. The young people regularly walked five or six miles, and in summer carried their stockings and shoes, if they had any, in their hands, both going and returning.

I believe that no churches or houses of worship were erected in the country until about 1790. Even in winter the meetings were held in the open air. A place was selected which partially sheltered the congregation from the weather, where a log pulpit was erected and logs furnished the audience with seats. Among the men who attended public worship in the winter, ten were obliged to substitute a blanket or a coverlet for a great-coat, where one enjoyed the luxury of that article. So great was the destitution of comfortable clothing, that when the first court of common pleas was held in Catfish, now Washington, a highly respectable citizen, whose presence was required as a magistrate, could not attend court without first borrowing a pair of leather breeches from an equally respectable neighbor who was summoned on the grand jury. The latter lent them, and having no others, had to stay at home. This scarcity of clothing will not seem surprising when we consider the condition of the country at that time, and that most of these settlers brought but a scanty supply of clothing and bedding with them. This stock could not be refurnished until flax was grown and made into cloth.

Those who are reared in contact with the ledgers, the claims, the lawsuits, and the bankruptcies of this contentious age, can form but a faint idea of real pioneer hospitality, in which half of the scanty supply of a needy family was often cheerfully served up to relieve the necessity of the still more needy traveller or emigrant family. From feelings and acts of this kind, as from seeds, has sprung much of the systematized benevolence in which many of our enlightened citizens are engaged.

The labor of all the settlers was greatly interrupted by the Indian war. Although the older settlers had some sheep, yet their increase was slow, as the country abounded in wolves. It was therefore a work of time to secure a supply of wool. Deerskin was a substitute for cloth for men and boys, but not for women and girls; although they were sometimes compelled to resort to it. The women had to spin, and generally to weave all the cloth for their families; and when the wife was feeble and had a large family, her utmost efforts could not enable her to provide them with anything like comfortable clothing. The only wonder is — and I shall never cease to wonder—that they did not sink under their burdens. Their patient endurance of these accumulated hardships did not arise from a slavish servility or insensibility to their rights and comforts. They justly appreciated their situation, and nobly encountered the difficulties which could not be avoided. Possessing all the affections of the wife, the tenderness of the mother, and the sympathies of the woman, their tears flowed freely for others' griefs, while they bore their own with a fortitude which none but a woman could exercise. The entire education of her children devolved on the mother; and notwithstanding the difficulties to be encountered, she did not allow them to grow up wholly without instruction, but, amidst all her numerous cares, taught them to read and instructed them in the principles of Christianity. To accomplish this, under the circumstances, was no easy task. The exciting influences which surrounded them made the boys restless under restraint. Familiarized, as they were, to hardships from the cradle, and daily listening to stories of Indian massacres and depredations, and to the heroic exploits of some neighboring pioneer who had taken an Indian scalp, or, by some daring effort, had saved his own; ignorant of the sports and toys with which children, in other circumstances, are wont to be amused, no wonder they desired to emulate the soldiers or engage in the scarcely less exciting adventures of the hunter. Yet even many of these boys were subdued by the faithfulness of the mother, who labored to bring them up in the fear of God.

If the reader would reflect upon the difficulties of emigration at that early day and those of the present, he must cast his eyes upon the rugged mountain steeps, then an almost unbroken and trackless wilderness, haunted by all sorts of wild and fierce beasts and poisonous reptiles. He must then observe that the hand of civilization has since crossed them by the smooth waters of canals, or the gentle and even ascents of turnpikes and railroads, and strewed them thick with the comforts of life. He may then have a faint idea of the difference of the journey; and as to the difference of living after removal then and now, let him consider that then almost every article of convenience and subsistence must be brought with them,—or rather could neither be brought nor procured,—and must necessarily be erased from the vocabulary of housekeeping. Let him think what has since been done by the power of steam in ascending almost to the very sources of the various ramifications of our rivers, carrying all the necessaries and many of the luxuries of life, and depositing them at points easy of access to almost every new settler; and he will see that if settling is now difficult, it was distressing then. When he further reflects upon the abundant and overflowing products of the West, compared with the absence of agriculture, arts, and manufactures in those early days, and now that not only our largest rivers and gigantic lakes, but the ocean itself, by the power of increased science, are all converted into mere ferries, he will at once conclude that the emigrants to Liberia, New Holland, Oregon, or California, can know nothing of privation compared with the pioneers of the West. If poverty or suffering exist, benevolence seeks it out and relieves it, whether it be far off or near, whether in Greece or the islands of the sea.

COMMERCE OF THE WEST.

HORSE-PACKING — ITS TERMINATION — EMIGRATION TO KENTUCKY—MARKET TO NEW ORLEANS—DANGERS AND DIFFICULTIES OF THE TRAIL TO NEW ORLEANS.

When our emigrants had struggled through the first summer, and the Indians had returned to their homes, the leading men set about supplying the settlements with salt and iron. These indispensable articles could only be obtained east of the mountains, at some point accessible by wagons from a sea-port. Winchester and Chambersburg were salt depôts. One man and one or more boys were selected from each neighborhood to take charge of the horses which the settlers turned into the common concern. Each horse was provided with a pack-saddle, a halter, a lash-rope to secure the load, and sufficient feed for twenty days, a part of which was left on the mountains for a return supply. The owner of each horse provided the means of purchasing his own salt. A substitute for cash was found in skins, furs, and ginseng; all of which were in demand east of the mountains. With these articles, and a supply of provisions for the journey, they set out, after selecting a captain for the company. Notwithstanding the fatigues to be endured, (the entire return journey having to be performed on foot), no office was ever sought with more importunity than was this by the boys who were old enough to be selected on this expedition. Not only salt, but merchandise, for the supply of the country west of the mountains, was principally carried on pack-horses until after 1788.* It was necessary to balance the loads with great care in order to preserve the backs of the horses from injury. If well broke to packing, they would travel twenty-five miles a-day.

* Packing continued to be an important business in Kentucky until 1795. The merchants of that State, for mutual conveniènce and protection, each provided with as many horses and drivers as his business required, repaired to the place of rendezvous, organized themselves,

After the first peace with the Indians, this mode of importation ceased; and the packers who had been the lions of the day, were succeeded by still greater lions, the *keel-boatmen*, who will be noticed hereafter.

Emigration continued to Western Pennsylvania. Even the most exposed districts increased in population, and many of the emigrants of 1785 and '86, were what was then considered rich. They introduced into the country large stocks of cattle, sheep, and hogs, cleared large farms, built grist and saw-mills, and gave employment to many poor settlers. But notwithstanding the brightening prospects, the healthy climate and good soil, many of the settlers became restless and dissatisfied with their location, which they believed inferior to Kentucky, or some other country still further off in the West. Numbers sold their improvements in the fall of 1786, and prepared for descending the Ohio, with their families, in the spring. The various hardships which they had encountered in providing a home for their families, seemed to increase their enterprise, and to inspire them with a desire of new adventures. Their anticipated home was as much exposed to the tomahawk, as the one which they were about to leave; besides, the hazard of descending the river 500 miles in a flat-boat was very great. The capture of the boats and the destruction of whole families frequently occurred. But these dangers did not lessen the tide of emigration which set down

---

appointed officers, and adopted regulations for their government. Every man was well armed, provisioned, and furnished with camp equipage. The expedition was conducted on military principles. The time and place of stopping and starting were settled by the officers, and sentries always watched by night. This company of merchants carried to the East, furs, peltries, ginseng, flax, linen cloth, and specie (the latter obtained from New Orleans in exchange for tobacco, corn and whiskey). These articles obtained a ready sale in Philadelphia or Baltimore for dry-goods, groceries, and hardware, including bar-iron and copper for stills. These caravans could transport many tons of goods, and, when arranged by experienced hands, the goods would be delivered without injury in Kentucky.

the river from 1786 to 1795. Few of these emigrants were well to live. They had sold their land in Pennsylvania for a small sum which they received in barter, generally in copper for stills, which was in great demand. A good *still* of one hundred gallons would purchase two hundred acres of land, even within ten miles of Pittsburg, and in Kentucky could be exchanged for a much larger tract.

The erection of mills gave a great impulse to the industry of the settlers of Western Pennsylvania. New Orleans furnished a good market for all the flour, bacon, and whiskey, which the upper country could furnish; and those who, in 1784, had suffered for want of provisions, in 1790 became exporters.

The trade to New Orleans, like every enterprise of the day, was attended with great hardship and hazard. The right bank of the Ohio, for hundreds of miles, was alive with hostile Indians. The voyage was performed in flat-boats, and occupied from four to six months. Several neighbors united their means in building the boat, and in getting up the voyage: some giving their labor, and others furnishing materials. Each put on board his own produce at his own risk, and one of the owners always accompanied the boat, as captain and supercargo. A boat of ordinary size required about six hands, each of whom generally received about sixty dollars a trip, on his arrival at New Orleans. They returned either by sea to Baltimore, when they would be within 300 miles of home, or more generally through the wilderness, a distance of about 2000 miles. A large number of these boatmen were brought together at New Orleans. Their journey home could not be made in small parties, as they carried large quantities of specie, and the road was infested by robbers. The outlaws and fugitives from justice from the States resorted to this road. Some precautionary arrangements were necessary. The boatmen who preferred returning through the wilderness, organized and selected their officers. These companies sometimes numbered several hundred, and a great proportion of them were armed. They were provided with mules to carry the specie and provisions, and some spare ones for the sick. Those who were able purchased mules or Indian ponies for their use; but few could afford to ride. As the journey was usually performed after the sickly season commenced, and the first six or seven hundred miles was through a flat, unhealthy country, with bad water, the spare mules were early loaded with the sick. There was a general anxiety to hasten through this region of malaria. Officers would give up their horses to the sick, companions would carry them forward as long as their strength enabled; but although everything was done for their relief which could be done without retarding their journey, many died on the way, or were left to the care of the Indian or hunter who had settled on the road. Many who survived an attack of fever and reached the healthy country of Tennessee, were long recovering sufficient strength to resume their journey home. One would suppose that men would be reluctant in engaging in a service so perilous to health and life, without extraordinary compensation. But such were the love of adventure, and recklessness of danger, prevalent with western young men, that there was no lack of hands. The sight of 50 Spanish dollars in the hands of a returned boatman was a powerful incentive to those who, perhaps, never had a dollar of their own.

But we hasten to introduce to the reader some account of the first minister of the gospel who fell in the battle-field of Christian conflict in the West, and found the first minister's grave in the Valley of the Mississippi.

LIFE AND TIMES

OF THE

REV. JOSEPH SMITH,

ONE OF THE FIRST MINISTERS OF WESTERN PENNSYLVANIA.*

To be employed as instruments in laying the foundations of flourishing States and well-regulated kingdoms, has ever been regarded as securing a just passport to honor and renown. There is another achievement that claims a niche not much lower in the temple of fame, and, doubtless, in many instances, will reach a still higher place in the temple not made with hands. A right direction given to communities in the early stages of their formation, as to the standard of public and private morals, and the prevalent tone of religious sentiment, especially when those communities are destined to germinate into mighty and wide-spread republics, is a work not likely to be entrusted by Divine Providence to ordinary men, and seldom achieved by ordinary hands. It is not always easy to settle this question of precedence between those who have secured for their country Magna Chartas and

* In the preparation of this paper, we have been essentially aided by the Rev. Dr. Elliott, who kindly furnished several facts and incidents in addition to those supplied by his biographical notice of the subject of this memoir, appended to his valuable "Life of Macurdy." We are also indebted to the Rev. Dr. William Wylie, for a number of anecdotes and dates; some things, also, we gathered from aged persons living in the bounds of Cross creek, and Buffalo, and from others in Ohio.

free constitutions, and those who have trained a people to become capable and worthy of enjoying such blessings. Who will say that the old English barons in Runnymede did more for British freedom than Cranmer, and Knox, and their compeers? or that *Lord Somers*, regarded as the main instrument in securing the present English constitutional government, was a greater benefactor to his race than Robinson, the humble minister of the exiles in Holland, who aided in training and sending forth the first race of noble pilgrims that landed on Plymouth Rock? However such respective claims to the grateful remembrance of posterity may be settled, surely we cannot regard without special interest the work of those who were first employed in sowing the seed of the kingdom in this mighty republic. And if, as is commonly believed, the vast Valley of the Mississippi,* soon about to possess the majority of our population, will control the destinies of this land, and if we believe that the religion of the Bible alone can save our land from utter anarchy, and moral desolation and ruin, is there not an interest of a peculiar character attached to the self-denying toils, and struggles, and dangers of those who were first honored as instruments in diffusing that religion in the western world—an interest scarcely yielding to that with which we invest the character and work of M'Kemie, and Andrews, and their associates?

That portion of the Valley of the Mississippi which was first yielded up by the aboriginal tribes to the settlement and home of the Anglo-Saxon race, and which has been the most abundant hive for other sections of the West, is Western Pennsylvania. For, after the encroachments of the French and their Indian allies were successfully repelled, and the treaty of peace, signed at Fontainbleau, November 3d, 1762, secured to the British crown this long-disputed section of the West, emigrants from Eastern Pennsylvania, Virginia, Scot-

* This phrase is often, perhaps most frequently, used to denote that portion of North America whose waters are drained by the Mississippi, and not merely the region bordering that river.

land, and the North of Ireland, began to pour in, and, in the course of twelve or fifteen years, formed extensive settlements through what now constitutes the counties of Fayette, Westmoreland, Indiana, Allegheny, Greene, and Washington. For a considerable time, there was no settled ministry of the gospel, seldom even a missionary, among them. Yet a large proportion of these early pioneers were the children of the Church. They had been baptised, and brought up in its bosom; and some of them had, previous to their emigration, entered its communion. For a few years their situation was critical and perilous in the extreme. Had their religious interests fallen into unfaithful or incompetent hands, or had they been even a little longer neglected, to all human appearance the result must have been of fearful moment to themselves and their posterity. But God had purposes of mercy for these offspring of his people. He was *at this very time* preparing a class of *no ordinary men** to enter this field, and lay the foundation of our western Zion, that vast building that is still rising higher and higher, and that our children's chil-

* The following quotations from Doddridge's "Notes on the Life and Manners of the first Western Settlers," seem not out of place here. This Mr. Doddridge was an Episcopal clergyman, and a brother of the late distinguished Philip Doddridge, Esq., a member of Congress from Western Virginia. These "Notes" were published in a small volume, many years ago; but I quote from them as I find them in the Appendix to Kircheval's History of the Valley of Virginia, chapter 31, page 403. "The ministry of the gospel has contributed, no doubt immensely, to the happy change which has been effected in the state of our western society. At an early period of our settlements, three Presbyterian clergymen commenced their clerical labors in our infant settlements — the Rev. Joseph Smith, the Rev. John M'Millan, and the Rev. James Power. They were pious, patient, laborious men, who collected their people into regular congregations, and did for them all that their circumstances would allow. It was no disparagement to them that their first churches were the shady groves, and their first pulpits a kind of tent, constructed of a few rough slabs, and covered with clapboards. He who dwelleth not exclusively in temples made with hands, was propitious to their devotions."

dren will not see completed. Within the compass of three or four years, James Finley, James Power, John M'Millan, Joseph Smith, Thaddeus Dod, and J. Clarke, all were found at their stations in this singularly important field. Some of them had been out in the new settlements for a few months as missionaries, and then returned to their eastern homes or churches. Indeed, as to full pastoral and ministerial work, they almost entered abreast upon the mighty harvest. Every one of those named above, deserves an extended memoir. We select, for our first biographical notice, the fourth name in the list; not because it designates the first laborer in the vineyard, but because, with the exception of Mr. Finley and Mr. Clarke, he was the oldest, and, without exception, the earliest called to his rest, and perhaps the mightiest of them all in wielding the sword of the Spirit. But few fragments of reminiscences can now be gathered of this race of ministers. The motto of England's greatest Chancellor, "prodesse potius quam conspici," seems to have been theirs, and of none of them more than of the subject of this paper. In Dr. Hodge's Constitutional History of the Presbyterian Church, vol. ii., p. 343, it is stated, "In 1769, John M'Creary and Joseph Smith were added to the roll (of the Presbytery of New Castle). Both of these were distinguished men. The latter, pre-eminent for piety and energy, was one of the fathers of our Church in Western Pennsylvania."

This devoted servant of God, Mr. Smith, was born in 1736, in Nottingham, Maryland, not far from the Susquehanna river. His father's farm was on the road leading from that river to Wilmington, Delaware, near what is called the *Rising Sun*. His parents were natives of England, professors of religion, and regarded as very pious and exemplary persons. Of his early education, and of his first religious exercise of mind, nothing is known. It would appear that he was out of his minority when he turned his thoughts towards the scholastic preparation which was required for entering the gospel ministry. For, as he graduated at Princeton in 1764, he was then 28 years of age. Nassau Hall, our first collegiate Presbyterian school of the prophets, was then enjoying the presidency of *Dr. Samuel Finley*, to whose saintly piety, and triumphant death, the eloquent pen of Dr. John M. Mason has given a world-wide fame. His name is attached to Mr. Smith's diploma.* At Drawyers, August 5th, 1767, Mr. Smith was licensed by the Presbytery of New Castle, to preach the gospel. No information has been obtained as to his theological training. He appears to have acquired considerable knowledge of the original languages of Scripture. The Hebrew Bible, the Greek Testament, Leigh's Critica Sacra, and Pool's Synopsis, were his companions during his subsequent life. On the 20th of October, 1768, he accepted a call from the congregation of Lower Brandywine, and was ordained and installed their pastor, April 19th, 1769. He had married Miss Esther Cummins, daughter of William Cummins, merchant, of Cecil County, Maryland, a short time before he was licensed. However questionable the wisdom of this order of events in a minister's history in most cases, we can hardly doubt that in the case of Mr. Smith, then

---

* We give the old ante-Revolutionary form, with all the signatures, as a literary curiosity, in the following exact copy of Mr. Smith's *Diploma*.

"Praeses et Curatores, — Collegii Neo-Caesariensis, — Omnibus et Singulis has literas lecturis: Salutem in Domino.

"Notum sit quod nobis placet, Auctoritate regio Diplomate commissa, *Josephum Smith*, Candidatum primum in Artibus Gradum competentem Examine Sufficiente primo approbatum, titulo, graduque artium liberalium *Baccalaurei* adornare. Cujus Sigillum commune Collegii *Neo-Caesariensis* huic membranae affixum, Nominaque nostra subscripta Testimonium sint.

	SAMUEL FINLEY, D.D. Praeses.	
Datum in Aula Nassovica	GULIELMUS TENNENT,	Curatores."
Sexto Calendas Octobris	RICHARDUS TREAT,	
Anno Ærae Christi	GULIEL. P. SMITH,	
Millesimo Septingentesimo	SAML. WOODRUFF,	
Sexagesimo quarto.	JOHANS. BRAINARD,	
	ROBERTUS OGDEN,	

nearly, if not quite, thirty years of age, it was not very unsafe or imprudent. His wife was a lady of remarkable piety, intelligence, and refinement of manners, and proved to be a help-meet, indeed, till the day of his death, surviving him more than twenty years.

Difficulties having sprung up in the congregation relative to the site of a church, the pastoral relation between him and that people was dissolved on the 26th of August, 1772. At the same meeting of the Presbytery, he received a call from the congregations of Rocky Creek and Long Cane, South Carolina. It is not improbable that he had visited some of the southern churches, soon after he was licensed, by appointment of his presbytery, or of his synod, just as Dr. Power and Dr. M'Millan, afterwards his fellow-laborers and co-presbyters in the West, are reported to have done, when licentiates of the same Presbytery. This call from the South he declined, and accepted an appointment as a supply to his former congregation for one year. About this time he began to preach in Wilmington, Delaware. This proved the occasion of great dissension among the people, as the Rev. William M'Kennan was already preaching in that place. After a season of much excitement, during which various petitions and remonstrances were carried up to the Presbytery on the subject, that body, on the 12th of August, 1773, put into his hands a call from the *Second Church of Wilmington.* This action of the Presbytery seems clearly to exonerate the subject of this sketch from any blame or censure in his course at Wilmington. This very significant call he held in his hands till the fall of the next year. In the meantime, this congregation of Wilmington having united with that of Lower Brandywine, in seeking his pastoral labors, he accepted this united call, and became their pastor, October 27th, 1774. In these churches he labored until April 29th, 1778, when, at his request, the pastoral relation was dissolved. In the minutes of the Presbytery, it is added, "by reason of the difficult state of our public affairs." This expression alludes to the distracted state of the country, and especially of that part of Delaware, being then involved in some of the most harassing and bloody scenes of the Revolutionary war. Some time in the preceding August, General Howe had landed a formidable British army, at the head of Elk river. On the 11th of September, General Washington, with the American forces then under his command, met his country's foes near the Brandywine, which stream has given its name to that memorable battle. The fearful cannonading on that field of slaughter was distinctly heard in the comparatively neighboring town of Wilmington, and perhaps shook many a window there on that day. Mrs. Smith who was in very feeble health at the time, soon after gave birth to their fourth child. The nervous excitement produced by the roar of the cannon, and its horrid associations, threatened to prove fatal to both mother and child; but they were mercifully preserved, the mother to sustain and increase the usefulness of her husband while he lived; the feeble infant, prematurely born, to become, in future years, the wife of one minister, and the mother of another.

Soon after these events, Mr. Smith, urged, no doubt, by an imperative sense of duty, as a husband, parent and minister, retired with his family into the Barrens of York, a district of country now, perhaps, partly included in Adams County. Here he resided for a little more than a year; but it was a memorable year in his history, as will presently appear. For some time he preached the gospel with great success, "in the region round about." Though he had no thought of remaining there, he labored as incessantly as though it were his chosen field for life, and his ministry was abundantly fruitful. One of his neighbors and spiritual children had recently married, and returned home late in the week with his young wife. Several of his neighbors, with their wives, much to the annoyance of the young man, paid them a complimentary call on the Sabbath day, just as they were preparing to set out for the church, which was quite near. These unseasonable visitants were Quakers. The young man succeeded, however, in persuading them to go with him to hear their new minister, Mr. Smith, of whom he gave them such an account as to awaken their curiosity. The result was the hopeful conversion of several of the party.

Early in the following spring, Mr. Smith paid a short visit to Western Pennsylvania. The Rev. John M'Millan had removed, with his family, to that region a few months before. The Rev. James Power had already been residing there since the fall of 1776. How far his mind was influenced by his intercourse or correspondence with them, is not now known. Before this great event of his life, however, he was called to experience a severe preparatory trial. He was taken sick, and lay for some time under the pressure of a severe and dangerous fever, at the point of death. The people met, as they were wont, in a large barn, to hold their prayer meeting, on a Sabbath day. Tidings came that there was scarcely a hope of his recovery. It was requested that prayer should be offered in his behalf. The first man who led in their devotions, forgot his case, the second said but little, and so, the third. His friend, *James Edgar*, then a young man, afterwards distinguished for his piety, his usefulness, and his great influence, both in church and state, in Western Pennsylvania, was at that prayer meeting; he left it, with agonized feelings, to repair to the house of Mr. Smith, and to see him, as he feared on his deathbed. As he approached the house, he met an old lady, who was considered among them a mother in Israel. Mr. Edgar eagerly asked her about Mr. Smith. "He is worse," said she. Mr. Edgar's heart sunk within him. "But," added she, "he will not die, for the Lord hath told me to-day, that he will raise him up, and send him out to the West, to preach the gospel." This she uttered with great confidence and vivacity. Soon after this, and while Judge Edgar was still sitting by the bedside of Mr. Smith, a manifest change took place in the appearance and symptoms of his beloved minister, and he began to recover rapidly from that hour. We mention this singular, but well-attested fact, and the remarkable language of the old lady, without comment, only observing, that however it may have an air of fanaticism, it seems to illustrate a feature of the religious character and sentiment of those days, not unlike those of the old Puritans and Scottish Reformers. In D'Aubigne's Life of Cromwell, the reader will find some very just and scriptural views on this subject. In the case above stated, we suppose this lady did not mean, nor did Mr. Edgar so understand her, that she had any express revelation from heaven, but only a strong and firm persuasion from the liberty and enlargement of soul she enjoyed, in pouring out her heart for her minister at the feet of her Saviour.

In this connexion, it may be proper to mention, that shortly before their removal from Wilmington, as Mr. Smith and his wife were returning from an evening walk, about sundown, in the outskirts of the town, and near an adjoining wood, they both distinctly heard strains of sweet and melodious music over the tops of the trees, that seemed to them to rise and float away into the distant skies. They listened to it for some minutes. They often spoke of it, especially Mrs. Smith, but rather confidentially: she was far from being a weak or superstitious woman. Whatever might have been the cause or source of this music, conveyed, possibly, by some peculiar law of acoustics, from a distant band in the British or American camp, similar to that which has been noticed at a point off the coast of Rio Janeiro, where the sound of bells and of music from the city, though out of sight, is distinctly heard — however we may account for it, why may we not regard it as under a special providential direction, and designed, as we have no doubt it served, to encourage and cheer them in the prospect of setting out, at no distant day, with their family of helpless children, to the wilds of Western Pennsylvania?* In this sickness, from which he was raised

* We are surprised to find so excellent a writer as Dr. Mosheim speaking rather sneeringly of "*the pious sort of mistake*" that the

up from the very jaws of death, he doubtless received a fresh baptism of divine influence, designed to prepare him for his future work. His illness, from some of the circumstances mentioned, must have been in the summer or fall of 1778.

Early in the following spring, in April, 1779, we find him in Western Pennsylvania, on a short visit, where he labored for a few weeks in a part of what is now Washington County, then quite a frontier settlement. After remaining for some time breaking to these people in the wilderness the bread of life, he returned, and soon a call was sent after him to his Presbytery. This call is dated June 21st, 1779, and is a remarkable document. The following is an accurate copy:

A call from the United Congregations at Buffalo and Cross Creek, to the Rev. Joseph Smith, a member of the Presbytery of New Castle.

WORTHY AND DEAR SIR, — Having, under the direction of Divine Providence, been removed into this new country where the blessing of the gospel has never been enjoyed in the stated ordinances, or but seldom; but being of late favored with an opportunity of hearing you, reverend sir, to our satisfaction, and we trust the edification of our souls; we do unanimously agree to invite, beseech, and pray you to take the pastoral care, under God, of our souls. For encouragement we do promise, if you should accept of this our call, to yield all due subjection in the Lord, by regularly attending on the Word preached, and ordinances administered by you, and by endeavoring to improve them, through divine grace, for the edification of our souls; and by submission to the due exercise of discipline, if our faults should at any time deserve censure. And that you may be free from the incumbrances of the world, so as to attend upon your ministry, we do promise you a competency of the good things of this life,

---

Christians made; he, considering the *shower*, as he calls it, which rescued the Roman army from destruction, a mere happy coincidence, and *not* any *special interposition* of Divine Providence, in answer to the prayers of Christian soldiers. See Mos. Eccl. Hist. 2d Cent. p. 1. ch. i.

with which God has blessed us; particularly we promise to pay yearly and every year, during your incumbency among us, the sum of one hundred and fifty pounds, Pennsylvania currency (money equal in value to what it was in the year 1774), viz.: seventy-five pounds from each congregation—they employing your ministerial labors equally.

And now, reverend sir, when we consider the great loss youth sustain, by growing up without the stated means of grace; the formality likely to spread over the aged, and the great danger of ungodliness prevailing amongst both: there being divers denominations of people among us who hold dangerous principles, tending to mislead many weak and ignorant people: we cannot but renew our earnest entreaties that you would accept this our hearty call. That the Glorious Head of the Church may direct you to what may be most for his glory, and your future comfort and usefulness—is the earnest prayer of your humble suppliants.

We, the inhabitants of the upper and lower congregations of Cross Creek, do promise to pay or cause to be paid unto the Rev. Joseph Smith, annually, during his regular incumbency among us as a gospel minister, the several sums annexed to our names, respectively: and whereas money is become of less value, and every article has arisen to an extravagant price: therefore we do hereby agree that the said sums shall be annually regulated by five men, chosen in each congregation; and be made equal in value to what the said sums would have been in the year 1774.*

Witness our hands, June 21, 1779.

---

* The depreciation of the paper currency, or continental money, had, in 1779, become a very serious burden to the people; and all over the country, great ingenuity was exercised to discover a remedy. Embargoes, commercial restrictions, tender laws, and limitations of prices were all tried—but in vain. Prices still sank. "I had money enough, some time ago," said a merchant of those times, "to buy a hogshead of sugar: I sold it again, and got a great deal more money than it cost me; yet, when I went to market again, the money would not get me a tierce. I sold that too, at a great profit; yet the money received would only buy

Then follow six columns of names, amounting to 204: and the amount of their subscriptions is £197 5s. 6d.: thus abundantly exceeding the amount (£150) promised in the call. It is evident that they followed no special form in the construction of this paper; and the uniting of the call and the subscription paper into one document, gives it quite an original character. We need hardly say that there are some passages in this call of a most solemn and touching character. Altogether, it is a curious original paper, evincing great ability and fervent piety. Most probably, it was drawn up by Judge Edgar; though of that we have no direct evidence. It appears also that a call was sent to him from Peter's Creek; but on the 27th of October, 1779, he signified to the Presbytery his acceptance of the call to Cross Creek and Buffalo; and the next year, 1780, moved into the bounds of the latter, and became, in due time, their regular pastor. Here he spent the remainder of his life—twelve years.

Mr. Edgar, of whom we have already spoken, had removed also into Cross Creek congregation, a year or some months before, and became one of his most efficient elders. Perhaps no pastor was ever more blessed with a bench of devotedly pious elders, than was Mr. Smith. They were indeed men "mighty in prayer." Sustained by such men, and by a remarkably praying people,* he was "instant in season and out

---

a barrel. I have now more money than ever; yet I am not so rich as when I had less."—*Hist. Pitts., p.* 145.

* It is said that through the summer, during the interval of public worship, you could stray in no direction through the surrounding forest, without hearing the voice of secret prayer; and if you would return to the church, you could hear the low sound of a whisper from the pulpit, where the pastor, who seldom came out of it during such intervals, was likewise wrestling with the angel of the covenant. This fact has been attested by several unquestionable witnesses. The Rev. Dr. James Hervey, some years ago, stated to the Synod of Wheeling, that when a very small boy, he one Sabbath, during "intermission," being near the door of Mr. Smith's church, went in. The house was vacated, but he heard Mr. S. engaged in prayer in the pulpit; and it gave him an awful and

of season." A revival of religion soon began, which never ceased till the day of his death, and for some years after—a revival of twelve or fifteen years! Incredible as this may now appear, there are still living credible and intelligent wit-

---

indelible impression of the presence of God filling the house. This was the first deep and abiding awakening of his conscience. Mr. S. had indeed, from an early period of his labors, a race of "wrestling Jacobs," and "mothers in Israel," that we fear cannot be easily found now. The eminent piety of a large number of Western Presbyterians is affectionately remembered by thousands of their descendants to this day. When, more than thirty years ago, we read in Dr. Miller's sermon, preached at the ordination of the late lamented Dr. Nevins, of Baltimore, some remarks about cities tending to produce intensity of character, and therefore favorable to the production of the most eminent piety, we hesitated, and we hesitate still, to give an unqualified assent to his views. A distinguished minister of our Church (the late Dr. Mathews, of the New Albany Theological Seminary) remarked to us, after reading Dr. Miller's statements, that the pious John Newton seemed to differ from him; for he had said, somewhere in his works, that were Great Britain searched, by an angel, for the most pious person, he would possibly find that person an old woman, sitting at her spinning-wheel in some retired corner of the kingdom. It often occurred to us to ask when and where do we find the brightest monuments of holiness. Who and what was Enoch, "who walked with God?" Who were Abraham, Isaac, and Jacob? and where did they dwell? It will be remembered also that God chose for his covenanted people, a pastoral and agricultural life. The whole genius of the Mosaic institutions, as Michaelis has clearly shown, was designed to make and keep the Jews a rural people. [A pastoral and agricultural people; not strictly a rural people, in the modern sense of the term.] It is a natural inference that such a state is on the whole most favorable to piety. Who also were the Waldenses, and where did they live? The history of the Culdees of Scotland and Ireland may likewise be cited for illustration. And the more modern history of the Covenanters and of the Huguenots through the South of France, will, perhaps, occur to many as furnishing materials for a decision on this point. But our own country has had many illustrious proofs of a deep and fervent piety, that never drew any aid from the busy haunts of men. In Virginia are many rural spots, for ever sacred to the memory of those who lived near to God, and "quite on the verge of heaven." But without designing any invidious comparison, I would select the early race of Western Presbyterians, as presenting nesses of that fact. It is true there were periods of comparative declension; but during all this time, scarcely one Sabbath occurred when some new cases of conviction or conversion did not become known. And this, too, in the midst of the trials and perils of frontier life, when they were often in imminent danger from savage foes—when, sometimes, they were compelled to retire to forts or block-houses to protect themselves from the merciless tomahawk. Sometimes a fresh outpouring of the Spirit would take place, while they were actually gathered in Fort Vance, to shelter themselves from some new invasion of the Indians. But these troubles were not very frequent, nor of long continuance.

It was a remarkable circumstance, that between Mr. Smith's congregations and the Ohio, and along up and down the river, for thirty or forty miles, there was early settled, or "squatted" rather, a peculiar population, many of them from Eastern Virginia—well suited, from their habits and training as hunters, and from their adoption of Indian modes of warfare, to fight with the savages, and to act as a life-guard, as a protecting *cordon*, to Mr. S.'s people and the interior settlements. Here were the Wetzells, the Bradys, and the

complete proofs that cities are not necessary to produce intensity of Christian character. Martin Luther used to say that his three masters were Prayer, Meditation, and Temptation. All these were the masters, in an eminent degree, of our first ministers and their people in Western Pennsylvania. The piety in our city churches may be eminent: the advantages for cultivating it and for calling it into habitual and healthful action are certainly great. Christians in cities, by constant intercourse, too, may be much benefited. The habitual exercise of pious sentiments and affections, adorned by social refinement, and an easy, graceful familiarity with all the conventionalities of city life, may throw a peculiar sweetness and charm around the person and character; especially in the view of those who have themselves lived in cities, and whose refined taste would be often scandalized by the unpolished roughness of rural life. The apostolic piety of Mr. Smith, and many of his people, constitutes, at any rate, an eminent illustration of what the great Reformer's three masters would do, in training a people for heaven, amidst the toils and perils of frontier life.

Poes, and other names that figure in all the narratives of early western adventures. It is remarkable, by the way, that some of these famous frontier Nimrods signed the call to Mr. Smith—among others, the names of Andrew Poe and Adam Poe, each subscribing £1, are found. Thus God provided for his people a singular class of protectors, between them and the Indian settlements.

A glorious work of grace began and long continued in that vineyard, which God had so strangely fenced around. The following extract from a letter of Judge Edgar to Mr. Leiper, dated Oct. 22, 1802, will be read with interest by many, and may here be appropriately introduced:

"In April, in the year 1779, the Rev. Joseph Smith visited this country, and preached several times in the bounds of that which afterwards became formed into the congregations known by the names of Buffalo and Cross Creek. In June, a call was signed and sent down to the presbytery to him. That fall he accepted, and moved into them in December, 1780. In this winter, 1781–2, the Lord, by his Spirit, began to work. Attention and some serious thoughtfulness appeared among the people, in both congregations. The exercises of social prayer were attended to, in some parts. The summer of '82 was very remarkable. The gale increased. Many were under deep conviction of sin and danger until harvest, without much appearance of relief: few of the distressed had got relief; so that some of those that had religion formerly, were made to lament that the children were come to the birth, but few or none bringing forth. Indeed, at this time the number of God's people were very few [of that description] *that knew anything about the travail pains*, or *agonizing*, that Christ might be formed in the souls of the distressed the hope of glory. However, a gracious God was pleased to discover his glory shining in the gospel, to many of the convinced, before the sacrament was administered, that fall; which was the first time it was administered in these congregations. As well as I can recollect, about fifty in each congregation were added to the Church on that occasion, giving comfortable evidence of a work of grace on their hearts. The most of them to this day continue on, though some few instances there are of falling back. The work rather increased for three years. At the sacrament in Cross Creek in May and June, 1787, it was perhaps the most remarkable. On Monday evening, the power of God appeared bowing many. The people did not all get away from the meeting-house green until long after night, and came back on Tues day. This was the most solemn day I had ever seen at this time, in the house of God. Yet there were not more than two or three instances of crying out aloud. I cannot say there was much decline appeared for six or seven years after the work began. Our dear pastor died on the 19th of April, 1792. God continued his presence all that time, adding numbers to the Church every year."

Besides Mr. Smith's abundant labors on the Sabbath, and his frequent preaching through the week, during particular seasons of spiritual harvest, he instituted, at his own house, a Wednesday evening prayer-meeting, to which persons would come from a distance of from three to fifteen miles. These meetings would sometimes extend to a late hour in the night. But no weariness nor drowsiness seemed to attend them. Many, now in heaven, will, perhaps, never forget those prayer-meetings. He was not a man of robust health. In person he was tall and slender, of fair complexion, of a slight look askance, of one eye. It will be remembered that this was a peculiarity of Whitefield, and that gave him increased power over his audience, as many thought he was looking directly at them. Whether this was the case with Mr. S., we have not understood. It is abundantly testified, however, that there was a piercing brilliancy about his eyes, when he became animated, that was peculiarly impressive. His dress was always neat and becoming. His voice was remarkable alike for the *terrific* and the *pathetic*, and, as Dr. Kirkland said of the celebrated Fisher Ames, "now like the thunder, and now like the music of heaven." When his theme was the terrors of the law, or the horrors of hell, or the glories of heaven, he appeared to many of his people as though he had just come from the spirit-land. "I never heard a man," said the Rev. Samuel Porter, "who could so completely unbar the gates of hell, and make me look so far down into the dark bottomless abyss, or, like him, could so throw open the gates of heaven, and let me glance at the insufferable brightness of the great White Throne." His favorite subjects were the importance and necessity of regeneration, and the immediate necessity of faith in Jesus Christ. His ordinary manner of speaking had nothing of rhapsody in it. It was rather that of animated conversation. Indeed, his sermons were generally written out with some degree of fulness. Many of the skeletons, which he used on ordinary occasions, are so well drawn out, that, with but little addition, they would be fit for the press. He would often rise to an almost supernatural and unearthly grandeur, completely extinguishing in his hearers all consciousness of time and place, and verifying Cicero's strange description of the highest kind of eloquence—"aliquid immensum, infinitum que." John Foster's account of the peculiar power of fascination which the celebrated Robert Hall could sometimes exert over his audience, has often reminded us of what our aged fathers have told us of Mr. Smith.

When the above was written, six months ago, for the Presbyterian Magazine, we felt apprehensive that it would be deemed an exaggerated and extravagant account of Mr. S. as a preacher. Two persons of highly cultivated minds, who had often heard him, have recently testified to us, after reading the foregoing remarks, that they altogether fall short of giving any conception of the peculiar power of Mr. Smith's eloquence. "It was altogether different," said one of them, "from Dr. M'Millan's manner. *He* was sometimes awfully solemn and impressive. But Mr. Smith's manner had a strange kind of power about it, totally indescribable." "Neither you nor any man on earth that never heard him," said the Rev. C. Dodd to us, "can form any idea of his wonderful power." "Permit me to say," says another aged servant of God, "I have formed an estimate of him higher than posterity, even his descendants, can form of him. Even if his sermons had been correctly written as they fell from his lips, they could not now be appreciated. And why? Because neither the stenographer nor the printer has any types by which to express his tones, his emphasis, his holy unction, the holy vitality of his soul. Who can now rightly appreciate the characters of Whitefield and the Tenants, by their simple sermons, which have been printed? Printers have no types for souls. When Mr. Smith commenced his pulpit exercises, if his flight was upwards, he was immediately out of the sight of the growling critic, who became like the huntsman's dog, when he has lost the track! Or when, arrayed with divine and awful majesty, he uncovered the bottomless and wide-extending pit of wo, whose billows of fire are ever lashed into fury by the almighty breath of an incensed, slighted Saviour, the sinner lost his coat of mail, retreated in terror, or fell prostrate, imploring for mercy. Mr. Smith's mind was early disciplined by classical studies and collegiate drillings, so that, when his ardent soul became fledged with heaven's plumage, he was prepared to soar, without a seeming effort or premeditated measurements, above the flight of common minds. He never elaborated his sermons by logical, syllogistic formulas, or mere theological didactics. Every truth he presented had the perspicuity and force of an intuitive axiom, and conclusions were drawn by every listener; so that the speaker would have lost time, and chilled the kindling flame, by the introduction of a "therefore," or a "quod erat demonstrandum." The traveller, in a tornado, is not occupied with the philosophy of pneumatics, nor the floundering mariner with the philosophy of the tides. Such was the condition of Christless sinners under the preaching of Mr. Smith. No doubt he was a classical scholar; but the cold ratiocinations of logic—the crucibles of the chemist—the black-board and the chalk, were left far behind. His baptised soul had been led to that fountain whence all science flows. Nothing short of imperious necessity, and that for Christ's sake, could ever have nailed him to a common-school bench, or chained him to the presidential chair of a college." "When he was taken up from us, much of his spirit fell upon a Hughes, a Marquis, a Patterson, a M'Gready, a Brice, &c. But Smith was the giant; and no one was found capable of putting on and wielding his whole armor."*

* Rev. Dr. Lindley.

Old Col. R. of Virginia, used to say that he liked that preacher best, who could make him wish that he could creep into an augur hole before the preacher was done.

The celebrated Robert Morris, the great American financier, who saved the credit of his country, and ruined his own, once told Dr. Rush that "he liked that kind of preaching that drives a man into a corner of his pew, and makes him think the devil is after him." He would have been delighted with Mr. Smith. See Hazard's Register, vol. xii., p. 249.

If it might be said that preaching was Mr. Smith's great forte, it is questionable whether his usefulness out of the pulpit was not even greater. He was a man of prayer, and often spent special seasons in that exercise. It was not uncommon for him to rise in the night and engage in intercessory prayer for his people, and especially the youth of his congregation, and his own children. For this purpose, he kept a cloak at the foot of his bed, during cold weather, in readiness to throw around him when he wished to get on his knees. His wife and himself would often observe special fast days, for the conversion of their children. And they were almost all the subjects of Divine grace, while quite young. One of them, and it was the one born the day after the battle of Brandywine, was received into the fellowship of the Church at ten years of age. A large session, of unusual Christian experience and discrimination, were unanimous in their vote, to receive her. He was faithful in catechising and conversing with his children. Sabbath evenings were generally spent in this way. Gathering them round the fireside after the usual recitation of the Shorter Catechism, he would talk most earnestly and affectionately to them about the interests of their souls, and would sometimes close with solemn warnings, telling them that "he would take the stones of the chimney to witness against them," &c. Yet there was nothing severe or morose in his character. On the contrary, it was one of his peculiar excellencies, that he could win the friendship and affection not only of his own children, but of all the children and youth of his church. Some of them have testified that they were unconscious of the flight of time when Mr. Smith was among them. There was a peculiar charm about his cheerfulness and his talent for social intercourse with the young. He was seldom depressed or in low spirits. But this steady cheerfulness seemed to be fed by communion with God, and the hope of heaven. Praise generally employed his lips, when he first opened his eyes in the morning. He was fond of singing, and he loved to sing a verse or two before he rose. One of these verses was,

> "Ye little birds of heaven,
> On every bough that sing,
> Ye shame me with your early notes,
> While on your morning wing."

Another was

> "Not many suns shall set,
> Not many mornings rise,
> Till heaven unfold its glories all,
> To my admiring eyes."

Yet though a cheerful, happy man, he had often his trials and sorrows. Besides those common to the lot of humanity, he and his family, in the earlier years of their western history, were sorely tried by frequent alarms about the Indians. At certain periods, he, in common with his people, when committing themselves and their little ones at night, to the care of the Shepherd of Israel, knew not but that before the morning's dawn, their cabin-houses might be wrapped in flames, and themselves massacred, or led off into captivity. On one occasion he had to bring a communion service, at King's Creek, to an abrupt close on the announcement of the approach of a body of Indians from the mouth of Mill Creek, to mount his horse, and with many of his people, both men and women, to ride in haste, near twenty miles. Pecuniary embarrassments, which, no doubt, in a great measure proceeded from the perilous condition, or entire suspension of trade and commerce, produced by these "forays" of the savages, pressed sorely upon Mr. Smith and his people. Here we cannot forbear to introduce a very singular account of a providential interposition for the relief of Mr. Smith, at a very alarming crisis in his affairs, when his faith must have been greatly tried. In justice to the Rev. James W. Miller, to whom the public was indebted many years ago, for this statement, we will give the narrative in his own language.

"Our story will carry the reader back 'to the period' when all north of the Ohio River was an almost unbroken wilderness—the mysterious red man's home. On the other side, a bold and hardy band from beyond the mountains had built their log cabins, and were trying to subdue the wilderness. To them every hour was full of peril. The Indians would often cross the river, steal their children and horses, and kill and scalp any victim who came in their way. They worked in the field with weapons at their side, and on a Sabbath met in a grove or rude log church, to hear the word of God, with their rifles in their hands. To preach to these settlers, Mr. Joseph Smith, a Presbyterian minister, had left his parental home east of the mountains. He, it was said, was the second minister who had crossed the Monongahela River. He settled in Washington County, Pennsylvania, and became the pastor of the Cross Creek and Upper Buffalo congregations, dividing his time between them. He found them a willing and united people, but still unable to pay him a salary which would support his family. He, in common with all the early ministers, must cultivate a farm. He purchased one on credit, promising to pay for it with the salary pledged to him by his people. Years passed away. The pastor was unpaid. Little or no money was in circulation. Wheat was abundant, but there was no market. It could not be sold for more than twelve and a half cents in cash. Even their salt had to be brought across the mountains on pack-horses, was worth eight dollars per bushel, and twenty-one bushels of wheat had often to be given for one of salt. The time came when the last payment must be made, and Mr. Smith was told he must pay or leave his farm. Three years' salary was now due from his people. For the want of this, his land, his improvements upon it, and his hopes of remaining among a beloved people, must be abandoned. The people were called together, and the case laid before them; they were greatly moved; counsel from on high was sought; plan after plan was proposed and abandoned; the congregations were unable to pay a tithe of their debts, and no money could be borrowed. In despair, they adjourned to meet again the following week. In the mean time, it was ascertained that a Mr. Moore, who owned the only mill in the county, would grind for them wheat on reasonable terms. At the next meeting it w s resolved to carry their wheat to Mr. Moore's mill: some gave fifty bushels, some more. This was carried from fifteen to twenty-six miles, on horses, to mill. In a month word came that the flour was ready to go to market. Again the people were called together. After an earnest prayer, the question was asked, 'Who will run the flour to New Orleans?' This was a startling question. The work was perilous in the extreme; months must pass before the adventurer could hope to return, even though his journey should be fortunate; nearly all the way was a wilderness, and gloomy tales had been told of the treacherous Indian. More than one boat's crew had gone on that journey and came back no more. 'Who, then, would endure the toil and brave the danger?' None volunteered: the young shrunk back, and the middle-aged had their excuse. The scheme at last seemed likely to fail. At length a hoary-headed man, an elder in the church, sixty-four years of age, arose, and, to the astonishment of the assembly, said, 'Here am I—send me.' The deepest feeling at once pervaded the whole assembly. To see their venerated old elder thus devote himself for their good melted them all to tears. They gathered around *Father Smiley* to learn that his resolution was indeed taken; that, rather than lose their pastor, he would brave danger, toil, and even death. After some delay and trouble, two young men were induced, by hope of a large reward, to go as his assistants. A day was appointed for starting. The young and old, from far and near, from love to Father Smiley, and their deep interest in the object of his mission, gathered together, and, with their *pastor at their head*, came down from the church, fifteen miles away, to the bank of the river, to bid the old man farewell. Then a prayer was offered up by their pastor, a parting hymn was sung. 'There,' said the old Scotchman, 'untie the cable, and let us see what the Lord will do for us.' This was done, and the boat floated slowly away. More than nine months passed, and no word came back from Father Smiley. Many a prayer had been breathed for him, but what was his fate was unknown. Another Sabbath came; the people came together for worship, and there, on his rude bench before the preacher, composed and devout, sat Father Smiley. After the services, the people were requested to meet early in the week to hear the report. All came again. After thanks had been returned to God for his safe return, Father Smiley rose and told his story; that the Lord had prospered his mission, that he had sold his flour for twenty-seven dollars a barrel, and then got safely back. He then drew a large purse, and poured upon the table a larger pile of gold than most of the spectators had ever seen before. The young men were paid, each a hundred dollars. Father Smiley was asked his charges. He meekly replied that he thought he ought to have the same as one of the young men, though he had not done quite as much work. It was immediately proposed to pay him three hundred dollars. This he refused to receive till the pastor was paid. Upon counting the money, it was found there was enough to pay what was due Mr. Smith, to advance his salary for the year to come, to reward Father Smiley with three hundred dollars, and then have a large dividend for each contributor. Thus their debts were paid, their pastor relieved; and, while life lasted, he broke for them the bread of life. The bones of both pastor and elder, I believe, have long reposed in the same churchyard; but a grateful posterity still tells this pleasing story of the past."*

---

* Mr. William Smiley was an elder in Upper Buffalo Church — was a Scotchman, of a strong mind, very shrewd, and eminently pious. His manners were somewhat blunt; and he had an integrity and honesty about him which would not allow him to connive at anything which he thought to be wrong. He disliked everything which in any way set aside the claims of religion, and did not give it its proper place in the business of life or the enjoyment of the social circle. While attending the General Assembly at Carlisle, he was invited to spend a social evening at the house of General ———, who was also an elder and a pious man. The next day he was asked by an acquaintance, who met him, how he enjoyed himself. "Not very well," he replied, that "they gave him cursed tea." — "Cursed tea!" said his friend; "how was that?" — "Why," said he, "it was not blessed — of course it must have been cursed, that is all." He referred to the fact that the tea had been handed round without a blessing having been asked. Such was his judgment of the fashionable mode of tea-drinking. During the same Assembly, the Rev. Mr. ———, a vain man, of very moderate abilities, preached from I. Tim., i. 15, "This is a faithful saying, &c." Several other ministers had preached on the preceding days. The next day after he had preached he was walking with Father Smiley, and took occasion to ask him how he liked the sermon of Mr. ———, and the sermon of Mr. ———, who had preached on the previous days. Mr. Smiley put him off with a general answer. "Well, then, how did you like my sermon?" asked his interrogator. — "Why," said he, "I did not like it at all." — "Why not?" said the preacher. — "Because," rejoined Smiley, "you said nothing about closing with Christ."—"That," said the preacher, "was not in the text."—"It was as much in the text as what you did say," replied Smiley. This put an end to the colloquy, and it is not likely that the reverend gentleman would soon again seek to elicit a compliment from the honest Scotchman. Father Patterson

Mr. Miller states in his outset, that he received this account from Mr. Grimes, an elder of Buffalo; and we will add, that we have taken considerable pains to ascertain, from various other sources, that it is all substantially correct. Such were the dealings of God with His servant, and well might he, ever after this, feel assured that "the Lord will provide."

Mr. Smith was a laborious and faithful pastor. In visiting and catechising his people, and in his efforts to seek out those who were neglecting the ordinances of religion, he was most diligent. The tide of emigration, especially from Virginia, poured around him considerable numbers of a profane, Sabbath-breaking class. He was skilful in devising successful methods of access to every sort of persons, even to some that but few would have thought it worth while to approach. In this respect, he knew no man after the flesh, and would at once "beard the lion in his den." He may have sometimes failed, but no such instance of failure is now remembered. When once at the house of one of his elders over night, and rising early in the morning, he observed a house some half mile distant, and persons walking back and forth, near it. He inquired of his elder who lived there? He was told that it was a man who had come there some months before. Mr. Smith asked if he came to church. The elder said that he did not, but that his wife and daughters came sometimes. Mr. Smith said he would go and see them, and telling the elder not to wait breakfast for him, he set off immediately. On arriving at the house, he found the man and his family at home. He introduced himself as the minister who preached at Buffalo, and as such he called to see him. The man said he knew him, although he had not been to church; but his wife and children sometimes went. Mr. Smith called the family together, and talked with them on the subject of religion. After some time he asked the man if he had family

---

was walking near to them at the time, and overheard this conversation, very much to his gratification.

worship that morning. He replied he had not. "I suppose," said Mr. Smith, "you pray in your family, of course." He admitted that he did not. "Then," said Mr. Smith, "you ought to do it, and the sooner you begin, the better. You must begin immediately." He then asked for a Bible, and read and remarked upon a suitable passage, and then asked the man to pray; and without giving him time to express his assent or dissent, kneeled down forthwith. A long silence ensued; Mr. Smith then turned to the man, and urged him to pray. He still remained silent. Again urged by his importunate visitor, to pray, under this process, his mind deeply agitated, he at length cried out in agony, "O Lord, teach me to pray, for I know not how to pray." "That will do," said Mr. Smith, as he rose from his knees, "you have made a good beginning, and I trust you will soon be able to extend your petitions." The result was such as Mr. Smith predicted, for the tradition is, that from this time forth he became a man of prayer, and he and his family became consistent and active members of the Church.*

He was anxious from the first, after he settled in the West, to look out for, and aid in preparing some young men to preach the gospel.† He is believed to have been the first

* Dr. Lindley says, in one of his letters, "The ruling passion of his warfare was innocent contrivances to catch flanking parties and strolling individuals in the gospel-net. He was an eagle-eyed spy and scouter upon the trails of the enemy, and was very successful in the capture of individuals, as well as taking them in squadrons. Though he made no pretensions to brute force, he feared none of the Devil's emissaries, on this side of Hell."

† We give another passage from Doddridge's "Notes." "From the outset, they prudently resolved to create a ministry in the country, and accordingly established little grammar schools at their own houses, or in their immediate neighborhoods. The course of education which they gave their pupils was indeed not extensive; but the piety of those who entered into the ministry more than made up the deficiency. They formed societies, most of which are now large and respectable, and in point of education, their ministry has much improved. About the year 1792, an academy was established at Canonsburgh, in Washington

who moved in this matter. The Rev. Thaddeus Dodd had, as early as 1783 or '4, moved into the village of Washington, and taught the town school or academy, in the old Court-House, for about a year, and returned to Ten Mile, where he had previously resided. During that time, two or three young men, having the ministry in view, received instruction from Mr. Dodd, among whom were James Hughes and John Hanna. But the first school that was opened with a special view to the training of young men for the sacred office, is believed to have been begun by Mr. Smith, at Upper Buffalo, as early, at least, as 1785. The subject had pressed heavily on his mind for some time before. There was one difficulty in his way. He had no suitable house. But he had recently erected a house adjoining his dwelling-house, to serve as a kitchen and out-house. If his wife would be willing to surrender that for a while, and fall back on their former hampered domestic system, it could be done. He stated the case to her. She cordially acquiesced in the plan, and warmly seconded his views. Almost immediately the first Latin school was begun. Messrs. M'Gready, Porter, and Patterson, began their course. Soon after, James Hughes, and Brice, who had already been with Mr.

County, in the western part of Pennsylvania, which was afterwards incorporated under the name of Jefferson College. The means possessed by the Society, [the Presbyterian Church, doubtless, he means,] for the undertaking, were indeed but small; but they not only erected a tolerable edifice for the academy, but collected a fund for the education of such pious young men as were desirous of entering into the ministry, but were unable to defray the expenses of their education. This institution has been remarkably successful in its operations. It has produced a large number of good scholars, in all the literary professions, and added immensely to the science of the country. Next to this, Washington College, situated in the county town of the county of that name, has been the means of diffusing much of the light of science through the Western country. Too much pains cannot be bestowed on those good men who opened these fruitful sources of instruction for our infant country, at so early a period of its settlement. They have immensely improved the departments of theology, law, medicine, and legislation in the western regions."

Dodd, joined them. This school for the languages and sciences was continued some time, and then, by some mutual arrangement, was transferred and re-organized, near Canonsburgh, under the care of Dr. M'Millan. It was therefore the real nucleus, the larva out of which grew eventually, first, the Canonsburgh Academy, and then Jefferson College. This view of the case will, perhaps, be called in question. It has been commonly supposed that such a school was long before in operation, under the direction of Dr. M'Millan, and that the school at Chartiers, for preparing young men for the ministry, did not succeed that of Mr. Smith, or in any sense was the same school, transferred from Buffalo to Chartiers. We will endeavor to state fairly a few things that may serve to guide us to a right decision on this point.

In the first place, the records of the Presbytery of Redstone show that there were no licentiates under their care, who had received their previous scholastic or theological training from Dr. M'Millan, till long after the above period, and that all the first ministers had received their instruction, either from Mr. Dodd or Mr. Smith. The Redstone Presbytery was the only Presbytery then west of the mountains. Now it is strange, if, indeed, there was such a school at Dr. M'Millan's, where young men were instructed in the languages and sciences, before or for some years immediately after, or during 1785, that not one of them can now be found, and that there is no mention of such in the minutes of the Presbytery. The same thing will appear upon examining the Appendix (containing brief biographical notices of all the first ministers in Western Pennsylvania) affixed to Dr. Elliott's life of Macurdy.

In the second place, we would mention the express testimony of Mrs. Irwin, an aged, but very intelligent lady, now residing near Marysville, Ohio, who stated to us, in substance, as follows (and her pastor, the Rev. Mr. Smith, testifies that it has been her unvaried statement for many years, and has no doubt of her memory being perfectly good in this case,) "that she was between twelve and fifteen years of age, living near Mr. Smith's, one of his spiritual children, took a great interest, then, in what Mr. Smith did in this matter, and all her life after, familiarly remembered the following facts: that in 1785, Mr. Smith, of Buffalo and Cross Creek congregations, opened a school for assisting and training young men for the gospel ministry; that Mr. M'Gready, Mr. Brice, Mr. Porter, and Mr. Patterson, began their course then with him, Mr. James Hughes soon after joining them; that Mr. M'Gready came from Dr. M'Millan's, with whom he had been living, not as a student, but as a laborer on his farm; that five congregations, through the ladies, united in furnishing these students (with the exception of Mr. M'Gready) with clothing, viz., Buffalo, Cross Creek, Chartiers, Bethel, and Ten-Mile; that they made up summer and winter clothing for several of these young men (coloring linen for summer wear in a dye made of new-mown hay!) that this was the first movement made for preparing young men for the ministry; that there was no such school, at this time, at Chartiers, nor until after the one at Buffalo was discontinued; that Mrs. M'Millan and the Chartiers ladies took their share in this effort to sustain this school at Buffalo, Mr. M'Gready coming from Dr. M'Millan's to the school." This is very explicit testimony; and to every word of it Mrs. Irwin testified, in substance, to the writer.

In the third place, we give the following statement, furnished to us by Dr. Cephas Dodd, the venerable pastor of Amity, Washington county, and son of Rev. Thaddeus Dodd. He was sufficiently old, at the time, to remember distinctly the facts which he states. "There was an agreement made between Mr. Smith and Mr. Dodd, by which they engaged, alternately, to superintend the education of certain young men, who had the ministry in view. Mr. Dodd had a large cabin erected near his dwelling, which was occupied as a school-room, and they boarded in his family. Of these, were Messrs. James Hughes, John Brice, Robert Marshall, and John Hanna, and afterwards David Smith, son of Mr. Smith, all of whom afterwards entered the ministry. They were with Mr. Dodd from about 1783 to 1786, and pursued their studies for the remainder of the time with Mr. Smith. It is thought that Dr. M'Millan was also a party to the above arrangement, but for some cause the aforesaid young men were never under his tuition. There were others, as Messrs. Patterson, M'Gready, and Porter, who were instructed solely by Mr. Smith." There may seem some slight discrepancy between the view presented by Dr. Dodd, and some of the foregoing testimony; but the most essential difficulty is easily removed by remembering that Mr. Dodd's school was, all along, an *English school*, and instruction in the languages merely an appendage to it, for the accommodation of two or three young men; whereas Mr. Smith's school was a real Latin school, got up especially for training young men for the ministry, and concentrating the aid and patronage of all the churches, Dr. M'Millan's church included.*

We may, in the *last* place, refer to an extract from a letter of Dr. M'Millan to Dr. Carnahan, dated March 26th, 1832. Towards the close of that interesting letter he says, "I am now in my eightieth year; I have outlived all the *first set* of ministers who settled on this side of the mountains, viz., Rev. Messrs. James Finley, James Power, Jas. Dunlap, J. Clarke, Joseph Smith, and Thaddeus Dodd; and all of the *second set* who were raised up in this country, viz., Joseph Patterson, James Hughes, John Brice, James M'Gready, Wm. Swan, Samuel Porter, Thomas Marquis, and J. M'Pherrin." There is Dr. M'Millan's list of the *second set;* and *none* of these

---

* The statement above given respecting the character of Mr. Dodd's school, the writer is assured by the Rev. C. Dodd and the Rev. Jacob Lindley, is not altogether correct. This school of Mr. Dodd, though with an English department, was prominently a classical, mathematical and scientific school. The silence of Mr. Doddridge, and a statement of the Rev. William Wylie, D. D., together with an expression of the Rev. Joseph Patterson, (see his Life,) had misled us.

did he train or instruct, till after the school at Buffalo ceased, or was transferred to Chartiers.

An earlier passage in this letter has given rise to what we believe an error respecting the date of Dr. M'Millan's *Latin school.* It is as follows: "When I determined to come to this country, Dr. Smith enjoined it upon me* to look out for some pious young men, and educate them for the ministry; for, said he, though some men of piety and talents may go to a new country first, yet, if they are not careful to train up others, the country will not be well supplied. Accordingly, I collected a few who gave evidence of piety, and taught them the Latin and Greek languages. Some of them became useful, and others eminent ministers of the gospel. I had still a few with me when the academy was opened in Canonsburg, and, finding that I could not teach and do justice to my congregation, I immediately gave it up and sent them there."

Now, this passage furnishes nothing in conflict with all that we have said, and, we think, *proved.* If the Doctor refers to a period *prior* to the school at Buffalo, as some seem to have understood him, but of which he says nothing, then *who were those* he thus trained, and who afterwards became ministers? It is manifest their names are not found on the records of the Presbytery of Redstone, nor in that list which he himself calls the *second set* of ministers. It is evident that either this passage in the Doctor's letter has been misunderstood, when it has been brought to prove that his Latin school was the first, or is only another illustration of "lapsus memoriæ" in an octogenarian! [This letter, by the way, gives no evidence that Dr. M'Millan had any direct agency, or at least took any active part, in getting up the academy at Canonsburg. On this we have other evidence that he opposed that location, but it is aside from our purpose to introduce it now.] It seems in itself not unlikely that this enterprise should begin

* He no doubt gave the same injunction to Mr. Smith and others, if he had the opportunity.

with Mr. Smith, as he was a thorough classical scholar, and fifteen years older than Dr. M'Millan, and the pastor of two very large churches, where a great number of youth had been hopefully converted to God under his ministry.* That he

* We would also invite attention to the following statements from the Rev. Joseph Patterson, and from his son, the Rev. Robert Patterson, as in harmony with the entire view we have given above, though by no means written for that purpose. The first is an extract from a prefatory note to a volume of letters written by the Rev. Joseph Patterson: "In the fall of 1785, being thirty-three years old, it was thought best, with the advice of the Presbytery of Redstone, that I should endeavor to prepare for the gospel ministry. There being no places of public education in this country, I, with a few others, studied with the Rev. Joseph Smith, of Buffalo congregation, Washington county, Pa. Being partially absent from my family," &c.

The other statement will be found in the following extract from a letter of the Rev. Robert Patterson to the Rev. M. Brown, D. D., dated Oct. 1st, 1846: "Between 1780 and 1790, and chiefly in the latter part of these ten years, some of the few Presbyterian clergymen living west of the mountains in Pennsylvania, were in the habit of giving instruction in the languages and sciences to young men, whose object in their studies was the gospel ministry. The Rev. Messrs. Joseph Smith and John M'Millan were distinguished in their devotion to this cause. They both settled in congregations in Washington county, Pa. Mr. Smith had a small building erected in a corner of the garden, called "the students' room," too small to be dignified with the name of a *hall.* And Mr. M'Millan had a small log cabin built near his log dwelling-house, known to this day by the appellation of the "log cabin." In these primitive seminaries were educated some men who became eminently useful and successful in the Church. Among them may be named the Rev. Messrs. William Swan, Samuel Porter, James Hughes, John Brice, David Smith, Joseph Patterson, and others whose names do not occur to my memory. It should be here stated, that, for want of suitable places elsewhere, the students generally lodged in the minister's family, without profit, and sometimes at considerable expense to the household. In this service and toil, the wives of these two godly ministers heartily concurred. I knew them well, and they were both eminently mothers in Israel.

"For some time in the latter part of 1790, instruction in these small seminaries had been suspended," &c.

Both these statements substantially confirm the account given by cheerfully handed over the subsequent management of this important interest to Dr. M'Millan, and co-operated with him, after the transfer, in building up the school, we have not a doubt. Indeed, as chairman of the committee appointed by the Synod of Virginia, (and truly this place was rightly assigned to him who had done so much in starting the enterprise,) he brought in a report which was adopted by the Synod at their session in Winchester, Oct. 1st, 1791. That report contains these two interesting items:

"The committee appointed to form a plan for promoting the education of persons for the ministry of the gospel, report: The Synod having considered the same, and made such amendments and additions as were judged necessary, agreed to it as follows: 'Taking this measure, therefore, under serious consideration, the Synod recommend that there be two general institutions for learning, conducted under the patronage of this body—the one to be established in Rockbridge county, in this State, under the care of the Rev. Wm. Graham; the other in Washington county, Pa., under the care of the Rev. John M'Millan. The principles upon which these institutions are to be conducted, are to be as follows,'" &c. Thus the prominent part which the subject of this memoir took, from first to last, may be clearly seen. While Mr. Smith lived, the institution at Canonsburg was under the care of his presbytery, and remotely of his synod (of Virginia). And so it continued for many years after his death.* It is no part of our design to trace the subsequent history of this

---

Mrs. Irwin and Dr. C. Dodd; whilst the latter statement of the Rev. R. Patterson shows how erroneous has been the prevailing theory about the earlier and prior origin of the "log cabin" school, and about the Canonsburg academy growing out of it. It indeed rather grew out of Mr. Johnson's school, or Mr. Miller's school; and Dr. M'Millan gave up his school in consequence, in part, of this academy being thus begun. (See further on this subject in the Life of Dr. M'Millan.)

*We have since ascertained that this statement, as will hereafter appear, is not quite correct.

earliest western Presbyterian school of the prophets. For reasons no doubt deemed satisfactory, it has long since passed out of the control of the Church. It is no longer under ecclesiastical supervision, and, indeed, never was, we believe, as a college. Its earlier history, from the peculiar relations to it of the subject of this memoir, we have thought proper to notice. Mr. Smith never met the Synod of Virginia again. Before that time he was called to his rest.

Still abounding in labors, at home and abroad, and wearing out in his master's service, the spring of 1792 found Mr. Smith at his post. His health, though never vigorous, gave no token of his approaching end. He was in his pulpit on the first Sabbath of April, and was at Cross Creek, according to his alternate course, on that day. His text was Gal. i. 8, "Though we, or an angel from heaven, preach any other gospel than that which we have preached, let him be accursed." He took occasion, from this text, to give them a summary sketch of his twelve years' preaching. It seemed like the winding up of the whole of his ministry. It was universally remarked that he spoke as though he had a presentiment that it was to be his last sermon. He seemed to them as though he was just going to the judgment-seat of Christ. The whole place was like a Bochim. How much more were his people affected, when it was found that he required assistance to get from the pulpit to his horse! He was obliged to remain for a day or two in the neighborhood, and then was conveyed home on a sled. Carriages with wheels were almost unknown then.

His disease was inflammation of the brain. His sufferings, though short, were severe. In the earlier stages of his disease, he was in deep waters. At one time a cloud of great darkness came over him. His affectionate people poured in to see him. He asked them to pray for him. To a number of young people, whom the Lord had given him as his spiritual children, and who were permitted to approach his bedside, he said, "My dear children, often have I prayed for you when you were asleep in your beds; now is your time to pay me back. Oh, pray for me, that the Lord would shield me from the fiery darts of Satan. Deep calleth unto deep, and all his billows he maketh to pass over me." In such language, we have been told by one of that group that then stood by his bedside, did he express the anguish of his spirit; but the conflict was soon over, and all was peace. His last day was spent in the land of Beulah. As long as he could speak, it was in the accents of triumph and holy joy. On the 19th of April, 1792, Mr. Smith finished his course on earth, and died in the faith. The tidings of his death spread a gloom over a widely extended community. Such were the feelings of his own people, that, as many of them testified, it was a common remark among them, that the sun did not seem to shine with his natural brightness for many days afterwards. Truly a great man had fallen in Israel. The following lines, composed by the Rev. Thaddeus Dodd, are to be found on the stone that covers his mortal remains in the graveyard at Upper Buffalo:

"What joys malignant flushed the powers of Hell!
But Zion trembled when this Pillar fell,
Lest God, who his ambassador withdrew,
Should take away his Holy Spirit too;
Then some vain hireling, void of special grace,
Be brought to fill this faithful pastor's place."*

* The following lines were found among Mr. Dodd's papers, composed by him as an affectionate tribute to the memory of his departed friend and brother:

"Hark! hark! methinks I hear the solemn toll,
Which might reverberate from pole to pole;
That dear beloved man, whom oft we heard,
And every truly gracious soul revered,
That man of God—the man we often saw,
In his great Master's name proclaim his law,
In terms which might have moved a heart of steel,
And almost made an adamant to feel
The terrors of God's wrath—and when he show'd
The way of peace, pointing to Jesus' blood,

The congregation where he lived and died still survive in the successive generations that have arisen. Their candlestick is not yet removed. It is true, that by emigration, they have furnished an immense number as materials for new churches all over the West: could their statistics in this matter be gathered, it would, it is believed, awaken in every pious mind astonishment and gratitude. In this respect, the influence of his ministry has been extended down till the present time; and over the Western States, and with multitudes, wherever the traveller wanders through Ohio and other States, he will find the name of Joseph Smith pronounced with reverence and affection. It will be seen also by the statistics of the General Assembly, appended to their Minutes, that his old churches are still amongst the most flourishing of Western Pennsylvania. If Kidderminster, the place where Richard Baxter laboured so ardently and so successfully, has still a chosen people, after the lapse of two centuries, need we wonder that the Lord is still very gracious to the descendants of that pious race, that, more than seventy years ago, were gathered in our western wilderness, under the ministry of such a man as Joseph Smith, who "lured to brighter worlds, and led the way."

Mr. Smith was a faithful preacher of the terrors of the law; and, on this account profane people gave him the soubriquet of *Hell-fire* Smith. In this connexion we may mention a well-accredited fact, though all the details are not now preserved. Mr. Smith was on his way to the General

---

Hard was the wretch, a senseless rock the heart,
That in the Saviour would not have a part;
Sweet invitation dwelt upon his tongue,
Enough t' have drawn an infidel along.
In him seraphic zeal and manly sense,
A mind informed, and sacred eloquence,
Warm (not enthusiastic) heavenly love,
To souls below and his great Lord above,
Joined in sweet concert: Unto him was given
The art of converse, tasting strong of heaven."

Assembly, and tarried during the Sabbath in a congregation where vital religion was at a very low ebb. The minister, having heard of Mr. Smith's style of preaching intimated to him that he would be glad if he would give his people one of his more moderate sermons, as it would better suit their taste. Mr. Smith, after giving out an impressive hymn and offering an unusually fervent prayer, arose to preach, and as he rose uttered with a strong voice the words, "Fire! fire! fire!" The congregation, as we may well suppose, were alarmed and agitated, and eagerly glanced their eyes towards every part of the building, above and around. "If the very mention of the word," continued the preacher, "so startles you, if the mere apprehension of it, excited by the voice of a stranger, so disturbs you, what will it be to encounter the reality? 'Who can dwell with everlasting burnings?' This is my text." He delivered one of his most alarming and awakening discourses. It was the means of an entire change in the spiritual views and ministerial labors of the pastor, and the commencement of a revival of religion in the congregation. The minister often mentioned the circumstance freely, and with flowing tears and expressions of gratitude to God for having sent his servant among them.

At one of the first communion seasons in the western wilderness, Mr. Smith was present. An immense concourse of people were drawn together from a widely extended settlement. The services were conducted in a grove, adjoining the meeting-house; which house, by the way, would hardly have contained a tithe of the people that usually assembled, on such occasions. This recourse to a grove was quite a common arrangement for many years afterwards. There are thousands yet living who well remember the solemn, delightful scenes witnessed and enjoyed beneath the canopies of western forests; and we doubt not, the reminiscences of Heaven sometimes wander back to such rural spots, where "Heaven was begun below!" But to return: the sacramental service which, at that time, was generally more protracted than in our day, was at length closed, late in the afternoon of a long summer day. Mr. Smith rose to deliver a closing address; but the attention of the audience was disturbed: considerable numbers having many miles to go in order to reach their homes, were rising and dispersing; some setting out on foot, some going to their horses, some disengaging their bridles from the branches of the trees, some preparing to mount, some already mounted, and riding in different directions — presenting altogether a picturesque and striking scene. Mr. Smith, surveying the whole aspect before him, and raising his clear and remarkably piercing voice to a loud and thrilling pitch, commenced, after this manner: "One word to those who are now retiring, and who cannot remain longer with us. We are told that when this supper was celebrated for the first time, none retired from the place until all was over, but Judas. If there be any Judases here, let them go! but let them remember, that what they have heard and seen here to-day, will follow them to their homes and to hell, if they go there!" The effect, it is said, was like an electric shock; they all, with scarcely an exception, returned to their seats and hung upon his lips with fixed attention, until the benediction was pronounced.

The following is an extract from *his will*:—"I give and bequeath to each of my beloved children, a *Bible*, to be paid for out of my personal estate, and in so doing, mean to intimate to them, as I am a dying man and in the sight of God, that it is ten thousand times more my will and desire that they should find and possess the pearl of great price hid in the field of the Scriptures, than enjoy anything else which I can bequeath to them, or even ten thousand worlds, were they all composed of the purest gold and all brim-full of the richest jewels, and yet be ignorant of the precious treasures in God's word, that are entirely hid from the most eagle-eyed and quick-sighted men that are properly of this world." We cannot forbear to add that there is good reason to hope that all his children are now with him in heaven.*

* Indeed it is worthy of admiration and praise, that the Lord was truly a covenant God to him and to his seed after him. He trained in

After all that has been said, we know of nothing better suited to give us a full view of the depth and fervency of his piety than the following letter, written more than two years before his death, and addressed to a young minister, though not a very young man, whom he had trained for the sacred office, and who was now just settled as a pastor in an adjoining field.*

"*Rev. and Dear Sir*, — Grace, mercy, and peace be with you and yours. It might, perhaps, look too much like flattery, to tell you how much I long to see you, and the desire I have for your success in the great work which your divine Master has lately intrusted you with. Dear sir, let me remind you, and myself with you, that such is the greatness, the extreme difficulty of a minister's work, and the awfully-important consequences of every sermon, of every sentence he delivers in the name of the Eternal God, that every man of the sacred character, who knows what he is about, must often tremble at the thought, and cry out with the Apostle, 'Who is sufficient for these things?' Who is fit to stand so near to, and personate so glorious and dreadful a God? Who is fit to manage this office, so as to give a good account of it upon the strictest inquiry? Who can discharge it, answerable to that boundless eternal felicity, or extremest everlasting misery, which will enure upon the manner of his executing it? O, what acquaintance with God,

---

the nurture and admonition of the Lord *five daughters*, one, who died a peaceful and happy death, in the very bloom of womanhood; the four others became the wives of ministers. These ministers were the Rev. Dr. Welch, of Dayton, the Rev. James Hughes, first President of Miami University, the Rev. Joseph Anderson, lately deceased in Missouri, and the Rev. Dr. William Wylie, of Newark, Ohio. One of his sons died whilst preparing for the ministry. Another, the Rev. David Smith, lived to the age of thirty-two; after preaching with great success, for about nine years, he literally fell in his Master's work, with his armor on, and "*vici*" on his shield, in the midst of an extensive revival of religion in his congregation. Several of Mr. Smith's grandchildren became ministers of the Gospel, some of whom are now in the field.

* Mr. Smith had been appointed to deliver the charge to Mr. Patterson at his ordination; but was prevented from attending on that occasion. And though another had performed that service in his stead, he, in this letter, perhaps at Patterson's request, sent him the substance of what he had intended and prepared to say in the charge. See Records of 26th Meeting of Presbytery.

what application of mind, what skill, what prudence, what tenderness, what care, what fortitude and courage, does such an one need! In short, if we consider and well survey the important ends of our office, how extremely difficult it is; what discouragements and oppositions we have to encounter, from ourselves, from those we preach to, from the missionaries of hell, who, with a zeal that may reproach our lukewarmness, exert themselves to propagate the contagion of vice, and occasion those to relapse who seemed upon the recovery by our instrumentality, —I say, can we consider this, the important and tremendous ends of our office, and yet yawn and indulge a slothful inactivity in the pursuit of them? Surely, no: but we must be crying out, O, that we could get free from the stupifying influence of sin and sloth! and keep our spirits deeply impressed with the dread importance of eternal things! O, that we were always duly sensible of the worth of the immortal soul! then would we be as watchful over our flocks as their guardian angels.

"But, alas! from hell, too, do our ministrations meet with the most powerful opposition. The very office itself, and ministers for the sake of it, are the butts against which Satan, by his instruments, levels his sharpest darts, well knowing that here are laid the strongest batteries against his kingdom. And, therefore, without doubt, the most faithful ministers are the most assaulted.

"Oh, it is well that the mighty conqueror hath said, 'Lo! I am with you always, even unto the end of the world.' In this one blessed promise we find all necessary provision. The officers he employs, in every age, are still entitled to the benefit of this provision, as well as those of the first age. Here, then, my dear son, brother, and friend, while you take heed to fulfil your ministry, you have the greatest encouragement. Though you may be often ready to faint, and so left to feel your weakness and dependence, yet, on the whole, you shall find strength proportioned to the difficulties of your work. For you are a fellow-worker with Him whose designs shall not be frustrated by all the powers of hell. When our dear Lord put you into the ministry, I doubt not at all but he counted it the greatest honor he could put upon you in this mortal life; and he justly expects that you should form the same estimate of it. See that you endeavor always to realize this, and it will much sweeten your work, and raise your grateful wonder. See also that you keep your mind believingly attentive to this promise, 'Lo! I am with you,'—to qualify and succeed you in whatever work I call you to, 'Lo! I am with you,'—to comfort you by my grace and Spirit, when your heart is grieved,' Lo, I am with you,'—to defend and strengthen you in every trial, though all men should forsake you; and while He stands with you, there can be no just cause of fear or fainting. When you are exposed to danger, it will comfort your heart that Christ holdeth the stars (his ministers) in his right hand, and none can pluck them thence. If any hurt them, they must strike them *there*. And, therefore, you can suffer nothing but what He permits for gracious ends, and from destructive evils you are altogether safe.

"And now, my dear sir, as you are appointed an instrument to plant the Heavenly world, may you be honored in begetting many souls to Christ, and saving those who shall be your crown of rejoicing in the day of our dear Lord Jesus. Nor will you fail of endless glory, though your hearers should perish by their own fault. From, dear sir,

"Your obedient, affectionate friend,

"JOSEPH SMITH.

"Cross Creek, Jan. 16, 1790.

"REV. MR. PATTERSON."

Such were the views and sentiments of this western pioneer of the gospel ministry, and "though dead, he yet speaketh." If the foregoing account of this eminent servant of God be rendered in any measure instrumental in promoting amongst the rising ministry an increased degree of devotion to their sacred work and of love to the souls of men, it will be an abundant compensation for the time and trouble expended in the preparation of this article. To the divine blessing, for this purpose, we commend our humble offering. If this paper shall meet the eye of any of the descendants of the venerated subject of this Memoir, may it contribute to quicken their steps heavenward. J. S.

Note.—The partner of Mr. Smith's joys and sorrows, who was truly a crown to her husband, Mrs. Esther Smith, survived him for twenty-eight years, and did not reach the goal of her life till she had almost touched the boundaries of fourscore. She was a remarkable woman. Often it might be said "she was an Israelite indeed, and a mother in Israel." She was the daughter of Mr. William Cummin, merchant, of Cecil County, Maryland. Early in life she knew the Lord, and devoted herself to him. In the twenty-second year of her age she was united in marriage to the subject of the foregoing memoir. They had eight children — three sons and five daughters; all hopefully the children of God. Six of them gave comfortable ground of hope that they entered the heavenly rest of God's people before their mother. Mary, the wife of the Rev. James Hughes, and Esther, the wife of the Rev. William

Wylie, D. D., survived her. But both have long since joined their pious parents in the heavenly Inheritance, as we confidently and joyfully hope. Mrs. Smith lived with, and sustained, and blessed her husband, more than twenty years, saw him triumphantly depart, and pursued her widowed pilgrimage for a still longer period, before she in turn reached the margin of Jordan, on whose banks she had seen her husband enjoying the visions of the Celestial City. The latter part of her life, particularly after her removal to the State of Ohio — for, having selected the family of the Rev. James Hughes as her earthly home, she went with them to Ohio — was peculiarly useful. Being without any particular charge or incumbrance, she spent a great part of her time among the poor, afflicted, and those who were under exercise about the state of their souls. She did much to relieve and procure relief for their distress. A steady member of female praying societies, she did much to unite Christian females of different denominations in these societies; one of which she attended weekly until a few days before her decease, when she became too weak to walk. She gradually declined, without much pain or sickness. Near the close of life, she sometimes wondered why *the Lord continued her so long in the world:* she feared that she had in some way offended him; and this was a reason why *he did not take her home to himself.* She said, a short time before her death, that she had no hope but through the perfect righteousness of Christ. She had so often (she thought sincerely) given herself to the Lord, she believed he would not cast her off. She slept sweetly in Jesus on the morning of the 7th of October, 1820, in the 78th year of her age, while the family were engaged in their morning devotions, in which the following hymn was sung, though her death was not at that time immediately expected:

"Ye fleeting charms of earth, farewell:
Your springs of joy are dry:
My soul now seeks another home;
A brighter world on high.

"Farewell, ye friends, whose tender care
Has long engaged my love;
Your fond embrace I now exchange
For better friends above.

"Cheerful I leave this vale of tears,
Where pains and sorrows grow:
Welcome the day that ends my toil,
And every scene of woe.

"No more shall sin disturb my breast;
My God shall frown no more;
The streams of love divine shall yield
Transport unknown before.

"Fly, then, ye interposing days;
Lord, send the summons down:
The hand that strikes me to the dust
Shall raise me to a crown."

CHAPTER II.

MANNERS, CUSTOMS AND DOMESTIC CIRCUMSTANCES OF EARLY FRONTIER LIFE.

WE cannot suppose that some account of the manners and customs and domestic circumstances of the people among whom our early ministers labored, would be unacceptable—or be deemed out of place in this work. On this subject, however, we shall draw largely, though not exclusively, upon Doddridge's "Notes on the Life and Manners of the first Western Settlers." In a few cases, Mr. Doddridge's descriptions are not alike applicable to every section of the early settlements. He was more conversant, from his residence, with the habits and manners of the Western Virginians; yet, though the inhabitants of the "Pan-Handle," perhaps, principally sat for the picture drawn by his graphic pen, much of his account is equally applicable to all Western Pennsylvania eighty years ago. They were all involved in the same privations, and were obliged to adopt similar personal and domestic usages. The settlers had to depend, for many years, principally for their necessaries, such as iron, nails, salt, and many other things, upon the towns of Chambersburg, Hagerstown, and Winchester; whither they resorted with their pack-horses, carrying furs, ginseng, snake-root, &c., to barter. In 1787, several stores, with what was then considered good stocks of goods, were established at different points, by enterprising men; who found it their interest to supply the articles necessary for a new country. The people themselves being thus accommodated, soon gave up their own eastern trips for such supplies. The merchandise, salt, &c., were still brought out on pack-horses: two men would manage ten or fifteen horses, carrying each about 200 pounds, by tying one to the other in single file—one of the men taking charge of the lead-horse, to pioneer; and the other the hinder one, to keep an eye on the proper adjustment of the roads, and to stir up any that appeared to lag. Bells were indispensable accompaniments to the horses; by which their position could be more easily ascertained in the morning, when hunting up, preparatory to a start. Some grass or leaves were inserted into the bell, to prevent the clapper from operating during the travel of the day.

The first wagon-load of merchandise that was brought over the mountains on the southern route, or that now nearly traversed by the national road, was in 1789. They were for Jacob Bowman, who had settled at Brownsville, as a merchant, in 1787, and is deceased but a few years ago. The wagoner was John Hayden, who also resided in Fayette County until his death. He drove four horses, brought out about 2000 pounds, for which he received $3 per 100, and was nearly a month making the trip to and fro, from Hagerstown, Maryland, a distance of about 140 miles. By means of the great improvement in the road, six horses will now haul 7000 or 8000, between the same places, in seven days, for $1 per 100.—*Day's Hist. Coll., p.* 343.

The perilous character of the roads across the mountains—and for some years there were but two, that of Braddock's, and the other cut for General Forbes, leading from Bedford, by Ligonier, to Pittsburg, rendered the management of a loaded wagon no child's play. So precipitous was the descent on the northern route, that it was usual to attach a small sapling, with all its brushy boughs, to the hinder part of the wagon, to act as a drag, to the foot of the mountain. These, in time, accumulated there, by the road-side, to the great puzzlement of those travellers who were not aware of the cause.

The task of making new establishments in a remote wilderness, even in a time of profound peace, is sufficiently difficult; but when, in addition to all the unavoidable hardships attendant on this business, those resulting from an extensive and furious warfare with savages are superadded—toil, privation, and sorrow are carried to the full extent of human endurance. Such was the wretched condition of the western settlers, in making settlements here. To all their difficulties and privations, the Indian war was a weighty addition. This destructive warfare they were compelled to sustain almost single-handed; because the Revolutionary contest with England gave full employment to military strength and resources on the east side of the mountains.

Their buildings were of the rudest kind. A spot was selected, on which to erect a house. On an appointed day, a company of choppers met, felled trees, cut them off at proper lengths; a man with a team hauled them to the place; this, while a carpenter was in search of a straight-grained tree, for making clapboards for the roof. The boards were split, four feet long, with a large prow, and as wide as the timber would allow: they were used without shaving. Some were employed in getting puncheons for the floor of the cabin. This was done by splitting trees about eighteen inches in diameter, and hewing the faces of them with a broad-axe. They were half the length of the floor they were intended to make. These were the usual preparations for the first day. The second day, the neighbors collected round, and finished the house. The third day's work generally consisted in "furnituring" the house—supplying it with a clapboard table, made of a split slab, and supported by four round legs, set in auger holes. Some three-legged stools were made in the same manner. Some pins stuck in the logs, at the back of the house, supported some clapboards which served for shelves for the table furniture, consisting of a few pewter dishes, plates and spoons; but mostly of wooden bowls, trenchers, and noggins. If these last were scarce, gourds and hard-shelled squashes made up the deficiency. The iron pots, knives and forks were brought from the east side of the mountains, along with salt and iron, on pack-horses.

A single fork, placed with its lower end in a hole in the floor and the upper end fastened to the joist, served for a bedstead, by placing a pole in the fork, with one end through a crack, between the logs in the wall. This front pole was crossed by a shorter one within the fork, with its outer end through another crack. From the first pole through a crack between the logs of the end of the house, the boards were put on, which formed the bottom of the bed. Sometimes other poles were pinned to the fork, a little distance above these, for the purpose of supporting the front and foot of the bed, while the walls were the supports of its back and its head. A few pegs around the walls for a display of the coats of the women, and hunting-shirts of the men; and two small forks or buck's horns to a joist, for the rifle and shot-pouch, completed the carpenter work. The cabin being finished, the next ceremony was "the house-warming." Did our first ministers know anything of such modes of living? Yes—every one of them, perhaps, without exception. Take Dr. M'Millan's account of the matter, as a specimen. "When I came to this country, the cabin in which I was to live was raised; but there was no roof on it, nor any chimney nor floor. The people, however, were very kind, and assisted me in preparing my house, and on the 16th of December I removed into it. But we had neither bedstead nor tables, nor stool, nor chair, nor bucket. All these things we had to leave behind us; as there was no wagon road at that time over the mountains; we could bring nothing but what was carried on pack-horses. We placed two boxes on each other, which served us for a table, and two kegs answered for seats, and having committed ourselves to God in family worship, we spread a bed on the floor, and slept soundly till morning. The next day a neighbor came to my assistance. We made a table and a stool, and in a little time had everything comfortable about us." The Doctor's bedstead and other fixtures were, no doubt, such as Mr. Doddridge describes.

The diet of our first settlers, says our author, was mainly

"hog and hominy." Dr. M'Millan says, "that for weeks together they had no meal, and lived on potatoes and pumpkins as a substitute for bread." Johnny-cake and pone were the bread for breakfast and dinner; mush and milk, a standard diet for supper. When milk was not plenty, which was often the case, the substantial dish of hominy had to serve the place of them; mush was frequently eaten with sweetened water, molasses, bear's oil or the gravy of fried meat.

Their dress was partly Indian, and partly of civilized nations. The hunting-shirt was universally worn. This was a kind of loose frock, reaching half way down the thighs, with large sleeves, open before, and so wide as to lap over a foot or more when belted. The cape was large, and sometimes handsomely fringed with a ravelled piece of cloth of a different color from that of the hunting-shirt itself." Both, however, were generally of that description of cloth called "Linsey-woolsey." The most common color was blue, and had a far neater appearance than those ugly-looking, red-flannel "waumuses"—now much worn in the winter by the farmers. "The bosom of this dress served as a wallet to hold a chunk of bread, cakes, jirk, tow for wiping the barrel of the rifle, or any other necessary for the hunter or warrior. The belt which was tied behind, answered several purposes, besides that of holding the dress together. In cold weather the mittens, and sometimes the bullet-bag, occupied the front of it. To the right side was suspended the tomahawk, and on the left the scalping-knife in its leathern sheath."

The hunting-shirt was generally made of linsey—sometimes of coarse linen, and a few, of dressed deer-skins. These last were generally cold and uncomfortable in wet weather. The shirt and jacket were of the common fashion. A pair of drawers or breeches and leggins were the dress of the thighs and legs. Buckskin breeches, yellow or black, were much worn by our ministers in those days.* We have seen in our

* When these *skins* were properly dressed, they looked as well as the finest Leeds black broadcloth.

boyish days, not less than four or five of them thus dressed. Dr. M'Millan long retained his preference for this article of dress.*

Meeting in the streets of Canonsburg, one day, Joe Dunlap, then a wild and thoughtless son of the venerable President of the College, the Doctor said to him, "Joe, can you tell me the difference between you and old Satan?" "Yes," said Joe, "I wear pantaloons, and Satan wears buckskin breeches." He did not intend to insult the Doctor, by such an answer. He knew the good man would laugh heartily at his jest.

But to proceed with Mr. Doddridge's further account of the dress of the times:—"A pair of moccasins answered for the feet much better than shoes. These were made of dressed deerskins. They were mostly made of a single piece, with gathered seams along the top of the foot, and another from the bottom of the heel, without gathers, as high as the ankle joint, or a little higher. Flaps were left on each side, to reach some distance up the legs. These were nicely adapted to the ankles, and lower part of the leg, by thongs of deerskin, so that no dust, gravel or snow could get within the moccasin. The moccasins in ordinary use cost but a few hours' labor to make them. In cold weather, the moccasins were stuffed with deer's hair, or dry leaves, so as to keep the feet comfortably warm.

"In latter years of the Indian war, the young men became more enamored with the Indian dress throughout, with the exception of the watch-coat. The drawers were laid aside, and the leggins made longer, so as to reach the upper part of the thigh. The Indian style of toilet was adopted. This was a piece of linen or cloth nearly a yard long, and eight or nine

---

* In a list of the different trades in Pittsburg in 1792, there is mention of "1 *Skin-dresser and Breeches maker.*" It was doubtless a good business then; and probably our ministers patronised the establishment. For though their wives could "gar ould clathes to look amaist as weel as new," we never heard that they had much skill at working in leather.

inches broad. This passed under the belt before and behind, leaving the ends of the flaps hanging, before and behind, over the belt. These flaps were sometimes ornamented with some coarse kinds of embroidering work. To the same belt which secured this cloth, strings which supported the long leggins were attached. When this belt, as was often the case, passed over the hunting-shirt, the upper part of the thighs, and part of the hips, were naked. The young warrior, instead of being abashed by his nudity, was proud of his Indian-like dress."

The latter part of this account refers, we have no doubt, exclusively to the region along the Ohio, bordering on the Indian country.

"The linsey-woolsey petticoat and bedgown, which were the universal dress of our women in early times, would make a very singular figure in our days. A small home-made handkerchief, in point of elegance, would ill supply the profusion of ruffles with which the necks of our ladies are now ornamented. She went barefooted in warm weather, and in cold, their feet were covered with moccasins, overshoes, or shoepacks, which often would make but a very sorry figure beside the elegant morocco slippers, often embossed with bullion, which at present ornament the feet of their daughters and grand-daughters."

A lady dressed *now*, as to neck and feet, as here described, and just as we have seen forty years ago, would create as much surprise, as one in the style of still earlier days. Such are the whims of fashion.

The coats and bedgowns of the women, as well as the hunting-shirts of the men, were hung in full display on wooden pegs, round the walls of their cabins; so that while they answered, in some degree, the place of paper-hangings or tapestry, they announced to the stranger, as well as neighbor, the wealth or poverty of the family in the articles of clothing. This practice prevailed for a long time. It is said that such a display of female attire annoyed the worthy old Bishop Asbury so much the first night he lodged in the West, that he could not sleep till they were all taken down.

The sight of a splendid wardrobe or clothes-press would have astonished many of our grandmothers as much as "Punch" describes the Frenchmen, staring at a washstand!

"The ladies handled the distaff, [we suppose he means the spinning-wheel, big and little,] shuttle, sickle, weeding-hoe, scutching-knife, hackle, and were contented if they could obtain their linsey-woolsey clothing; and covered their heads with sun-bonnets made of 6 or 700 linen." The quality of linen was graded according to the number of threads in what was called a "cut." The coarser fabrics contained only 6 or 700 threads in a cut; while the finer sort, approaching the superior qualities of Irish linen, would contain 10 or 12 and even 1800 such threads.

Cotton fabrics were but little known, or in demand. Such as were brought into the country, of which, to some extent, *Sunday shirts* were made, were of the most flimsy description,* and all of foreign importation. Flax was universally cultivated. When ripe, it was usually pulled by the women and boys, as this operation always occurred in harvest, when the men were occupied with their grain or hay. And those who 'pulled' it, after the seed was threshed out of it, perhaps towards the heels of harvest, by the men, then spread it out 'to rot' for some weeks, on some green pasture fields; and after a number of weeks, it was taken up, ready for the application of the 'brake' and 'swingling knife.' The former instrument required the muscular arms of stout men. The latter was often, perhaps most generally, wielded by the women. 'Skutching frolics,' or gatherings of neighbors to skutch or swingle flax, were very common, and afforded much innocent amusement and recreation to the young people, blended with pretty hard work. The old ladies generally took charge of the 'hackling' of the flax. Hackling and

* It required some caution, on return from church, in hot weather, when the boys were required to lay them off, to go through the operation without tearing them to pieces. For they stuck to the skin like the shirt of Nessus.

goose-picking days required much patient toil. Our grandmothers, even on those days, were still 'at home' to their visitants; for they knew nothing of modern fashionable lying in high life.

"One important pastime of our boys, was that of imitating the notes or noise of every bird and beast in the woods. This faculty was not merely a pastime; but a very necessary part of education, on account of its utility in certain circumstances. The imitations of the gobblers, and other sounds of wild turkeys, often brought the keen-eyed, and even watchful tenants of the forest within the reach of the rifle. The bleating of the fawn brought its dam to her death in the same way. The hunter often collected a company of mopish owls on the trees about his camp, and amused himself with their hoarse screaming; his howl would raise and obtain responses from a pack of wolves, so as to inform him of their neighborhood, as well as guard him against their depredations. This imitative faculty was sometimes requisite as a measure of precaution in war. The Indians, when scattered about in a neighborhood, often collected together by imitating turkeys by day, and wolves or owls by night. In similar situations, our people did the same. I have often witnessed the consternation of a whole neighborhood, in consequence of a few screeches of owls. An early and correct use of this imitative faculty was considered as an indication that its possessor would become, in due time, a good hunter, and a valiant warrior.

Throwing the tomahawk was another boyish sport; in which many acquired considerable skill. The tomahawk, with its handle of a certain length, will make a given number of turns in a given distance. Say in five steps, it will strike with the edge, with the handle downwards—at the distance of seven and a half, it will strike with the edge, the handle upwards, and so on. A little experience enabled the boy to measure the distance with his eye, when walking through the woods, and strike a tree with his tomahawk in any way he chose.

The athletic sports of running, jumping, and wrestling, were the pastimes of boys in common with men. A well-grown boy, at the age of twelve or thirteen years, was furnished with a small rifle and a shot-pouch. He then became a fort-soldier, and had his port-hole assigned him. Hunting squirrels, turkeys, and raccoons, soon made him expert in the use of his gun." Mr. Doddridge then proceeds to mention the prevalence of "story telling"—and the kind of fictions that were common in those days. They were generally of the "Valentine and Orson" school. He then offers some remarks that do much credit to his judgment and good sense, and in justice to him, we will let him be heard. "Civilization has indeed, banished the use of those ancient tales of romantic heroism; but what then? It has substituted in their place the novel and the romance. It is thus that, in every state of society, the imagination of man is eternally at war with reason and truth. That fiction should be acceptable to an unenlightened people is not to be wondered at, as the treasures of truth have never been unfolded to their minds; but that a civilized people themselves, should, in so many instances, like barbarians, prefer the fairy regions of fiction to the august treasures of truth, developed in the sciences of theology, history, natural and moral philosophy, is truly a sarcasm on human nature. It is as much as to say that it is essential to our amusement, that, for the time being, we must suspend the exercise of reason, and submit to a voluntary deception."

"In the section of country where my father lived," says Doddridge, "there was for many years after the settlement of the country, 'neither law nor gospel.' Our want of legal government was owing to the uncertainty whether we belonged to the state of Virginia or Pennsylvania. The line which at present divides the two states was not run until sometime after the conclusion of the Revolutionary war. Thus it happened that during a long period of time we knew nothing of courts, lawyers, magistrates, sheriffs or constables. Every one was therefore at liberty to do whatever was right in his own eyes."

"As this is a state of society which few of my readers have ever witnessed, I shall describe it as minutely as I can, and give in detail those moral maxims which, in a great degree, answered the important purposes of municipal jurisprudence." And we will also here add that what Mr. D. states on this subject will serve to throw light upon the *moral character* and *condition* of a very large portion of that field which the members of the Redstone Presbytery occupied, especially during the earlier period of their labors.

"In the first place, let it be observed that in a sparse population, where all the members of the community are well known to each other, and especially in a time of war, where every man capable of bearing arms is considered highly valuable as a defender of his country, public opinion has its full effect, and answers the purposes of legal government better than it would in a dense population and in time of peace. Such was the situation of our people along the frontiers of our settlements. They had no civil, military, or ecclesiastical laws; at least, none that were enforced; and yet 'they were a law unto themselves,' as to the leading obligations of our nature in all the relations in which they stood to each other. The turpitude of vice and the majesty of moral virtue were then as apparent as they are now; and they were then regarded with the same sentiments of aversion and respect which they inspire at the present time. Industry in working and hunting, bravery in war, candor, hospitality, and steadiness of deportment, received their full reward of public honor and public confidence among our rude forefathers, as well as among their better instructed and more polished descendants. The punishments which they inflicted upon offenders, by the imperial court of public opinion, were well adapted for the reformation of the culprit, or for his expulsion from the community.

The punishments for lying, idleness, dishonesty, and ill-fame, generally was that of "hating the offender out," as they expressed it. This mode of chastisement was like the ατιμία of the Greeks. It was a public expression, in various ways, of a general sentiment of indignation against such as transgressed the moral maxims of the community to which they belonged. This commonly resulted either in the reformation or banishment of the person against whom it was directed. At house-raisings, log-rollings, corn-huskings, and harvest-parties, every one was expected to do his duty faithfully. A person who did not perform his share of labor on these occasions was designated by the epithet of "lazy Lawrence," or some other title still more opprobrious; and when it came to his turn to require the like aid from his neighbors, the idler soon felt his punishment in their refusal to attend his calls.

Although there was no legal compulsion to the performance of military duty, yet every man of full age and size was expected to do his full share of public service. If he did not do so, he was "hated out as a coward." Even the want of any article of war equipments, such as ammunition, a sharp flint, a priming-wire, a scalping-knife, or tomahawk, was thought disgraceful. A man who, without a reasonable cause, failed to go on a scout or campaign when it came to his turn, met with an expression of indignation in the countenances of all his neighbors, and epithets of dishonor were fastened upon him without mercy.

Debts, which make such an uproar in civilized life, were but little known among our forefathers at the early settlement of this country. After the depreciation of the Continental Paper, they had no money of any kind: every thing purchased was paid for in produce or labor. A good cow and calf was often the price of a bushel of alum salt. If a contract was not punctually fulfilled, the credit of the delinquent was at an end. Any petty theft was punished with all the infamy that could be heaped upon the offender. A man on a campaign stole from his comrade a cake out of the ashes, in which it was baking. He was immediately named the "bread rounds." This epithet of reproach was bandied about in this way: when he would come in sight of a group of men, one of them would call "Who comes there?" Another would answer, "The bread rounds." If any one meant to be more serious about the matter, he would call out "Who stole a cake out of the ashes?" Another replied by giving the name of the man in full. To this a third would give confirmation by exclaiming "That is true, and no lie." This kind of "tongue-lashing" he was doomed to bear for the rest of the campaign, as well as for years after his return home. If a theft was detected in any of the frontier settlements, a summary mode of punishment was often resorted to. The first settlers, as far as I knew of them, had a kind of innate or hereditary detestation of the crime of theft, in any shape or degree; and their maxim was that "a thief must be whipped." If the theft was of something of some value, a kind of jury of the neighborhood, after hearing the testimony, would condemn the culprit to Moses' law; that is, to forty stripes, save one. If the theft was of some small article, the offender was doomed to carry on his back the flag of the United States, which then consisted of thirteen stripes. In either case, some able hands were selected to execute the sentence, so that the stripes were sure to be well laid on. This punishment was followed by a sentence of exile. He then was informed that he must decamp in so many days, and be seen there no more, on penalty of having the number of his stripes doubled.

"For many years after the law was put in operation in the western part of Virginia, the magistrates themselves were in the habit of giving those who were brought before them on charges of small thefts, the liberty of being sent to jail, or taking a whipping. The latter was commonly chosen, and was immediately inflicted; after which the thief was ordered to clear out. In some instances, stripes were inflicted, not for the punishment of an offence, but for the purpose of extorting a confession from suspected persons. This was the torture of our early times, and no doubt was sometimes very unjustly inflicted.

"If a woman was given to tattling and slandering her

neighbors, she was furnished, by common consent, with a kind of patent-right to say whatever she pleased, without being believed. The tongue was then said to be harmless, or to be no scandal."

"These people were given to hospitality, and freely divided their rough fare with a neighbor, or stranger, and would have been offended at the offer of pay. In their settlements and forts they lived, they worked, they fought and feasted, or suffered together, in cordial harmony. They were warm and constant in their friendships. On the other hand, they were revengeful in their resentments. And the point of honor sometimes led to personal combats. If one man called another a liar, he was considered as having given a challenge, which the person who received it must accept, or be deemed a coward; and the charge was generally answered on the spot by a blow. If the injured person was decidedly unable to fight the aggressor, he might get a friend to do it for him. The same thing took place on a charge of cowardice, or any other dishonorable action. A battle must follow, and the person who made the charge must fight either the person who received the charge, or any champion who chose to espouse his cause. Thus circumstanced, our people in early times were much more cautious of speaking evil of their neighbors, than they are at present.

"Sometimes pitched battles occurred, in which time, place, and seconds were appointed beforehand. I remember having seen one of those pitched battles in my father's fort, when a boy. One of the young men knew very well, beforehand, that he would get the worst of the battle, and no doubt repented the engagement to fight; but there was no getting over it. The point of honor demanded the risk of battle. He got his whipping; they then shook hands, and were good friends afterwards.

The mode of single combats, in those days, was dangerous in the extreme: though no weapons were used, fist, feet and teeth were employed at will; but above all, the detestable practice of gouging, by which eyes were sometimes put out, rendered this mode of fighting frightful indeed. It was not, however, so destructive as the stiletto of an Indian, the knife of a Spaniard, the small-sword of a Frenchman, or the pistol of the American or English duellist. I do not recollect that profane language was much more prevalent in our early times than at present.

"What a contrast," says the historian of Western Pennsylvania, "does this picture of early simplicity present to the mind! Great, in many respects, have been the changes within the short period of half a century. Now, the inhabitants of the same region present all the luxuries and refinements of long-settled European countries. All the fashions of dress in the metropolis of Pennsylvania and other Atlantic cities, flourish here. The linsey and coarse linens have been exchanged for the substantial and fine fabrics of Europe and Asia — the hunting-shirt for the fashionable coat of broadcloth, and the moccasin for boots and shoes of tanned leather. The mechanics here are not surpassed by any in the East. Literature and science receive great attention. By the persevering hand of industry, 'the wilderness has been made to blossom,' and the aspect of the country has everywhere been changed. The horse-paths along which the first settlers, for many years, made their laborious journeys over the mountains for salt and iron, (and by which *all* the first *set* of ministers, with their families, reached their western homes,) were succeeded by wagon-roads; then by substantial turnpikes; and now by the flaming path of the iron steed. What was the *far back-woods* to these fathers, is now brought into proximity, by a few hours of easy travel, with the Atlantic cities. Not only have physical changes been wrought, but the rude sports of early times have disappeared. Athletic trials of muscular strength have given way to the more noble ambition of mental endowments, and skill in useful arts. To the rude and often indecent song, have succeeded the psalm, the hymn, and the swelling anthem. Yet we have no reason to boast;

in many respects, they were our equals; in some of the most substantial virtues, perhaps, indeed, our superiors. And well might those departed spirits, if permitted to behold our progress and our superior advantages, ask us, "What hast thou that thou hast not received?"

In the foregoing picture of early social life in Western Pennsylvania, which we have taken principally from Mr. Doddridge, we would not be understood, as we have heretofore intimated, to exhibit this as the only and universal state of society throughout the field of our first ministers. From a very early period of the settlement of this country, there was a numerous class of persons, possessing a degree of refinement and intelligence that would have no occasion to blush in the presence of any class of persons, native or otherwise, now to be found amongst us. Many of them contrived to gather around them some of the usual appendages of a higher social life. Though their dwellings at first were humble, their tables often displayed evidences of progress in the culinary art, upon which little advance is anywhere now to be found. And so, with their means of resting the weary traveller. Throughout a portion of Westmoreland, Fayette, and Washington counties, there were many gentlemen farmers, of refined, easy manners, courtly in their address, social and hospitable, always ready to receive our ministers on their weary journeys to distant meetings, or to the destitute settlements. Some of this class, with their wives and families, were, or became members of our churches. They were the "quality folks," as they were called by the people. Now, it is worthy of notice, that almost all our first ministers were the right sort of men to win the respect and esteem of this class, and not to repel them by any boorishness in their own manners. Their own intelligence, politeness, and refinement, gave them an easy and welcome admission into such circles, wherever they existed. Thus, with this class of families scattered around them through their respective fields of labor, they were greatly aided in their efforts at the general improvement of the domestic and social state of the country. It may seem an extravagant statement, but we verily believe, that, almost in the very midst of such a state of society as Mr. Doddridge describes, there were to be found persons of the bland and courtly manners of the old school, such as can seldom now be found in circles of the highest pretension. John Randolph, speaking of the decline of this class of gentlemen of the "old school," once said that he knew of but one real gentleman left in all Virginia; and that was an old, gray-headed slave. In Western Pennsylvania, sixty years ago, there were gentlemen, and ladies too, such as he referred to; and in some instances they were warm-hearted, intelligent Christians.

In addition to this class, there was a still more numerous class of plain, substantial Scotch-Irish people, who, though somewhat blunt and unpolished in their manners, yet for real kindness of disposition, integrity, and hospitality, are not excelled by any of their descendants. Too much praise cannot be bestowed upon the female sex of this middle class. There was a quiet energy of character, a patient endurance of the hardships of frontier life, and a cheerful submission to domestic privations, which entitle them to the grateful remembrance of the present generation. Numbers of them were called to bear a prominent part in many a bloody scene and perilous adventure with their savage neighbors. A volume could not contain all the thrilling stories that have been told of female sufferings, of female prowess, and of female presence of mind and promptness to seize upon happy expedients, in moments of imminent peril. Then, in more peaceful times, woman was a most efficient fellow-laborer in building up our western Zion. If Paul, in writing to his Christian brethren of Philippi, desired that help should be afforded "to those women that labored with him in the gospel," no doubt our early ministers, from their experience of similar co-operation, could sympathize with him in such grateful reminiscences. And they trained their children to fear God, to tell the truth, to reverence the Sabbath and house of God, to work hard, and to be honest in all their dealings. Though we have now better-educated mothers, we are compelled to doubt whether we have, on the whole, *better* mothers. If there is more refinement and intelligence now, is there not more feebleness of character, more dependence on the conventionalities of modern social life, and greater physical, if not mental imbecility? There are noble exceptions, doubtless. But is there not something still wanting in our modern system of female education? In their successful attempts to polish and refine the female character, may the ladies not divest themselves of many of the substantial qualities of our early western mothers? They become more lovely and charming. But do they become more capable of fulfilling their "mission?" We like the views of Mr. Dymond, the Quaker philosopher, on this subject. See his "Essays on Principles of Morality," p. 152, Collins's edition.

REVD CHARLES BEATTY.
First Presbyterian Missionary, West of the Mountains.

P. S. Duval & Co. steam lith. press Phila.

CHAPTER III.

WHEN WERE THE FIRST EFFORTS MADE TO INTRODUCE THE GOSPEL IN THE WEST?

THE trials and sufferings of the early settlers in the West, must have enlisted the sympathies of their friends and their countrymen, generally, east of the mountains. Our own people of the Presbyterian church, we have no doubt, shared largely in the anxieties and prayers of their pious friends and the churches they had left behind, when they took their lives in their hands and came out to pitch their tents in the howling wilderness. It is interesting and instructive to review the various proceedings of the synod of New York and Philadelphia (our highest judicatory till 1789), in reference to the West. At the *first meeting* of that body, upon their happy reunion in 1758, we find a record respecting the appointment of a solemn fast; that shows not only their sympathy for the suffering people of the frontier settlements, but also in what light they regarded the war with the French and Indians that was then spreading its desolating ravages over the western settlements. This is their language: "Considering the calamities of war, and dangers that threaten us from *savage* and *anti-christian* enemies, the ravages and barbarities committed *on our borders*, and how much our success depends on this campaign"—perhaps the campaign under General Forbes, just about, at that time, to set out for the re-capture of Fort DuQuesne, "and being sensible that God has been greatly provoked by our ingratitude for mercies received, the decay of vital religion, the prevailing of vice and immorality in the land, and the contempt of gospel light, liberty and privileges, we judge ourselves loudly called upon to repentance and humiliation; and accordingly the synod recommend that a day of fasting and prayer be observed by all the congregations under our care, to deprecate the wrath of God, to pray for a blessing on his Majesty's armaments by sea and land in order to secure a lasting and honorable peace, and in particular for the success of our intended expeditions in America," (there were *three* then in progress; one against *Louisburg*—another against *Ticonderoga and Crown Point*, and the third against *Fort Du Quesne*,)—for the *prosperity* of his *Prussian Majesty's* arms and advancement of the *Protestant interest;* for the overthrow of *anti-christian errors*, *superstition*, and *tyranny;* and the universal spread of pure and undefiled religion. And it is ordered that the members within the bounds of this province, observe it on the 16th of June next, being the day appointed by this government for that purpose," &c. (Records, p. 290.) It is manifest that the synod regarded this war in part, if not mainly designed to promote the interests of Antichrist, and to extend the boundaries of the man of sin. It is likewise worthy of notice that President Davies, in his Fast-day Sermon called "the Crisis," preached two years before, in reference to this same war—regarded it much in the same light. "Who can tell," says he, "but *the present war* is the commencement of this grand decisive conflict between the lamb and the beast; *i. e.*, between the protestant and popish powers? The pope first received his principality and secular authority from Pepin, one of the kings of France; and there seems to be something congruous in it, that France should also take the lead, and be, as it were, the general of his forces, in the last decisive conflict for the support of his authority. This is also remarkable and almost peculiar to *the present war*, that protestants and papists are not blended together in it, by promiscuous alliances; but France and her allies are all *papists*, and Britain and her allies are all *protestants*."

But the sympathies and the action of the synod terminated not here. We find two years after, 1760, the *Rev. Messrs. A. M'Dowel and H. Allison* are allowed to go out as chaplains to the West, with the Pennsylvania forces. And in the two successive years, they petitioned the governor of Pennsylvania, and the Assembly, in behalf of the captives among the savages to the West—earnestly imploring their attempts to recover them. (See Records, pp. 312, 315.) In 1763, the synod took another step to supply the spiritual wants of the frontiers. They recommended to all their Presbyteries *to propose one or more of their candidates* that they think proper to be sent to their *frontier settlements*, and that they let their candidates know that they intend to propose them as such, to the synod, "that so our synodical appointments may be more punctually fulfilled" (p. 324). But we find another record of greater significance still, illustrating the interest the synod took for this western region, in 1763. It seems that the "Corporation for poor and distressed Presbyterian ministers," &c., had, at their meeting, November 16, 1762, agreed to appoint some of their members to wait on the synod, at its next meeting, and in their name to request that some missionaries be sent to preach to the *distressed frontier inhabitants*, and to report their distresses, and to let them know when new congregations are forming and what is necessary to promote the spread of the gospel among them, and that they likewise give information as to what opportunities there may be of preaching the gospel to the Indian nations among them. The Board also proposed to pay the necessary expenses of such missionaries. The synod accordingly appointed the Rev. Messrs. Beatty and Brainerd (brother of the missionary,) to go as soon as they can conveniently on this mission. The length of time is not mentioned; but it is evident, from the amount of supplies they assigned to their pulpits in their absence, that they were expected to spend several months in this service, (Records, p. 326.) But they were prevented from going; as they reported at the next meeting of synod, 1764, "the whole design of the mission being entirely frustrated by the breaking out of the Indian war." This was what was called Pontiac's war, producing one of the most awful periods of distress ever before or after experienced in Western Pennsylvania. Though the French War was now over, the savages, instigated, it is believed, by their late allies, carried on their ravages on the frontiers, even worse than ever. The Indian chieftain Pontiac was ostensibly at the head of this widely extended Indian war. But the Canadian French Catholics were at the bottom of it all. "The whole country west of Shippensburg became the prey of the fierce barbarians. They set fire to houses, barns, corn, hay, and everything that was combustible. The wretched inhabitants whom they surprised at night, at their meals, or in the labours of the field, were massacred with the utmost cruelty and barbarity; and those who fled were scarce more happy. Overwhelmed by sorrow, without shelter or means of transportation, their tardy flight was impeded by fainting women and weeping children. On the 25th July, 1763, there were in Shippensburg, 1384 poor, distressed back inhabitants, viz., men, 301; women, 345; children, 738; many of whom were obliged to lie in barns, stables, cellars, and under old leaky sheds, the dwelling-houses being all crowded." (Hist. West. Penn.) Such is the frightful picture given us of the state of the country, during that summer that these missionaries were to have spent in preaching the gospel in Western Pennsylvania. But the signal victory gained over the Indians by Colonel Boquet, at Brush Creek, or rather at Bushy Run, in Westmoreland County, during the following autumn—so dismayed the savages that they not only gave up all further designs against Fort Pitt and the surrounding country, but withdrew from the frontiers, far beyond the Ohio, and left our people, for a while, again at peace.* Then the Synod, in 1766, renewed the appointment of Mr. Beatty,

* Yet the synod *this very year*, 1763, renewed their efforts for our Western frontiers. It is recorded, May 24—"As the Synod have the *mission to the frontier much at heart*, therefore, lest it miscarry, it is ordered that if either Mr. Beatty or Mr. Brainerd fail of going, Mr. Kirkpatrick shall go in the place of the person who fails."

and instead of Mr. Brainerd, gave him Mr. Duffield as his associate; directing them to spend two months on this mission. They accordingly came out, and were in Pittsburg in September. The historian of Pittsburg gives the following account of this visit:

"In the summer of 1766, the Rev. Charles Beatty, the grandfather of the Rev. C. C. Beatty, D.D., of Steubenville, was appointed, by the Synod of New York and Philadelphia, to visit the frontier inhabitants, in order that a better judgment might be formed of what assistance it might be necessary to afford them in their present low circumstances, in order to promote the gospel among them, and also to visit the Indians, in case it could be done safely. On Friday, the 5th September, late in the evening, he arrived at Fort Pitt. He immediately waited on Captain Murray, the commandant, who received him and his companion, Mr. Duffield, politely, and introduced them to the Rev. Mr. M'Lagan, the chaplain to the 42d regiment. The officers were all very kind to them, invited them to their tables, gave them a room in the fort, and supplied them with bedding, so that they were as comfortable as could be expected. On Sabbath, 7th September, Mr. M'Lagan invited him to preach in the garrison, which he did; while Mr. Duffield preached to the people, who live in *some kind of a town* without the fort, to whom Mr. Beatty also preached in the afternoon." The writer adds: "we infer, from the expression 'some kind of a town,' that Pittsburg must have been a poor affair indeed." —*Hist. Pitts.*

These brethren accordingly reported to the Synod, at their next meeting, 1767, that they had complied with the order of last Synod, in going on a mission to the frontiers. We have no doubt that this was a refreshing visit to many of God's dear suffering people in this region. They appear to have been the right sort of men for such an important work—men eminently devoted to the cause of Christ and of missions. There is much reason to believe that, on their return to their churches and to the Synod, they gave a fresh impulse to prayerful efforts in behalf of the religious interests of the West. For they reported that "they found on the frontiers numbers of people earnestly desirous of forming themselves into congregations, and declaring their willingness to exert their utmost to have the gospel among them, but in circumstances exceedingly distressing and necessitous from the late calamities of war in their parts; and also that they visited the Indians at the chief town of the Delaware nation, on the Muskingum, about 130 miles beyond Fort Pitt, and were received much more cheerfully than they could have expected; that a considerable number of them waited on the preaching of the gospel with peculiar attention, many of them appearing peculiarly concerned about the great matters of religion; that they expressed an earnest desire of having further opportunities of hearing those things; that they informed them that several other tribes of Indians around them were ready to join with them in receiving the gospel, and earnestly desiring an opportunity."

The Synod were so favorably impressed with this account, that they appointed, instanter, Messrs. Brainerd and Cooper to pay a visit to the frontier settlements and the Indians, and spend at least three months in their mission, and forbade them *to take any money from the frontier settlements* for their ministerial labors among them. The Synod also, at this meeting, "laying to heart the unhappy lot of many people in various parts of the land, who at present are brought up in ignorance, and are perishing for lack of knowledge; who, on account of their poverty, or scattered habitations, are unable, without some assistance, to support the gospel ministry among them: considering, also, that it is their duty to send missionaries to the frontier settlements, who may preach to the dispersed families there, and form them into societies for the worship of God, and being moved with compassion towards the Indians," &c., entered upon a new and much more systematic plan of carrying on the work of missions—enjoining annual collections in all the churches—directing Presbyteries to appoint treasurers—appointing themselves a general treasurer—requiring annual reports, &c. In fine, it is evident that the Synod were, at this meeting, baptized afresh with a missionary spirit; and it was probably largely owing, under God, to the instrumentality of Messrs. Beatty and Duffield. And who knows but that James Finley first formed the purpose, then and there, of spending his life eventually, if God should spare him, amongst that people of whom he now heard so afflicting an account? for he was at that meeting.

The prospect now appeared, indeed, to brighten; but alas! many long years of trial and sorrow must roll round before the West is supplied with faithful laborers in its growing and spreading harvest! At the next meeting of Synod, 1767, Messrs. Cooper and Brainerd reported "that they did not execute their mission among the Indians on the Muskingum and *other parts*, as ordered at last Synod, by reason of the discouraging accounts brought in by the interpreter, Joseph, sent out, as mentioned in our last-year's minutes, and other discouraging circumstances. It seems that, being discouraged as to the prospect of that part of their work which related to the heathen natives, they did not feel warranted to undertake that part of their appointment which related to the frontier settlements. And so another year passed without a visit to our people in the West. Hitherto, those appointed by the Synod were entrusted with the two-fold work of both Domestic and Foreign Missions. The failure of the latter, during the last year, producing a sad failure of the former, also put the Synod, perhaps, upon the appointment of eleven of their most prominent members, lay and clerical, to devise a distinct and general plan in regard to missions among the Indians. They also appointed Mr. Anderson "to take a tour on the western frontiers of Pennsylvania; to set off as soon as possible, and preach in the vacancies on the frontiers at least *twelve* Sabbaths; for which he is to receive twenty shillings for every Sabbath that he preaches on the other side of the Kittatinning Mountains; and to take his directions from

Donegal Presbytery." Whether this appointment was fulfilled, or whether it brought him into what are now the western counties of the State, we do not learn from the records of the ensuing year, 1769. The Synod, however, ordered the Presbytery of Donegal to supply the Western Frontier with ten sabbaths of ministerial labor; but whether it was fulfilled we cannot learn, as there is no recorded report. Mr. Niles, however, was then appointed to labor in part in Western Pennsylvania, but failed through sickness. Mr. Finley, also, was then (1771) appointed to spend two months "at least over the Allegheny Mountains;" which he reported fulfilled at the next meeting, 1772; p. 426. This excellent man, we doubt not, gave full proof of his ministry amongst the dispersed sheep of the house of Israel, and amongst the famishing lambs of the flock. If he was at Pittsburg during that tour, he found a little village of twenty houses, and perhaps 120 people. In other places, he would find the people, just at this time, harassed with the conflicting claims and jurisdictions of the two states of Pennsylvania and Virginia; a matter which soon after increased to a fearful flame of excitement, and was no doubt a great hindrance to the progress of the gospel. But he came not among them to discuss the merits of that question; and whether with Virginians or Pennsylvanians, he would know nothing among them save Christ, and him crucified. In 1772, the Donegal Presbytery were appointed "to send either Mr. Craighead or Mr. King to Monongahela and other places adjacent, to supply as long as they can." Which this Presbytery report the following year as complied with, but do not state which of these ministers they sent, nor how long he labored. Then in the next succeeding year, 1775*, Mr. Forster, also, was appointed to supply six Sabbaths in the frontier parts of Pennsylvania in

* "Mr. Samuel Smith, a probationer under the care of the Newcastle Presbytery, was appointed to supply four months between this and the next meeting of Synod on the frontier parts of Pennsylvania and in Virginia, if his state of health shall admit of it."

the months of September and October. But the records of the next year are silent as to his complying or not complying with this mission. In 1776, the Synod appointed Mr. Carmichael to supply two months — October and November — in the north and west parts of Pennsylvania; and the Presbytery of Newcastle were ordered to supply his pulpit four Sabbaths, and gave the same Presbytery leave to ordain Mr. Power *sine titulo*, "as he purposes to remove to the western parts of this province." Up to this date we have traced the history of the various proceedings of the Synods of New York and Philadelphia in reference to this field. We see from the recital of facts on their records, that, *for near twenty years before the first ordained minister removed to the West*, the then supreme judicatory paid almost unremitting attention to this important section of their territory. Several devoted men came out, and no doubt labored faithfully, in trying to gather the sheep in the wilderness. Still, down to our last date, it was yet indeed a wilderness, and much of it long continued so; but it was beginning "to blossom as the rose." In a few more years, seven faithful men are found at their stations in this vast field, and henceforward the Synod is exonerated from farther care, except that which they have for all their churches.

Some further account of the Rev. Charles Beatty may very properly find a place here. We have had occasion to call special attention to this devoted servant of Christ, when we endeavored to trace the history of the Synod's efforts and action, in behalf of the spiritual wants of the West.

Charles Beatty, one of the first regular Presbyterian missionaries to Western Pennsylvania, was a man of no ordinary character and worth. It is evident, from the early records of our Church, that he occupied a prominent position among the brethren and fathers of his day. He was born in the County of Antrim, Ireland, about the year 1715. His father, John Beatty, was also a native of Ireland, of the Scotch-Irish stock, and was an officer in the British army. His mother,

Christiana Beatty, whose maiden name was Clinton, was of English descent. His father died when he was very young; and his mother, with her brother, Charles Clinton,* their families, and several others of their relatives and friends, resolved to emigrate to America. They were induced to leave the country of their birth, principally in consequence of the oppressive acts of the Established Church towards the Dissenters. They were Presbyterians. They embarked for Philadelphia in the latter end of May, 1729; but owing to a peculiar and disastrous train of circumstances, did not arrive until the month of October, when they were landed at Cape Cod.† They resided in the vicinity of that place until the spring of 1731, when they removed, with their families, to a part of Ulster, now Orange County, New York, where they formed a flourishing settlement.

Mr. Beatty's inheritance was the manly and religious training which the Scotch-Irish are accustomed to give their children. His education, however, was above the common grade. In Ireland he had been sent to a classical institution, and had obtained a good knowledge of the languages, before he emigrated to this country. Providence designed the young student for a useful career in a distant land, and gave him the early advantages and opportunities which prepared him for

---

* Charles Clinton was the father of George Clinton, Governor of the State of New York, and Vice-President of the United States, and grandfather of De Witt Clinton, also Governor of New York.

† They engaged a ship at Dublin, commanded by a Captain Rymer, and had her bound to them for the faithful performance of their agreement. For several days before they landed, their allowance was half a biscuit and half a pint of water for twenty-four hours. Several of the passengers died of famine, among whom was a daughter of Christiana Beatty, and a son and daughter of her brother, Charles Clinton. It was believed by the passengers that the Captain had been bribed to subject them to privation and hardship, for the purpose of discouraging emigration. Cape Cod was the first land seen by them on the American coast; and there the Captain was induced, by a considerable sum of money, to land them.

influence in future life. Like many a faithful servant of Christ, Mr. Beatty was not rich in this world's goods, though far from being of a low origin; for few families in this country were of a higher or better lineage. With a noble energy and independence of spirit, he became, for a season, a pedlar, seeking thereby the requisite means to qualify himself, the sooner, for whatever business or station the Providence of God might open to him in future life. This business brought him, in his excursions, to the Log College, at Neshaminy, then under the care of the celebrated William Tenant. His acquaintance with that excellent man led to his entering upon a course of study with a view to the gospel ministry. Of this remarkable passage in his history we shall have more to say hereafter. Suffice it now to say, that here he pursued his studies at a most eventful time.

The Presbyterian Church was agitated by the different views entertained about the degree of closeness and searching stringency to which candidates for the ministry should be subjected, in inquiries about their *experimental acquaintance* with religion—which ultimately ended in the schism of 1745. The Log College was the training place of the revival men. Its influence was for the purity of the Church, and for the salvation of souls. It resisted the formality of a dead orthodoxy, and inculcated the necessity of a living zeal in the Christian ministry.

Mr. Beatty was probably an inmate of the Log College when Whitefield first visited Philadelphia; and no doubt heard that great man when he preached the gospel in the old grave-yard of Neshaminy, where the old church formerly stood. Trained up under such influences, Mr. Beatty united zeal to orthodoxy, and became a burning and a shining light. He was licensed October 13th, 1742, by the Presbytery of New Brunswick, which took the lead on the new side, and which had withdrawn—or rather had been exscinded—from the Synod two years before. In this year, the increasing infirmities of old Mr. Tenant induced him to seek a release

16

from his pastoral charge; and in the following year a call was presented from Neshaminy to Mr. Beatty, and he was ordained December 14th, 1743. The last time that Mr. Tenant sat in Presbytery was at this ordination of his pupil.

About this time, in consequence of the publication of Brainerd's "Journal" of missionary labors among the Indians, a missionary spirit seems to have been kindled among the ministers of the Presbyterian Church, in connection with the Synod of New York and New Jersey. Under this influence, both Mr. Beatty and Mr. Treat, of Abington, left their congregations, and went on a mission to the Indians. Previous to the unhappy schism in the Synod of Philadelphia, in 1745—which led to the formation of the new side Synod of New York and New Jersey—the Presbytery of New Brunswick had withdrawn, as already stated; and any further notice of it is not found in the Records of Synod, after 1741. But Mr. Beatty's name does not *then* appear.

At the first separate meeting of the new-side synod in 1745, he is reported among the members of the New Brunswick Presbytery as *present;* and then, as such, regularly at all the subsequent meetings for eight years, till we come to the year 1753, when he is thenceforward reported as a member of the Abington Presbytery. In 1754 he was appointed, along with Mr. Bostwick and others, to spend three months as a missionary in Virginia and North Carolina, which mission he reported at the next meeting of synod in 1755 as fulfilled. In the following year it appears that, having been invited to become chaplain for a season to the Pennsylvania troops that were about to be sent to the northern and western frontiers of the State, under the command of Dr. Franklin, he sought advice of the synod whether he should accept of this appointment. It appears that, at a meeting of the commission of synod, they were informed that a motion had been lately made to him by the government of Pennsylvania to go out as chaplain with their forces upon the frontiers, and he desired that some provision might be made for the supply of his pulpit. The commission, accordingly, had appointed Abington Presbytery to supply four Sabbaths, the Presbytery of New York three Sabbaths, the Presbytery of New Brunswick four Sabbaths, and the Presbytery of Newcastle five Sabbaths. In this case, he did not apply for advice. But it is manifest that the commission had expressed their cordial concurrence. But now, having sought and obtained the advice of the synod, it seems probable that he entered upon the service soon after; for it was in the earlier part of this year that Franklin set out with the troops. During that campaign, we have this rather amusing notice from the pen of the Philosopher-General:

"We had for our chaplain a zealous Presbyterian minister, Mr. Beatty, who complained to me that the men did not generally attend his prayers and exhortations. When they enlisted they were promised, besides pay and provisions, a gill of rum a day, which was punctually served out to them, half in the morning and half in the evening; and I observed they were punctual in attending to receive it: upon which I said to Mr. Beatty, 'It is perhaps below the dignity of your profession to act as steward of the rum; but if you were to distribute it out, only just after prayers, you would have them all about you.' He liked the thought, undertook the task, and, with the help of a few hands to measure out the liquor, executed it to satisfaction; and never were prayers more generally and more punctually attended. So that I think this method preferable to the punishment inflicted by some military laws, for non-attendance on divine service."—*Day's Hist. Coll.*

At the following fall meeting of synod, he "desired to know their mind with respect to his going chaplain to the forces that may be raised in the province of Pennsylvania, if he shall by the government be called to that service." The synod judged it to be his duty, and, in the event of his going, appointed ample supplies for his pulpit. (*Rec.* p. 275.) He was present at the meeting of synod in 1757, and also in

1758—the last separate meeting of that synod. At that meeting, informing the synod that Col. Armstrong had asked him to serve as chaplain to the first battalion of Pennsylvania Provincials, Mr. Beatty asked advice of the synod as to his duty in this matter. They unanimously advised him to go. Two days afterwards, the synods, after a separation of thirteen years, were again united; and Mr. Beatty's name is found among the "present." Thenceforward we find him occupying a prominent place in the proceedings of the united synod, (and moderator of the body in 1764,) till his name finally disappears, perhaps shortly before he was called to his rest. He had been appointed a trustee of New Jersey College in 1763, and continued its ardent and efficient friend till his death; indeed, sacrificed his life in endeavoring to promote its prosperity; for he died in Barbadoes, August 13th, 1772, whither he had gone to solicit funds for the college. Dr. Alexander, in his "Log College," says, "Mr. Beatty was an able evangelical preacher, and was much esteemed for his private virtues and public labors. He seems to have much of a public spirit and a popular address." We will conclude our present paper with an extract from Dr. Miller's "Life of Dr. Rodgers," respecting the subject of the above notice, and a remark or two suggested by Dr. M.'s statement.

"The Rev. Charles Beatty, a native of Ireland, obtained a pretty accurate classical education in his own country; but his circumstances being narrow, he employed several of the first years of his residence in America in the business of a pedlar.* He halted one day at the Log College. The ped-

* Dr. Miller, though a model of politeness and refinement, does not mince his language in giving this anecdote. He might have used the expression "itinerant merchant," and spoken of his "carrying goods for sale into country neighborhoods." But it seems he preferred the plain, old-fashioned term, "pedlar." He used to tell us at Princeton of a new translation of the New Testament once published in England, in which the author, instead of the old expression, "a certain rich man," employed the words "a certain opulent gentleman." The late

lar, to Mr. Tenant's surprise, addressed him in correct Latin, and appeared to be familiar with that language. After much conversation, in which Mr. Beatty manifested fervent piety and considerable religious knowledge, as well as a good education in other respects, Mr. Tenant said 'Go and sell off the contents of your pack, and return immediately and study with me. It will be a sin for you to continue a pedlar when you can be so much more useful in another profession.' * He accepted Mr. Tenant's offer, and in due time became an eminent minister of the gospel. He was chaplain in the army, under Dr. Franklin, on the Lehigh. He died at Barbadoes, whither he had gone to solicit benefactions for New Jersey College." We cannot but admire the spirit of energy and self-reliance which Mr. Beatty had previously displayed; and then his prompt and cheerful acceptance of Mr. Tenant's pro-

---

Rev. Elisha M'Curdy, who, perhaps, had more of the spirit and fire of the early preachers than any of his cotemporaries, was once a *road-wagoner*, and always spoke of himself as such, and never was known to talk of his having "engaged in the transportation business." Nor did John Newton ever speak of his once having been a "mariner," but a common sailor in a slave ship! We confess it would greatly diminish our respect for any of the descendants or relatives of Beatty, or M'Curdy, or Newton, if we were aware they would feel hurt by having the plain old-fashioned expressions adopted about the former employments or pursuits of their ancestors. Shades of Roger Sherman and Daniel Sheffy! to what are we republicans, and followers of the reputed Son of the Carpenter, coming, in this ambitious age of family pretensions! We shall next, perhaps, hear the Apostle Peter called "a piscatorial merchant," instead of a "fisherman."

* This language is changed, but not improved, we think, by the writer of the "Biographical Sketch of Charles Beatty," in the Presbyterian Magazine for 1852, p. 413, in the following manner: "You must quit your present employment. Go and sell your merchandize, and return immediately and study with me. It will be a sin for you to continue in this profession when you may become qualified for the ministry and be useful in winning souls!" We appreciate the probable motive of the writer in giving this "various reading," but differ with him in our judgment and taste—perhaps erroneously.

posal. We do not wonder that he became, through future life, no ordinary man. Too many of our young men are apt to run into the one or the other of two extremes. Some yield to a tame helplessness and inertness of character — what Dr. Speece, of Virginia, expressed by a homely word—"granny-ism." They seem to think it a great hardship to be thrown on their own resources, and often evince great reluctance to make any effort to help themselves along in their education. Others cherish a morbid feeling of dislike to the offer of any aid from the church. They imagine they become, in that case, a species of paupers — mere "charity students." No view of the case can be more false than this. Who ever dreams that, when our country sustains the expenses of training young men at West Point for her future service, should she need them, she is performing an act of *charity?* And if the church, in her wisdom, makes provision, by her Board of Education, for training young men for the gospel ministry, and *for her service*, and thereby provides for her own more rapid growth, inviting poor and pious young men to accept her aid, that thereby they may the sooner become ready to serve her in her great mission, is it not folly and presumption in any young man practically to impeach the collected wisdom of the church, and to decline her proffered assistance? saying, in effect, "It is true I wish to preach the gospel; but unless I can get into the ministry by my own efforts, I will not serve God in the gospel of his Son; or, at at least, I will suffer a few more years of my short life to pass away, though the church is inviting me to hasten to her work, and sinners are daily going down to eternal death!" Ought not such a young man to review the motives which have ever led him to turn his thoughts to the ministry? Of one thing we are sure: he will never become a *Charles Beatty.*

We have thought the above tribute was due to the memory of a man whose name has been seldom pronounced (except as belonging to his greatly respected relative) by any now living in the bounds of the old Presbytery of Redstone — a man whom God, through his church, first sent to preach the gospel amidst the wilds of the West.

Since the above was written, we have been favored with the perusal of the whole Journal of Mr. Beatty when on his tour to the West; but, though exceedingly interesting, we find nothing further to extract from it that is of essential importance to our purpose. For the earlier part of this memoir, we are indebted to the writer referred to in the last note.

CHAPTER IV.

STATEMENTS ABOUT THE REDSTONE PRESBYTERY.

THERE are some general facts and circumstances connected with the history of the old Presbytery of Redstone, and the period to which it belongs, worthy of notice. The following remarks, somewhat miscellaneous, ought not, perhaps, to be overlooked.

1. This presbytery, as the sole undivided presbytery of the West, extended through a period of twelve years, its first meeting being on the 19th of September, 1781, and its last on the 18th of October, 1793. It held forty-one meetings. Nine times it met at Pigeon Creek, six times at Chartier's, five times at Rehoboth, four times at Roundhill, three times at Dunlap's Creek, twice at Mount Pleasant and Bethel, and once at Buffalo, Peters's Creek, Lebanon, Pittsburg, Laurel Hill, Upper Racoon, Short Creek and Three Ridges, James M'Kee's, Fairfield, and Long Run. There was but one "pro re nata" meeting during all that time, which met in Winchester, by order of the Synod of Virginia, at the time. Its object was simply to receive Mr. Barr's application for a dismission to the Presbytery of Carlisle.

It will be seen by the foregoing statement, that the greater number of their meetings were held without the bounds of the present Redstone Presbytery. They met twenty-two times in what are now the bounds of the Ohio and Washington Presbyteries, twice in the bounds of the present Blairsville Presbytery, and seventeen times within the bounds of the present Redstone Presbytery. This old presbytery originally consisted of but four members; three of whom, Mr. Dod, Mr.

M'Millan, and Mr. Smith, were settled out of its present bounds. A very large majority of the churches, also, were beyond the present limits of the Presbytery. But the vacancies to which supplies were furnished in 1782 and 1783, (there were none appointed at their first meeting in 1781,) were all in the bounds of the present Redstone, except one, the Ohio Court-house, a place that stood some miles west of the present town of Washington, and that vanishes and appears no more in the subsequent lists of supplies. But the next year, 1783, ten Sabbaths of supplies were sent without the present bounds, and only four within. In 1784, seventeen Sabbaths were given to vacancies and missionary fields without the present bounds, and only seven within. The disparity becomes greater every year as we advance, and as the amount of supplies increases from year to year. In 1788, there were thirty supplies given to the territory now embraced by Redstone Presbytery, and eighty-eight to churches and regions without. This enormous increase of the supplies granted, was owing to their having now, for the first time, two licentiates, Messrs. Hughes and Brice, who were licensed April 16th, 1788. In the above statement, we have mentioned only those that are expressly named. But this by no means gives the full amount of supplies furnished by the Presbytery. A very large proportion of these supplies were "at discretion." For instance, in 1783, when this part of their work fairly began, there were only fourteen Sabbaths assigned to places expressly named, while there were ten additional Sabbaths at discretion; making in all, for that year, twenty-four Sabbaths of supplies.

2. The next thing to which we would direct attention is the vast amount of labor, of this missionary character, which these fathers performed. They had all, without exception, two pastoral charges, from eight to twelve miles apart. They organized the Presbytery, as we have before stated, with four members, and received into their body, within the first three years, three additional members, Messrs. Clarke, Dunlap, and

Finley. Six years after their organization, Mr. Barr was added to their number. But he remained only three or four years, and seems to have been of no advantage to their cause, rather retarding their progress. For a short time during 1786, two Irishmen, father and son, perhaps, by the name of Morrison, came among them, and labored a while in some of the vacancies; they proved to be no acquisition, but, on the contrary, sources of much vexation and trouble; and the brethren felt, doubtless, that they were well rid of them, when they left. An excellent man, the Rev. Jacob Jennings, M. D., from the Dutch Reformed Church and Synod of New Jersey, joined them in 1791, and was regularly received in 1792; he was a valuable acquisition. But about the same time, a wandering star, by the name of Thomas Cooly, professing to have come from a presbytery of Charleston, S. C., and also with "a dismission and testimonials from a number of dissenting ministers in England," came among them, and was employed for a short time in their vacancies. But they were not satisfied with his credentials, and referred them to the Synod, who in turn referred them to the General Assembly. The Presbytery then declined to give him further employment till the General Assembly would decide about the matter, or Mr. Cooly could more satisfactorily clear up his case. The General Assembly judged his credentials forged, and the Presbytery had much trouble, as in the case of the Morrisons, in neutralizing the mischief done in various vacancies, and setting their people right in respect to these men. They were also much vexed with a Mr. Mahon, who came from the Carlisle Presbytery, towards the close of their history. He wished to be ordained and installed as pastor in Pittsburg; but they were not satisfied, on examining him upon experimental religion and cases of conscience; upon which he applied for a dismission back to the Carlisle Presbytery, which they granted, no doubt very willingly.

But there was one stranger who came among them for a short time, in 1787, the Rev. Wait Cornwell, from an association in Connecticut, who seems to have been a very pious, devoted man. He assisted Mr. Smith during a great revival of religion in Cross Creek, in April of that year, and spent a few months in visiting the vacancies and missionary regions of the Presbytery, under their direction, and then returned; and we hear no more of him. There is reason to believe that he rendered important service, at a time when their destitute churches and vacancies had grown on their hands, to a wonderful degree.

A short time before they adjourned to meet no more, Mr. Thomas Moore, from New England, appeared among them, a man of great worth, who, in after years, labored in what are the bounds of the Blairsville and Washington Presbyteries, and eventually removed to Ohio, where he died a few years ago, having joined the New School Presbyterians, however, a short time before he died. He was a Hopkinsian in theology, somewhat ultra in his Calvinism, and in the prominence he gave it in his preaching. He was a very pious and most valuable man, of strong, vigorous intellect, and uncompromising in his denunciations of coming wrath, against sinners and hypocrites in the church. His labors resulted in numerous conversions, both at Salem, in Blairsville Presbytery, and at Upper Ten Mile, in Washington Presbytery, where many of his spiritual children may yet be found. He was, perhaps, the most awful scourge of Arminianism that we ever had among us.

Now with the above exceptions, those beloved men, Clarke, Smith, M'Millan, Power, Dodd, Dunlap and Finley, labored, in season and out of season, in this mighty field, widening and widening every year—the importunate calls from vacancies growing louder and more numerous, at every meeting of Presbytery—for *seven years*, (from 1781 to 1788,) nearly fifty places needing their aid, (their names are all before us,) and yet all this time, there was not a single permanent accession to their number from Presbyteries east of the mountains. With the exception of Mr. Cornwell, who remained but a short time, all the additional help they received was not only transient, but of little value, some of it positively a hindrance. Where were the bowels of compassion among other Presbyteries, and with the young licentiates and ministers east of the mountains?

This view of the matter gives us the means of appreciating still more highly the character of those whom Dr. Hodge, in his Constitutional History, calls "a noble set of men." Now look at the amount of time these men gave to this extra work on their hands—in 1782, 12 sabbaths of supplies; in 1783, 24 sabbaths; in 1784, 27 sabbaths; in 1785, 34 sabbaths; in 1786, 40 sabbaths; in 1787, 30 sabbaths; and in 1788, when they, at length, have two licentiates, their appointments for supplies reach the number of 127 sabbaths!

Truly these men "sowed in tears." We must not forget that, during all this time, they and their people were harassed, more or less, by the savages on their borders making continual inroads, burning and desolating all before them, and sometimes murdering whole families. They came in on their settlements from various points on the Ohio and Allegheny rivers. It could seldom be known when or where they would strike—sometimes over towards the Ohio, sometimes coming in from Venango, along on the Loyalhanna; they (these ministers) would be compelled to flee to forts with their helpless families. In some instances, their meetings were broken up. In many cases, at particular periods, every man went armed to their places of worship, and in some cases stacked their guns at the door, and appointed a sentinel. This state of things did not entirely subside till nearly a year after their *last united meeting.* For it was not till Wayne's decided victory, in 1794, that all further danger from this quarter ceased.

A very large portion of what then composed the territory of the Presbytery was liable, at no previous period, perhaps, to more danger, than after the disastrous campaigns of Harmar and St. Clair, in 1790 and 1791. The Presbytery, at their meeting held at Bethel, December 22d, 1791, appointed a special fast day—a day of fasting and prayer—"particularly on account of the situation of our country with respect to the savages." This is an interesting fact in their history, and it is fully and satisfactorily illustrated by the history of that year. (See the 46th Note on the Records.) And yet, in the midst of this state of things had these brethren to labor. They often preached and had protracted meetings in forts, especially in the earlier part of their history, on their western bounds. Here, also, the Spirit of God was often poured out; and a revival influence which was begun in forts extended, in more than one instance, to the churches, during the following weeks and months.

3. Let us consider the amount of toil and exposure endured in their fulfilling the supplies appointed. Often would they have to travel from fifteen to fifty miles, and be away for some days from their families. The roads were often of the worst description, and sometimes no roads at all. A blind path, but seldom used must be followed, when every neighborhood road to a mill or a smith's shop, being much more distinct, would be almost sure to mislead them. There were few or no pointers or finger-boards in those days—no bridges across creeks and runs—the fording places often uncertain and not easily found. Yet they never met with a disaster in these missionary excursions; and their families were kept safely beneath the "overshadowing wings." Indeed we can ascribe it to nothing but a very special providence exercised over these brethren and their families, during these periods of their frequent separation—similar to that which was spread over the ancient people of God, when all the males went up to Jerusalem, from every part of the land, to attend the great annual festivals, leaving their families perfectly exposed to their foreign enemies. So long as they were faithful to His covenant, God "made their enemies to be at peace with them." These ministers were called, not only to distant points to preach and catechise the children, but also to preside

at meetings of sessions, to settle difficulties, to administer discipline, to reconcile adverse parties, and to preserve churches from breaking into factions and fragments. Two of them were aged men before they entered the field. Mr. Clarke was sixty-four years of age when he united with the Presbytery. Mr. Finley was sixty. With these men, their days of active toil and endurance, one would have thought, were past. Yet to their honor it will be found that they took an equal share in the labor of supplies. Mr. Finley appears to have preserved, till the age of seventy (when he died), much of his juvenile buoyancy and activity; and performed an immense amount of pastoral labor, over a field, fifteen miles long, and eight or ten miles broad. The others were much younger men. Dr. M'Millan was twenty-nine years of age when the Presbytery was organised; Mr. Dodd, thirty-one; Mr. Power, thirty-five; Mr. Dunlap, thirty-eight, when he joined the Presbytery. Mr. Smith was forty-five at its formation. It was, perhaps, a most auspicious circumstance that they had all been in the ministry some years, in other fields. They were not inexperienced men. They could avoid any errors that might have occurred in their previous course, and in other fields. They were much better able to count the cost—and even to endure hardships as good soldiers. They were capable of being wise counsellors to their people in all matters whatever.

4. On one subject which greatly perplexed their people, and no doubt, for a time, hindered the progress of the gospel, these brethren were at times much harassed: we refer to the conflicting claims of the two States of Pennsylvania and Virginia, to a large portion of their field. In many cases this led to disputes and broils, and litigations. In some places, there was great uncertainty as to land titles. To such an extent did this grow at one time, that thousands of the early settlers had serious thoughts of getting up, and seeking a quiet home elsewhere. A man by the name of Jackson entered into an extensive combination for this purpose, and

drew after him many followers, even of the people of our communion. This scheme was to go and possess themselves of a quiet settlement further west, where they would be free from these conflicting claims of jurisdiction. It happily, however, fell through, and proved only a flash in the pan. It may well be supposed that, especially through Washington County, this would be a source of much trial to the faith and patience of ministers and people. Some of our ministers, indeed, had had some experience of this very kind of trouble in the region whence they came. The Nottingham settlement had passed through a similar trial. Party spirit ran high, and broke forth in acts of violence. Many of those who had emigrated from that region could well remember that until *Mason and Dixon's* line had been run, people knew not whether they were Marylanders or Pennsylvanians. A considerable part of Nottingham fell to the Maryland side. Mr. Finley himself, lived in Maryland, while his church, a few miles off, was in Pennsylvania. His brother, Dr. Samuel Finley, with his church, was altogether in Maryland. Messrs. Finley, M'Millan, Power, and Smith, had, therefore, from their earliest days, some acquaintance with this sort of trouble; and therefore knew how to deal with it when it came upon them afresh in the West.

5. This Presbytery, during the twelve years of its undivided state, consisted, as to its clerical members, of pastors. There were no ministers then without charges—none engaged in secular pursuits—none who were merely presidents or professors in colleges, academies, or seminaries. When they assembled, they came together, from their respective fields of labor, all earnest men, and intent on doing their work, as presbyters, promptly, but faithfully. There was not a toad-eater among them. The toadyism and servility often witnessed in later times, (when certain members of our ecclesiastical judicatories follow, without questioning, some Diatrophes "who loveth to have the pre-eminence,") were unknown in those early, unambitious times. They would have stared with

astonishment at the forwardness and garrulity of many unemployed ministers at the present day, who seem to feel that "the care of all the churches" rests on their shoulders, and who, professing great dread of cliques or caucusses, are continually getting, or keeping them up, themselves. They knew nothing, in those simple days, of electioneering. We never heard of one of these old fathers bustling around, at any of their meetings, asking, "Whom shall we make Moderator?" or "Whom shall we send to the Assembly?" There were no triflers, or buffoons, or merry-andrews among them. You would never see one or more of them sitting back from the others, while the examination of candidates was in progress, amusing themselves in jocular conversation, and, after a few minutes, though not having heard a word from the candidates under examination, popping up and calling out, "Moderator, I move that the further examination on this part of trial be arrested;" or, "I move that this examination be sustained."

Such trifling, in the discharge of a solemn presbyterial duty, was unknown to our fathers. They were generally men of great gravity of manners, and their dress and demeanor secured for them uniformly much respect, and, with younger people, even a kind of dread. When they first settled in the western country, the young people, and especially children, were filled with a degree of awe in their presence. One of them mentioned an extreme case of the kind, that was rather ludicrous. Meeting, in a lane, a boy who was mounted on a horse, with a bag of grain under him, he observed that the lad, who had perhaps never seen a minister dressed in black clothes before, was shying off, so as to endanger his bag by coming into contact with a corner of the fence, called out to him, "Don't be afraid, my son; I'll not hurt you." "The deil trust you!" said the boy, evidently in a tremor of alarm. Yet we would much mistake the character of those good men, were we to imagine that they thought it a sin to laugh. Some of them were men of considerable wit, and, in its proper place, all of them indulged in a hearty, joyous spirit. More cheerful men never lived; but, with few exceptions, they never compromised their clerical dignity, either in or out of presbytery.

Whilst there was a great difference in the manners and constitutional temperament of these seven brethren, they were truly a band of brothers. They never strove together but to provoke each other to love and good works. A more harmonious ecclesiastical body never existed. They were of one mind and one heart. Indeed, most of them had drunk at the same fountains in their training; the Fogg's Manor Academy and New Jersey College. They had in early life enjoyed the ministry of such men as Samuel Finley, Samuel and John Blair, and Mr. Strain—men of a thorough evangelical spirit. They had also, in early life, witnessed and enjoyed powerful revivals of religion, and had come from a region eminently blessed with frequent outpourings of the Holy Spirit. There was also a remarkable missionary spirit among them in the Newcastle Presbytery. The happy reunion that had taken place between the Synods of New York and Philadelphia, twenty-three years before the organization of the Presbytery of Redstone, had had sufficient time to work out its blessed results, and to restore harmony among the churches in that region, whence our ministers generally came. They therefore had an opportunity to imbibe some of the excellencies of both the old parties. With the new side, they were revival men, and insisted upon strict and close examination on the subject of personal piety, in regard to applicants for admission to the communion of the Church, and especially for admission into the sacred office of the gospel ministry. They, with the old side, insisted much on the importance of doctrinal and catechetical instruction, and of thorough education, as far as practicable, in candidates for the ministry. They were strict disciplinarians, and held in the highest importance the early religious training of children and youth. They were most conscientious observers of the Sabbath, and of family worship, morning and evening, seldom or never omitting either reading or singing, as parts of that duty.

6. When they entered upon their respective fields of labor, they found an immense amount of ignorance, ungodliness, and profanity, sufficient to have appalled the stoutest heart. True, there were scattered through most of their churches some very pious people. But many had grown up in utter neglect of religion, and the ordinances of God's house. But God sustained his servants; according to their day was their strength afforded. They were generally blessed with vigorous health; and so were their families. There arose also a noble race of laymen, men of vigorous intellect and of devoted piety. These men were most valuable helps to our ministers. Few ministers now, perhaps, have such sessions as were found in the Presbytery, eighty years ago. Several of these men had, in their younger days, been brought into the communion of the Church during glorious revivals in East and West Nottingham, in Fagg's Manor, and in New Jersey, and were thorough revival men. We have mentioned New Jersey. Did she make any contribution to the settlements and ministers of the West! Yes—one of the most valuable of all our early settlements, and one of the noblest of our first ministers. We will now introduce them to the reader.

A SKETCH OF THE LIFE

OF THE

REV. THADDEUS DOD.

THE south-western part of Washington County, bordering on Virginia, embraces a fine agricultural region, lying on either side of Ten-mile Creek. This creek was so named from the circumstance of its entering the Monongahela ten miles above Redstone Creek. At an early period in the settlement of the country, this section attracted the notice of emigrants from New Jersey. Two respectable elders of the Presbyterian Church from Morris County, of that State, removed to the West about the same time and settled on the waters of Ten-mile. Their names were Jacob Cook and Demas Lindley. The period of their emigration is supposed to have been as early as 1773. Each of these worthy men drew around him, in a short time, a considerable settlement, known for many years after by the name of Cook's Settlement and Lindley's Settlement. Mr. Lindley, in the fall and winter of 1774–5, erected a fort and Block-house long known by his name. In fact, it was one of the best forts and most formidable garrisons between the Monongahela and Wheeling. Before we proceed further, it may be as well to afford the reader some idea of what is meant by a *Fort*. It was usually not only a place of defence, but the residence of a small number of families belonging to the same neighborhood. As the Indian mode of warfare was an indiscriminate slaughter of all ages and both sexes, it was requisite to provide for the safety of the women and children, as well as that of the men. The fort consisted of cabins, and block-houses, and stockades. Divisions or partitions of logs separated the cabins from each other. The walls on the outside were ten or twelve feet high; the slope of the roof being turned wholly inward. A very few of the cabins had puncheon floors. The greater part were earthen. The block-houses were built at the angles of the fort. They projected about two feet beyond the outer walls of the cabins and stockades; their upper stories were about eighteen inches larger every way than the under one, leaving an opening where the second story began to prevent the enemy from making a lodgment under the walls. In some forts, instead of block-houses, the angles of the fort were furnished with bastions. A large folding gate, made of thick slabs, on the side nearest the spring, closed the fort. The stockades, cabins, bastions, and blockkouse-walls, were furnished with port-holes at proper heights and distances. The whole of the outside was made completely bullet-proof. "It may be said," says Mr. Doddridge, "that necessity is the mother of invention; for the whole of this work was made without nails or a single spike of iron, and for this reason: such things were not to be had. In some places less exposed, a single block-house, with a cabin or two, constituted the whole fort. Such places of refuge may appear very trifling to those who have been in the habit of seeing the formidable military garrisons of Europe and America. But they answered the purpose, as the Indians had no artillery. They scarcely ever took one of these forts when the inmates were duly apprised of an intended attack. Into such forts as these did our early ministers, with their families, sometimes flee. There they preached the gospel; there, sometimes, the Spirit of God was poured out, and precious souls were born into the kingdom. But to return from this not unnecessary digression: such a fort as above described was Mr. Lindley's;

and nowhere in the West was one more required or more serviceable.

In the fall of 1777, the Indians had made a most formidable attack on Fort Henry, at the mouth of Wheeling Creek. This was one of the most memorable events in the Border Warfare. In Howe's Hist. Coll. of Virginia, p. 400, a thrilling narrative of that affair, taken from the American Pioneer, drawn by the pen of Mr. Kiernan, may be found. The whole West, for weeks and months together, after this event, was all alive with almost daily expectation of savage forays. Only a few weeks after, and while in and around Fort Lindley all was apprehension and anxiety, there arrived a young man of sallow complexion, of slender form, black hair, and keen, penetrating, dark eyes, not unknown to some of the inmates of that fort; and his arrival gave them no ordinary joy. It was the Rev. Thaddeus Dod.* He had come from the same state and county whence most of the dwellers in the garrison had emigrated. To Mr. Lindley it is believed he was well known. We are altogether incapable of entering into the feelings of that little forted band. Perhaps they had not heard for months from their native place. There were no mails then. Seldom a newspaper reached them. The previous season had been one of more than usual hardship and solicitude to them. What gladness pervaded many a heart that day of his arrival! "How beautiful upon the mountains," perhaps they would exclaim, "are the feet of him that bringeth glad tidings, that publisheth peace!"

Mr. Dod had been ordained, sine titulo, by the Presbytery of New York, in view of his purpose of emigrating to the West, and of preaching the gospel in the frontier settlements. One tradition has it that he had brought his family with him across the mountains; but hearing, no doubt, of the recent attack on Fort Henry, and other indications of increasing Indian hostilities, he left them east of the Monongahela.

* Mr. Dod had been out a few weeks in the early part of the summer.

If this is correct, it is probable Mr. Dod had passed Mr. Power, then residing at Dunlap's Creek settlement, on his way; and may have left his family in that settlement, though of this we are left to conjecture.*

Entering at once on his Master's work, he preached on the following Sabbath in the fort, and administered the sacrament of Baptism. Several children were baptised. It was probably the first time, he had ever administered the ordinance. At any rate it was the *first time* it was ever administered there. It is remembered by one of those children who was then a little boy, standing by his father's side, as a most solemn and melting occasion. He afterwards became a minister of the gospel, and believes that that solemn hour was fraught with unspeakable blessings to his soul. Mr. Dod continued to preach at the garrison and at Cook's settlement and other places, as he had opportunity—visiting his family occasionally. There is an impression that for some period, he withdrew, whether with or without his family, and labored for some time in the region of Springfield and Frankfort, east of the mountains in Virginia. The statement of the Rev. Dr. J. Lindley is, that in 1778, he brought his family over, and commenced forming congregations — one called Lower Ten-mile—the other, Upper Ten-mile, each about ten miles from Washington. They constituted, however, but one church, having but one bench of elders, amongst whom, Messrs. Lindley and Cook were prominent members. The former was a descendant of the Puritans. One of his distant forefathers had accompanied the Rev. John Robinson, when in 1608, he emigrated from England to Holland. Francis Lindley had come with his family along with the band of pilgrims, that in 1620 landed on Plymouth Rock. It is supposed that the father of Demas Lindley emigrated from New England to Morris County, N. J. From such a pious race came this excellent man, who, for many years, occupied

* Since the above was written, we have learned that he brought his family no further than Patterson's Creek, Hampshire County, Va.

a prominent place in our Western Zion, and was one of the first magistrates of Washington County. Of the other, Jacob Cook, we have heard less, but have understood that he was a man of great worth. These men, and several others from New Jersey, had come from the very midst of the spirit and power of those revivals which followed the labours of Whitefield, and the tenants in their native state. With such coadjutors, but infinitely above all, with the presence and blessing of God, Mr. Dod entered upon his most trying field of labor. In many respects his post was the *forlorn hope.* It was by far the most perilous of the frontier posts of our Western Zion. Indians were continually making inroads upon that region. Yet here in a short time a glorious revival took place in Lindley's Fort, and more than forty persons were made happy in believing.

Mr. Dod settled on a farm, three miles from the fort. Near the fort, some years after, a meeting-house was built of hewn logs. Here, under the protection of the fort, families could step out and worship God, without fear and trembling. Much of the preaching before, and even after, the building of this house and of another at Amity, was at private houses. Dr. Lindley relates that "While Mr. Dod was preaching in the house of Caleb Lindley, in the year 1783 or 1784, tidings came that the Indians had murdered a family of the name of Death, on Wheeling Creek, some eighteen miles from us. Services closed immediately; and several young men promptly started with their guns to the spot of the murder, to bury the dead, or to follow the Indians, if practicable. Francis Dunlavy, I know, one of Mr. Dod's scholars, and I think John Brice, started in this company. These young men started on the run, in Indian style and I recollect Dunlavy was foremost." This incident may serve to illustrate what often occurred with most of our first ministers, while engaged in preaching the gospel.

It was a considerable time before Mr. Dod and his session thought it advisable to administer the sacrament of the Lord's supper. Different times had been thought of; but it was still necessary, as he briefly noticed in his Journal, to defer it. At length, however, such a season was enjoyed. And it was the harbinger of many others. Some of these communion seasons were very remarkable. His brethren, Messrs. Smith, M'Millan, and Power, were each of them present, on different occasions. He, in his turn, aided them. There seem to have been a peculiar intimacy and congeniality of spirit between him and Mr. Smith. Whether their acquaintance began at Princeton, we do not know. It is not probable, however, for Mr. Smith had graduated in 1764, and Mr. Dod not until 1773. They were, however, baptised into one spirit. Yet they appear to have been men of quite different temperaments. Mr. Smith was a Boanerges. Mr. Dod was a "Son of Consolation." We do not mean that there was any tameness of character about him. He was a thorough *revival* man, in the best sense of the expression. His preaching was with great power, in the demonstration of the Spirit. It was mighty, through God, to the pulling down of the strongholds of Satan. He assisted Mr. Smith at Cross Creek, during the great revival which began in the fall of 1781, as is noticed in the Western Missionary Magazine.

Mr. Dod possessed a highly cultivated and well-disciplined mind. His power of *concentration*, and of holding his thoughts directly upon any point or subject of investigation, amidst any amount of external interruption, was, perhaps, never exceeded. Not only was he an accurate classical scholar, thoroughly grounded in the Latin, Greek and Hebrew languages, but he was an excellent mathematician. In this respect, he probably excelled all his brethren. Whilst there is evidence, in the few fragments of his writings which he has left, of his familiarity with the original languages of Scripture, there are still living witnesses of his uncommon proficiency in the sciences. If he had a passion for any department of human knowledge, we are inclined to believe, from what we have heard, it was for the *exact sciences*.

A more clear-headed and skilful mathematician we have, perhaps, never had in the West. "He was the only man," says one of his pupils, "that I have met with who could explain every line and figure on Gunter's scale." He was in the practice of making his students construct for themselves Gunter's scales out of dog-wood, so as to be thoroughly prepared, by the scale, to work out every thing belonging to surveying and navigation. No wonder the late Chief Justice Kirkpatrick, a prominent member of the Board of Trustees of Princeton College, upon a young man of the name of Dod * being nominated to the vacant chair of Mathematics, remarked that though he did not know *him*, he knew *Thaddeus* was a good mathematician, and he believed that all that bore the name of Dod had good mathematical heads. He was willing to support the nomination just made, or words to that effect.

But we are anticipating a little. We ought to have mentioned that Mr. Dod, soon after his settlement in the West, joined to his more delightful employment of preaching the gospel, the office of an instructor of youth. This was more or less the case with all our first ministers. It was a matter of necessity. But the Lord greatly blessed them in this important work.

In 1781, Mr. Dod's neighbors, with one consent, turned out and put up a Log Academy, considerably larger than any dwelling-house then in the neighborhood. The interest taken by the settlement in the enterprise reflects great credit upon them, in view of the trying times in which they lived. They consisted, indeed, of many persons considerably in advance of the Scotch-Irish, in point of education. They had brought their New Jersey and New England tastes with them. From a very early period, they loved good taste in public speaking, and in church music. Fifty years ago, better singing could be heard at Upper and Lower Ten-mile than any where in Washington County.

* We have since learned that it was the late lamented Professor Dod.

The Rev. Thomas Moore was one of Mr. Dod's successors in Upper Ten-mile—a man of highly cultivated intellect, and of a refined and abstract style of preaching, that could only have been relished by a people of considerable mental improvement. We mention this fact, at present, merely as evidence that there was nothing strange in Mr. Dod's people taking so earnest an interest in getting up a first-rate classical and scientific school. There was a department in this school, it is true, for the more elementary branches. But its main character was as stated. Here, in 1782, *began the first classical and scientific school in the West.*

In the course of a year or two, James Hughes, John Brice, Robert Marshall, John Hanna, Daniel Lindley, Jacob Lindley, David Smith, and Francis Dunlavy, (who all became ministers of the gospel,) some of them quite small, began their studies, partly in English, and partly in Latin and Mathematics. There were also several boys who afterwards became eminent men in various walks of secular life, who were here trained, especially in the sciences. Some of them became first-rate surveyors. Among them may be mentioned Daniel M'Farland, Joseph Eddy and Thomas Stokely. M'Farland, with his father, and Stokely, were amongst the most eminent land speculators we ever had in the West. Two of those in the first list we mentioned, afterwards pursued their studies with Mr. Smith, when, in the fall of 1785, he opened the Latin School, called "The Study," designed more particularly and exclusively for training young men for the gospel ministry. These young men, being of Mr. Smith's pastoral charge, were probably led to change their school, more from motives of convenience and economy than any thing else.

In view of the facts above stated, we are now led to believe that Mr. Dod justly claims the precedence, in his efforts to promote the cause of education; while Mr. Smith's school at Buffalo may have been the first with a more special and exclusive reference to the training of young men for the service of the church. Soon after, the "Study" at Buffalo was *fol-*

lowed by the "Log Cabin," at Chartiers. For most of those with Mr. Smith, and some who had been with Mr. Dod, went over to Dr. M'Millan's school, and composed a part of those with whom, he informs us, (giving their names,) *his school began.* Of this further notice will be taken in the life of Dr. M'Millan.

What portion of his time Mr. Dod gave to instruction in his school, we cannot tell. His pastoral field was large, and required and received his diligent attention. He was likewise appointed by the Presbytery to supply various destitute settlements, especially Muddy Creek and the South Fork of Ten-mile. Several gracious outpourings of the Holy Spirit were afforded to Ten-mile, during Mr. Dod's ministry. In the Western Missionary Magazine for September, 1803, it is expressly stated that while the gracious work was going on in Cross Creek, Upper Buffalo, Chartiers and Pigeon Creek, "The Lord also poured out his spirit," particularly on Bethel and Lebanon, under the ministry of the Rev. John Clark, and on "Ten-mile, *under the ministry of the Rev. Thaddeus Dod.*"

On the 20th of January, 1789, Mr. Dod was appointed the first *Principal* of *Washington Academy*, at Washington, Pennsylvania, which Academy had been incorporated by the Legislature of Pennsylvania, September 24th, 1787,* and was afterwards, in 1806, merged into *Washington College.*

This appointment evinces the high estimation in which his literary and scientific qualifications were held. But in consequence of the loss of the building by fire† in which this school at Washington was held, Mr. Dod, who had removed with his family to Washington, returned again to Ten-mile and resumed his former employments. There seems no doubt,

* Having an endowment, also, of 5000 acres of land.

† It was the old Courthouse, that had been converted into an academy or schoolhouse. By this fire Mr. Dod lost a number of valuable books; a serious disaster to a minister at that early period.

that had it not been for this Providential occurrence, — the temporary suspension of the Washington School, — it would have speedily risen to a high eminence, and would have superseded and prevented altogether the movement soon afterwards made to get up the Academy at Canonsburg. Our ministers, generally, and some of the most prominent citizens of the West, were, up to this time, looking to Washington. Dr. M'Millan, Mr. Smith, Mr. John Corbley, the eminent Baptist minister of Muddy Creek, and several others, were either trustees of Washington Academy, or warmly enlisted in its interests. And Mr. Dod was the man whom they had chosen to conduct it. But God seeth not as man seeth. He had other purposes to accomplish; and his devoted servant, Dod, was not to finish his life in Washington. His few remaining days were to be spent in the field to which God had at first called him. And here he labored till his death, which occurred May 20th, 1793. When he found his sickness was unto death, he said "I must examine carefully the ground of my hope. I may deceive myself: the heart is very deceitful, and Satan is very subtle;" or words to that effect. After remaining for a considerable time engaged, apparently, in thorough self-examination and in prayer, his countenance was observed, at length, to grow radiant with joy. The first utterance he gave was "O, I am so glad I was born to die!" Other expressions, not now remembered, followed. As he lay with his face towards the wall, he was heard to say "Ha! I expected you; but you may go back." Mr. Carmichael, his elder, here asked him what he meant. He said that he had just experienced an assault of the fiery darts of Satan, but that he was quickly relieved. Mr. C. asked him, "Can you now bear your dying testimony to the gospel you have preached to us?"—"Yes, I can!" he promptly replied. In this happy frame his spirit winged its flight to its Everlasting Rest. "The path of the just is as the shining light that shineth more and more unto the perfect day."

Mr. Dod preached the opening sermon at the first organization of the Presbytery of Redstone, in 1781, from Job xlii. 5, 6. He lived till a few months before its last undivided meeting, in 1793. He was one of its brightest ornaments, and was indeed a chosen vessel of the Lord. He survived his brother, Smith, only about thirteen months. They were first called to die, as they had lived, for their Master. And now of that little band of four ministers, with which the Presbytery was formed, half were gone. But already the Presbytery had grown to a large size, and were just about to be divided into two presbyteries.

Mr. Dod, beside his other natural and acquired gifts, was possessed of considerable poetic powers; and had he cultivated his genius in this respect, it would have attained to some distinction. He thus presented the rare and almost incredible combination of mathematical talent, classical taste, and poetic imagination. But Christian, deeply devout and spiritual, was his highest style. He was a man of modest, humble, yet prepossessing manners. As he possessed an uncommon memory and great acuteness of mind, he must have been a most agreeable companion. His pupils held him in the highest respect, and he had the happy faculty of infusing into those who were capable of it, an intense love of science and literature. When we consider his various traits of character, and the very remarkable combination of talents found in him, we cannot but admire the orderings of Providence that assigned to such a man such a perilous and self-denying charge. Often were he and his family driven to the neighboring fort by the savages of the wilderness. In one instance, during Mr. D.'s absence, Mrs. Dod and her little children, upon the alarm of approaching Indians, fled and concealed themselves, for several hours, amongst the high weeds in an adjoining ground. They were thus concealed, if we remember rightly, upon Mr. Dod's return; and either it proved a false alarm, or the Indians had taken another direction. Here often was he compelled also to leave them exposed when engaged in supplying distant congregations! But the Almighty arm of a Covenant God was over him and his. Yet an eminent servant of God, John Corbley, a Baptist minister, settled in a comparatively adjacent settlement, with whom Mr. Dod appears to have lived on terms of much Christian fellowship, and who was frequently with him at Lindley's Fort, was called to a severe trial, which must have awakened the tenderest sensibilities of Mr. and Mrs. Dod. The following narrative was given by Mr. Corbley, in a letter to the Rev. Mr. Rogers, of Philadelphia, in the year 1785:

"On the second Sabbath of May in the year 1782, being by appointment, at one of my meeting-houses, about a mile from my dwelling-house, I set out with my dear wife and five children, for public worship. Not suspecting any danger, I walked behind 200 yards, with my Bible in my hand, meditating; as I was thus employed, all on a sudden, I was greatly alarmed with the frightful shrieks of my dear family before me. I immediately ran with all the speed I could, vainly hunting a club as I ran, till I got within 40 yards of them. My poor wife, seeing me, cried to me, to make my escape. An Indian ran up to shoot me. I then fled, and by so doing, outran him. My wife had a sucking child in her arms. This little infant they killed and scalped. They then struck my wife several times, but not getting her down, the Indian who aimed to shoot me, ran to her, shot her through the body, and scalped her. My little boy, an only son, about six years old, they sunk the hatchet into his brains, and thus dispatched him. A daughter, besides the infant, they also killed and scalped. My eldest daughter, who is yet alive, was hid in a tree about 20 yards from the place where the rest were killed, and saw the whole proceedings. She, seeing the Indians all go off, as she thought, got up and deliberately crept out of the hollow trunk; but one of them espying her, ran hastily up, knocked her down and scalped her; also her only surviving sister, on whose head they did not leave more than an inch round either of flesh or of skin, besides taking a piece of her skull. She and the aforementioned one are still miraculously preserved; though as you must think, I have had and still have, a great deal of trouble and expense with them, besides anxiety about them; insomuch that as to worldly circumstances, I am almost ruined. I am yet in hopes of seeing them cured. They still, blessed be God, retain their senses, notwithstanding the painful operations they have already and must yet pass through.

["MUDDY CREEK,
Washington County, July 8, 1788."]

Such a horrid scene thus occurring but a little distance, as in those days accounted, from Mr. Dod and his family, must have been a severe trial to their faith, and have driven them nearer to the overshadowing Wings.

It would have afforded us great satisfaction to give some extracts from Mr. Dod's diary, in which he portrays the nature of his early Christian experience. It is in the hands of his son, the Rev. Cephas Dod, the senior pastor of Amity, or Lower Ten-mile; who, it is hoped, will give it to the public in connexion with a more extended memoir of his excellent father; on which, it is understood, he is now engaged. Many important particulars we have been unable to give in this paper, for want of the materials which are in the hands of his son; and we could neither with propriety ask him to surrender them to us, nor wait for the use of his memoir, without delaying our progress in the preparation of this work for the press. We may have fallen into errors in several particulars. We are indebted to the Rev. Dr. Jacob Lindley, William Darby, Esq., and the Rev. Dr. William Wylie, for the larger portion of materials of the foregoing sketch. Two of them were his pupils, and were well acquainted with him.

Since the above was written we have been favored with the perusal of what Dr. Cephas Dod has written of his father, and are glad to find no serious discrepancy in our respective accounts of this dear servant of God.

CHAPTER V.

HOUSES OF WORSHIP, SACRAMENTAL SEASONS, STOVES AND BAPTISM, CATECHISING, ETC.

FOR many years the people in Western Pennsylvania were compelled to construct houses of worship of a very humble and unpretending character. Nor were they liable to the charge of dwelling in ceiled houses, while the house of the Lord lay waste. Their own dwellings were generally log cabins. In many instances, newly married couples boldly ventured into this perilous region, and commenced their new life in log cabins, amidst hardships, dangers and privations which few in our day would be willing to encounter. Their dwellings, in many instances, were of the humblest description, and their *fixtures* inside and out corresponded. The man who, in Fayette County, erected a good two-story house of hewn logs, immortalized himself; and the place was known for fifty years afterwards as "the high house," even when other dwellings, all around, towered above it, in every sense.

They early bestirred themselves to do what they could in erecting meeting-houses. These were also but cabins of a larger size. The pompous formalities of laying corner-stones, or of a dedication service, were innovations of more ambitious times. How far these things, and the introduction of organs, &c., are consistent with the principles of Presbyterianism, and the genius and simplicity of the Christian dispensation, might be a subject for serious consideration, leading even good men to very opposite conclusions. The second set of churches were still but log houses—though the logs were hewn, and with a good shingle roof over them.

As the settlements grew, and their meetings became more thronged, their houses could not comfortably accommodate

Log Cabin Meeting House.

A Meeting House of 2nd Class.

A Meeting House of 3d Class.

First Presbyterian Church, Pittsburg, Pa.

Lith: of P. S. Duval & Co. Ph.

the people—during the summer especially, on sacramental occasions. Many congregations, during the whole summer, when the weather was pleasant, worshipped in groves. These groves were commonly in the immediate vicinity of the churches. Usually a hill-side was selected, where the trees were large and free from undergrowth. A platform, six or eight feet wide and ten or twelve feet long, was erected, about four feet from the ground, on the upper side. This was boarded up a few feet above the platform, having an open doorway, or place of entrance. At the back, on the lower side, the boarding extended much higher, and was connected with the roof, or covering, sloping off from the front. This *tent*, as it was called, was usually placed some distance down the hill-side, on descending ground; seats of logs, or slabs, were arranged in front of the tent, along up the side of the hill for some distance, spreading off considerably to the right and left of this tent-pulpit. Usually a long log, hewn only on the upper side, extended from near the pulpit, directly up through the area of the seats. This was elevated about the common height of a table, supported sometimes by straddling legs, but most generally by blocks of wood. On either side were similar logs, but much lower, for seats, placed sufficiently far from the higher, or table-logs, as to give room for walking between them. Sometimes, also, two other log-tables, with their seats diverged at right angles, to the right and left, all converging to a point some six or eight feet in front of the pulpit, but leaving sufficient room for an ordinary walnut or deal table to occupy the point of convergence, and to have free passage around.* These log tables were occupied exclusively by communicants, during the progress of that solemn service. Before that service began, and at other times, they served as a part of the ordinary sitting.

A passing stranger, if not altogether a heathen or a publican, would readily recognise the sacramental sabbath by ob-

* More frequently, perhaps, *two* log tables, parallel to each other, ran up in front.

serving these extended log tables, covered with snowy linen, all radiating from the large common table, containing the vessels of the sacred symbols, and all covered with white napkins. The "tout-ensemble" was strikingly picturesque. The seats were, of course, without backs, except where the trees furnished that luxury; and such choice seats were reserved for aged ladies and the infirm.

Let the reader now endeavor to fall back in fancy to these early times; and to conceive himself, on some beautiful sabbath morning, approaching such a scene. He sees, perhaps, a few cleared fields, in most of which the deadened timber is still standing; but the greater part of the landscape is the leafy forest—we say *leafy*, for we will suppose it is early in the month of June, and all nature is glowing in the freshness of early summer. The music of the feathered tribe, heard through the woods, blended with the occasional tinkling of cow-bells, is grateful to his ears, and in harmony with the day and the scene. By some turn in his road, a full view along the hill-side of the scene around the tent opens before him. The people are assembling from all directions—many on horseback, more on foot. Neither gig, nor barouche, nor buggy, nor carryall is seen. Such means of conveyance were unknown in those days. Some are seen on the ground, or on the logs, putting on their stockings and shoes—for they have walked many miles barefoot, carrying these articles wrapped in their kerchiefs, *in their hands*. This circumstance engages his attention but for a moment. He sees the gathering crowds pouring in, from all directions, towards the tent. He hears the continual neighing of horses, some near, and some afar off. Perhaps he distinguishes, especially, the louder and peculiar tone of some old equine Nestor, that approaches, in its depth and grandeur, to the sublime. If Dr. Allison, in his delightful work on Taste, has taught us to notice the sublimity of the distant lowing of cattle in the stillness of a summer evening—what would he have said of the neighing of horses, blended with the repose of the sabbath landscape, spread around the stirring scenes of a communion season amidst our early western forests.

We will suppose the reader looks around on earth and heaven. Upward, all is bright and sunny. A single hawk or eagle is perhaps far up in the skies, slowly wheeling in his gyrations, and seeming, if possible, to share in the gladness of the general scene. The vast assembly gradually gather round the spot appropriated to the solemnities of that glorious day. They all become, at length, quietly seated. After a short pause, he sees the men all uncovering their heads, and the whole assembly rising to their feet; for the minister has risen in the tent, come forward to its front, and spread his hands in token of prayer. Then the psalm succeeds; and oh, what singing was there! Messrs. Mason and Hastings would have been scandalized, perhaps; but Professor Silliman, who was so delighted with the universal outburst in the Tron Church, when he was in Scotland, would have been in raptures, had he heard the notes of praise that swelled up through the umbrageous forests around an early western sacramental scene, and made all the welkin ring; for those old-fashioned people had understood in a literal sense the Psalmist, "Let the people praise thee, let all the people praise thee." Another longer prayer, another psalm, and then the sermon—but we will not task the reader further. Let him, in fancy, sit and hear the successive services of that long summer day. Let him witness those long tables, successively filled and vacated four, five, six, and sometimes seven times, by the approaching and retreating crowd of communicants. The communion seasons of our fathers were, from an early period, exceedingly interesting. The Thursday preceding was commonly observed as a day of fasting and prayer. And there was always public worship on Saturday and Monday, in connexion with these occasions. The ministers, of course, aided each other; and many people from surrounding congregations and distant settlements attended. The families residing in the vicinity of the place were usually thronged with lodgers.

Though there was much, in all the circumstances of these meetings, calculated to produce a species of religious dissipation, we cannot but believe they were eminently profitable and refreshing seasons, and greatly aided in extending the influence of the gospel through those early settlements. The extension of the services through several successive days contributed to suspend or lighten the influence of their worldly cares, and to break up, for a time, their anxieties and all their little petty vexations of domestic life. They promoted, also, Christian friendship, and enlarged the sphere of their social intercourse and of their Christian sympathies. They paved the way for many happy marriages and many auspicious nuptials. Above all, they proved seasons of special intercourse with heaven, and of foretaste of its joys, to many of those greatly tried and often sorrowing Christians who, in their frontier life, were frequently in heaviness through manifold temptations. It is worthy of special notice, also, that a very large proportion of those who were brought from darkness to light, and from the power of Satan unto God—traced their first religious impressions to these sacramental seasons. The taste and usages of modern days have formed us to habits that would make us feel dissatisfied with the tedious length of the services on those occasions. We would be apt to exclaim "What a weariness is it!" But our forefathers felt not so. They would be as much disgusted at the brevity with which such services are hurried over in many places now-a-days. Whether there is not too great a disposition to conform to the taste and wishes of an ungodly world in respect to the length of sermons and sacramental services in our day, merits serious enquiry. The far greater frequency of communion seasons now, compared with those of early times, is not, we are aware, to be left out of view; and perhaps justifies a much greater brevity in all the exercises than was then practised. In this, as in most other things, *in medio tutissimus ibis* is a wise direction. Even their ordinary services were more protracted. We must remember, also, that throughout the entire winter their houses were without stoves or any fire. It was not till ten or twelve years after the old Presbytery of Redstone held its last meeting at Long Run, in 1793, that stoves were introduced. And it was not without great opposition, even from some physicians. The attempt to introduce fire into meeting-houses produced, in some places, even a greater commotion than the introduction of Dr. Watts' Psalms and Hymns.

We have spoken of the communion season during the earlier history of our ministers and churches in Western Pennsylvania. For many years, it was not usual to administer the Lord's Supper more than twice a year, and, indeed, generally, as the ministers had more than one pastoral charge, only once in each congregation. But a very large proportion of all the members of their whole charge attended; riding, or walking, as many were compelled to do, ten or fifteen miles. The sermon on the fast-day (which was usually the previous Thursday) was generally long, and was a prayerfully prepared and affecting exhibition of the grounds and reasons for humiliation and prayer. In early times, the services on this day were well attended; the congregations were usually quite as large as on ordinary Sabbaths. There is no doubt that this usage was well suited to the state and character of those times, and greatly promoted the piety and spirituality of the churches, and prepared them to ascend the mount of ordinances on the ensuing Sabbath, and to draw near to God. If the exercises on that day, and indeed during the entire solemn convocation, would appear to us protracted to tediousness, they harmonized with the perhaps better tastes and feelings of our fathers. We may have gone farther than we are aware into an opposite extreme, paring and clipping away many things, which, if not essential, are highly appropriate and edifying. It is to be feared that, in these matters, ministers are tempted to consult a worldly policy, and to regard with too much deference the tastes and wishes of impenitent men, especially if they happen to be wealthy pew-holders.

Where weariness begins, it is true, edification ends. But Dr. Nesbit's sarcastic remark, "lang sermons are a great affliction to the ungodly," is also true. A good deal of what we complain of and protest against, has, perhaps, been introduced into our Church by those who never were thorough Presbyterians; and though we have been graciously delivered from this alarming source of innovation and mischief, it has never yet, perhaps, been sufficiently ascertained how many "notions" are still permitted to remain, to the scandal of the Church, and to the keeping up of a fastidious dislike of our old-fashioned Presbyterian usages. Our forefathers were probably inclined to be prolix. The people, however, were satisfied. They would have been greatly pained at the way in which matters are often conducted on these "high days" of the Church of God.

The *action sermons*, as they were called, on communion Sabbaths, were generally preached by the pastors or resident ministers; this was considered peculiarly proper. And we must remember that perhaps fully one-half of the audience were not his ordinary hearers. Then followed what was called *fencing the tables*. This was often tedious, occupying an hour or more. Not unfrequently there was a regular review of all the sins forbidden in each of the ten commandments. And it was remarked by the profane, that the preacher never stopped till he had solemnly debarred from the ordinance every one of his people, and himself to boot. Our old ministers, however, seldom indulged in such lengthened details as the *seceders* were said to be in the practice of doing, forbidding and debarring various classes of offenders, that were not to be found among them, such as stage-players and visitants of theatres; and yet it must be confessed that, too often, our venerable fathers took this occasion to pour out a great deal "de omnibus rebus, et quibusdem aliis." There are few ministers now, in this section of the Church, including our brethren of the secession, who would not subscribe to the sound and judicious views of Dr. Dick, in his lectures on theology:

"*Fencing the tables* is merely an expedient suggested by human prudence, and is not supported by scriptural precept or apostolical example. It is therefore a vulgar prejudice to account it essential to the ordinance, and to imagine that it adds anything to its perfection or solemnity. The truth is, that to aid his people in examining themselves, should be the object of a minister from the beginning to the end of the year, and that he should study so to divide the word of truth, that all may be furnished with the means of ascertaining their state and character, before they assemble to celebrate the Supper. But, although this part of the service is not necessary, is not adopted in many Christian societies, and might be laid aside without in any degree impairing the original institution, at which it was not observed, yet there is no doubt that it has been productive of good, and might have produced more, if it had been judiciously conducted. Ministers should beware of the two extremes, of being too easy or too severe; of being too easy, lest they embolden the profane; and of being too severe, lest they discourage the pious. There is danger to be apprehended from their boundless charity, and from their gloominess and narrow-mindedness. The word of God is the only standard of character; and as it excludes all who are living in sin, so it invites all who love the Saviour, although their love should be as a grain of mustard-seed. The plan at present pursued in our church is preferable to that of our predecessors, who, taking the decalogue as their standard, excommunicated sinners of every description and degree, many of whom were well known not to be present, and would have disclaimed the privilege which was publicly denied them. What had they to do to judge them who were without? Ought they not to judge them alone who were within?" This extract from the late distinguished professor of Theology in the Secession body, though longer than we had intended, we could not withhold; as it may perhaps be read by many with satisfaction, who may not have access to that noble work.

The practice of distributing tokens to communicants on Saturday or Sabbath morning, previous to the communion service, universally prevailed, and was, no doubt, introduced into this country from Scotland and the north of Ireland. When at our early sacraments, so large a proportion of intending communicants were from surrounding churches, it seemed a highly proper custom. It is now, to a great extent, discontinued. It may well be doubted whether any real advantage can be shown, from the continuance of this confessedly human device, in any of our churches now. We are familiar with all that has been alleged in its defence. We are aware of the circumstances which seemed to render it necessary in early times. But even then, the evils, at least the embarrassing inconveniences, sometimes resulting from it, might well have raised the question whether they did not outweigh any good that was secured. On the whole, this custom so prevalent once in our Western churches, we think, is now more honored in the breach than the observance.

The ordinance of infant baptism was generally administered on the Sabbath, at the house of God, at as early a time after the birth of the child, as it suited the convenience of parents to attend public worship. The practice of confining the administration of this ordinance to Mondays of Communions, they did not sanction or approve. It appears, from the minutes of the Presbytery, that at their spring session, in 1792, a recommendation of the Synod of Virginia—of which they were then a part — came before them, in respect to which they adopted the following minutes: "The Presbytery taking into their serious consideration the recommendation of Synod respecting periodical baptism, cannot see sufficient ground from scripture authority for their compliance therewith." Is it not likely that these fathers also preferred their own usage on this subject, because, by the more frequent public administration of that ordinance, an opportunity would be better afforded to remind parents and children present, almost continually of their solemn obligations?

They were all in the habit of engaging parents to strict and solemn promises, in reference to the religious training of their children. When an attempt was made to introduce a laxer system among them, and a reference was made to them on the subject, August 12th, 1788, in this form, "Whether ministers ought, in the administration of baptism, to require the parents to promise to perform certain duties, or only to recommend the performance of them. 'The Presbytery were unanimously of opinion that it is the duty of ministers, not only to recommend, but to require of parents a solemn promise that they will, through grace, conscientiously perform certain duties which are usually mentioned on such occasions.'" Such were their views and practice in those earlier times, in regard to the ordinance of baptism. We would further add that they not only bound these solemn vows upon the consciences of parents—but they took care to ascertain how far they complied with their engagements. Especially did they attend to the catechetical instruction of all the children and youth of their congregations. The children expected, as a matter of course, to be examined on the shorter catechism, in the course of the pastor's family visitation, and were generally ambitious to secure his approbation by their recitations; and of course were usually well prepared for his visits.

It is very apt to excite surprise upon examining any of the letters, papers, or records of those early times that these early fathers wrote so small a hand, and crowded so much into a little space. This was the case with Finley, M'Millan, Power, Smith, and Dod. We have not seen any specimen of the hand-writing of Clarke, and Dunlap; but have been told that they were no exceptions in this respect. This may have arisen from their custom of preparing small forms or skeletons, such as they could conveniently insert in their little pocket Bibles, which they used altogether in those days. A modern fine Quarto Bible in the pulpit would have been a curiosity too exciting to admit of much attention to the sermon—at least for a few weeks. But perhaps this peculiarity in their writing arose from the necessity of economising paper, which was scarce and very dear.* Book-stores were unknown. How they ever succeeded in getting over the mountains such works as Pool's Synopsis, Henry's Commentary, Stackhouse's Bible, and Ridgeley's Body of Divinity—all folios—has puzzled us to divine. Of the smaller works, such as Boston's Fourfold State, Baxter's Saint's Rest, Alliene's Alarm, Baxter's Call, Pilgrim's Progress, Ambrose's Looking unto Jesus, Flavel's Touchstone, Owen on Prayer, and many others, you would generally find two or three of these in almost every Presbyterian family.

Neither our ministers nor people had any religious Newspaper in those days; no Magazines nor Reviews. The "Western Missionary Magazine" was started in 1802; but did not survive the third year. It is well worth looking after, as it contains a very considerable amount of valuable matter, especially about the early revivals in Western Pennsylvania, in Kentucky, and in New England.

But they had no post-offices—no newspapers of any kind, except what came casually to hand, brought out by travellers, traders, merchants, and others. The first Newspaper ever published in the West was "The Pittsburg Gazette," which began July 29th, 1786.† There was no regular mail across the mountains for several years after the Redstone Presbytery was organized.

The first regular post from Philadelphia to Pittsburg was started in 1788—and one from Virginia to Bedford—the two to meet at Bedford.‡ We would think it an intolerable hardship now to be deprived of mails and newspapers, especially our weekly "Advocates," "Presbyterians," and "Banners."

---

* Messrs. Johnson and Sharpless established the first paper-mill in the West, in 1797; on Redstone Creek, Fayette County, Pa. (See Hazard's Register, Vol. 13, page 224.)

† The first editor was John Scull, Esq., who died, February 8th, 1828, in Westmoreland, in the 63d year of his age.

‡ History of Pittsburg.

We would not depreciate the value of periodical literature; but if our forefathers had it not, they at least escaped the temptation of wasting too many precious hours over that kind of reading, to the neglect of more solid and substantial food. And if the people now have much more general intelligence, through the means of the newspaper press, their knowledge has grown, in many cases, more superficial, especially in religious matters, than that possessed by many of their fathers. If they had no papers, many of them had a few good books, which they often perused. Some of them were familiar with Fisher's Catechism; and in an examination on theology, would have put to the blush many a candidate before Presbyteries of our day.

Great attention was paid to the "Shorter Catechism." It was usually taught in all the schools. And pious parents required a recitation of it in their families, by old and young, on Sabbath evening. To have neglected this matter would have been regarded as heathenish. Their singing was generally of a very plain description. But it was with a heartiness and earnestness that showed they meant something by it. "Praising God by a committee," in other words, the use of choirs, was unknown to them. The singing at the church was generally led by one or more persons in front of the pulpit; and very commonly a smaller pulpit was constructed in front of the minister's, a few feet lower, called the Clerk's desk. If the sounds they occasionally made were somewhat nasal, it disturbed nobody. The lines were "parcelled" out—sometimes one at a time—generally two—and in this we have certainly gained some advantage. But in those days psalm-books were scarce, and many would have been scandalized had any attempt been made to sing without "giving out" the lines.

We have little respect for that kind of spirit that would flout at their more simple usages, or suppose that our old ministers were utterly wanting in taste and refinement, because they did not correct or change these customs. How much better, and more in accordance with the true design of this part of public worship, the methods of those times, than what is witnessed often now, in town or city churches, calling themselves evangelical too, when a choir, with or without an organ or bass viol, almost entirely monopolise the singing; and professors of religion turn almost half-way round in their seats to look up and listen to the choir. 'Tell it not in Gath, publish it not in the streets of Askelon.' This is often now witnessed in many of our churches.

In those times, the people all rose in time of prayer, except the aged and infirm, and stood devoutly till its close. The indecent practice of multitudes now, either not rising at all, or almost immediately popping down again on their seats, was unknown in the times of the old Redstone Presbytery.

There was one custom that then prevailed, which was well adapted to the plainness and simplicity of the times, the restoration of which we would almost advocate. When anybody became drowsy or weary with sitting, it was perfectly allowable to get up and stand awhile. And persons of every age and both sexes adopted this custom; so that, on a warm summer day, you might see twenty, fifty, or sixty people, young and old, standing bolt upright, in various parts of the congregation. By this means, sleep was resisted, and drowsiness thrown off. Subjected to various toils and hardships, many, in those days, found it exceedingly difficult, after a week of hard work, to keep themselves awake on the Sabbath, while at church. The services were somewhat long — the sermon would often reach the length of an hour and a half. Their prayers, too, were often long. In the summer, an hour's intermission between sermons was common. Their communions were often held out in a grove. Indeed, the services, in many places, were conducted at what they called a tent, during the whole summer, when the weather permitted. It was customary for many to take their little Bibles with them, and to note the text, and the text-proofs quoted.

The people were generally very plainly clad, and in summer seldom wore coats at meeting. Even our old ministers generally divested themselves of their coats, when they rose to announce the text. Their custom was, generally, during the period of the year when they preached twice, to make one of the discourses a part of a series of lectures, or expository sermons, on some portion of the Bible. The Psalms, the Prophecy of Isaiah, or one of the Epistles, would be taken up and treated seriatim in this way. The great advantage to themselves and to their hearers, in this course, need not be dwelt upon. It is much to be lamented that it has gone so much out of use; but we rejoice to see that it is recently recommended from high quarters of ministerial influence. As to the amount of study and preparation necessary for such a course of lectures, we believe it requires more study and diligence to make a good lecturer, than a good text-preacher.

These early fathers were humble, devoted, prayerful men. They studied much, considering their toils and hardships. They redeemed much time to prepare beaten oil for the sanctuary. They were not ambitious to shine as pulpit stars, or to blazon their learning or talents. There was not a D. D. among them, nor was there while that old Presbytery lasted. And yet they were all good scholars and divines, had graduated at Princeton, and were well-grounded in literature.

A SKETCH OF THE LIFE

OF THE

REV. DR. JOHN M'MILLAN.*

THE Rev. Dr. John M'Millan was born at Fagg's Manor, Chester County, Pa., on the 11th of November, 1752. His parents, (whose names were William M'Millan and Margaret Rea,) came from the north of Ireland to the United States about the year 1742, and were first located at Fagg's Manor. Here his mother died in 1768. The father married again,† and some time during the War of the Revolution removed to the Western country, where he died July 2d, 1792, aged 75 years. His father and mother were both pious; the latter was eminently so. They had eight children—five sons and three

* This sketch, down till Dr. M'Millan's first visit at Chartiers, was written by the Rev. Lemuel F. Leake, and published in the Presbyterian Advocate, in 1845. With his consent, we have employed it, without addition or curtailment. We have even received considerable aid from him, in the subsequent part of this Memoir. We are also much indebted to a printed, but unfinished sketch of the Doctor's life, by the late Rev. Matthew Brown, D. D. It is much to be regretted that Dr. Brown did not turn his attention to this Work, before the growing infirmities of age arrested his further progress. Doubtless he could have furnished a valuable Memoir of Dr. M'Millan, together with an interesting history of Jefferson College. Thanks are due, also, to a brother, who gave us the use of Dr. M'Millan's Journal, in his own handwriting. This was a most unexpected favor, as we had despaired of ever seeing it.

† His father's second wife was the mother of Professor Miller, late of Jefferson College.

daughters. Two of the sons died young. The names of the sons who attained to mature age were Thomas and William. William was the father of the Rev. William M'Millan, D. D., who, at the time of his death, was President of Franklin College, New Athens, Ohio. The daughter's names were Mary, Jane and Margaret. John, who was the youngest but one, survived all the rest of the family.

Like Samuel and John of old, and many others of distinguished usefulness in the Church of God, the subject of these notes was a son given in answer to special prayer. Before the birth, his father, having lost an infant son, whose name was John, solemnly vowed to the Lord,* that if he would give him another son, he would call his name John, and devote him to the work of the gospel ministry. In consequence of the birth of this son, who was thus given in answer to prayer, and who was named John, in fulfilment of his father's vow, many, no doubt, as in the case of the son of Zacharias, were made to rejoice; for he too, as he afterwards appeared, was the appointed instrument of God to turn many who were disobedient to the wisdom of the just—to make ready a people prepared for the Lord.

Having made the necessary proficiency in English studies, young M'Millan commenced his classical course at the highly celebrated Academy at Fagg's Manor, his native place. This seminary, which had been founded, and for some time continued, by that eminent scholar and divine, the Rev. Samuel Blair, was now under the direction of the Rev. John Blair, not less distinguished than his kinsman and predecessor. Here such men as President Davies, Alexander Cummins, Robert Smith, James Finley, John Rogers, and others, some of whom were among the master spirits of the age, and the most distinguished ministers of the day, had their elemental training. The plan of education pursued in such seminaries

* Although, in Dr. M'Millan's MS., the father only is mentioned—yet, as his mother was an eminently devout woman, she doubtless had her own exercises of faith and prayer, in reference to the same subject.

as this had, indeed, less of show than that adopted in the gymnasiums, and high schools, and institutes of such lofty pretensions, to which the spirit of boasted improvement, and we may add, the fastidious taste of the present age, have given birth: but it is believed it had far more solid worth, and was better adapted to the development of mind. It was better suited to lay a foundation for ripe scholarship. And unless we err in judgment, the mode of discipline then in practice was calculated to shed a more healthful influence upon the exercise and right improvement of the moral powers. Unless we are deceived, the result has shown that there is far more sciolism, and far less fixedness of strength of moral principle, among nominally educated men of the present day, than at the time to which we refer. And for all the practical and important purposes of life, such an education as was chiefly or wholly obtained at such institutions as the Academy at Fagg's Manor, or the Log College on the Neshaminy, was far more valuable than that which has the sanction of the "Facultates Artium," and the "Sigillum latum Curatorum," of many of the Colleges and Universities, of pompous pretensions, in our day.

Under circumstances thus favorable for mental and moral culture, John M'Millan continued to pursue his studies at the Academy in Fagg's Manor, until the removal of Mr. Blair, his distinguished Preceptor, to Princeton College.* From Fagg's Manor, when he was about fifteen years of age, he was sent to the grammar school at Pequea, Lancaster County, Pa. This institution was of kindred character with that which he had left. It will form an index of its repute to know that it was, at this time, under the instruction and superintendence

* To this venerable institution Mr. Blair was called, by the Trustees, in 1767. Here he occupied the Chair of Professor of Moral Philosophy and Theology until the accession of Dr. Witherspoon to the Presidency, in 1769. Mr. Blair was chosen to the office of Vice-President of the College. (See Note D. appended to Dr. Green's Discourse to Baccalaureate, pp. 363 and 394.)

of such a man as the Rev. Robert Smith. It was here the privilege of Mr. M'Millan to enjoy the literary and scientific advantages of such a school; but it was his higher privilege still, to attend upon the religious instruction and the ministry of this servant of the Lord, so eminent for his zeal, his ability, and his success in his Master's work.*

The residence of Mr. M'Millan at Pequea forms a period in history of deep and prominent interest. His timidity of temperament, which was characteristic and peculiar, and which to himself was often extremely distressing, had hitherto kept out of view his moral worth. The native vigor of his mind could no longer entirely be concealed. The keen eye of that wise observer of human nature, his instructor, Mr. Smith, saw through all the darkening disparagements of an exterior, forbidding as it was, the indications of talent that gave much promise of future usefulness. He would often apply to his pupil, M'Millan—referring especially to the character of his mind — a plain but expressive adage, the import of which is "he is better than he looks." By the kind, and soothing, and judicious attention of Mr. Smith, he was encouraged; and he soon gave evidence that was decisive, that he possessed

---

* Mr. Smith was of Scottish descent. His parents, when he was a child, emigrated to America, about the year 1730. In his fifteenth or sixteenth year he was hopefully made a subject of God's special grace, through the instrumentality of the preaching of Whitefield, whose preaching was so remarkably blessed, both in Britain and in this country. He pursued his classical and theological course of instruction under the direction of the Rev. Samuel Blair, of Fagg's Manor. In 1750, he was licensed, and was ordained the pastor of the church of Pequea in 1751. In the year 1784, he received the honorary degree of D. D. from the College of New Jersey. After having acquired high distinction as a classical teacher, as an instructor in theology, and as a minister of the gospel, he closed a life of great usefulness in his 63d year. See a sketch of his life and character in the Assembly's Magazine, Vol. 2, Number for January, 1806. The writer of that sketch says of Dr. Smith, "He was certainly among the most able theologians, the most profound casuists, and the most convincing of successful preachers of his age."

an intellect of a high order. But the part of his history while yet at Pequea, of greater interest still, remains to be told. While a pupil here, it pleased God to visit the congregation of Mr. Smith with a special outpouring of his Spirit. Almost the whole school was made to feel the influence of this blessed work. The result was, that a majority of the pupils in the school was hopefully converted. "Some of them," to use Dr. M'Millan's words, "became blessings in their day, and were eminently useful in the Church of Christ." It was under the overshadowing of this visit of mercy and grace that his own soul was made the subject of religious impressions that were deep, powerful, and abiding. He was now, probably, about sixteen or seventeen years of age. And although in that very brief and general statement which he has left in manuscript of his own history, he has expressed no opinion of the precise time of his conversion, yet it is probable that it was about the period of his renewal into the divine image. He speaks, indeed, of a subsequent time, particularly when he was in college, to which we shall hereafter advert, when his views of eternal things were clearer and more satisfactory. But probably these were the result of the actings of a more matured principle of holiness, of a more vigorous faith, of a brighter and more joyful manifestation of his interest in the Saviour, made to his own soul; the more powerful witnessing of the Spirit that he was a child of God—rather indicative of the advancement in the heavenly life, than of the soul's first entrance upon it.

In describing his exercises of mind at the time of the Revival at Pequea, Mr. M'Millan thus speaks: "It was here that I received my first religious impressions; though, as long as I can remember, I had at times some checks of conscience, and was frequently terrified by dreams and visions in the night, which made me cry to God for mercy. But these seasons were of short duration: like the morning cloud and the early dew, they soon passed away. I knew that I was a lost, undone sinner, exposed to the wrath of a justly offended

God. I could do nothing for my own relief. My convictions were not attended with much horror, though I felt that I deserved hell, and that in all probability it must be my portion; yet I could not feel that distress that I ought to feel, and which I thought that I must feel, before I could expect to obtain relief. I felt, also, much pride and legality mingled with all the duties I attempted to perform." "In this situation," he further adds, "I continued till I went to college." Here, although he himself appears not, at this time, to have entertained a clear hope that he had passed from death unto life, we think we can see the workings of a mind in a state similar to that of the Apostle, described in the latter part of the 7th chapter of the epistle to the Romans; where we have doubtless delineated the exercises and views of a soul new-born: "For we know that the law is spiritual; but I am carnal, sold under sin: for the good which I would, I do not; but the evil which I would not, that I do, oh wretched man that I am," &c.

In the consideration of the case of Mr. M'Millan, thus early called (if we may date his conversion about this period,) into the kingdom of grace; and called, too, in a season of the special and powerful outpourings of the Spirit; we are reminded of what we believe to be God's most usual method of furnishing instruments of great usefulness in the church. While genuine conversion at any time of life, and under any circumstances, is an event as desirable and important as is the salvation of the deathless soul, and causes much joy among the angels of God, yet there is ordinarily little hope of exerting extensive influence for good where the energies of youth are wasted, and the mind is debased and paralyzed by a long course of sin. But when the mind is early brought under the influence of grace, and especially when its first spiritual breathings are in the atmosphere of a revival, other circumstances being equal, much fairer promise is given of a healthful and vigorous youth in piety. And when, as in the case before us, strong native talent is thus moulded, and directed, and ennobled by sanctifying grace, and the life be long continued, and Providence spreads out a favorable field, and leads to its occupancy, there is reason then to anticipate much efficiency in doing good.

At witnessing this great and important crisis in Mr. M'Millan's history, so great and important, viewed both in its temporal and eternal bearing and connexions, we may well suppose his pious parents would feel an intense interest.* As has been remarked, this son had been given to them in answer to their prayers; and even before his birth they had solemnly devoted him to the Lord: and all along the hazardous path of childhood and youth, they had doubtless watched over him with a solicitude which none but parents of their character and circumstances could feel. It was, too, with considerable effort, and at much worldly sacrifice, that they furnished the means of sustaining him in his academical course.† But after all the pious care in training him up for God, and the expense incurred in furnishing the means of literary improvement, unless he should be made a subject of God's special grace, he must and ought not only to stop short of the ministry, but his talents and acquirements might only prepare him for doing more extensive mischief in his day and generation, and for a deeper and more appalling condemnation in the world to come. While, therefore, they would feel it their duty and privilege, in humble dependence on God for the

* Whether his mother was now alive, is not certainly known. She appears, from what we can gather from the records, to have lived till after he went to the academy at Pequea. But whether her decease took place shortly before or subsequently to the supposed period of his conversion, cannot be determined. But if her sainted spirit were now in heaven, her interest and her joy were not the less intense because unearthly.

† The pecuniary circumstances of Dr. M'Millan's father were only moderate; and to defray the expenses of his son's education, he was often straitened and subjected to considerable difficulty. Even his sisters, much to their honor, engaged in the labors of the field to help forward their brother in obtaining his education.

blessing, to employ all the instrumentalities at their command for securing the object of their hopes, their bosoms would often beat with the heavings of strong desire that God would be gracious to their son—that Christ might be formed in his heart the hope of glory; with what emotions would they then contemplate those buddings of grace so full of promise and hope. Their covenant-keeping God has now, in the hopeful conversion of their son, given them fresh proofs that he is the hearer of prayer. And now their trust in him is strengthened, and they feel that it is scarcely too much to hope that their son, through the mercy of the Lord, will one day become a faithful minister of the New Testament;—and that having instrumentally turned many to righteousness, he would at last shine as a star in the kingdom of his Father forever. Say, pious parent, would not the hope of seeing your son crowned with the richest diadem of earthly royalty be poor and low, compared with such anticipations?

Mr. M'Millan continued at the academy in Pequea until the spring of 1770, when he entered the college at Princeton, New Jersey. He was in his eighteenth year. And as the circumstances under which he had pursued his more early course of study had been propitious, so now he had the privilege to enjoy the advantages in an institution so signally blessed of God, and so famed as a nursery of piety and sound learning as Nassau Hall; an institution which has had at its head men of the first order, and which reckons among its alumni, in proportion to the whole number, more names of eminence in the church and in the state than, perhaps, any other college in the land. The time, too, in which Mr. M'Millan enjoyed its advantages was one of the brightest periods in its history. It was now under the direction and care of that great and good man, Dr. Witherspoon;—a man in whose character was exhibited a very rare assemblage of greatness and worth; whose memory is revered not only as a preacher, as a divine, and as the head of a distinguished seminary of learning, but whose great practical wisdom, and whose unflinching patriotism, are known to have shed such an influence for good on the political institutions and destinies of his adopted country.

In the summer of 1768, Dr. Witherspoon, at the unanimous, the urgent, and repeated call of the trustees, came over from Scotland and took charge of the college. It was about two years after this that Mr. M'Millan entered as a student here; and during the time of his continuance at this place, which was two years and a half, the mind of the instructor, which was in the full vigor of its exercise, would scarcely fail to impress something of its own character on the mind of the pupil: and, accordingly, in tracing the subsequent career of the subject of this notice, we shall probably not be mistaken in supposing that we are able to see striking indications of the results of that influence which was now brought to bear upon him. However this may be, we certainly do not err when, in reference to the part he was afterwards to act on the great theatre of life, especially in reference to the place in the Lord's vineyard which he was afterwards to occupy, we attach high importance to that holy and heavenly influence he was made to feel while he was at this favored institution. We refer to the influence of a season of refreshing with which the college was visited shortly after Mr. M'Millan was a student there. Concerning his exercises at this season, so fraught with mercy to his own soul, and to the souls of others, he has himself left the following brief records:

'I had not," he states in his MS., "been long here until a revival of religion took place among the students. I believe, at one time, there were not more than two or three but what were under serious impressions. On a day which had been set apart by a number of students as a day of fasting and prayer, while the others were at dinner I retired into my study; and while trying to pray, I got some discoveries of divine things which I had never had before. I now saw that the divine law was not only holy, just, and spiritual, but also that it was good; and that conformity to it would make me happy. I felt no disposition to quarrel with the law, but with myself, because I was not conformed to it. I felt it now easy to submit to the gospel plan of salvation; and felt a calm and a serenity of mind to which I had hitherto been a stranger. And this was followed by a delight in contemplating the divine glory in all his works; and in meditating on the divine perfections, I thought that I could see God in everything around me."

Thus while he was at college, we again see the agency of God strongly and visibly marked; his spirit concurring with his Providence in maturing young M'Millan's preparation for his future work. He was afterwards to be extensively engaged in forming the minds of others. Especially was he to be called to the high trust of training young men to the gospel ministry. He was, too, to be a revival man—a revival man not in the grossly perverted sense in which that appellation has been often employed in our day. Not one, who, by his wild and wicked extravagance, spreads abroad fire-brands, arrows and death, in the church;—not one who, under the influence of pride and self-seeking, resorts to all sorts of trickery to get up an excitement—nor yet one, who, though well meaning, yet led on by his misguided zeal, becomes frantic in religion, and imparts his frenzy to others. His was not to be the unenviable fame of manufacturing misnamed revivals —revivals that curse the church and ruin souls, and dishonor God and outrage the cause of truth and righteousness—that so caricature religion itself, that the very name revival becomes at length, a term of reproach, and an object of unmingled scorn. He was to be the distinguished instrument, in God's hand, in effecting and promoting such revivals as have resulted in the enlargement of the church, by the accession, it is believed, of hundreds of genuine converts, and in the great increase of practical godliness; which, in a word, have shed a mighty and a lasting influence for good, on all the most precious interests of Zion, and on the general community. That he might thus be well furnished for purposes so important, was he thus schooled in the Providence and grace of God, who sees the end from the beginning. And when afterwards he was called to act, as his history will tell, he brought up to the work a mind and a heart, which gave full proof of the early training he had received.

Mr. M'Millan having completed his course at Princeton College, was, at the Commencement in the fall of 1772, admitted to the first degree of the arts in that institution. He now returned to Pequea, with a view to the prosecution of a regular course of study in theology, under the direction of the Rev. Dr. Robert Smith, who, as before stated, had been his classical instructor, immediately previous to his entering the college. At that time, and for more than thirty years after, there were no regularly organised theological seminaries in our country.* And although the professorship of theology had been formally conferred upon the Rev. Mr. Blair at Princeton, shortly before, and was at this time filled by Dr. Witherspoon, in connexion with the presidency; and although there had been for some time previous, and there was now, a class in theology at Princeton, as preparatory to the ministry; and although there were at other colleges similar classes—yet these classes were usually quite small. By far the greater number of those who had the ministry in view, either chose, or were led by their circumstances to pursue their theological course in a more private way. And if, under the direction of some intelligent, judicious and devoted pastor, with the privilege of access to a library, which, though moderate in size, was well selected; their opportunities were less splendid and the form of their preparation was less imposing; yet in some important respects, their real advantages were superior. From the necessity of the case, they were obliged to think more for themselves. What they read, they digested better, and made it more their own. They were less in danger of knowing superficially, everything in theology and its kindred sciences. Their time was less occupied, and their attention was less frequently diverted by the mere etiquette of system—a system unsuited, perhaps, in many of its details,

* The Theological Seminary under the patronage of the Congregational Church, founded at Andover, Massachusetts, in 1808, and the Theological Seminary established at Princeton, New Jersey, in 1812, are the oldest in the United States.

to their own peculiar cast of mind, and thus calculated to cramp its energies and hinder the cultivation of habits of close, patient, and successful thinking. But this is not all—students in theology, under such circumstances, would see the various and important duties of the pastoral office carried out in their practical details, and thus they would acquire the elements of an experience on this subject, so valuable to them in after life, and which they could not so well and so easily learn by any other course of preparation. [Students in theology would thus enjoy advantages somewhat resembling those of medical students attending Clinical Lectures.—J. S.]

There were several considerations that influenced Mr. M'Millan to select Pequea as the place of his theological study. It was associated in his mind with many interesting recollections. It was, as we have supposed, the birthplace of his renovated nature. He had here more pious friends, with whom, in the freshness of his piety, he had taken sweet counsel. It was not far from his father's residence. His means were not ample. Here the style of his living was plain and simple. He was strongly attached to Dr. Smith; a man in whose character were blended so many excellencies, and who, under God, had been an instrument of so much good to himself. And in choosing Dr. Smith as his theological teacher he showed his good sense, as well as his warmth of feeling; for he scarcely could have made a better choice. The writer of the sketch of Dr. Smith's life, to which we have before referred, says, "Many of his classical pupils, as well as others, returned to him from college, to complete their theological studies under his direction in whom they were sure to find an able instructor and an excellent model of practical preaching. To have enjoyed the theological training of such a man, Dr. M'Millan was accustomed to regard as one of the happiest and most important providential arrangements of his life.

The exercises of Dr. M'Millan's mind, as recorded by himself at this period of entering upon the study of theology, as immediately preparatory to the preaching of the gospel, were such as might be expected. In reference to the work of the ministry, the great Apostle of the Gentiles was constrained to say, "who is sufficient for these things?" And that man who rushes upon his work without many a solemn pause, without a strong sense of the dread responsibilities which it involves, and without a deep feeling of his own unworthiness and his own insufficiency, runs before he is sent. He is not called of God, as was Aaron. It is manifest that he is a profane and an impious intruder into the sanctuary of the Lord. And at this day the church needs to employ special caution that she lay hands suddenly on no man. At this day, when a religion of show and of mere forms, courting an alliance with the spirit of the world, seeks with special energy to usurp the place of genuine godliness, piety, decisive and deep-toned, is especially needed. It is true, that in our church the ministry has not thrown about it the meretricious lure of livings and sinecures established by law. Although it is here untinselled with the pomp and power of earthly emoluments, which a lordly, prelatical assumption claims for it, yet, without a mind well balanced, without a piety intelligent and vigorous, men may be influenced, by motives most unworthy, to seek the sacred office. Zealous, but weak young men, who are pious, may form a wrong estimate of their powers, and greatly err in supposing that this is the field in which they can do most good. Increased facilities for acquiring an education, afforded by the charitable funds, the partiality of friends, and even the rivalship of instructors and of public institutions, may present undue encouragement. And men who are not pious may yet propose to themselves a comparative ease, and a comparative elevation in rank and authority, in entering the ministry in our church, humble as are its claims under the form of Presbyterian parity, and in view of all the self-denial with which it is associated by those who rightly regard it. And thus, without special vigilance on the part of the church, there is great danger lest an increased proportion of incompetent, and even wicked men, be set apart to the work.

In the case, however, of Mr. M'Millan, we have no surprise, when upon this subject we hear him utter such language as this: "At the time,"—the time when he began to study theology at Pequea, under the direction of Dr. Smith,—he remarks, "I had great difficulties in my own mind about undertaking the work of the gospel ministry. However, I at last came to the conclusion to leave the matter wholly with God. If he opened the way, I would go on; if he shut it, I would be satisfied. And I think if ever I knew what it was to have no will of my own, it was about this." In reading this record, we are forcibly reminded of the shrinking back of Moses from the work to which God was calling him. "And he said, O my Lord, send I pray the hand of him whom thou wilt send." And of his sense of dependence when, at a subsequent period, he said, "If thy presence go not with me, carry me not up hence." We think we here see the movements of a mind jealous of itself with a godly jealousy. A mind which, under a conscious sense of unfitness for the work, is afraid to go forward, but yet dares not go back; and which, at length, giving itself up to be guided and blessed of God, merges all its purposes and desires in his sovereign pleasure. At what time precisely Mr. M'Millan was received as a candidate for the gospel ministry, under the care of the Presbytery, is not known. It was probably soon after he commenced the study of theology. We, however, know that he passed through his trials for licensure under the direction of the Presbytery of Newcastle, and was licensed by that body as a probationer to preach the gospel at East Nottingham, Pennsylvania, on the 26th of October, 1774. When he was licensed to preach, he was within a few days of 22 years of age. And now he entered upon the work which for nearly 60 years constituted his most delightful employment. On the Sabbath immediately subsequent to his licensure, as appears from his Journal, now before us, he preached at Fagg's Manor, his native place. Through the whole ensuing winter and spring, and every Sabbath, without exception, he preached principally in the vacancies in Newcastle and Donegal Presbyteries. We have no information as to the results. His Journal at this time is little more than a naked statement of times and places. When we recollect his youth, and the little preparation he had probably been able to make, and if his practice of writing out and memorizing his sermons was then the same as in after life, we have evidence of laborious zeal in his Master's service. We have here a fair specimen of that patient, and laborious, and persevering industry, surmounting all difficulties and discouragements, for which afterwards he was so distinguished.

In the summer of 1775, he took a tour through the settlements of Virginia, between the North and South mountains, in Augusta and Rockbridge Counties. In July, he crossed the mountains between Staunton and the head of Tygart's valley, preaching in the various settlements through which he passed, until he came to Chartiers. In this journey he experienced great privations and difficulties. In the country through which he passed, there were no roads but paths and Indian trails, crossed by others — the population very sparse — the people living in huts — and those often twenty miles apart. The following extract from his Journal will give a specimen of the trials of those pioneers, and early emigrants in general:

"This morning crossed the Laurel Hill—came to Mr. Barker's about 12 o'clock. Here my company left me; and Mr. Barker, who had promised to accompany me to the next house, which was about thirty miles distant, not having his horse at home, I was forced to tarry there till five o'clock, when the horse coming home, we set off. Nothing remarkable happened, save that Mr. Barker shot a doe, part of which we carried with us. Night coming on, and being far from any house, we were forced to think of taking up our lodging in the woods: we sought for a place where there was water, unsaddled our horses, hobbled them with hickory bark, and turned them to the hills: we then kindled a fire, roasted part of our venison, and took our supper: about ten o'clock, we composed ourselves to rest. I wrapt myself in my great coat, and laid me on the ground; my saddle-bags served me for a pillow.

Thursday.—This morning we rose very early, ate our breakfast, got our horses, and set to the road again. About noon, we arrived at Ezekiel York's. Here my company left me, and I had to take the woods alone: crossed two hills which, if they were in some parts of the world, would be called lofty mountains; and after travelling what they call twelve miles, through an almost pathless way, I came to the glades. My lodging, this night, was not much better than the night before. I had a deer-skin and a sheet spread under me, some clothes above me, and a pillow was laid for my head. This, however, I put under my haunch, to keep my bones from the floor, and I placed my coat under my head.

Friday.—I left the glades, and travelled ten miles to one Coburn's. Here I got some grain for my horse, which was the first he had since Wednesday morning. They told me I was then about ten miles from Colonel Wilson's, where I intended to tarry the remainder of the week: but this day being very wet, the road difficult, and houses scarce, I lost my way very often. Some places I could get no directions. And what directions I got, I could not follow, because of the multitude of paths that are every where through the woods. About sunset I came to a plantation, where I intended to tarry all night: but when I came to the cabin, it was waste. I searched all about, but could find no inhabitants. I then took another path, which led me to a cabin; but there was nobody at home, and the door was barred. I then took my horse again, and went further along the path, to see if there was any other cabin nigh; but could find none. The night being dark, and very rainy, I therefore resolved to return to the fore-named cabin. When I came there, I found the cabin still barred, and nobody at home. I, however, unsaddled my horse, and turned him into a field which lay convenient. Finding it impossible to open the door, I climbed the wall, and went into a hole in the roof, which served instead of a chimney. I then opened the door, brought in my saddle, kindled a fire; and after I had ordered my affairs as well as possible, I laid myself down on a sort of bed, and slept very contentedly till morning.

Saturday.—This morning I buckled on my wet clothes, got my horse, barred the doors, and left my lonely lodgings, not knowing which way to steer. But before I had gone many rods, I met the owner of the cabin returning home. I told him the story, got directions of the road, and came to Mr. Wilson's in time for breakfast.

The 1st of August.—Preached at Mount Moriah; but the day being rainy, there was only a small congregation. However, they seemed pretty attentive, and a few tears were shed by some. In the evening,

I returned to Colonel Wilson's, and tarried there till Wednesday morning, part of which time I spent in writing.

Wednesday.—Rode about fourteen miles, and preached at John Armstrong's, on Muddy Creek, to a small congregation. There I remained till Sabbath morning. But the weather being rainy, and the house small, I got but little done.

The second Sabbath of August.—Rode about four miles down the river, and preached at John M'Kibbon's, on Dunlap's Creek, and lodged with him all night.

Monday.—Finished my first sermon, and began a second, on Luke, 14—23.

Tuesday.—I spent the forenoon in writing, and then went about four miles to Mr. Adams', where I spent the remainder of the day.

Wednesday.—Preached at James Picketts', to a pretty large congregation, and then rode about five miles, to David Allen's.

Thursday.—Spent the forenoon in conversation with my old acquaintances, and in the afternoon preached to a number of the neighbors.

Friday.—Travelled about twelve miles, to Edward Cook's, where I tarried till Sabbath.

The third Sabbath of August.—Preached at Pentecost's, to a very small congregation. The people had been dilatory, and had not given a proper warning. I tarried here till Wednesday, when I rode about six miles further, and lodged that night with my brother-in-law.

Thursday and Friday—Spent in visiting friends and acquaintances.

Saturday Morning.—I travelled about sixteen miles, to John M'Dowell's, on Chartiers, where I stayed till Monday morning.

The fourth Sabbath of August.—Preached at John M'Dowell's.

Monday.—Rode about six miles, to Patrick M'Cullough's, on Pidgeon Creek.

Tuesday.—Preached at Arthur Forbise's, and lodged with Patrick Scott."

He preached also at Thomas Cook's, on the following day. Then returned to his brother-in-law's—remained over Sabbath, (the first Sabbath of September,) and preached at a meeting-house, on the banks of the Monongahela. The second Sabbath of September he preached at Fort Pitt, lodging with Mr. Ormsby. Thence he set out homeward, and reached his father's house in October, 1775. He then attended Presbytery, and was again appointed to visit Augusta and Westmoreland. Accordingly, in November, he took his second journey to Virginia, passed through Winchester and Staunton, and continued in Augusta until January, 1776. We give another extract from his Journal, respecting this visit to Virginia; which, while it may be passed over by some of our readers, will, perhaps, be read with interest in that quarter, should this Work ever wander so far South.

"*Tuesday*, (after the second Sabbath of November, 1775.)—Got my horse shod—set out on my journey for Augusta—passed through York, and after travelling about 26 miles, we came to the Buck, where we tarried all night.

Wednesday.—Got free lodging last night—this day passed through M'Allister'stown, Lytle'stown, and Taneytown; and, in the evening, after having travelled 43 miles, came to Bentley'stown, where we tarried all night.

Thursday.—Passed through Fredericktown—crossed Monockosy and Potomac, and lodged at Mr. Harper's. This day we travelled about 31 miles.

Friday.—After having travelled about 34 miles, and passed through Winchester, we came to John Gilkeson's. But he having a husking frolic, we thought it improper to tarry all night. However, we left our horses there, and walked over to Robert Wilson's. I thought to have taken off my boots, as they were inconvenient to walk in, but upon examining my saddle-bags I found I had no shoes.

Saturday.—The Sabbath drawing near, I found that I could not reach any other congregation in time to give the people any warning. Therefore, concluded to remain until Monday.

Sabbath, (the third in November.)—Preached at Opequon meeting-house, and lodged with John Gilkeson.

Monday.—Passed through Stephen'sburgh, Stoverstown, and Millerstown—crossed Shenandoah, and after travelling 48 miles, we came to a Dutchman's, where we tarried all night.

Tuesday.—We rode this day 35 miles—crossed the North river, and lodged at widow Watson's.

Wednesday.—About noon, came to Staunton; where, it being Court time, I met with a number of my old acquaintances, who professed great joy to see me. I stayed in town till towards evening, and then rode to John Trimble's. This day I travelled about 22 miles.

Thursday.—Continued at Mr. Trimble's.

Friday.—Went to John Moffat's.

Saturday.—Returned to Mr. Trimble's; and, in the evening, Benjamin Brown brought me a pair of shoes, for which I paid him 8*s*.

Sabbath, (the fourth in November.)—Preached at the North mountain, and lodged with Matthew Thompson.

Monday.—This day I rode in company with John Thompson about 16 miles, to see my uncle on Back creek; found them all well.

Tuesday.—This morning proving very stormy, we thought it most convenient to return again to the settlements, and accordingly I took leave of my relations; and though it snowed excessively, we set to the road, and in the evening came again to Matthew Thompson's.

Wednesday.—Went to Hugh Torbet's—from thence to Alexander Mitchell's, where I tarried all night.

Thursday.—Came to Joseph Blair's.

Friday, (1st Dec.)—Rode to John Moffat's in the evening—got a tooth pulled by Wendal Bright—tarried here until Sabbath, and began to write a sermon on Matthew xvi. 26.

Sabbath, (the first in December.)—Preached at the Stone meeting-house; and, in the evening, rode in to Staunton, in company with Mrs. Reed—lodged at Mr. Reed's.

Monday.—I left town—called at Mr. Trimble's, and lodged with Mr. Moffat. This evening I began a sermon on Luke xiii. 5.

Tuesday.—This day I spent chiefly in study.

Wednesday.—This day I moved my camp to Wm. M'Pheeter's,

Thursday and *Friday.*—Continued at the same place, spending my time chiefly in study, and finished my sermon on Luke xiii. 5."

Thus the journal proceeds; and by its statements we can trace his course, his labors, and his studies, on his way back—down the valley—and thence to Winchester; and thence, in the depths of winter, over the Alleghany mountains. On New Year's day, 1776, he had preached at Peter Hanger's to a large assembly, and next day set out down the valley; and having preached on the first Sabbath of that year at Opequon, and lodged at night with Mr. Holliday, he set off on Tuesday for the mountains. Mr. Gray went with him part of the way—dined at Mr. Hog's, and lodged that night at Robert White's. The second Sabbath of January he spent in Romney: "This morning," when he was in Romney, "Mr. Manning, the parson of this parish, came, contrary to the expectations of the people, and would preach, though requested by the people not to do it. After he had gone through his service, as he calls it, and preached a short sermon, I also preached in my turn." His journey over the mountains was attended with much exposure and suffering. His horse one day got away from him, and compelled him to walk many miles, but he at length recovered him. At length he arrived at Chartiers and Pigeon creek. Here he preached on the fourth Sabbath in January, 1776, and on the following Sabbath at Chartiers. He continued dividing his time between these two places until the latter end of March, when he returned to Fagg's Manor.

His second visit seemed to have awakened great interest in these places. There are notices in his journal, of his congregations being often "numerous, very attentive, and much affected." Soon after his return—a call was prepared, presented, and accepted by him, at the Presbytery of New Castle, April 22d, 1776. He was then dismissed to join the Presbytery of Donegal, which met at Chambersburg, 19th of June, 1776, when he was ordained with a view to take charge of these congregations. The Presbytery of Donegal included the whole territory west of the mountains, and of course embraced the congregations of Chartiers and Pigeon Creek. After his ordination, he spent most of the ensuing summer in the neighborhood of Fagg's Manor. On the 6th of August, he was married to Miss Catherine Brown, (youngest child of William Brown, a ruling elder in the church of Upper Brandywine,) by the Rev. Mr. Carmichael. This excellent woman was peculiarly qualified to be his companion and helper in the important stations he was to occupy.

Mr. M'Millan did not immediately remove to the West, it being in the time of the Revolutionary war, and the Indians being troublesome, he was prevented from removing his family to his congregation until November 1778. He, however, "visited them as often as he could, ordained elders, baptized their children, and took as much care of them as circumstances would permit." After he at length ventured to bring them, he gives the following account of the new scene into which he and his family were now brought—in a letter to Dr. Carnahan, dated Chartiers, March 26th 1832.

"When I came to this country, the cabin in which I was to live, was raised, but there was no roof to it, nor any chimney, nor floor. The people, however, were very kind; they assisted me in preparing my house, and on the 16th of December, I removed into it. But we had neither bedstead, nor tables, nor stool, nor chair, nor bucket. All these things we had to leave behind us, as there was no wagon road, at that time, over the mountains. We could bring nothing with us but what was carried on pack-horses. We placed two boxes, one on the other, which served us for a table, and two kegs served us for seats; and having committed ourselves to God, in family worship, we spread a bed on the floor, and slept soundly till morning. The next day a neighbor coming to my assistance, we made a table and stool, and in a little time, had everything comfortable about us. Sometimes, indeed, we had no bread for weeks together; but we had plenty of pumpkins and potatoes, and all the necessaries of life; as for luxuries, we were not much concerned about them. We enjoyed health, the gospel and its ordinances, and pious friends. We were in the place where we believed God would have us to be; and we did not doubt but that He would provide everything necessary, and, glory to his name, we were not disappointed."

He immediately entered upon his arduous labors. The circumstances in which he was placed, rendered it necessary to work "with his own hands," chopping down timber, felling the sturdy oaks, and wielding the mattock, the hoe, and the plow. He was a man of vigorous bodily powers, and few of his neighbors could excel him in handling the axe and the maul.* He did not, however, suffer these necessary toils to prevent his careful preparation for his labors on the Sabbath. He studied carefully his sermons, generally wrote them out in full and committed them to memory. This was his practice through his whole future life. "Dr. M'Millan," says Dr. M. Brown in an unpublished sketch of his life, "having been now permanently located, entered upon the duties of his station, which were various and arduous, calling forth all his energies of body and mind.† For some time it was necessary to en-

* Dr. M'Millan once remarked to a friend, that he had not, from his earliest recollection, been confined half-a-day by sickness, during his whole life!

† Shortly after he settled at Chartiers, he made an appointment on the Sabbath, at Parkinson's Ferry, where Monongahela City now stands;

gage in providing the necessaries of life, and making such improvements in building, and clearing the ground, as were indispensable. These, however, he did not at any time allow to interfere with his more important duties as a minister of the gospel. He labored in two congregations, and carefully prepared written sermons, which he memorised.

He not only attended to the duties of his own extensive charge, but frequently was called to officiate in destitute places, organize churches and dispense the ordinances among them. His labors in the ministry were soon crowned with abundant success, as were those of his compeers; and in a few years the wilderness became a fruitful field. The Spirit of God accompanied the word preached, and converts were multiplied."

The following is the account which Dr. M'Millan gave to Dr. Carnahan in the letter already quoted, respecting the gracious visitations of Divine Influence to the field of his pastoral labors.—"The first remarkable season of the outpouring of the spirit which we enjoyed in this congregation, began about the middle of December, 1781. It made its first appearance among a few who met together for social worship, on the evening of a thanksgiving day which had been appointed by Congress. This encouraged us to appoint other meetings for the same purpose, on sabbath evenings; and the appearance still increasing, Sabbath-night societies were continued with little interruption, for nearly two years. It was then usual to spend the whole night in religious exercises;

---

and on the Saturday evening previous, at Ginger Hill, four miles west of the Ferry. At this latter place, his horse having been put out to pasture, strayed off and could not be found in the morning. After considerable search, without success, Mr. M'Millan proceeded on foot and fulfilled his appointment at Parkinson's Ferry, returned to Ginger Hill and preached there in the afternoon, agreeably to an appointment made the preceding evening; after which he walked home nine miles—having preached twice and walked seventeen miles in all.

Judge Gordon, of Monongahela City, informed us of a similar feat of the Doctor, not at all inferior to this.

nor did the time seem tedious, for the Lord was there, and his work went pleasantly on. Many were pricked to the heart with deep convictions; and a goodly number, we hope, were brought to close the happy match with precious Christ. At the first sacramental occasion after the work began, *forty-five* were added to the church; many of whom continued bringing forth the fruits of righteousness, and filling important offices in the church, until they were removed to the world of spirits. This time of refreshing continued in a greater or less degree till 1794. Upon every sacramental occasion during that period, numbers were added to the church, who gave comfortable evidence of their having obtained a saving change of heart. But as I neglected to keep a register of their names, I cannot now ascertain their number.

"The next remarkable season of the outpourings of God's spirit was in 1795. This, however, was not very extensive nor of long continuance; yet during this year about fifty were added to the church, most of whom continued by their walk and conversation, to manifest that they had experienced a real change of heart; and some of them became successful preachers of the gospel, though there were some lamentable instances of apostacy.

In the spring of the year 1799, the Lord again revived his work in this congregation. Many were at once awakened to a serious concern about their immortal souls, and made to inquire the way to Zion, with their faces thitherward, weeping as they went. Of those who were thus awakened, about sixty joined the church, and made a profession of religion. This revival, as well as that of 1795, was carried on without much external appearance, except a solemn attention and silent weeping under the preaching of the Word. From that time until the fall of the year 1802, religion was evidently on the decline; for though some were every year added to the church, yet they were generally such as had been brought under serious impressions in 1799, and there were few or none awakened. Sinners became more bold in sin, and floods of vanity and carnality seemed likely to carry all before them. Even the pious themselves became very weak and feeble in the cause of Christ, and much buried in the world—insomuch, that when God returned to build up Zion, it might in truth be said, we were as men that dream. Many stood astonished, not knowing what to make of it, and but few were prepared to meet the Lord, and bid him welcome. This work differed from former revivals only in this, that the body was more generally affected.* As far as I could observe, the bodily exercise never preceded, but always followed upon the mind's being deeply affected with some divine truth. Between fifty and sixty joined the church as the fruits of this revival †—a number of whom were students in the College, and now preaching the gospel of Christ to their dying fellow-men. Since that time, religion has been on the decline, though still we are not left without some tokens of the Divine presence. At every sacramental occasion some have come out from the world, and professed to take the Lord for their portion."

Such is the account which Dr. M'Millan, in his eightieth year, gave his friend of what the Lord had done for him, and with him.

We would remark that, like all his fellow-laborers, in those seasons, he exercised great prudence and care, giving no countenance, by precept or example, to any thing like extravagance or wild-fire—and watching with his session, care-

---

* "It was no unusual thing to see persons so entirely deprived of bodily strength, that they would fall from their seats, or off their feet, and be as unable to help themselves as a new-born child. I have seen some lying in this condition for hours who yet said they could hear every thing that was spoken; and yet their minds were composed and more capable of attending to divine things, than when their bodies were not thus affected."—*Manuscript of Dr. M'Millan.*

† After the close of the revival which began in 1802, though upon every sacramental occasion, some joined the church—yet nothing very remarkable took place until the year 1823, when God again visited this dry and parched congregation with a shower of divine influences.

fully, the entrance door of the church. He also labored diligently, all his life, in instructing his people, and catechising the children and youth. Meetings in different neighborhoods were held, for *doctrinal examination and instruction*, during the course of each alternate winter—the other winter would be devoted to *pastoral visitation.* At an early period, he directed his attention towards the preparation of suitable young men, of piety and talents, for the gospel ministry. It has been said, though he has not so stated himself, that his school began within a year after he removed his family to the West. If his efforts, in this way, were not quite so early as those of Mr. Dod and Mr. Smith, they were much longer continued; and it would appear that many of those who had been studying with the former brethren, repaired to Dr. M'Millan's, and were under his instruction, both as to part of their literary course and as to their *theological training.* He was selected by the Synod of Virginia *to manage and take charge of* the institution which, by their appointment, was entrusted to the superintendence of the Presbytery of Redstone.

This institution, with his consent, and the concurrence of the Presbytery of Redstone, though not by the direction or special authority of the Synod, was located, within a year after it was thus originated, in Canonsburg, and became merged into the Academy of that place in 1791–2. How far the original plan and object of the Synod were carried out by this measure we will not stop to inquire. Perhaps there were various interests to be consulted and to be harmonised by the direction which the whole matter took. The friends of ecclesiastical supervision should be cautious, we think, in censuring Dr. M'Millan and the Old Redstone Presbytery for not more literally carrying out the original device of the Synod of Virginia.

In regard to the other institution, placed under the care of Mr. Graham, in Rockbridge, matters took precisely the same course. That school was soon merged into Washington College, of Lexington.

Both institutions passed out of the hands and control of the church. No one has a right to condemn or complain, unless he is thoroughly acquainted with all the facts of the case. Indeed, for 60 years Jefferson College has been a thorough Presbyterian institution, and is so now.

Dr. M'Millan strove, in the outset, to have that school located near him. (See the Rev. R. Patterson's Letter to Dr. Brown, published in the Advocate, 1845.) If he yielded to the views of others, he no doubt acted conscientiously. If his own wishes were thwarted, and for a short time he felt his zeal for the academy a little abated, and did not take a very prominent or active part in its transactions for the first year or two, as we think is evident from its early Records, he subsequently lent his efficient and powerful patronage to this institution; and when it, at length, became a chartered College, he was its most steady and effectual friend, through his long life. Jefferson College owes an immeasurable debt of gratitude to Dr. M'Millan; and of course the cause of science and literature must ever regard him as one of its earliest and most valuable patrons and supporters. Those who preceded him a year or two, or at least were his coevals, in the enterprise of getting up "Latin schools," were soon called to their rest. Messrs. Dod and Smith were in their graves when the Academy at Canonsburg fairly commenced its career. The latter, there is reason to believe, was principally instrumental in getting the Synod to appoint Dr. M'Millan at the head of the Synodical institution that was merged into that Academy. When, a few years before, he gave up his school at Buffalo, for want of health, and the pressure of pastoral duties, in the midst of a constant and long-continued revival—the young men who were in his school went over to Dr. M'Millan's "Log Cabin." Among these were James Hughes, John Brice, James M'Gready, Samuel Porter, and Thomas Marquis. *Dr. M'Millan mentions these as his first scholars.* We have evidence that they had *previously* been with Mr. Smith, and some of them also with Mr. Dod.*

* It is singular how much error, especially of anachronism, has pervaded the fountains of future history about Jefferson College. Take, for instance, the following specimen from Day's Hist. Coll. of Pennsylvania, page 668:

"The Rev. Dr. M'Millan, justly called the father of the Presbyterian Church here, settled in the County about the year 1773, and was, for more than fifty years, the pastor of the Chartiers congregation, which he collected. With the commencement of his labors, he began to lay the foundation of a literary institution at Canonsburg, and which, with the blessing of God, he intended should be a nursery for the Church, as well as the State. This was the first literary institution west of the mountains. It originated in a small log cabin, where the first Latin School was taught by the Hon. James Ross, of Pittsburg, under the patronage of the Rev. Dr. M'Millan. The number of students having increased, a comfortable stone building was erected in 1790. The Canonsburg Academy was then instituted," &c.

Now this statement contains almost as many errors as there are lines in it. Dr. M'Millan, speaking of the origin of his school, says,* "Accordingly I collected a few who gave evidence of piety, and instructed them in the knowledge of the Latin and Greek, &c., viz.: James Hughes, John Brice, James M'Gready, Samuel Porter," &c. These were a part of the materials with which, he says, his school began. But these had been either with Mr. Dod or Mr. Smith, in their schools, before they came to this school at Dr. M'Millan's, in the years 1784–5. This is capable of the clearest proof, from various sources. Then this school which Dr. M'Millan collected, consisting of these young men, as he expressly states, could not possibly have begun till after 1785. This writer places the Doctor's settlement back two years before ever he saw the West. He moreover tells us, his school was nearly coeval with that date. And then he makes the Canonsburg Academy to originate in the log cabin school, and speaks of the latter increasing, so as to give rise to the other, and the erection of a new building, &c. Nothing can be more incorrect. The Academy did not originate in the Latin School at the "log cabin," but was begun independently of it, and superseded it, and caused its suspension. "I had still a few with me," says Dr. M'Millan, "when the Academy was opened at Canons-

* Original MS. of Dr. M'Millan, in our possession.

Dr. M'Millan was one of the original members of the Presbytery of Redstone when it was formed, in 1781. During the twelve years of its undivided state, he was most punctual in attending its sessions. He is scarcely ever reported absent. And when the Presbytery, in 1789, was attached to the Synod of Virginia, he attended the meetings of the Synod several times, though it cost him long and fatiguing journeys across the mountains. In 1793, he and Messrs. Patterson, J. Hughes, and Brice, were formed into the Presbytery of Ohio, of which he continued a member till his death. When the Synod of Pittsburg was constituted and held its first meeting, September 29th, 1802, "the Rev. James Power, who was appointed to open the Synod, being sick, it was opened by the Rev. John M'Millan with a sermon on Rom. viii. 6." He was often, also, a commissioner to the General Assembly. Perhaps no man has ever set a better example in his punctual attendance upon the judicatories of the church. And his thorough acquaintance with the business of such meetings always gave him immense influence. He was called to pass through many remarkable scenes, and to encounter some severe trials. In common with his brethren and their families and people, he, with his family, was, for many years after his settlement in the West, subject to great annoyance from their savage foes. He was more than once compelled to seek for himself, his wife and children, the shelter of a fort. And

burg, and finding that I could not teach, and do justice to my congretion, I gave it up, and sent them there." * Other errors here it is unnecessary to notice. See also "Life of the Rev. Joseph Smith," in this volume, p. 122.

* William Darby, Esq., in a letter dated "Washington [City], December 15th, 1850," says, "Through 1789, and part of 1790, I resided in the Murdock family, who resided in East Chartiers, directly opposite Mr. M'Millan's. That family, you know, were Seceders, and members of Mr. Matthew Henderson's congregation; therefore, as I attended with the members of the family, I passed with them, every Sabbath-day, past the house and school-house. I often passed there, however, on week-days. Though the Academy was then established in Canonsburg, the School was still in operation—but when discontinued, I cannot state."

here, like Messrs. Dod and Smith, he also often preached, and prayed, and labored for the salvation of souls. These brethren enjoyed some refreshing seasons in their forts and with their neighbors, confined like themselves. Like Paul and Silas, they "prayed and sang praises to God, and the prisoners heard them." It would be interesting to record the incidents of such a passage in the life of Dr. M'Millan; to give the details of his hurried departure with his family to the fort; to tell how the news reached them of their danger, and how, with the children, his wife and himself would hastily hurry away from their cabin, &c.: but the Doctor kept no journal of such things; and those who could have told us of these scenes are all gone to where the wicked cease from troubling.

This source of vexation and anxiety was scarcely removed by the final termination of all Indian troubles, in consequence of General Wayne's complete victory, when the troubles of the "Whiskey Insurrection" broke out in 1794. Few of our early ministers suffered more annoyance from this source than Dr. M'Millan; and none acquitted themselves more nobly than did he in the firm and decided stand which he took against that popular commotion, and in favor of order and obedience to the laws. But a full account of this we will give in another part of this work. We will only here remark that the West owes much to Dr. M'Millan for the effectual aid which he rendered in bringing that unhappy affair to a peaceful termination.

Another trial of the faith and patience of this eminent servant of God occurred in 1802; but one of a more domestic nature. Two young ministers of great promise had married two of his daughters. The Rev. John Watson, the first president of Jefferson college under the charter, had married his second daughter, Margaret. The Rev. Wm. Morehead had married his eldest daughter, Jane. For a time, the prospect for enlarged domestic and social enjoyment shone brightly on the Dr. and his family; but by the all-wise, yet deeply mysterious Providence of God, these two ministers, who had been married to two sisters by their father, on the same day—took sick on the same day—died on the same day—and were buried in the same grave at Chartiers! The two funeral processions, one coming from the house of Dr. M'Millan, the other from the village of Canonsburg, met at the same point where the roads united, a few hundred yards from the grave-yard. It was doubtless a sore trial to Dr. M'Millan, and his wife, and his bereaved children; but there is reason to believe it was a sanctified affliction to them all. Perhaps the usefulness and success of Dr. M'Millan's ministry were thereby greatly increased. And if he found abundant consolation in the progress and fruits of the glorious revival that had begun a short time before in his charges, this affliction, perhaps, was made instrumental in qualifying him anew for the arduous work before him, and in giving an impulse to the whole work. Thus does God magnify his grace in the afflictions of his ministers. "Whether we be afflicted it is for your consolation and salvation, which is effectual in the enduring of the same sufferings which we also suffer; or whether we be comforted, it is for your consolation and salvation." *

But Dr. M'Millan, two or three years after this, met with a source of annoyance and trouble of a very different character, and perhaps more trying to him than even the death of his sons-in-law, and the bereavement of his children.

In common with his brethren, he had been much annoyed years before, at different times, with ministerial adventurers who had come out into the western settlements — some of them irregular in their conduct — some of them suspended ministers, and one of them with forged credentials. The records of the old Presbytery of Redstone will show what trouble such men as Messrs. Barr and Hughey, and the Morrisons and Cooly, had given them and the churches. But about 1800, a man of the name of Birch, a Presbyterian minister from Ireland, came into the bounds of the Presby-

---

* 2 Corinthians i. 6.

tery, and for some time resided in Washington County. His conduct evinced that he was not only destitute of piety, but strongly suspected of habitual intemperance. Dr. M'Millan, whose failing all his life was a little too much bluntness of manner and expression, and who hated everything like hypocrisy and ministerial inconsistency of character, was tempted to express himself without much reserve as to his opinion of this man.* These things coming to the ears of Mr. Birch, he brought charges against Dr. M'Millan before the Presbytery of Ohio. The Presbytery acquitted Dr. M'Millan, with the exception of one expression which he had used, and to their censure for that he cheerfully and humbly submitted. Mr. Birch was dissatisfied with this issue of the matter, and gave notice of his intention to appeal to the higher judicatories of the church. But he changed his mind, and brought suit against Dr. M'Millan for slander in the civil court of Washington County. It was tried in October, 1804, and the suit was gained by Birch.† An appeal was immediately taken to the Supreme Court by Dr. M'Millan's counsel, the principal of whom was the Hon. James Ross, once the Doctor's pupil. Here the decision of the lower court was reversed, and Dr. M'Millan was acquitted. As the whole case is full of interest, and one which, in our judgment, does not in the least tarnish the memory of Dr. M'Millan, we will here give it, from Binney's Reports, Vol. I., p. 178.

"*M'Millan against Birch, In Error.*

"*Pittsburgh, Saturday, Sept.* 18*th*, 1806.

"This cause came before the Court by writ of error from the Circuit Court of Washington County. It was an action of slander brought by Birch against M'Millan, for calling him 'a liar, a drunkard, and a preacher of the Devil.' The declaration stated that the plaintiff was a

* The Presbytery of Ohio, after three successive examinations in 1800 and 1801, rejected him. See their records.

† After this most unrighteous verdict, the Presbytery of Ohio, Dec. 26th, 1804, reaffirmed, in strong terms, their justification and acquittal of Dr. M'Millan.

man of learning, integrity, and piety; and that for twenty-eight years last past, he had been, and then was, a minister of the gospel in the Presbyterian church, and had taken upon himself the orders of the same. It also laid a special damage in consequence of slander, viz., that the plaintiff was refused admission into the Presbytery of Huntingdon as a member. Pleas—*not guilty, act of limitation, and justification.*

"It was proved at the trial of the cause, that the plaintiff was a Presbyterian minister, regularly ordained in Ireland—that he came to the United States in 1798, and on producing his credentials to the standing committee of the Presbyterian church in Philadelphia, was permitted to preach there—that he afterwards came with his family to Washington County—that upon an application made to the Ohio Presbytery, he was rejected for want of *experimental knowledge;* and that he appealed from their sentence to the General Assembly, who, after examining and considering the case, did not pass any censure on the Ohio Presbytery, but determined that they found no ground why any Presbytery should not take the plaintiff up, and proceed with him agreeably to the rules and regulations in such cases provided.

"The plaintiff afterwards cited the defendant, who was also a clergyman, before the Presbytery of Ohio to answer for slander and for unchristian threatenings. The defendant appeared, and was heard in his defence. The Presbytery acquitted the defendant of the charges brought against him, except for calling the plaintiff 'a preacher of the Devil;' for which they reprimanded the defendant, and he submitted. The plaintiff appealed again to the General Assembly; but apprehending that he should not obtain a favorable decision, in consequence of his having committed some irregularities in Washington County, by administering the sacrament and ordaining elders in violation of the rules of the church, he gave up his appeal, and withdrew from the jurisdiction of the General Assembly: after which, the Assembly determined that they would have nothing more to do with him, and that he never had been in union with the Presbyterian church in the United States, so as to be authorized to preach as one of their ministers.

"The plaintiff proved also as laid in the Declaration that he failed in his application for admission into the Presbytery of Huntingdon.

"The words laid in the Declaration, or some of them, were spoken of and to the plaintiff, in the Presbytery of Ohio, while the defendant was making his defence against the plaintiff's charge.

"The cause was heard before Judges Yeates and Smith, in October, 1804, and the counsel for the defendant among other things objected,—1st, That the action could not be maintained by the plaintiff, for words spoken of him in his profession of a minister of the Presbyterian

Church, because the evidence showed that he did not hold that office;—and 2dly, That words spoken by defendant in Presbytery, while making his defence against the plaintiff's charge, were not actionable. Upon both points the court charged for the plaintiff and sealed a bill of exceptions. The jury found for the plaintiff.

Then follows a report of the arguments of counsel for plaintiff and defendant.

"Chief Justice Tilghman, then, after stating the facts, delivered the opinion of the court as follows:" (and this opinion is deeply interesting to us all; as it settles great principles, and is decisive, in all similar cases, to this time.)

"In arguing the case before us, the counsel for the plaintiff in error, (Dr. M'Millan), made four points which it will be necessary for us to consider. 1. That the words spoken are not actionable, applied to persons in general. 2. That they are not actionable when applied to the plaintiff on the evidence in this cause. 3. That exclusion from the Huntingdon Presbytery, is no temporal damage, nor such as the law will take notice of, or suffer damages to be recovered for. 4. That the words spoken in his defence before the Ohio Presbytery are not actionable." (The first three points the court did not sustain, showing reasons at length which we need not here transcribe.)

"I come now to the *last point*, the only one which is attended with difficulty. I will proceed to offer my reasons for thinking that the words spoken by the defendant when making his defence before the Presbytery *are not actionable.* I consider malice as an essential ingredient in slander. If I say of a man that he is a thief, or that he committed murder, the law implies malice in general; and it lies on me to show that there was no malice in my heart. This I may do in various ways. I may show that I used the expression when examined as a witness in a court of justice; or when I was concerned in a prosecution as attorney for the commonwealth; and although I was mistaken in the fact, no action lies. The occasion of my speaking, being called upon by others, and only acting in the course of my duty, preclude the idea of malice. So what is said by myself or attorneys in my defence in a court of justice, is not actionable; not only because of the occasion of my speaking, but also because the public good requires that every man should be allowed to speak freely in his own defence. It is the same with regard to what I say as plaintiff in an action; because there is as much reason why persons should enjoy freedom of *complaint* as freedom of *defence.* But if any man should abuse this privilege, and under pretence of pleading his cause, wander designedly from the point in question and maliciously heap slander upon his adversary, I will not say that he is not responsible in an action at law.

"This freedom of speech, in what is called a *court of justice*, is not confined to courts of *common law*. Cases have been cited to show that it is extended to proceedings in *ecclesiastical courts*, and proceedings before justices of the peace; and I have no doubt but it should be likewise extended to proceedings before referees.

"The objection in the case before us, is, that Presbyteries and General Assemblies are not courts of justice, because they have no authority to administer an oath; and a person swearing falsely could not be indicted for perjury. But although they are not courts of justice, they are bodies enjoying certain rights established by long custom, and not forbidden by law. They can inflict no temporal punishment, and their jurisdiction is founded on the consent of the members of the church. No extensive church can preserve decency, good order, or purity of manners, without discipline. It serves to correct a multitude of evils, which cannot and ought not to be subject to temporal cognisance. It corrects them, too, in a manner the most mild, the most private, and the least scandalous and injurious to religion; in a manner that may reform the offender without exposing him to the open scorn and ridicule of the world, circumstances which sometimes render men desperate. A jurisdiction of this kind, exercised only over those who consent to it, certainly must be productive of good effects; and it appears to me that the persons thus consenting and pleading their causes, either in a course of *complaint* or *defence*, fall within the principles applied to those who are speaking in courts of justice. If they conduct themselves in a decent manner, the occasion of speaking makes it improper that the law should imply malice. I repeat the remark made before, that if under the pretence of pleading a cause before a Presbytery, one should designedly and maliciously wander from the point, and slander his opponent, he would be responsible for his conduct in a court of justice.

"Let us apply these principles to the case before us. It was the plaintiff who first affirmed the jurisdiction of the Presbytery, and cited the defendant to answer before it. The defendant did not decline the jurisdiction. What then was he to do? He must either confess the words he had spoken of the plaintiff were false; which if he believed them to be true would be a great crime; or by acknowledging that he had spoken them, and endeavoring to justify them, render himself liable to an action in a court of law, which had been barred by the act of limitation; for this is a consequence if the words spoken there (in Presbytery) are actionable. Would these words have been spoken at the time if the plaintiff had not extorted them? And after extorting them shall he apply to a temporal court for damages? If the law is so, will not ecclesiastical jurisdiction prove traps for the unwary? May not the occasion of the defendant's speaking be fairly and candidly said to warrant the conclusion, that he spake not through malice, but in his own defence; or at least, ought it not to form an exception from the general rule, by which the law implies malice? The subject suggests a multitude of reflectisns; but I have said enough to explain the principles on which my opinion is founded.

"I am of opinion that the charge of the court was erroneous in the last point mentioned, in the bill of exceptions, and therefore the judgment must be reversed.

"Brackenridge J., concurred. Judgment reversed."

This opinion and decision of the court, though occupying more of our space than we can well spare, we have thought it right to give, not only because it is due to the memory of Dr. M'Millan, but on account of its own intrinsic merits. We cannot forbear to ask, however, if the rights of ecclesiastical courts are only "established by long custom, and not forbidden by law?" We had thought they were secured by the constitution, guaranteeing protection to churches in the exercise of discipline, and in the administration of their rules and regulations, so long as they do not attempt to infringe upon civil rights, or inflict temporal pains and penalties.

So far as we are aware, this vexatious suit, which thus issued in Dr. M'Millan's favor, was the end of his troubles from that quarter. We have heard that, either then or subsequently, Mr. Birch was received as a member of the Baltimore Presbytery, though he still continued to reside in Washington County. This gross irregularity was countenanced and sustained by a body that, though it has since risen to the highest respectability for its piety, missionary spirit, and noble efforts in the cause of church extension, was then counted the *fag end* of the Presbyterian Church.*

A few years afterwards, the Doctor was not a little worried and distressed with the case of Mr. Gwin, of Pigeon Creek,

* It is proper to add, however, that this irregularity had the sanction of the General Assembly.

who was suspended from the ministry on grounds similar to those in the case of Bishop Onderdonk, of New York. At first, Dr. M'Millan warmly engaged in the defence of Gwin, believing him innocent. But satisfied, at length, of his guilt, he took a decided stand for the discipline of the church. This case occupied the attention of the Presbytery of Ohio, the Synod of Pittsburg, and the General Assembly, for several years, and cost Mr. M'Millan and many others of his brethren no little trouble and sorrow.

A more serious source of annoyance to himself personally arose out of an attempt to unite the colleges of Jefferson and Washington, in 1817. There was much feeling on both sides. Heavy charges, after the failure of the negotiation between the Boards and their committees, were hurled back and forth. And the Doctor did not escape his share. But after the battle was over, and the smoke was dispersed from the field, we never heard that he was much hurt in any way. We know enough about the matter, in its whole extent, to be well aware that a much more detailed account than we are willing to give, or than any one now would choose to read, would be necessary, to understand its merits. We think it altogether unnecessary to go further into the matter, though it was, for a while, one of Dr. M'Millan's very serious annoyances.

Soon after this, in 1819, he lost his beloved wife. She died a peaceful and triumphant death, Nov. 24th, 1819. A few months after her death, March 18th, 1820, he wrote to the Rev. Dr. Johnston, of Newburgh, New York, once a favorite pupil, the following interesting and touching account of that important event in his life:

"I am now a lone widower. My wife left me and went to her husband, Jesus, on the 24th of November last. Through the greater part of her sickness she complained that she was much in the dark, and could not obtain that access to God which she thought she had in her former days. But on the Friday morning before she died, all her doubts were removed. She was raised quite above the fear of death, and longed to get away to her house not made with hands, eternal in the heavens. On that morning, as she lay ruminating on her situation, that text of scripture, John xvi. 33, (" These things I have spoken unto you that in me ye might have peace," &c.), was impressed with power on her mind. This encouraged her to hope that God would not leave her in the valley and shadow of death, nor suffer her to sink in the swellings of the Jordan. In a little while afterwards, she obtained such a view of the divine glory that she was but just able to support under it. It appeared to her that the glory of God filled the room; and the love of God was so shed abroad in her heart, and enkindled such a flame of love in her soul, that she longed to be absent from the body and present with the Lord. Her tongue was remarkably loosed, her heart was full, and she could not but speak forth the praises of her Redeemer. She exhorted all around her to secure an interest in Christ, and to make that the main business of their lives. To her pious friends who called to see her, she could not help telling what the Lord had done for her soul, as she said, to encourage them to trust in the Lord, and cleave unto him through all difficulties; assuring them that the manifestation which he had then made of himself to her was more than sufficient to recompense her for all the troubles and difficulties which she had ever met with in his service. After this she spake but little, but slumbered the greater part of her time, except when her pains were more than usually severe; and then she was frequently heard saying 'Come, Lord Jesus; O, come quickly, and take me to thyself!' Thus died the dear saint with whom I have lived forty years, three months, and eighteen days, enjoying as much comfort and happiness as usually falls to the lot of sinful mortals in the conjugal relation. But I hope in a little time to meet her again in the land of glory, where the term of our enjoyment shall not be measured by years and months and days, but shall continue to all eternity. I am now a poor, lone creature, and have none to sympathize with me in the ills inseparable from old age. My children treat me with all the tenderness that I can expect; but the young are no company for the old; they are entirely unacquainted with their feelings. The principal comfort which I now have is in preaching the gospel and attending to a divinity class." In a letter to his son, William M'Millan, Esq., he states that she requested to be buried in a particular spot in the graveyard, and gave as a reason that here, after an hour of agony in prayer, the Lord had visited her soul with special consolation and manifestation of his glory.

On April 21st, 1830, he sought and obtained a dismission from his pastoral charge; having long before been dismissed from Pigeon Creek. Already the formation of Centre church had considerably reduced Chartiers. Another organization—that of Canonsburg—was about to be formed, which would reduce the old mother church still more. Dr. M'Millan was opposed to this course, doubted the policy, and resisted it as long as he could. He loved the country and country churches—and, above all, old Chartiers. It was natural; it had grown to be a giant, from weak and tottering infancy, under his ministry. It was the child of his affections, of his youth, and of his old age. There many a pentecostal season had been witnessed and enjoyed. But what could the Presbytery do? It seemed all-important that there should be a church in Canonsburg: the interests of the place, the claims of the aged and the feeble, the spiritual welfare of the college, all seemed imperatively to require it. We think they did right in granting this new organization. But, so far as we know, Dr. M'Millan, when he found it was inevitable, yielded—though he first resigned the pastoral charge. There was a constitutional buoyancy of spirits, and a Christian spirit also, that combined to support him under this trial.

After he was dismissed from Chartiers, he still continued to preach as much as his health and opportunities would allow. About this time, a new, and more modern, and much finer pulpit was erected at Chartiers. But the Doctor never entered it—would persist in taking his stand below when he preached, or otherwise assisted in public worship. As the old pulpit, after its removal, stood awhile by the side or back of the house, he was more than once seen leaning against it in meditative posture, while a tear might be observed coursing its way down his aged cheek. He especially disliked the two flights of steps to the new pulpit, and said the Devil went up one pair, while the preacher ascended the other.*

* The Doctor was no patron or friend of the more ambitious improvements of modern times. When Gen. Morgan removed from Princeton, N. J., into the bounds of Chartiers congregation, at an early period, a part of his large and fashionable family were conveyed to the church in a fine carriage. Such a thing was quite an exciting event amongst these plain, rural people. The Doctor was annoyed, perhaps, more by the diverted attention of the people, than by the appearance of the carriage itself, and did not omit in the course of his sermon to intimate that people might travel on the *broad road* in *fine carriages*, as well as on horseback, or on foot. He was unfortunate in giving offence to the party concerned, and he lost his influence with this highly respectable family.

When the first *umbrella* made its appearance at Chartiers, it was in the hands of a lady, who passed near where the Doctor was standing conversing with others. He enquired, "What woman was that with a petticoat wrapped round a stick?" It is believed that he was among the last who adopted the use of that modern convenience. It may, perhaps, be known to few, that this article, which we no longer consider a luxury, but an indispensable means of comfort and protection, was, not thirty years before, first seen in the streets of London in the hands of the celebrated philanthropist-merchant, Jonas Hanway, and excited universal surprise and much derision, even from the nobility and gentry of England. See Frost's Lives of Eminent Christians, p. 470.

To show that our notions of luxury and effeminacy are altogether conventional, Dr. Miller, of Princeton, told us, in our seminary days, of a Highland Chieftain, who, with his son, being overtaken by night amongst the bleak mountains of Scotland, sought a place on the south side of a hill to bivouack, and prepared it, as well as they could, by removing the snow from the ground. The father went aside to hunt a stone or a piece of a rock for a pillow; on his return, finding that his son had rolled up a snow-ball for this purpose, and had already lain down, wrapped in his tartan of plaid, he kicked the snow-ball from

Lith. of P.S. Duval & Co. Philad[a]

Dr. Mc MILLAN'S LOG CABIN.

There are a few other incidents in his history, of minor importance. But we pass them over; and before we hasten to the closing scenes of his life, we must briefly speak of him as an Old School Presbyterian, as a preacher, and as a theological instructor.

As to the position which Dr. M'Millan held, in view of the rising conflict between the Old and New School, nothing can be more clearly proved, than that his sympathies were thoroughly with the Old School, till the day of his death. It may suffice, however, to give one extract from his farewell sermon to his Presbytery, and as it proved, in some measure, to the whole Presbyterian Church.

> "At the present day," says this departed saint, "I believe that the Church is in greater danger from those who style themselves peace-men, than from all the errors that abound in her; for those generally cast their weight into the scale of the errorists, and thereby not only countenance and encourage them in their errors, but weaken the hands of those who are laboring for the peace and purity of the Church. And it is my serious opinion, that our Church will never have peace and purity in union, until it is purged, by discipline, of the false doctrines which defile it, and the false measures which distract it."

"Here is our opinion," said Dr. Green, quoting the above passage in his December Number of the Advocate, for 1833, "expressed with admirable simplicity and perspicuity." Yes, Dr. M'Millan was not only thoroughly of the Old School in his views of both doctrines and measures, but he disliked and dreaded the compromising spirit of many of our ministers in high places, in those times.

As a public speaker, he possessed one qualification in high perfection, well suiting him for the earlier part of his career,

---

under his head, and exclaimed, "Tut! tut! mon, are ye becoming effeminate?"

The reader will find some curious and amusing things about the first appearance of umbrellas in Philadelphia—when they were scouted in the public gazettes, as a ridiculous effeminacy—in Watson's Annals of Philadelphia, Vol. I., p. 193.

when he so often preached in the woods and in the open air. He had a voice which, though not mellifluous, was yet powerful, and could sustain any amount of effort short of absolute screaming without ever breaking down or causing exhaustion. His manner was always solemn and impressive. Though he preached from memory, he had the faculty of delivering his discourses in so natural a tone of voice, that the hearer would suppose it was perfectly extemporaneous. On certain topics, he would often use the same language, word for word, that had been heard before. This was especially the case with some of his exhortations; and though heard ever so often, they always, somehow, seemed fresh to the hearer. We have heard many testify to this. But as to his matter, as a preacher, here we prefer to give the language of Dr. M. Brown, who was intimately acquainted with him, and had heard him scores of times for nearly a quarter of a century:

"The subjects which characterized his sermons were, the dreadful evil of sin; the awful danger of the sinner, exposed to the wrath of God; the character of God as holy and just, as well as merciful; the spirituality, purity, extent, and excellence of the divine law; the absolute need of salvation through the atoning sacrifice of Christ; the fulness, sufficiency, and freedom of the gospel salvation; the utter helplessness of the sinner; insufficiency of his own righteousness; the necessity of an entire change of heart, and absolute need of Christ for pardon and acceptance. These great points were pressed with all his solemnity and force, and pressed upon the sinner's conscience, who was urged, by all the solemnities of heaven and hell, immediately, and without delay, to make a surrender of himself to Christ as a lost and helpless sinner; that he was without excuse in refusing to receive Christ and the offered salvation; that his inability to believe, repent, and embrace the Saviour, was a moral inability; the result of depravity, a perverse will, a perverted taste; the inability of a wicked heart, at enmity with God; and that this, instead of being an excuse, was the essential crime."

"It was in the spring of 1831," says Mr. Leake, "that I first made Dr. M'Millan's acquaintance. His general appearance had at that time, probably, undergone considerable change. His manner in the pulpit was, however, as I have learned from those who knew him well, much the same that it had been in his earlier ministerial life. At that time, his countenance wore an aspect that had an approach to sternness; and, to a stranger, was rather forbidding. His complexion was unusually dark. His features were prominent, and strongly marked; and the *tout ensemble* of his face was expressive of the strong and masculine character of the mind within. His manner, both out of and in the pulpit, was characterized by what might almost be called a studied plainness. He held in such contempt all efforts at mere parade and show, that he was, perhaps, too little attentive to etiquette; and sometimes, in his intercourse with people of taste and fashion, he might have been charged with a seeming approach to rudeness." *

---

* William Darby, Esq., writes: "The personal appearance of Mr. John M'Millan I need not describe to you, or his demeanor. But the salutary influence of his character, spreading far beyond the limits of his congregation, I cannot omit. Stern he was, and uncompromising. Vice received his rebuke, let the object be what it might. When Mr. M'Millan came to this neighborhood, where his future days were spent, and his usefulness exerted, few men could be better calculated to suit the times, and very few had sufficient hardihood to disregard his reproof. Rough and rude were the manners of that country, at the age under review: yet there was, under this repulsive exterior, much sound moral principle and manly feeling; and I doubt whether there was in the country another man more respected than Dr. M'Millan."

These rebukes of Dr. M'Millan, of which Mr. Darby speaks, were sometimes instrumental in happy results. The Rev. Dr. William Neill, when a stout young lad at Jefferson College, took it into his head, as he was then altogether thoughtless and irreligious, that he would spend a portion of a fast day, on which there were no recitations in college, in a ramble through the wood, with his gun. His route brought him across the track of Dr. M'Millan, on his way to public worship. Enquiring of young Neill what he was doing, and being told that he

"In the pulpit," Mr. Leake continues, "he had ordinarily but little action. He made almost no gestures. At times, however, the agitation of his whole frame gave evidence of the mighty heaviness of a deeply impassioned soul. His whole manner was perhaps best adapted to the presentation of truths that were terrible and alarming. His rebuke of vice and sin was appalling; and few that listened to him were so hardened as not to quail under it. His descriptions of the wrath of God and the danger and doom of the impenitent were awful. He could, however, melt and move in the sweet strains of gospel grace. There was, ordinarily, nothing musical in his voice. As it fell on the ear of the stranger, it approached to harshness. We do not now hold up Dr. M'Millan to the decisions of modern criticism and modern taste as the beau ideal or as the model of pulpit eloquence. Nor do we mean to institute any general comparison between him and Whitefield. Yet Dr. M'Millan was sometimes truly eloquent. When absorbed by his subject, he could, unconsciously to himself, throw into particular words and phrases a deep-toned tenderness of pathos that was quite peculiar, that has more than once reminded us, at least, of Garrick's remark, that he would give a hundred guineas to be able to pronounce the interjection O! after Whitefield's manner. Dr. M'Millan's mode of sermonizing was, perhaps, rather formal. His regular discourses had, almost uniformly, three general divisions, with a number of subdivisions under each, and closed with a practical improvement. They seldom exceeded fifty or sixty minutes in delivery. He had a favorite saying, derived, perhaps, from his theological instructor, Dr, Smith, which he

---

was trying to kill pigeons, he remarked to him, "What a sad thing to see a poor sinner on his way to hell, killing the poor, innocent birds!" and then passed on. The young man at first was quite indignant, and offended at the remark. But he could not forget it. The more he thought of it, the more it worked itself into the depths of his conscience. His peace of mind forsook him, and he never recovered it, until, as a penitent sinner, he found his way to the feet of the Saviour.

often repeated: "No conversions are effected beyond the hour." He did not study ornament in his language. His style was simple. He never made truth do homage to rhetorical flourish. His sermons were always sensible and pious, full of matter, and perhaps sometimes surcharged with it. He excelled as a casuist. He showed great skill in separating the precious from the vile, in dislodging the hypocrite from his refuges of lies, and directing the enquiring sinner to a genuine resting-place. He had the best evidence that his preaching was of a high order of excellence. It had the signature of God's approbation. *Three* wide-spread and powerful revivals, at least, occurred under his ministry. And it is supposed that hundreds, and even thousands, were, through his instrumentality, converted and trained up for heaven. How enviable his honors! How rich the glories of his crown! "For they that turn many to righteousness shall shine as the brightness of the firmament, and as the stars for ever and ever."

As a theological teacher, Dr. Brown informs us that "perhaps about one hundred ministers were trained, more or less, in his school of the prophets; many of whom were eminently useful. The mode of instruction was by written lectures, containing a complete system of theology.* The system the students transcribed, and were expected to recite literally. The system itself was excellent, containing a concise discussion of all the principal doctrines, with copious notes and quotations from scripture. It was concise, condensed, *multum in parvo*, lucid, and forcible."

"The course pursued by Dr. M'Millan, especially at this early period, when books were difficult to be procured, had some importaat advantages. The minds of the students were

* It was rather in the form of written Questions and Answers. The work, of which there are many copies extant, would, if published, form a stout octavo volume, and might well be called M'Millan's Medulla. On the subject of natural and moral ability, its views are much the same with those of Dr. Lyman Beecher.

replenished with an accurate knowledge of all the important doctrines, and with a summary of the arguments in their support; a treasury of most important truth, condensed in the best manner, and expressed with simplicity, clearness, and force; and, being required to recite verbatim all the scriptural quotations, the mind was enriched from the treasury of divine truth. A solid foundation was thus laid, containing the great elements of the system of truth, which reflecting and intelligent students would of course enlarge and improve by study and reading different authors. It may be questioned whether, at any period before or since, there has been a larger proportion of profound and accurate theologians, and efficient, practical, and useful preachers of the gospel, than those trained in this theological school. Their voices have been heard in every part of the West and South, and not a few called to occupy important stations in the East, in cities and in colleges, while others have gone far hence to the Gentiles, and been instrumental in imparting divine truth to some of the millions who were sitting in darkness and the shadow of death." *

But we must hasten to the closing scenes of his life. Though he passed the ordinary boundaries of even old age, never, perhaps, was any man more exempt from its infirmities. His mental and physical faculties were but little impaired. "In April, May, and June of 1832, he took what he supposed to be his last visit amongst some of the old churches of the west—which he had been instrumental in gathering from the wilderness, and supplying with pastors. On the last Sabbath of April, and first Sabbath of May, he assisted in dispensing the Lord's Supper at Cross Creek, and at the Cross Roads (Florence,) and preached six Sabbaths in Raccoon congregation, where he assisted in administering the Lord's Supper on the third Sabbath of June. During this journey,

* This last statement is, perhaps, not correct, unless made in reference to the school, considered as continued by, and merged into, the Allegheny Theological Seminary.

he preached seventeen sermons with more than usual fervency; and it has been since found that his labors, during this journey, were blessed to the spiritual quickening and edification of God's people, and the awakening of many careless sinners, who have since joined themselves to the Lord. During the year 1832, he assisted in administering the Lord's Supper eleven times, and preached about fifty times; on occasions leaning on his crutch, and in the eightieth year of his age. During the year 1833, up to the 16th of November, the time of his death, he assisted in administering the Lord's Supper seventeen times, and preached on these occasions about seventy-five times, frequently twice in the same day, besides attending to exhortations, &c.!" Thus was he honored with the strength and with the opportunity to labor to the last, and die with the harness on.

He had, in his letter to Dr. Carnahan, a short time before he took the excursion above described, stated: "If my life and health be continued, I design this spring and summer to visit some of the old congregations which I helped to collect, and see how they do, and once more blow the gospel trumpet among them." His wish was gratified. He was even allowed to take a second excursion as far as Wheeling, the following and last summer of his life—spend some time among his old acquaintances and friends, and preach as there was opportunity. We have been kindly favoured by the Rev. Dr. Elliott with some particulars respecting this closing excursion of the venerable man, that cannot fail to be read with interest. "The last meeting of the Synod of Pittsburg which the Doctor ever attended was held at Pittsburg. This was only a few weeks before his death. He appeared to be then in excellent health and spirits, and participated actively in the business of the Synod. After its adjournment, he proceeded to Wheeling, where he remained some time, and preached frequently, and with much acceptance.* On his

* Dr. Herron informs us that he accompanied Dr. M'Millan on this excursion, in a steamboat to Wheeling—that, on their way, they met

return, he spent a night in Washington, at the house of an old friend, where he had long been accustomed to lodge. I was then the pastor of the church in that place. I spent part of the evening with him, and engaged him for breakfast the next morning. My family, who were unacquainted with the Doctor, looked for his arrival with some concern, and anticipated rather a comfortless meeting, from having heard a good deal respecting the gruffness of his manners. All, however, were most agreeably disappointed. Upon receiving an introduction to Mrs. E. and the children, he took each of them by the hand, saluting them in the most kind and affectionate manner. He appeared as gentle as a lamb, and his countenance beamed with benevolence. He took particular notice of the small children, invited their approach, talked familiarly with them; and, in a short time, he and they were on the very best terms. The patriarchal simplicity of his manner, and his humble, affectionate, and condescending spirit captivated us all; and although his visit was a short one, it left on our minds the most agreeable impressions in his favor.

Having made arrangements to proceed homewards by the stage at an early hour in the forenoon, as soon as he had breakfasted he bade us an affectionate farewell. I accompanied him to his lodgings, and, at the appointed hour, saw him in the coach which conveyed him to Canonsburg. Upon his arrival there he was taken violently ill, and in a few days breathed his last at the house of Dr. Leatherman, November 16th, 1833."

The following account of the closing scenes of his life, given

---

with an orthodox Quaker going to a yearly meeting in Ohio—had much conversation with him on the subject of experimental religion—that the Doctor was much gratified, and expressed to Dr. Herron his persuasion that the Quaker was a pious man—that at Wheeling, Dr. M'Millan preached several sermons on the text, "Come unto me, all ye that labor," &c.,—discourses of great excellence, and all entirely distinct in form and matter from each other.

by the Rev. L. F. Leake, will be read with interest: "He had spent much of the preceding summer and autumn in visiting the churches. During these events, he attended many communions and preached frequently, and, as was remarked, with unusual unction and power. In October he was at the meeting of the Synod held at Pittsburg. He preached twice during the session of that body, and seemed to enjoy fine health and spirits. After the meeting of Synod, in company with several clerical brethren, he went down the river by steamboat to Wheeling, Virginia. There he remained twelve or fourteen days, and preached almost every day and evening during that time. On Tuesday, the 5th of November, he reached Canonsburg by stage, on his return from Wheeling. Arrived at Canonsburg, he called at the house of a friend. Here he remained several hours and took a hearty meal. He seemed to be somewhat exhausted by his recent journey and labors, but was quite cheerful, and apparently in his ordinary health. In the evening he went over to the house which, for many years, he had made his lodging-place when in Canonsburg. Here he retired to bed, about his usual time. Soon after retiring he was taken ill, and suffered much bodily pain during the night. Next morning, at early dawn, he went down to the house of his physician and friend; and when he first met the physician, with his characteristic simplicity of manner, he said to him, "Doctor, I had a messenger sent for me last night, and I must go;" intimating, as was supposed, that his present disease would issue in death. Thus, although from the first attack he supposed his end was near, and this, too, on examination of the case, was the opinion of the physician, yet he considered it his duty to employ the means of relief. Here he remained, at the house of his physician, in Canonsburg, until he died. His death occurred about six o'clock on Saturday morning, November 16th, 1833. His disease was paralysis of the prostate gland; induced, as was supposed, by too great exertion—preaching too frequently—for his strength. Of this he was himself aware, but he did not regret it. He seemed to regard it as a high privilege to fall a martyr in a cause he so much loved. During the whole period of his sickness, which lasted ten days, with some short intervals of alleviation, his bodily sufferings were extreme, yet he uttered no complaint. He did not, on his bed of death, enjoy those distinguished manifestations of the divine favor which God sometimes, in such circumstances, vouchsafes to his faithful ministers; yet he was vastly sustained by the consolations and hopes of the gospel. In full view of his approaching death, and in the full view and vigorous exercise of his reasoning powers, he was not afraid to die. He knew in whom he had believed, and his mind was calm; his confidence in the Redeemer was unshaken, and his end was peace. The day subsequent to his death, which was Sabbath, his body was conveyed to the Chartiers Church, attended by a large concourse of people. Several ministers who were present took part in the religious exercises of the occasion. His remains were interred in the burying-ground adjoining. Here a marble slab, inscribed to his memory, covers the grave. This and all that is earthly will perish; but the records of eternity will save from oblivion the usefulness and worth of such a man as Dr. M'Millan."

Thus passed away from earth the last of the pioneers of the Western Presbyterian Church. When, fifty-two years before, the first Presbytery west of the Allegheny Mountains was organized, there were but four members. A few weeks before his death, he met the Synod of Pittsburg, embracing, at that time, eight Presbyteries, and more than 130 clerical members; covering the original field of the Presbytery of Redstone, together with an extensive region beyond the Allegheny and Ohio Rivers, that, in the days of the old Redstone Presbytery, was the home and the hunting-ground of the red man. In the lifetime of this man what had the Lord wrought! Could his vision have embraced the entire West on the day of his death, he might have seen numerous other Presbyteries and Synods raising their banners far and wide over the plains and rivers of the mighty valley of the Mississippi. And in the course of his pilgrimage he had witnessed the rise and progress of five new western states — Ohio, Indiana, Illinois, Missouri, and Michigan—containing, when he died, 1,610,473 inhabitants where scarce a single white man of the Anglo-Saxon race dwelt when he entered the West! The event of the first child of a white man born in Ohio did not occur till twenty years after Dr. M'Millan penetrated the frontier settlements. When he died, Ohio contained 937,903 inhabitants, by the census of 1830. Well might he exclaim, "Now lettest thou thy servant depart in peace, for mine eyes have seen thy salvation."

We cannot better close this extended paper than in the words of him to whom we are indebted for the earlier part of this sketch:

"In short, when we regard Dr. M'Millan's whole character, and the wide field of effort and usefulness, in all the important aspects of its condition, to which he was introduced; especially when, from the point of observation which we occupy, we contemplate the actual results of his labors and influence, a part only of which can be told or known this side of heaven, we have special cause to recognize the wisdom and kindness of God in furnishing an instrument so well adapted to the work."

Dr. M'Millan was the father of several children: three sons, William, John, and Samuel; and four daughters, Jane, Margaret, Mary, and Catharine. These all outlived their mother; and all except Samuel, the youngest, survived their father. William, the eldest son, lately deceased in Mercer County, Pennsylvania. John, the second son, is now on the homestead farm. Samuel died March 9th, 1826. Jane, the eldest daughter, married, first, the Rev. Mr. Moorehead, and then Mr. Harper. Margaret was first the wife of the Rev. Mr. Watson, then of Mr. Neil. Mary, wife of Mr. Weaver, died April 28th, 1839. Catharine, the widow of the Rev. Moses Allen, is now residing in Ohio.

CHAPTER VI.

THE RURAL STATE OF PRESBYTERIANISM SEVENTY YEARS AGO.

A REMARKABLE feature in the early Presbyterianism of the West was, during the whole period of the Old Redstone Presbytery, its exclusively *rural character*. When the Presbytery was organized, and for some years after, there were really no towns west of the Allegheny mountains — if we except a little hamlet outside of Fort Pitt, and a small cluster of cabins at Hanna's-town, in Westmoreland, the seat of justice for the entire west. It is true, under Virginia authority, there were two seats of justice located south of the Monongahela, and one north of that river, but there were no towns there. One of these Virginia Court-houses stood a few miles west of the present town of Washington. Washington itself did not then exist; but a miserable hamlet, consisting of a few cabins, called *Catfish*, after the Indian chief of that name who once dwelt there. Pittsburg was not fully laid out till three years after the first meeting of the Redstone Presbytery. It is true a very small portion of it, including a square or two, had been partially arranged for a town in 1765. But during the entire period through which the pilgrimage of this old Presbytery extended, it was a small insignificant place — for some years occasionally visited and supplied by our first ministers.

In 1786, "a church of squared timber and moderate dimensions was on the way to be built."* This church actually stood within the ground covered by the first Presbyterian church, and was suffered to stand until the brick building was

* History of Pittsburg, p. 203.

reared around it. This brick building, afterwards much enlarged, was demolished in 1853, and a splendid edifice is now rising on its ruins. The old Presbytery settled the Rev. Samuel Barr there as its pastor, but he remained but a short time. With this single exception, all our ministers and their people were in the country, residing far from the thronged habitations of man; and though, in process of time, the counties of Washington, Fayette, and Greene were organized, there were no churches nor ministers at the county towns — none at Greensburg, the seat of the mother county of Westmoreland, which was laid out not long after the burning of Hanna's-town.

The ground now occupied by Allegheny City was owned by the savages, and was considered then, and for many years after, as in the Indian country. Not a village then existed from Pittsburg to Brownsville, along the entire course of the Monongahela. There was not a town on the Ohio from its head to Wheeling, unless, perhaps, a hamlet at Beaver might claim that name. Our ministers and their people were all withdrawn from the busy haunts of men; and they had even scarcely any intercourse, except when, during the earlier part of the period referred to, they sought such places east of the mountains for salt and iron. In some cases, it is true, they were crowded together for a few weeks in forts, for their mutual defence and safety against the Indians — going out in parties during the day to attend to their crops or clearings, and taking their guns with them. With these exceptions, their most usual place of meeting, in any considerable numbers, was the meeting-house, or tent, on the Sabbath day. Yet it is true that, in smaller portions, they were often together — at house-raisings, at huskings, at harvests, at flax-dressings, at wood-choppings, and at musters. They were eminently a social people, and necessity and mutual convenience drew them much together. But they had no fondness for towns; a life, in such places, would have been intolerable to them.

Now in this state of society, so eminently rural, was the Presbytery organized. Our first seven ministers were all *Chorepiscopi*. We had no metropolitans there. Their labors were all in the country. The first ordained minister who settled west of the mountains, the Rev. James Power, had, for a number of years, a charge not less than thirty miles in length, and many miles in breadth. "Yet he was in the habit," says Dr. Carnahan, "of visiting every family under his charge, accompanied by one or more of his elders." The charges of his other six fellow-laborers were nearly as extensive: perhaps one or two of them even greater. Yet they all displayed the same diligence in visiting their people.

In process of time, as country towns and other villages sprang up, they carried the gospel from the country to town. There is here a very marked contrast between this order of things, and that which characterised the progress of the gospel in the early ages of Christianity. The country people in Western Pennsylvania were the Christians—the towns-people the pagans; not, indeed, in its grosser sense, but in respect to their early destitution of the stated means of grace and the ordinances of God's house, and in respect to their general rudeness and profanity. "Not a priest of any persuasion, nor church nor chapel," said Arthur Lee, of Pittsburg, in 1785. And he might have said the same of every village and town west of the mountains; but had he crossed the Monongahela, and penetrated into the country, he would have found large and devout congregations at Montour's Run and Raccoon — turning to the right, and still bearing westward, he would have found King's Creek (now Florence,) without a pastor, indeed, but regularly supplied and highly prosperous — turning to the left in his onward course, he would have been astonished at the large assemblies at Cross Creek and Buffalo — wheeling further to the left, he would have soon been at Chartiers, and then Pidgeon Creek—large and flourishing churches. The state of the country was then, indeed, very singular. Had a traveller, during almost the whole latter period of the Old Redstone Presbytery, confined his visits and his observations to towns and villages, he might have inferred that he had got into a heathenish land — "in partibus infidelium." Had some one, on the other hand, carried him round the country churches — especially in 1787, when in several of them there was a revival of religion — he would have thought that he had got into an earthly Canaan! Now what a singular feature of our early Presbyterian history was this!

In the third and fourth centuries, Christianity had taken possession of the cities and towns—heathenism and idolatry lingered in the country and retired hamlets. Indeed, when the gospel commenced its victorious march through the gates of Jerusalem, after the days of Pentecost—the Apostles and evangelists went, everywhere, first to the crowded and populous dwellings of men—to Ephesus, and Athens, and Rome, and to the other cities and chief towns of the Roman provinces. And this peculiar feature in the early history of Christianity, furnishes convincing evidence of its divine origin. Errors, heresies, and wild delusions of every sort, usually begin in retired and unfrequented parts of a country, shunning in their earlier development, publicity and searching investigation. But the gospel, "beginning at Jerusalem" and boldly marching into the seats of learning, science, philosophy, and human power, at once and everywhere challenged the most unsparing scrutiny into its claims of a Heaven-sealed testimony. It was not till the second and third century that the gospel, to any considerable degree, penetrated the country and the rural hamlets. The country bishops or pastors were a class of ministers that had at first no existence. "But as the bishop in the city could not extend his labors and inspection to all the churches in the country and villages, he appointed deputies to govern and instruct the new societies." (Mosheim's Eccl. Hist., B. 1, Par tII., Chap. 2.) The learned Gibbon tells us, (Note, near the end of Chapter 21st of his "Decline and Fall," &c.) that, "pagan and rural became almost synonymous, and the meaner rustics acquired that name which has been corrupted into peasants, in the modern languages of Europe." "And then when Christianity gradually filled the cities of the empire, the old religion in the time of Prudentius and Orosius, retired and languished in obscure villages: and the word pagans with its new signification" was thus applied. Here the case was widely different. The people, at first, were all in the country. And they were, to some extent, already a Christian people. This peculiar social condition did not, it is true, originate in the West; it was brought out from Eastern Pennsylvania—from Scotland, and from the North of Ireland. A free, quiet, industrious, rural population, in a high degree moral and religious—dwelling apart on their own farms, is a condition of society that never has existed but under the influence of enlightened Protestant Christianity.

The serf system of feudal times was a system of involuntary servitude. And so under all the ancient systems of government. Not even the Jews, in the most flourishing period of their theocratic commonwealth, knew anything of homestead farms and separate dwellings, scattered over hill and dale. They dwelt in towns and villages. And so now, in almost all popish countries; and so in all Mohamedan and pagan lands. But the grand peculiarity of Western Pennsylvania, never before in the history of the world illustrated by any similar example, was the existence of a highly moral, industrious, free, Christian yeomanry, without any towns whatever. Such was the character of the first garden of the mighty West. Thus in a sense which the poet did not dream of, "God made the country, and man made the town." And our towns and cities as they afterwards grew up, first obtained their supplies of gospel ordinances from the country. Our country bishops visited them, preached to them, baptised their children, and administered the Lord's supper to them—ordained their elders and watched over them with parental care The people of many of our now most flourishing towns, once belonged to country churches. For instance, those of Brownsville, to Dunlap creek; of Florence, to King's creek; of M'Keesport and Elizabeth, to Roundhill; of West Newton, to Sewickly; of Washington, to Chartiers and Buffalo; of Canonsburg, to Chartiers; of Uniontown, to the Tent church; of Connelsville to Tyrone and Laurel Hill—and so on, throughout the entire bounds of the Old Redstone Presbytery. It is worthy of notice how often Pittsburg, Washington, and Wheeling are suppliants at the door of the Redstone Presbytery, begging, by their commissioners, for supplies. Where our town and city churches have now grown large, independent and wealthy, let them not be high-minded, but fear, remembering "the rock whence they were hewn, and the hole of the pit whence they were digged." Let them not, like Jeshuron of old, "wax fat and kick," when some poor country church asks them, sometimes, for a pittance to help them along.

There is danger, on the other hand, of country churches and their pastors too, either wholly neglecting or taking but little interest in the spiritual wants of flourishing villages that spring up in their bounds. The reminiscences of old times, and strong attachment to old country churches, with their graveyards—the rural habits of many of our people; their aversion, at first, to go into towns to attend upon public worship, often occasion a reluctance to favor the erection of places of worship, or the organization of either parasitic or independent churches in villages. Other bodies more wise and politic, go in and build up churches and houses of worship in the heart of such towns. Sometimes, even when the point has been yielded, houses for worship are built out in the suburbs, at inconvenient distances to the townspeople; especially to females, in bad weather. Even our old ministers, from their long habits and prejudices in favor of the country, have been known to oppose strenuously the organization of churches in adjoining villages. It is worse than useless, it is wicked now to contend—because our church was once rural, that now in a widely different state of the country we must keep it so. Let town and country now act as did Abraham and Lot.—But we are not yet quite done with this topic.

There was one feature in the religious character of those early times, connected with the rural state and habits of our people, too important to be passed without notice. As they were strict observers of the Sabbath, they generally avoided all worldly conversation on that day. As they were much thrown together on their way to and from their places of worship, and whilst there, before the commencement of public worship, and during intermissions, they were led to converse much together, on various religious topics. But as they had no religious newspapers, or magazines, they were not, as now, supplied with topics from these sources. Doctrinal subjects, and those relating to experimental religion, and to the various exercises and trials of gracious souls — the sermon which they had heard—passages of Scripture which had been cited in the discourses, &c., offered a wide field, and never left them at a loss for matters of edifying discourse. Their "speech was always with grace, seasoned with salt." They looked upon such conversation as not only most opportune to the Sabbath-day, but as a means of grace—an ordinance of God. As they were a God-fearing people, "they spake often one to another." They were generally careful to improve all seasonable opportunities for such conversation, in company with children and young people. They appeared to think the divine injunction given to God's chosen people, under the old dispensation, still binding. "Thou shalt teach them diligently unto thy children, and shall talk with them when thou sittest in their house, and when thou walkest by the way, and when thou liest down, and when thou risest up." Many of them could heartily respond to the language of the Psalmist, "My goodness extendeth not to thee, but to the saints that are in the earth, and the excellent, in whom is all my delight." "I am a companion of all them that fear thee, and of them that keep thy precepts."

Like the disciples on their way to Emaus, "they talked together of all these things which had happened." Nor could they be persuaded that religious conversation was a mere abrogated Jewish ordinance and custom. They read, in their New Testaments, the solemn injunctions, "comfort yourselves together, and edify one another even as also ye do." "Warn them that are unruly, comfort the feeble-minded, support the weak," &c. "Exhort one another daily, while it is called to-day, lest any of you be hardened through the deceitfulness of sin." "Let us consider one another to provoke unto love and to good works—not forsaking the assembling of yourselves together, as the manner of some is, but exhorting one another." They found that these and similar passages prescribed a general duty, and an important work—not merely to ministers and ruling elders, but to the whole household of faith. Yet they were not in the practice of holding class-meetings, or of telling indiscriminately, in promiscuous companies, their own religious exercises. Few of them, indeed, said much about their own feelings, or the dealings of God with their souls—except to those with whom they were on terms of peculiar intimacy. Yet we venture to say, never were there a Christian people more accustomed to religious conversation, especially on the Sabbath, than were early Western Presbyterians. And it is surprising what delight they took in it, and what expertness and skill many of them acquired.* Many persons of otherwise very humble positions in secular life, were pre-eminent for their usefulness in this service. In most of the churches, there were several persons whose society was much coveted on this account. The young people were often greatly instructed and benefited, in this way. Their communion seasons afforded many opportunities for such pious conversations. Where considerable numbers would lodge, for the night, at

* Bishop Burnet, had he lived in those days, and mingled with some of our pious first settlers, would have been as much astonished at their religious knowledge, and edifying prayers, as he tells us he was, when he was among the peasantry of Scotland. See "His Own Times."

neighboring houses, they would be found in different groups, or all together, employed in this manner—generally closing with singing and prayer.

No one can understand the spirit of those times, who leaves out of view this very interesting and marked peculiarity of their social religious habits. Now the fact that our people, in those days, lived in the country, and were, on that account, brought together in the manner we have described, was intimately connected with this important feature. How greatly we have degenerated, in this respect! May it not be questioned whether our religious periodicals have really contributed much to keep up this ordinance of God? They have meant otherwise, doubtless. But from the secular character of large portions of them, it is doubtful whether their reading, in most of our families, does not rather increase the worldly tone of conversation in our day.

The above features of early Presbyterianism accounts for that character of our Western Zion which entitled her to the following testimony, at a later period:

"Pittsburg Synod," said Dr. Alexander, in 1833, "is the purest and soundest limb of the Presbyterian body. When we fall to pieces in this quarter, and in the far West, that Synod will be like a marble column which remains undisturbed in the ruins of a mighty temple. I do not know but that more of us will be obliged to seek an ultimate refuge in that region, from the overflowing of new divinity and new measures."—*Extract of a Letter to the Rev. Dr. Weed, in the Life of Dr. Alexander, p.* 477.

This passage might have found an appropriate place in a part of our Introduction—but it is not out of place as a pendant to this chapter. How much does Dr. Alexander's language, in those dark days of our Church, resemble the language of General Washington—already quoted in a note—in the dark days of our American Revolution!

A BIOGRAPHICAL SKETCH

OF THE

REV. JAMES POWER, D.D.

THE National Road, from Cumberland to Brownsville, traverses the celebrated old road called "Braddock's Trail." This was the first road ever opened across the mountains to the West, in 1755. As it descends the Laurel Hill, it presents, at various openings, by far the most sublime and glorious view of that vast valley which stretches onward and spreads out right and left, bounded to the vision only by the far distant horizon, touching the seemingly uprising earth. But the traveller is aware that, vast as the range of his vision is, he sees but a speck of the panorama. To one who has spent all his previous life on the "Atlantic Slope," the impressions must be new and almost overpowering; such as James Ross felt when he came suddenly upon a view of one of our western lakes, with its boundless waste of waters, and exclaimed "Oh, Eternity!" In such a position stood an emigrant, on the summit of the Laurel Hill, early in November, 1776. But he was not alone. Almost all that he held dear on earth were by his side: his wife and four little daughters. They were mounted on horses; his wife on one, he on another; his oldest daughter behind him, his youngest, almost a babe, seated on a pillow before him; the two other children comfortably and cozily sitting in a sort of hamper baskets, one on each side of a led horse. He was now about to enter the western world with his helpless family, and to make it his future home. Did that sight, when November had clothed the western forests, not with "the sere and yellow leaf," such phrase as English writers are fond of using in describing their autumn; but with all the rich and varied tints of the rainbow, such as are peculiar to the American woods in the fall of the year — did that sight deeply affect with joy and hope, or with despondency and fear, those young parents? What was their purpose? What could justify their removal from all the comforts of their eastern home, and their perilous adventure to seek a home in western wilds? The world smiles with approbation upon those who, in pursuit of wealth or renown, encounter the risk of losing health, and happiness, and life itself. Will it justify this man in his bold advance, with his wife and little daughters, upon all the perils of the wilderness? When they are told that all this wearisome journey, and this daring encounter of the trials and sorrows of frontier life, were simply that he might preach the everlasting gospel, and aid in laying the foundations of our western Zion, the world laughs with scorn. But Heaven smiled that day upon this emigrant family, and gave his guardian angels charge concerning them, and watched over them with sleepless care; through many a long future year, crowned their world-despised mission to the West with complete success, and, late in life, called them home to their final rest. Those four little daughters are believed, long since, to have joined their parents in heaven. The two little girls sitting so snugly in the wicker-baskets afterwards became ministers' wives, and bore their full share in the duties and toils of that responsible station, and then finished their course with joy and died in the faith. Three other daughters, that were born afterwards, have also gone to their rest, and another — for there were eight in all—still lingers, at a very advanced age, in Summit County, Ohio. But who was this man? It was the Rev. James Power, D.D.; the first ordained minister that ever settled, with his family, in Western Pennsylvania.

He was born in 1746, in Chester County, Pennsylvania. It was in Nottingham, the most western part of that county. His parents were pious people. His father was a substantial farmer, and had emigrated, early in life, fron the north of Ireland, and settled here amongst his countrymen, who composed the majority of the neighborhood. It is believed that he obtained his preparation for college at the Fag's Manor School, then in the hands of the Rev. John Blair, an eminent scholar, and one of the most distinguished and successful ministers of his day. At quite an early age, he went to the College of Nassau Hall, at Princeton, New Jersey, where he graduated in the fall of 1766. The president of that institution, the Rev. Samuel Finley, D.D., had died a few months before, in Philadelphia, July 16th, 1766. Dr. Finley had gone down to the city in quest of medical advice. But he never returned, grew much worse in health, and, after a few weeks, during which he bore a noble testimony to the consoling power of religion and the riches of divine grace, he died a most triumphant death. A large part of the Senior class, among whom was Mr. Power, went in a body from Princeton to Philadelphia to visit their beloved dying president. Dr. Mason gives no special account of that interview; but we had the statement from Dr. Powers himself.* It probably made an indelible impression on young Powers' mind, and helped to make him a western missionary. He was licensed by the Presbytery of Newcastle, June 24th, 1772, at Mill Creek.

His health, which never became very robust, was at this time feeble, and had somewhat retarded his progress in his studies preparatory to licensure. On the 23d of December, ensuing, his Presbytery gave him leave "to take a journey into some parts of Virginia." Though there is no record on the minutes about it, he manifestly took this journey; for in August following, he received a call from the united congre-

* He was one of the eight students who bore the corpse to the grave.

gations of Highbridge, Cambridge and Oxford, in Bottetourt County, Virginia. Why he declined this call, there is nothing left among his papers to show; and even whether he ever again visited that region, we cannot tell. He might, as Dr. M'Millan did, in a similar case, have passed first up the Valley of Virginia, and after laboring there for a short season, have bent his way across the mountains to Western Pennsylvania. For in the following summer, 1774, he was out west of the mountains, and spent three months in missionary labors, through all the settlements of what are now Washington, Allegheny, Westmoreland, and Fayette counties. This fact, the Rev. T. Hunt, his son-in-law, says he had repeatedly from Dr. Power himself, while his memory was perfectly sound and unimpaired. John C. Plummer, Esq., of Westmoreland County, also affirms that he frequently heard his father, and other aged persons, speaking of Dr. Power having been in that region before he came with his family, and having preached at the place where the first Sewickly church was erected"* — where the Associate Reformed church now stands.

After the expiration of this tour through Western Pennsylvania, he returned to the east, and preached as a stated supply for nearly two years, to a congregation in which the Rev. Dr. Magraw afterwards labored, probably West Nottingham, and at another place within the borders of Maryland. In the spring of 1776, he seems to have made up his mind to remove to the West. For on the 23d of May, the Presbytery of Newcastle asked and obtained leave of the Synod of New York and Philadelphia, to ordain him "*sine titulo,*" assigning to the Synod as the reason that "he was about to remove to the Western parts of this province." He was accordingly ordained at their next meeting, at Octorara on the 2d Tuesday of the following August. It was but a few months after this, that he removed to Western Pennsylvania with his family.

* Appendix to Life of Macurdy.

Dr. M'Millan, in his letter to Dr. Carnahan, written in 1832, states that Dr. Power settled at Mount Pleasant in 1781. This statement has given rise to the supposition that this was the period of his removal to the West. It may be that Dr. M'Millan refers merely to the period of his taking the regular pastoral charge of that congregation. But he labored there and at Unity, as well as at Laurel Hill; at Dunlap's Creek, Tyrone, and Sewickly, some years before. He was indeed, a sort of missionary pastor, for some years. But that he actually came out with his family in the fall of 1776, is ascertainted with absolute certainty in two ways. In the obituary notice of his daughter Rebecca, who was first the wife of the Rev. D. Smith, and afterwards of the Rev. T. Hunt, and who died in 1839, it is stated that she was born December 12th, 1776, about a month after her father had arrived with his family in the bounds of Dunlap's Creek congregation, and was the first child born in the family of a Presbyterian minister west of the Allegheny mountains. This statement is given in the obituary of Mrs. Hunt, written by Mr. Hunt, who was accurately informed as to the facts. In the second place, Rebecca, this first child born west of the mountains in a minister's family, was married in 1795—and was then as she always afterwards said, in her twentieth year. This brings us again precisely to the same period, 1776. Mr. Power, beyond all question then, was out in the west, with his family, either the last of October, or early in November of that year. Another tradition of that period is preserved. When Dr. M'Millan two years after, in 1778, was on his way with his family to Chartiers, he lodged a night with Mr. Power. And we may well suppose it was an interesting evening to their two families. "From the time of his arrival in the West, in the fall of 1776, until the spring of 1779, Dr. Power, according to the statements of some of his family conections, devoted his time to the work of supplying the destitute churches generally—although he lived at Dunlap's Creek, and regarded that as the principal point of his labors;

and it was not until the spring of 1779, that he became the regular pastor of Sewickly and Mount Pleasant congregations."*

A different opinion has prevailed with some, who have received the impression that he, almost immediately after his arrival from the East, began his pastoral labors at these places. This has arisen, we suppose, from the fact that he did, to some extent, begin his labors there, preaching, visiting, and catechising the children. But there is ample proof that, for some years, the range of his labors was much more extended; including Dunlap's Creek, Laurel Hill, Tyrone, and Unity. He was even more than once on a visit to the settlements in Washington County; for he baptized, during this period, Mr. Marquis's child, in Cross Creek, when he was there on his first visit. It is stated in the brief memoir of that excellent man, in the Appendix to the "Life of Macurdy," p. 287: "During this period, 1778, they were favored by a visit from the Rev. Dr. Power, who preached to them at Vance's Fort; on which occasion, Mr. and Mrs. Marquis presented their first child to God in baptism. This was the first sermon preached, and the first child baptized, in that region of country. The next year a church was organised, of which this pious couple became members."

It is also remarkable that when, some time afterwards, Mr. Smith visited them, and the meeting took place for an election of a pastor, Mr. Power had several votes — we suppose, without his leave or knowledge. These two men, rivals then, were to become closely allied in their future labors, and in the marriage of their children. But Mr. Smith did not live to witness the latter event. He (Mr. P.) probably organised Sewickly congregation very soon after his arrival in the neighborhood. Of the united congregations of Mountpleasant and Sewickly, he continued the pastor until August 22d, 1787, when he gave up Sewickly, confining himself thence-

* Appendix to Life of Macurdy.

forward altogether to Mount Pleasant. That congregation engaged to pay him yearly £120, as his salary. This relation extended on till April 15th, 1817; when, at his request, on account of advanced age and infirmity, it was dissolved. He lived on, however, among them, greatly venerated and beloved, thirteen years longer; strengthening the hands of his successor, the Rev. Dr. A. O. Patterson, and co-operating with him as far as his strength allowed. Never, perhaps, did a young pastor feel more entirely satisfied with the constant presence of his predecessor, and with his friendly counsel and support, than did Dr. P. If all old ministers could behave themselves as well as did Dr. Power in this respect, such pastoral charges or vacancies, instead of becoming objects of serious apprehension, and sometimes of absolute aversion, would be invested with an increased attraction. He died August 5th, 1830, in the 85th year of his age.

The following extract of a letter from Col. James Smith, dated Jacobs' Creek, September 8th, 1785, addressed to his sister in Franklin County, bears very favorable testimony to the ministerial character of Dr. Power, and shows the progress which the gospel had made in that part of the country, at the time in which it was written. Col. Smith was a man of vigorous intellect and decided piety, who had doubtless been profited by Mr. Power's ministry. He says: "We have half of Mr. Power's labors here. I think that he is a faithful and able minister of the gospel, especially for reclaiming backsliders, and for encouraging believers to continue steadfast in the Christian road. I have reason to bless God that he has ever been sent among us. I have had some happy days since I wrote you last. We had the sacrament of the Lord's Supper administered to us last Sabbath. We have a considerable number of apparently pious ministers in the western part of the world, where we heard lately nothing but the yells of savages and wolves, &c.; but now we have the word of God, with peace and plenty; and the ordinances of God's house duly administered. And I not only enjoy the external means of grace, but I have likewise an ear to hear the voice of the eternal Son of God, — so that I may justly say, the lines are fallen to me in pleasant places, I have a goodly heritage." *

Dr. Elliott closes his account of Dr. Power in these words: "Dr. Power appears to have been an excellent man, and a useful minister, of a remarkably mild disposition, and uniform deportment. He was a graceful speaker, and a polished gentleman—neat and exact in his dress and habits, and courteous in his manners. He had a remarkable faculty for retaining the knowledge of names and faces. The Trustees of Jefferson College testified their respect for him by conferring on him the Degree of Doctor of Divinity, in 1808. Besides the daughter already mentioned, he had two other daughters married to ministers—one to the Rev. William Swan, and the other to the Rev. Thomas Moore."

One who, from his boyhood, knew him well, and who was probably baptized by him, tells us, "He was of remarkably easy manners, and graceful in and out of the pulpit—at all times maintaining the high dignity of a minister of the gospel of Christ. He had no enemies. When he came to my father's house, he always spoke to the boys and girls, shook hands, and named them. When seated, he was apt to look at each individually, as if to identify them afterwards. He had a sweet voice, spoke with great ease, emphasizing very distinctly every sentence. He always appeared in his element when lecturing on a Psalm. He was plain and very neat in his dress." †

Dr. Carnahan says of him, "He was a polished, gentlemanly man—remarkably neat in his dress—a very correct and graceful speaker. His power of remembering names, and of recognising persons, was very remarkable. For several years he preached at three places, Mount Pleasant, Tyrone, an' Sewickly. From one extremity of his parishes to the

* Appendix to Life of Macurdy. † John Plummer, Esq.

Lith. of P.S. Duval & Co. Philad^a

THE HOUSE OF ONE OF OUR FIRST MINISTERS.

other was at least 30 miles. Yet he was in the habit of visiting every family under his charge, accompanied by one or more of his elders. And after he visited the families in a neighborhood, he called them together, and had an examination on the doctrines of the gospel—the heads of families, the young people, and the children, in separate divisions. I have heard of men and women, 60 years of age, saying the Assembly's Catechism, giving the proofs from the Bible, and the explanations of Fisher. His habit was, when he visited a family, to ask the names of the children, in the order of their ages, and also of domestics; and at future visits he was sure to recognise each member of the family, and to call each by name. Yet this man could not, some years before his death, recognise his own children, after a short absence, or distinguish one from another."

This last fact is remarkable; but, like Bishop Beveridge, *he never forgot the Lord Jesus Christ.* He died in great peace, at a patriarchal age.

Such was the man who renounced all the comforts of more refined society, and all the prospects of this world's emoluments and enjoyments, and became the first settled minister in the bounds of the Old Redstone Presbytery. He had buried his wife some years before his own death. She was a woman admirably adapted to her station—an excellent manager, taking off Mr. Power's hands much of the cares and distractions of his domestic affairs, and giving him time to devote himself to his Master's work.* They lived long and happily

* It is not very easy to form a just estimate of the cares and trials of this early pioneer. In a very few years after his settlement in the West, he had a family of eight daughters to provide for, and train up in the nurture and admonition of the Lord. But he and his brethren, Smith and M'Millan, were blessed with wives that were truly "gifts of the Lord." They were eminent not only for their piety and energy of character, but for their economical and judicious management of their households. "They did their husbands good, and not evil, all the days of their lives. They sought wool and flax, and wrought willingly with their hands. Their husbands were known in the gates, when they sat

together, and raised a lovely family of daughters, every one of whom married well, and, with one exception, raised families, now widely scattered over the West. May they all be gathered, at last, into the family above!

Since the foregoing was written, we have met with the following sketch, believed to be from the pen of Dr. Carnahan, published, not long since, in the Presbyterian Banner:

In his person Mr. Power was slender and erect, of a medium height, and at no period of life became corpulent. In his dress he was always plain, and at the same time remarkably neat; so that it was a matter of surprise that he could ride on horseback ten or fifteen miles in a rough country, over muddy roads, and appear in the pulpit, or rather on a preaching stand in the woods, as neat and clean as if he had the minute before come from his toilet. He always rode a good horse, and it was believed he was a good judge of that animal, and that he selected one with such a movement as would not

---

among the elders of the land. They looked well to the ways of their households, and did not eat the bread of idleness." Prov. 31. "*Their husbands were known in the gates, when they sat among the elders.*" In illustration of this—at a meeting of Presbytery, one of the members, giving reasons for absence from the last meeting, told them about his building a spring-house or smoke-house, and some other matters of a similar character, which prevented his coming to Presbytery. Whereupon Mr. Power expressed his regret that the brother should find, in such domestic cares, an excuse for absenting himself; and then remarked, that he himself had never staid away from Presbytery for such reasons, and hoped he never would. "No thanks to brother Power," said Mr. Porter, without rising from his seat, "for all his bragging about *his* punctuality. We all know what sort of a wife he has to manage for him, at home."

We have already stated that Mr. Smith's family furnished wives for *four ministers*—Dr. M'Millan's, also, for three. Dr. Power likewise supplied his full quota: for besides the two ministers already mentioned, the Rev. Thomas Moore and the Rev. William Swan found their partners in his family. It was rather a remarkable incident in Dr. Power's domestic history, that he himself performed the marriage ceremony *for two of his daughters, standing with their husbands before him at the same time.*

throw mud or dust on the rider. In his conversation and manners he was dignified and precise, seldom, if ever, indulging in anything like wit or levity. And yet he was sociable, and far from being morose or censorious.

His voice was not loud, but remarkably clear and distinct. His enunciation was so perfect that the whole volume of his voice was used in conveying to his hearers the words he uttered. When he spoke in the open air, as he frequently did, he could be heard at a great distance. You heard no rumbling and confused noise; but clear, articulate sounds. He always preached without notes; but from the arrangement of his discourses and the correctness of his language, it is probable his sermons were generally written and committed to memory. In his manner and style of preaching, he had nothing of the vehemence and terror of his cotemporary, the Rev. John M'Millan, nor of the pungent and alarming address of the Rev. Joseph Smith, of Buffalo, Washington County. His sermons were clear, methodical, expressed in words well selected, and delivered in a pleasing, rather than a forcible and striking manner. To the sober and judicious part of the audience who desired instruction in the doctrines and practical duties of the gospel, rather than strong appeals to the passions, his preaching was very acceptable.

No remarkable revival took place under his ministry, if we except that of 1802, which extended to every Presbyterian congregation west of the mountains in Pennsylvania. Nevertheless his ministry was successful in edifying Christians, instructing the young, and improving the morals of the community. Every year additions were made to the churches under his care. To the children and young persons of his charge, Mr. Power paid particular attention; and he was very successful in attaching them to him personally, and in turning their minds to the subject of religion. He embraced every suitable occasion to introduce the subject of religion; and especially when he met a young person alone, it is believed he seldom failed to make an affectionate and solemn appeal to the heart and conscience.

The wonderful talent which he possessed of remembering names and recognising persons to whom he had been once introduced, gave him a great advantage in performing parochial duties. When he visited a family, or, on any occasion, entered a house, he was in the habit of asking the names of the children and domestics. And such was his memory in this respect, that afterwards he would call each one by name, and recollect the relative ages of a numerous family. And if any one of the family was absent, he never failed to inquire for that one by name. The consequence was, that he appeared to feel, and no doubt did feel, an interest in each individual, and no one thought himself overlooked or neglected. He departed this life in 1830, at an advanced age. And it is a remarkable fact, that for three or four years before his death, he lost his memory and power of recognising persons to such a degree that he did not know his own children, who resided in the neighborhood, and who frequently visited him. How frail is man! The doctrines taught by Mr. Power were those of the Westminster Confession of Faith, and his mode of exhibiting them similar to that of the Tennents, Strain, Finley, and other distinguished men of that day. It may be remarked, that the people to whom Mr. Power ministered, were chiefly Scotch-Irish, or their descendents; that they were educated under Presbyterian influence; were familiar with the doctrines of the Westminster Confession of Faith, and especially the Shorter Catechism; and that they retained, in a good degree, the religious customs of their ancestors. The Shorter Catechism was learned at school, and it was recited every Sabbath evening at home by all the family, young and old. The pastor, accompanied by an elder, visited, as he was able, the families belonging to his charge, prayed with them, and gave them such instructions and advice as the case of each required. After he had gone from house to house in a particular district, he appointed a general meeting, at which all the families were expected to attend; and the heads of families, the young people, the children, in separate divisions, were examined as to their knowledge of the Catechism and the doctrines therein taught. The children repeated the Catechism, the young people and the heads of families were examined as to their understanding of the doctrines taught in the Catechism and the Scripture proofs. And to prepare for this examination, Fisher's Exposition of the Catechism was recommended and generally used. The whole was closed with an address suitable to the occasion, and prayer. The discipline of the church was extended to all baptized persons; so that if any gross immorality had been committed, they were required to make public confession, and profess penitence for their sin before they were admitted to the Lord's table, or could have their children baptized. Mr. Power punctually and faithfully continued these customs, and the effects were salutary. Young people were restrained from gross sins. Both old and young were excited to diligence in reading and studying the sacred Scriptures, and in reading other books explaining the doctrines and moral precepts of the Bible. And among those hardy pioneers you would find many much better instructed in the great truths of the gospel, although they heard a sermon only once a month, than among those at the present time who listen to two or three discourses every Sabbath, and perhaps one or more on other days in the week.

To appreciate the labors and self-denial of Mr. Power, and other ministers of the gospel who settled in Western Pennsylvania during the Revolutionary War, it is necessary to keep in mind the difficulties and dangers to which they were exposed. The journey over one hundred and twenty miles of mountains was not, seventy-five years ago, what it now is. There were no Macadamised roads, nor canals, nor railroads. A horse-path over rocks, and precipices, and marshes, was the only way of access to what was significantly called "the

Back Woods." Nor could the direct route through Chambersburg and Bedford be taken with safety. Parties of Indians prowled around that road, and slaughtered many families on their way to the West. On that route there are places whose names to this day indicate the barbarous acts of those times; such as "the Burnt Cabins," "Bloody Run," &c. To avoid the tomahawk and scalping-knife, the southern route, through Hagerstown, Hancock, and Cumberland, in Maryland, was usually taken, and thence, following Braddock's Road, over the mountains; and even this road was not suitable for wheel-carriages. At the present time, a journey to Missouri or Iowa can be performed in less time, and without half the labor and danger, necessary at that time to reach "the Back Woods." When the mountains were passed, accommoeations not very attractive were found. In the whole county of Westmoreland there was not a single stone, brick, or frame house, for several years after Mr. Power settled at Mount Pleasant. All the inhabitants lived in log cabins, more or less comfortable, according to the means of the occupant. The difficulty of obtaining articles necessary in carrying on farming operations was very great. Iron, with which that country now abounds, had to be carried on pack-horses over the mountains; and salt, which now may be purchased for twenty cents, could not then be had for less than five dollars per bushel. The want of mills to grind their bread was also severely felt. In addition to these difficulties, the inhabitants were not safe from attacks of the Indians. The accommodations for public worship were as rude and unsightly as the family dwellings. These good people did not wait until they were able to erect a stone or brick building, costing from two to twenty thousand dollars; nor did they send commissioners to ask aid from their wealthier brethren east of the mountains. They took their axes, cut down trees, and erected with their own nands a log building, to protect them from the snow in winter and the rain in summer. Except in inclement weather, they worshipped in the open air, under the shade of the native trees. These primitive churches, if so they may be called, were constructed entirely with the axe. No saw, or plane, or even a hammer to drive a nail, was used; for nails, or iron in any shape, were not employed. The roof was clap-boards, kept in their places by logs laid upon them, and the doors were of the same kind, fastened together with wooden pins. The windows were small openings cut in adjacent logs, and *glazed* with paper or white linen oiled with hog's lard or bear's grease. The seats were logs, cleft in the middle and raised a suitable height on blocks. Such was the original house in which Dr. Power preached in Sewickly congregation. It stood about one mile and a half north of the present place of public worship, on the road leading from Markle's mill, towards Pittsburg, about half-way between the Big and the Little Sewicklies.

Dr. Power had eight daughters and no sons. They were remarkably intelligent and active women. Three of them became the wives of Presbyterian ministers, and the others married respectable men in Westmoreland and Washington Counties. Dr. Power resided on a farm at Mount Pleasant; and, leaving the management of the farm and other domestic concerns to his wife and daughters, he devoted his whole time to the duties of his sacred office. On account of the peculiar circumstances of the country, Dr. Power received a very small pittance for his services; yet his farm was managed so judiciously, that within a few years after their removal to the West, his family lived in a very comfortable and respectable manner.

Few men have lived so blameless and exemplary a life as Dr. Power. He had few, if any, peculiarities of character. Plain, simple, and polished in his manners, he made himself agreeable and respected by all classes of society, and closed his long life without a spot on his moral and Christian character.

It may not be deemed irrelevant to append, as a sequel to our Biographical Sketch of Dr. Power, some account of a tragical scene which occurred within the field of his labors, during the earlier period of his Western life. We refer to the *Burning of Hanna's-town* by the savages, and the thrilling tragedies connected with it. Most of our early ministers and their families experienced no ordinary suffering and anxiety from these human demons, ever thirsting for the white man's blood. Messrs. Dod, M'Millan and Smith had each their trials in this way. But, perhaps, none of them ever spent a day of greater anxiety than did James Power, on the 13th of July, 1782. He had now been nearly eight years residing, with his family, west of the mountains. His field was, at first, widely extended through Fayette and Westmoreland Counties. He had removed, and settled in the latter County. One of his regular places of supply was Unity, a congregation some six or seven miles north-east of the present town of Greensburg, not then, however, in existence. Not more than three or four miles from Unity was the seat of justice for all the West, that acknowledged the jurisdiction of Pennsylvania, Hanna's-town. Around it, and through the whole settlement, were living many of Mr. Power's people. He had been in its vicinity on the Sabbath previous. The story we have now to relate was given to the public some years ago, but has been heard, perhaps, by few of our readers. Mr. Power was near the scene at the very time. It will illustrate some of the trials to which our first ministers and their families were exposed.

During the whole time of the Revolutionary war, and for some time after it ceased, as we are informed by Mr. Finley in the History of the Western Insurrection, the country was cruelly wasted by perpetual savage depredations. The frontier was equally exposed on all sides round the whole extent of the country, except, perhaps, on the east a few miles near Youghiogeny river. The whole of what is now Westmoreland and Allegheny Counties, except a few townships, was either actually laid waste, or the inhabitants obliged to shelter themselves in forts. The then county-town (Hanna's-town,) was attacked in the time of court, and though the records were preserved, yet the town, with most of the property it contained, was burnt: and a number were also killed, or taken prisoners. The following, from the Greensburg Argus, of 1836, detailing the particulars of that event, will be read with interest by those who have not heretofore met with it:—

"About three miles from Greensburg, on the old road to New Alexandria, there stand two modern-built log tenements, to one of which a sign-post and a sign is appended, giving due notice that at the 'Seven Yellow Stars' the wayfarer may partake of the good things of this world. Between the tavern and the Indian gallows-hill on the west, once stood Hanna's-town, the first place west of the Allegheny mountains where justice was dispensed, according to the leading forms, by the white man. The county of Westmoreland was established by the provincial legislature on the 26th of February, 1773, and the courts directed to be held at Hanna's-town. It consisted of about thirty habitations, some of them cabins, but most of them aspiring to the name of houses, having two stories of hewed logs. There were a wooden court-house and a jail of the like construction; a fort stockaded with logs completed the civil and military arrangements of the town. The first prothonotary and clerk of the courts was Arthur St. Clair, Esq., afterwards general in the revolutionary army. Robert Hanna, Esq., was the first presiding justice in the courts; and the first court of common pleas was held in April, 1773. Thomas Smith, Esq., afterwards one of the judges on the supreme bench, (made his debût in the profession which he afterwards illustrated and adorned,) brought quarterly from the east the most abstruse learning, to puzzle the backwoods lawyers; and it was here that Hugh Henry Breckenridge, afterwards also a judge on the supreme bench, made his debût in the profession which he afterwards contributed to elevate by his genius and learning.

"The road first opened to Fort Pitt by Gen. Forbes and

his army, passed through the town. The periodical return of the court brought together a hardy, adventurous, frank, and open-hearted set of men from the Redstone, the George's creek, the Youghiogeny, the Monongahela, and the Catfish settlements, as well as from the region now in its circumscribed limits, still called 'Old Westmoreland.' It may well be supposed that, on such occasions, there was many an uproarious merry-making. Such men, when they occasionally met at court, met joyously. But the plough has long since gone over the place of merry-making, and no log or mound of earth remains to tell where Justice held her scales.

"On the 13th of July, 1782, a party of the townsfolk went to O'Conner's fields, about a mile and a half north of the village, to cut the harvest of Michael Huffnagle.

"The summer of '82 was a sorrowful one to the frontier inhabitants. The blood of many a family had sprinkled their own fields. The frontier, northwest of the town, was almost deserted; the inhabitants had fled for safety and repose towards the Sewickly settlement. At this very time, there were a number of families at Miller's station, about two miles south of the town. There was, therefore, little impediment to the Indians, either by way of resistance, or even of giving warning of their approach. When the reapers had cut down one field, one of the number who had crossed to the side next to the woods, returned in great alarm, and reported that he had seen a number of Indians approaching. The whole reaping party ran for the town, each one intent upon his own safety. The scene which then presented itself may more readily be conceived than described. Fathers asking for their wives and children, and children calling upon their parents and friends, and all hurrying in a state of consternation to the fort. Some criminals were confined in jail, the doors of which were thrown open. After some time it was proposed that some person should reconnoitre, and relieve them from uncertainty. Four young men, David Shaw, James Brison, and two others, with their rifles, started on foot through the highlands, between that and Crabtree creek, pursuing a direct course towards O'Conner's fields; whilst Captain J——, who happened to be in town, pursued a more circuitous route on horseback.

"The captain was the first to arrive at the fields, and his eye was not long in doubt; for the whole force of the savages was then mustered. He turned his horse to fly, but was observed and pursued. When he had proceeded a short distance, he met the four on foot—told them to fly for their lives—that the savages were coming in great force—that he would take a circuitous route and alarm the settlements. He went to Love's, where Frederick Beaver now lives, about a mile and a quarter east of the town; and assisted the family to fly, taking Mrs. Love on the horse behind him. The four made all speed for the town, but the foremost Indians obtained sight of them, and gave them hot pursuit. By the time they had reached the Crabtree creek, they could hear the distinct footfalls of their pursuers, and see the sunbeams glistening through the foliage upon their naked skins. When, however, they got into the mouth of the ravine that led up from the creek to the town, they felt almost secure. The Indians, who knew nothing of the previous alarm given to the town, and supposed that they would take it by surprise, did not fire, lest that might give notice of their approach: this saved the lives of David Shaw and his companions. When they got to the top of the hill, the strong instinct of nature impelled Shaw to go first into the town, and see whether his kindred had gone into the fort, before he entered it himself. As he reached his father's threshold and saw all within desolate, he turned and saw the savages with their tufts of hair flying in the wind, and their brandished tomahawks; for they had emerged into the open space around the town, and commenced the war-whoop. He resolved to make one of them give his death-halloo, and raising his rifle to his eye, his bullet whizzed true; for the stout savage, at whom he aimed, bounded into the air and fell upon his face. Then, with the speed of an arrow, he fled for the fort, which he entered in safety. The Indians were exasperated when they found the town deserted; and after pillaging the houses, they set them on fire.*

"Although a considerable part of the town was within rifle-range of the fort, the whites did but little execution, being more intent on their own safety than solicitious about destroying the enemy. One savage, who had put on the military coat of one of the inhabitants, paraded himself so ostentatiously that he was shot down. Except this one, and the one laid low by Shaw, there was no evidence of any other execution but some bones found among the ashes of one of the houses, where they, it was supposed, burnt those that were killed. There were not more than 14 or 15 rifles in the fort; and a company having marched from the town some time before in Lochley's ill-fated campaign, many of the most efficient men were absent; not more than 20 or 30 remained. A maiden, Jennet Shaw, was killed in the fort; a child having run opposite the gate, in which there were some apertures, through which a bullet from the Indians occasionally whistled, she followed it, and as she stooped to pick it up, a bullet entered her bosom; she thus fell a victim to the kindness of her heart. The savages, with their wild yells and hideous gesticulations, exulted as the flames spread, and looked like demoniacs rejoicing over the lost hopes of mortals.

"Soon after the arrival of the marauders a large party of

* Dr. Power had left home that morning to attend a meeting, or an appointment of some kind, in the direction of Hanna's-town. The news of the invasion and attack of the Indians, and the burning of the town, was received by Mrs. Power some hours before the return of her husband. They were hours to her of intense agony, as she knew not but that he was murdered and scalped by the savages. Mrs. Schraeder, a near neighbor, was the only person with her, besides her four or five little daughters. This lady, lately deceased at the age of 92, told us she never witnessed more distress in a family, than she that day witnessed. Such were some of the trials of our early ministers and their wives.

them were observed to break off by what seemed concerted signals, and march towards Miller's station. At that place, there had been a wedding the day before. Love is a delicate plant, but will take root in the midst of perils, in gentle bosoms. A young couple, fugitives from the frontier, fell in love, and were married. Among those who visited the bridal festivity were Mrs. H——, and her two beautiful daughters, from the town. John Brownlee, (who then owned what is now the fine farm of Frederick J. Cope), and his family, were also there. This individual was well known in frontier forage and scouting parties. His courage, activity, generosity, and manly form, won for him, among his associates, as they win everywhere, confidence and attachment. Many of the Indians were acquainted with his character; some of them, probably, had seen his person. There were, in addition to the mansion, a number of cabins rudely constructed, in which those families who had been driven from their homes resided. The station was generally called Miller's town. The bridal party were enjoying themselves in the principal mansion, without the least shadow of approaching danger. Some men were mowing in the meadow—people in the cabins were variously occupied — when suddenly the war-whoop, like a clap of thunder from a cloudless sky, broke upon their astonished ears. The people in the cabins and those in the meadows, mostly made their escape. One incident always excites emotions in my bosom, when I have heard it related. Many who fled took an eastern course, over the long steep hills which ascend towards Peter George's farm. One man was carrying his child, and assisting his mother in the flight, and when they got towards the top of the hill, the mother exclaimed they would be murdered; that the savages were gaining space upon them. The son and father put down his child that he might the more effectually assist his mother. Let those disposed to condemn keep silence, until the same struggle of nature takes place in their own bosoms. Perhaps he thought the savages would be more apt to spare the innocence of infancy than the weakness of age. But most likely it was the instinct of feeling, and even a brave man had hardly time to think under such circumstances. At all events Providence seemed to smile on the act; for at the dawn of the next morning, when the father returned to the cabin, he found his little innocent curled upon his bed, sound asleep, the only human thing left amidst the desolation. Let fathers appreciate his feelings; whether the Indians had found the child and took compassion on it, and carried it back, or whether the little creature had been unmolested, and when it became tired of its solitude, had wandered home through brush and over briers, will never be known. The latter supposition would seem most probable from its being found in its own cabin and on its own bed. At the principal mansion the party were so agitated by the cries of women and children, mingling with the yell of the savage, that all were for a moment irresolute; and that moment sealed their fate. One young man of powerful frame grasped a child near him, which happened to be Brownlee's, and effected his escape. He was pursued by three or four savages. But his strength enabled him to gain slightly upon his followers; when he came to a rye field, and taking the advantage of a thick copse, which, by a sudden turn, intervened between him and them, he got on the fence and leaped far into the rye, where he lay down with the child. He heard the quick tread of the savages as they passed, and their slower steps as they returned, muttering their guttural disappointment. That man lived to an honored old age, but is now no more.

"Brownlee made his way to the door, having seized a rifle; he saw, however, that it was a desperate game, but made a rush at some Indians who were entering the gate. The shrill, clear voice of his wife, "Jack, will you leave me?" instantly recalled him, and he sat down beside her at the door, yielding himself a willing victim. The party were made prisoners, including the bridegroom and the bride, and several of the family of Miller. At this point of time, Captain J—— was seen coming up the lane in full gallop. The Indians were certain of their prey, and the prisoners were dismayed at his rashness. Fortunately he noticed the peril in which he was placed, in time to save himself. Eagerly bent upon giving warning to the people, his mind was so engrossed with that idea that he did not see the enemy until he was within full gunshot. When he did see them and turned to fly, several bullets whistled by him — one of which cut his bridle rein; but he escaped. When those of the marauders, who had pursued the fugitives, returned, and when they had safely secured their prisoners, and loaded them with plunder, they commenced their retreat.

"Heavy were the hearts of the women and maidens, as they were led into captivity. Who can tell the bitterness of their sorrow? They looked, as they thought, for the last time upon the dear fields of their country and of civilized life. They thought of their fathers, their husbands, their brothers; and as their eyes streamed with tears, the cruelty and uncertainty which hung over their fate, as prisoners of savages, overwhelmed them with despair. They had proceeded about half a mile, and four or five Indians near the group of prisoners in which was Brownlee, were observed to exchange rapid sentences among each other, and look earnestly at him. Some of the prisoners had named him; and whether it was from that circumstance, or because some of the Indians had recognised his person, it was evident that he was a doomed man. He stooped slightly to adjust his child on his back, which he carried in addition to the luggage which they had put on him; and as he did so, one of the Indians who had looked so earnestly at him, stepped to him hastily and buried a tomahawk in his head. When he fell, the child was quickly dispatched by the same individual. One of the women captives screamed at this butchery, and the same bloody instrument and ferocious hand immediately ended her agony of spirit. God tempers the wind to the shorn lamb, and he enabled Mrs. Brownlee to bear that scene in speechless agony and woe. Their bodies were found next day by the settlers, and buried where they fell. The spot is marked to this day in Michling's field. As the shades of evening began to fall, the marauders met again on the plains of Hanna's-town. They retired into the low grounds about the Crabtreee creek, and there regaled themselves on what they had stolen. It was their intention to attack the fort the next morning before the dawn of day.

"At nightfall, thirty yeomen, good and true, had assembled at George's farm, not far from Miller's, determined to give that night what succor they could to the people in the fort. They set off for the town, each with his trusty rifle, some on horseback, and some on foot. As soon as they came near the fort, the greatest caution and circumspection was observed. Experienced woodsmen soon ascertained that the enemy was in the Crabtree bottom, and that they might enter the fort. Accordingly, they all marched to the gate, and were most joyfully welcomed by those within. After some consultation, it was the general opinion that the enemy intended to make an attack the next morning; and, as there were but about 45 rifles in the fort, and about 55 or 60 men, the contest was considered extremely doubtful, considering the great superiority of numbers on the part of the savages. It became, therefore, a matter of the first importance, to impress the enemy with the belief that large reinforcements were arriving. For that purpose, the horses were mounted by active men, and brought full trot over the bridge of plank that was across the ditch which surrounded the stockading. This was frequently repeated. Two old drums were found in the fort, which were new braced, and music on the fife and drum was kept occasionally going during the night. While, marching and countermarching, the bridge was frequently crossed on foot by the whole garrison. These measures had the desired effect. The military music from the fort, the trampling of the horses, and the marching over the bridge, were borne on the silence of the night over the low lands of the Crabtree: and the sounds carried terror into the bosoms of the cowardly savages. They feared the retribution which they deserved, and fled shortly after midnight in their stealthy and wolf-like habits. Three hundred Indians, and about sixty white savages, in the shape of refugees, as they were then called, crossed the Crabtree that day, with the intention of destroying Hanna's-town and Miller's station. The next day, a number of the whites pursued the trail as far as the Kiskeminetas, without being able to overtake them.

"The little community, which had now no homes but what the fort supplied, looked out on the ruins of the town with the deepest sorrow. It had been to them the scene of heartfelt joys — embracing the intensity and tenderness of all which renders the domestic hearth and family altar sacred. By degrees, they all sought themselves places, where they might, like Noah's dove, find rest for the soles of their feet. The lots of the town, either by sale or abandonment, became merged in the adjoining farm; and the labors of the husbandmen soon effaced what time might have spared. Many a tall harvest have I seen growing upon the ground; but never did I look upon its waving luxuriance, without thinking of the severe trials, and the patient fortitude, and the high courage which characterised the early settlers.

"The prisoners were surrendered by the Indians to the British in Canada. The beauty and misfortune of the Misses H—— attracted attention. An English officer — perhaps moved by beauty in distress, to love her for the dangers she had passed — wooed and won the fair and gentle Marian. After the peace of '83, the rest of the captives were delivered up, and returned to their country."

We have never understood what proportion of those engaged in the scenes above described were of Dr. Power's people. It is certain, that many of them were his constant hearers when he preached in that part of his charge.

So far as we have learned, this was the greatest, but not the last of the trials to which Dr. Power and his family and people were subjected from these marauders of the forest. We have recently learned from one who had it from the lips of Dr. Power himself, that he on that day was at Unity meeting-house; it being their fast-day previous to an intended communion on the ensuing Sabbath — that most of the men, as was the common custom, were there with their guns — that tidings came, either before or soon after the service commenced, of the attack and burning of Hanna's-town by the savages, and that the congregation immediately dispersed,— the communion was necessarily deferred. Of this circumstance, about the fast-day meeting at Unity, Mrs. Schroeder was not, we suppose, informed. She only knew that Dr. Power had gone in that direction to attend some meeting. Being herself a member of the Lutheran church, it is not strange that she did not know more particularly the occasion of Dr. Power's absence.

great moderation, there were still multitudes who, under the popular error, had no sense of shame in indulging in alcoholic liquids to excess. The trade in this article was then an important branch of commerce, and its manufacture one of the most extensive branches of national industry."

The people through the Western counties—unable to raise the means of paying their taxes by the sale of their grain, which would not bear portage, east of the mountains, on horseback, and which could not be carried to New Orleans, but with great danger and uncertainty—were driven, almost by necessity, to reduce the products of their farms to portable size, by distillation. They were compelled to become distillers; and a distillery was erected on almost every third or fourth farm through Westmoreland, Washington and Fayette Counties. The people used it themselves freely, morning, noon and night, especially in harvest, and on all occasions when they were exposed to severe toil, or the inclemency of the weather. Our ministers and elders used it, as well as their people. Yet they were not intemperate. No instance ever occurred, in the history of the Old Redstone Presbytery, in which either a minister or elder ever needed to be subjected to the slightest act of discipline, on this account. And there is no instance on record, in their minutes, of any case originating in this cause coming before them, by complaint or appeal from sessions.

When we remember the prevalence of the custom of using whiskey or brandy—when we learn that it was the universal custom, whenever a friend or neighbor called, to set out the bottle, as a common act of civility—when we call to mind the frequent exposures of the early settlers to the violence of the elements—when we remember how many causes of anxiety and sorrow pressed upon them continually, tempting them with the delusive promise of recruited strength, or of relief from distress, to resort to the consolations, or the delights, of the bottle—when it is borne in mind that liquor was freely used as a medicine, in various forms, and recommended by physicians—when we consider that, in those days, liquor was freely used at all meetings of every kind, that a man could not be *born*, *married*, or *buried*, without the presence and free use of whiskey—it is really wonderful that intemperance did not come in like a flood upon the church, and the world. Yet it is really due to our fathers—both ministers, elders and people—to testify, upon the most credible evidence, that intemperance was *not the vice* of those times, at least *among our people.* We once thought otherwise. But a more careful examination of the subject has satisfied us that this was not the case. The *Whiskey Insurrection*, it is true, occurred in the bounds of the Redstone Presbytery. But, in the first place, this arose from no special fondness for the intemperate use of the article. It was simply the result of a delusion respecting their rights, and an impression that they were wrongfully and oppressively taxed in the very article which alone they could turn to account in trade and commerce, and thereby secure to themselves and families the *very necessaries of life.* They regarded the excise tax as odious and oppressive. They neither loved nor used whiskey more than the people of other sections of the United States. But, in the second place, *very few of our people* joined in *that unhappy movement;* and all our ministers opposed it strenuously and successfully among their people. One of the historians of that Insurrection, Mr. Findley, states, in reference to the meeting held at Couche's Fort, "While they were deliberating what was to be done, the Rev. Mr. Clarke, a venerable and very old clergyman, expostulated with them on the impropriety of the enterprise, and used his utmost endeavors to dissuade them from it."

Judge Brackenridge says, "Great pains were taken—particularly by the clergy, in various congregations. The Rev. Samuel Porter, and the Rev. John M'Millan, and others, had, from the first, borne a decided testimony against the forcible opposition to the laws. Previous to the day of giving the test of submission, Mr. M'Millan, having appointed a day for giving the sacrament of bread and wine, adjourned the celebration, until it could be known who would submit—meaning to exclude those from the ordinance who should remain obstinate, and refuse this declaration of fidelity. He attended himself on the day of submission, and used his immediate influence."

Some account of that extraordinary event may, with propriety, find a place in this Work. For though the actual denouement of the "Whiskey Insurrection" did not take place *till the year after the Old Presbytery* of Redstone ceased to exist—yet its causes, and the circumstances which led to that unfortunate issue, are to be found scattered through several previous years: and their bearing upon the interests of religion, and of the church, was not inconsiderable.

An intelligent survey of the moral and religious state of the country during the last years of the Presbytery, cannot be taken without some acquaintance with that singular chapter in the history of Western Pennsylvania. Soon after the exciting occurrences of '94, Mr. Findley, long a member of Congress from Western Pennsylvania, wrote and published his account of them, entitled "The History of the Insurrection." This work was soon followed by another from the pen of Judge H. Brackenridge, entitled "Incidents of the Western Insurrection." These works, taken together, furnish a tolerably complete account, yet have been charged with much partiality and injustice in particular cases. Judge Lobingier has also given to the public his reminiscences and views of that exciting period, in which important corrections of the errors or partial statements of Messrs. Findley and Brackenridge may be found. Dr. Carnahan has likewise furnished a valuable paper on the subject to the New Jersey Historical Society. We propose to give the very clear, able, yet comprehensive account of the "Insurrection," from the pen of the Hon. Judge Wilkeson, first published in the American Pioneer; adding some concluding remarks from Dr. Carnahan's Lecture. Even those to whom the subject is familiar will read the Judge's account of it with interest:

"The federal constitution, which had recently been adopted, was not generally approved of in this section of the country. Many believed that the new government would usurp the power of the states, destroy the liberties of the people, and end in a consolidated aristocracy, if not a monarchy. It was even alleged by many that the reason why General Washington had refused to entrust the defence of the frontiers to the people themselves, was his desire to increase the regular army, that it might be ultimately used for destroying their liberties.

The defeat of General St. Clair's army exposed the whole range of the frontier settlements on the Ohio to the fury of the Indians. The several settlements made the best arrangement in their power for their own defence. The government took measures for recruiting, as soon as possible, the western army. General Wayne, a favorite with the western people, was appointed to command; but a factious opposition in Congress to the military and financial plans of the administration delayed the equipment of the army for nearly two years. While General Wayne was preparing to penetrate the Indian country in the summer of 1794, the attention of the Indians was drawn to their own defence, and the frontiers were relieved from their attacks. But Western Pennsylvania, though relieved from war, seemed to have no relish for peace. Having been some time engaged in resisting the revenue laws, her opposition was now increased to insurrection.

The seeds of party had been widely sown, and had taken deep root in the western counties. Every act of the general government which manifested a spirit of conciliation towards the British (who were charged with inciting the Indians to war on the frontier), was regarded with marked disapprobation. The Irish population which prevailed in the country generally sympathised with the French, and felt the most lively interest in the French Revolution, and the highest respect for their diplomatic agents in this country, who were then engaged in collisions with our government. The neutral policy which was adopted in relation to France and England was unpopular. Democratic societies were formed in every part of the country, and the measures of the government denounced; especially the act laying a duty on distilled spirits. This temper of disaffection was inflamed by the extensive circulation of newspapers, the organs of the French party, and of speeches of members of Congress in the French interest and opposed to the administration. The ordinary means of counteracting the influence of these mischievous publications were limited. The newspapers which defended the policy of the government had but little circulation in the West, and the friends of the administration neglected, until it was too late, to disabuse the public mind.

The resistance to the excise law from its first enactment had been so decided and general that the president, desiring to remove its most objectionable features, recommended to Congress a modification of the act. This was done. The concession, however, served only to increase the opposition. Every expedient was adopted to avoid the payment of the duties. In order to allay opposition as far as possible, General John Neville, a man of the most deserved popularity, was appointed Collector for Western Pennsylvania. He accepted the appointment from a sense of duty to his country. He was one of the few men of great wealth who had put his all at hazard for independence. At his own expense he raised and equipped a company of soldiers, marched them to Boston, and placed them, with his son, under the command of General Washington. He was the brother-in-law to the distinguished General Morgan, and father-in-law to Majors Craig and Kirkpatrick; officers highly respected in the western country. Besides General Neville's claims as a soldier and a patriot, he had contributed greatly to relieve the sufferings of the settlers in his vicinity. He divided his last loaf with the needy; and in a season of more than ordinary scarcity, as soon as his wheat was sufficiently matured to be converted into food, he opened his fields to those who were suffering with hunger. If any man could have executed this odious law, General Neville was that man. He entered upon the duties of his office, and appointed his deputies from among the most popular citizens. The first attempts, however, to enforce the law, were resisted. One or more deputies were tarred and feathered; others were compelled to give up their appointments to avoid like treatment. The opposers of the law, having proceeded to open acts of resistance, now assumed a bolder attitude. An assemblage of several hundred men proceeded in the night to General Neville's house and demanded the surrender of his commission; but finding him prepared for defence, they attempted no violence. He had not doubted that there was sufficient patriotism in the country to enable the civil authorities to protect him in the discharge of his duty; but in this he was mistaken. The magistrates were powerless. Their authority was set at defiance.

Although a large majority of the disaffected never dreamed of carrying their opposition to the measures of government to open resistance, yet they had aided to create a tempest which they could neither direct nor allay. The population received a large increase, yearly, of Irish emigrants, who had been obliged to leave their own country on account of opposition to its government; besides which, there was a large floating population, who had found employment in guarding the frontiers, and who had nothing to lose by insurrection. Both of these classes joined the insurgent party, and even forced them to adopt more extreme measures than they had at first contemplated. They at length proceeded so far as to form an organized resistance to the law. Meetings were held and officers were appointed in the most excited districts. Several hundred men volunteered to take General Neville into immediate custody. His friends in Pittsburg, being apprised of these movements, advised that measures should be adopted for his protection. But they were greatly mistaken in the amount of force which would be requisite. Major Kirkpatrick, with only a dozen soldiers from the garrison at Pittsburg, repaired to General Neville's house, which was that very evening (July 15, 1794), surrounded by about five hundred men. The General, yielding to the importunity of friends, had, on the approach of the insurgents, withdrawn from his house, accompanied by his servant. The assailants demanded that the General and his papers should be given up to them. On being refused, a fire was commenced, which was continued some time, until Major M'Farland, an influential citizen, who was one of the assailants, was shot.

Gen. Neville's house was situated on an elevated plain which overlooked the surrounding country. A range of negro houses was on one side, and barns and stables on the other. These were fired by the assailants, and when the flames were about to communicate with the dwelling-house, the party within surrendered. The soldiers were dismissed. The son of General Neville, who came up during the attack, was taken prisoner, but, with Kirkpatrick, was released on condition of leaving the country.

This violent outrage produced a strong sensation. It was in the season of harvest, when the people of the surrounding country were collected in groups to aid each other in cutting their grain. During the day, it became known that preparations were making to take General Neville. As he could call to his aid nearly a hundred of his faithful slaves, who had learned the use of arms in the Indian war, it was believed that he would defend himself. Few, if any, of the immediate neighbors of the General were engaged in the attack; but, instead of going to his defence, they collected from a distance of several miles around, and selected the most favorable positions in the neighborhood for listening to, or seeing the anticipated attack. At about 10 o'clock in the evening, I witnessed the commencement of the fire at a distance of two miles, and saw the flames ascending from the burning houses, until the actors in the scene became visible in the increasing light. It was a painful sight, especially to those who had experienced the hospitality of the only fine mansion in the country, to see it destroyed by a lawless mob, and its inmates exposed to their fury. Even those who were opposed to the measures of the administration, and had countenanced resistance to the execution of the excise law, were overwhelmed at this appalling commencement of open insurrection. Meetings were proposed by the friends of order, for the purpose of concerting measures for their own security; but so much time was lost in deliberation, that the insurgents became too strong to be resisted.

Men of property and influence, who had become compromitted in the destruction of General Neville's house, exerted themselves to involve the whole country in open resistance to the laws. Several officers of the government and others, whose influence was feared, were forced to leave the country. The mail was robbed, and the names of several writers found in it were added to the list of the proscribed. Those who were thus expelled their country dared not take the usual road across the mountains, but were compelled to proceed by a dangerous and circuitous route through the wilderness.

The insurgents seemed resolved that there should be no neutrals in the country. Immediately after the first outbreak, they called a general meeting of the militia at Braddock's field, to decide upon the measures which should be farther taken in relation to the excise. Seven or eight thousand assembled, and an attorney from Washington assumed the command. He was a blustering demagogue, and destitute of the courage and decision necessary to direct an insurrection. The leaders had no plan digested for future action; nor could this extraordinary assemblage, whose grotesque appearance it would require a Falstaff to describe, tell for what purpose they had come together. A committee was appointed to deliberate. Hugh Henry Brackenridge, a distinguished lawyer of Pittsburg, who filled a large space in the country, and was known as an opposer of some of the measures of the administration, and therefore presumed to be in favor of resistance, was appointed on this committee. Possessing great powers of persuasion, he succeeded in preventing the committee from recommending energetic measures, and urged moderation until the effect of their past resistance should be known. The report of the committee merely recommended the holding of a meeting, by delegates, from the several towns in the country, at Parkinson's ferry, a few weeks ensuing. On receiving this report, much dissatisfaction was manifested; the assembly, however, dispersed, two or three thousand men only marching in a body to Pittsburg. A portion of these proposed to burn the place, but the kindness of the citizens in supplying them with provisions, and the influence of the more respectable of their associates, induced them to leave the village unharmed. They contented themselves with burning the mansion of Major Kirkpatrick in the vicinity. Many of the most active insurgents traversed the country, to insure a general election of delegates to the convention, which was to be held in the month of August. In the meantime, the people were in a state of great alarm — parties of the most reckless of the insurgents, freed from all restraints of law, paraded the country, and threatened destruction to all tories and aristocrats, (epithets applied to all who would not join them.) In the face of all these dangers, however, many of the towns sent, as delegates, friends of law and supporters of the administration.

The President, desirous to avoid the use of force, had appointed three commissioners to repair to the western country, and offer pardon to all offenders who would return to their duty, and submit to the laws. These commissioners arrived about the time of the meeting of the convention. Some of the delegates to the convention were men of distinguished ability, at the head of whom was Albert Gallatin. Although a foreigner, who could with difficulty make himself understood in English, yet he presented with great force the folly of past resistance, and the ruinous consequences to the country of the continuance of the insurrection. He urged that the government was bound to vindicate the laws, and that it would surely send an overwhelming force against them, unless the proposed amnesty was accepted. Mr. Gallatin placed the subject in a new light, and showed the insurrection to be a much more serious affair than it had before appeared. The ardor of the most reckless was moderated. A conference was had with the government commissioners, and the question, whether the country should submit or not, was earnestly discussed. A strong disposition was manifested to accept of the terms proposed. The acts of violence which had already been committed, made some of the leaders tremble in view of what might follow. The machinery of the so-called democratic clubs was found not to work so well in this country as in Paris; and lynch law, executed by a set of desperadoes, was proved to be a poor exchange for the protection of law regularly administered. Many who had been seduced from their allegiance repented of their folly, and would gladly have retraced their steps; but this was not easy to do: they dreaded the vengeance of their associates. "The sons of liberty," as the insurgents styled themselves, could not bear traitors; and those who forsook their party, were exposed to, they knew not what, acts of violence and outrage. For, notwithstanding the returning good sense of many, there were others who still entertained such deep-rooted prejudices against the administration, and who had imbibed such wild notions of liberty, that they desired the separation of the West from the Union. They were deceived by exaggerated accounts of the disaffection which prevailed throughout Pennsylvania, Kentucky, and western Virginia. It had been represented from these places, that if western Pennsylvania would successfully resist for a few months, their cause would be espoused by a party so strong as to set the general government at defiance.

Although the convention was in favor of submission, yet as

its constituents had not delegated to it the power of settling that question, it was concluded to refer it back to the people, who in town meetings should decide it for themselves.

Early in September, the gratifying news was received that General Wayne had gained a signal victory over the combined force of the Indians on the Maumee. This news operated favorably for the government. It not only removed the dissatisfaction to which the great delays attending the campaign had given rise, but it was the best possible illustration of the benefits to be derived from the protection of the general government, which had been greatly underrated. As a permanent peace with the Indians was now considered certain, this increased the desire for tranquillity at home.

The citizens convened in town-meetings to consider the terms of submission proposed by the government, printed copies of which had been distributed through the country. In some townships, the meetings failed entirely; in others, they were interrupted and dispersed before having accomplished any business. But in a large majority of the townships the attendance was general, good order was preserved, and the submission papers were generally signed. These results inspired the friends of government with courage, and greatly dispirited the insurgents. By the first of October, tranquillity and good order were in a great measure restored.

But as the malcontents were still sufficiently numerous to resist the execution of the revenue laws, the government marched forward the army which they had for some time been organising, consisting of about 14,000 militia from Virginia, Maryland, New Jersey, and Pennsylvania. An unusual quantity of rain having fallen during the autumn, the army suffered greatly on their march, particularly several regiments composed of mechanics, merchants, and others from the cities, who were not inured to such hardships. They became so disheartened that if the passes of the mountains had been disputed by only 1000 resolute insurgents, the army might have been greatly embarrassed, if not defeated.

But they met no resistance either in the mountains or in the infected districts. Bradford, and a few others who had the most to fear, fled to the Spanish country on the Mississippi; others, equally guilty, but less notorious offenders sought security in sequestered settlements. "Not a dog wagged his tongue" against the army, which advanced to Pittsburg and took up their quarters.

General Hamilton, Secretary of the Treasury, who represented the government, had his quarters soon thronged with informers, and those who had suffered from the insurgents, and sought compensation. A kind of inquisitorial court was opened, in which testimony was taken against individuals denounced for treasonable acts or expressions. Many of the informers, influenced by prejudice or malice, implicated those who had been guilty of no offence against the government.

After a few days spent in these "star-chamber" proceedings, the dragoons were put in requisition; and the officers furnished with the names of the offenders, proceeded with guides, of whom there was no lack, to arrest them. Such of the proscribed as apprehended no danger, were soon taken; and without any intimation of the offence with which they stood charged, or time for preparation, about 300 were carried to Pittsburg. Here many found acquaintances, and influential friends, who interposed in their behalf, and obtained their immediate release; others, less fortunate, were sent to Philadelphia for trial, where they were imprisoned for ten or twelve months, without even indictments found against them. But few of the really guilty were taken, while many who had committed no offence against the laws, but unfortunately had fallen under the displeasure of an informer, suffered the punishment due only to the guilty. The following may serve as an instance:

A lieutenant of the army, while it was halting at Pittsburg, visited his uncle in the vicinity, and accompanied him to a husking party, when, on using the term rebel as applicable to the citizens generally, he was rebuked by a respectable old man of the party. The officer replied insolently, upon which a young man (for young men in those days always felt bound to protect the aged) interposed, and would have treated him with deserved severity, had not my father begged him off. The officer returned to Pittsburg, and the next day both of those who had offended him at the husking were arrested. The young man found friends who procured his liberation; but the old man, notwithstanding efforts were made for his release, was carried to Philadelphia and imprisoned for more than six months without trial.

I believe that but a single individual was tried; this was one of the mail-robbers, who was convicted of treason and sentenced to be hung, but was finally pardoned.

The army remained at Pittsburg only long enough to recruit from their fatigue and receive their pay. Many of them, disgusted with a soldier's life, obtained their discharge, and either settled in the country, or purchased horses on which to return home. A few battalions only of the army were retained in the country through the winter; the remainder resumed their march and recrossed the mountains."

Here we might close our extended extract from Judge Wilkinson's account of the Whiskey Insurrection. But though what follows is not necessary to complete the narrative, it is so much to our purpose in several other respects that we think the reader will not regret its insertion here.

"The insurrection for a time threatened the most disastrous consequences; and if it had not been promptly crushed, might have subverted the government; yet it was not without its advantages. Its suppression tested the patriotism of the people and their attachment to the constitution, points on which there had been much doubt, both at home and abroad. The practical experiment of raising a large army by draughts of militia from several states, and marching them in an inclement season, under great privations, several hundred miles, to suppress a revolt, was a most gratifying evidence that the government was founded in the affections of the people, and that however they might differ about the mode of its administration, yet the government itself would be sustained.

Nor was it the government alone that profited by the insurrection; the rapid growth of the country west of the mountains may be dated from that period. Although the country had for years abounded in stock and provisions, yet there was no home market where either could be sold for cash. There was but little money in circulation, and of course but little stimulus to industry. The price of a cow in barter was about five dollars, and of a good horse from ten to twenty dollars; wheat was about thirty cents a bushel. But the army created a demand both for provisions and horses, which increased their value from one hundred to three hundred per cent. Nearly a million of dollars of government money was paid out in the country. Had Western Pennsylvania been compelled to refund this amount, as the penalty of her revolt, she would still have been a gainer. A large accession of settlers from the army, greatly increased the price of land; money became plenty, and a cash home-market was established.

But the prosperity which resulted from the insurrection did not wipe away its reproach. The character of the people suffered greatly, and the more so, as the actual causes of this insurrection were misunderstood and misrepresented. It has generally been believed that the Western people were so devoid of patriotism, and so insensible to the blessings of a free government, that they refused to be taxed for its support; and that they regarded whiskey so necessary an article of consumption, as to be unwilling to have its price enhanced by a duty. These opinions do them great injustice. Although the citizens generally were in the habit of drinking whiskey, yet, strange as it may appear at this day, *they were not drunkards*. The custom of the country was to furnish whiskey in harvest; and at all collections of neighbors, to aid each other in log-rollings, raising cabins, or husking corn, whiskey was indispensable. The prevailing forms of hospitality could not be carried out without it. If one neighbor called on another, to make a visit, or do an errand, the bottle and a cup of water were invariably presented to him, after being first tasted by the host, who drank to the health of his guest. Women treated their visitors with whiskey, made palatable with sugar, milk and spices. It was used as a medicine in several diseases, and proved an unfailing remedy in some. Among laborers the bottle was passed around, and there was always some kind-hearted man to see that the little boys were not forgotten. Morning bitters were generally used, and a dram before meals. But this common use of liquor was not limited to Western Pennsylvania; it prevailed in all the new settlements, if not over the United States.

There was nothing disreputable, at that day, in either drinking or making whiskey. Distilling was esteemed as moral and as respectable as any other business. It was early commenced, and extensively carried on in Western Pennsylvania. There was neither home nor foreign market for rye, the principal grain then raised in that part of the country, and which was a profitable and sure crop. The grain would not bear packing across the mountains. A horse could not carry more than four bushels of it, but could carry the product of twenty-four bushels, when converted into high wines, which found a market east of the mountains, and could be used in the purchase of salt, goods, &c. The settlers, at an early day, calculated that the whiskey trade would become a great source of wealth to the country, when the right of way to New Orleans should have been settled, and that market fully opened to their produce. Monongahela whiskey was reputed to be superior to any in the United States, and had the preference in every market. There was, very naturally, a general disposition to engage in distilling, as the only business which promised sure gain; and the people of Western Pennsylvania regarded a tax on whiskey in the same light as the citizens of Ohio would now regard a United States tax on lard, pork, or flour.

There were many aggravating circumstances calculated to render the whiskey tax odious, and to array the Western people in hostility to the government. For years they had suffered unspeakable hardships and privations; the government had neither protected the frontiers from Indian massacres, nor paid the militia service of the settlers; and the Western posts had been suffered to remain in possession of the British, contrary to the treaty of peace. Thus exposed and deprived of the advantages of peace, which were enjoyed by the rest of the United States—destitute of money, and the means of procuring it—a direct tax appeared to them unjust and oppressive. Unjust, because they had not received that protection which every government owes to its citizens; oppressive, because the tax was levied on the scanty product of their agricultural labor, and was required to be paid in specie, or its equivalent, which could not be furnished. Whether these opinions were well founded, or not, it is doubtful whether the law-abiding descendants of the pilgrims would have quietly submitted to the law under just such circumstances. The settlers cultivated their land for years, at the peril of their lives. Like the Jews under Nehemiah, their weapons of defence were never laid aside; and when, by extraordinary efforts, they were enabled to raise a little more grain than their immediate wants required, they were met with a law restraining them in the liberty of doing what they pleased with the surplus.

The policy of laying a direct tax on the products of labor found few advocates in the Western country, and many violent opposers. It was contended that the tax on whiskey was but the commencement of a system of taxation as odious and oppressive as that of the British government, which had given rise to the War of the Revolution; and that if the system was carried out, independence would prove but an empty name. It was argued, that if rye could not be converted into whiskey without a license from government, wool could not be converted into a hat, nor a hide into boots, without their special permission; and that it was against just such assumptions of power that the American people had rebelled, and had continued for seven years to pour out their blood freely, rather than submit to the evils and degrading consequences of British taxation. They had fought for liberty, and not for a change of masters; and while the wounds they had received in battling against tyrants were scarcely yet healed, it is not astonishing that they should regard with abhorrence the swarm of government officers which every where beset them, spying into their domestic affairs, and demanding, with official arrogance, more than a tithe of their hard labor. This was too much to be borne by men who were imbued with the wild spirit of liberty which then pervaded our country. Whatever might have been the necessities of government, or however defensible the principle of direct taxation, a more critical time to make the experiment could not have been selected. Our whole country was agitated with political discussions. The political volcano which had broken out in France, and was sweeping over Europe like a sea of lava, threatening to overwhelm, in its fury, all forms of government, cast its frightful glare across the Atlantic, and so perverted the political vision, as to make law appear like tyranny, and anarchy like liberty."

Dr. Carnahan closes his lecture on this subject with these judicious remarks:

"Many important salutary lessons might be deduced from the narrative given; but I will merely suggest a few topics on which each one can reflect at his leisure.

First.—In a country so extensive as the United States, with such a diversity of climate and soil, leading the citizens to such a variety of pursuits and occupations, it appears to me impossible to raise a revenue to sustain the government by direct or internal taxation. The Constitution of the United States declares that "all duties, imposts and excises shall be uniform throughout the United States;" that is, the same articles shall be taxed alike throughout our extensive territory. The consequence will be, that taxes not felt at all in some places, will press heavily on others, as did the excise on whiskey in Western Pennsylvania, and will tempt the people to rebel. We have great reason to be thankful that the duties on importations from foreign countries are sufficient to pay the expenses of our government. In this case, every individual is at liberty to purchase or not to purchase foreign goods, and of course to pay, or not to pay, at his pleasure, the expenses of our General Government.

Second.—We see the disastrous consequences of mob law: the innocent are as likely to suffer as the guilty.

Third.—When a number of persons combine together to do wrong, reason is dethroned, and argument is of no avail. You may convince each individual of his error; but he will not and he dare not break ranks. He is afraid of his neighbor; and his neighbor may be as desirous as he is to back out, but he dare not; and this feeling may pervade the whole community, and no one will dare to express his real sentiments. This truth was illustrated by the Committee of Safety refusing to vote openly at the meeting at Brownsville.

Fourth.—In a commotion such as that in Western Pennsylvania, froth and bubbles will rise to the surface of the agitated waters, and swell and glitter in the sunbeams for a short time, and then burst and vanish from the sight. Witness D. Bradford, and other leaders of the Western Insurrection.

Fifth.—Those who are the most turbulent and outrageous when surrounded by a multitude agreeing with them in sentiment and feeling, are usually the most dastardly and sneaking when danger comes. Witness those who fled from the country when the army was crossing the mountains.

Sixth.—On this occasion Washington manifested his usual wisdom, in calling out an army so large as to render opposition hopeless, and by this means avoiding the effusion of human blood.

Lastly.—This occurrence was salutary as an example, showing that the Federal Government was not a rope of sand, which might be broken at the will of any section of the country, whenever any State or part of a State thought a particular law unjust or oppressive.

CHAPTER VIII.

THE BRIGHT SIDE OF THE PICTURE.

WE have now thrown together several topics which seemed to require notice in order to understand and appreciate those times of the Old Redstone Presbytery. In giving "the lights and shadows" of those days through which our fathers passed, we may seem to have had most to say about the "shadows." We have not adverted much to the brighter side. We have shown that all our first ministers were a very laborious set of men. They were the very reverse of the character given by the witty Dr. Jortin of a clergyman of his acquaintance: "invisible six days, and incomprehensible on the seventh." It would be a great mistake, indeed, were we to conclude, in view of all that has been now written, that these old ministers and their people were a joyless, unhappy, or gloomy race. The very reverse would be more true. Though they sowed in tears, they reaped, even here, in joy. We have scen some of the fountains of consolation that were opened to them in the wilderness, and the streams that followed them in the desert. We have mentioned their communion seasons and their protracted meetings, even in the forts. We have adverted to their health, and that of their families, and to the protecting care of Divine Providence over them in all their journeys. We might have mentioned that in very few instances did our people suffer in life, or limb, or liberty, from their savage foes. Perhaps no entire Presbyterian family was ever massacred or led into captivity, though often exposed and in imminent danger. This is a remarkable fact that has often been mentioned by many yet living. We might speak of other sources of satisfaction and enjoyment which that pious race had, either in possession, or in prospect for their children. But the greatest of all blessings which they enjoyed, were the frequent and copious outpourings of the holy Spirit upon the churches, converting multitudes to God, and bringing in vast numbers of the rising youth into the church. We quote the following as some specimen of what we mean, from the "Western Missionary Magazine," for September, 1803:—

"In the latter part of the year 1781, the Lord began a gracious work in the congregations of Cross Creek and Upper Buffalo, under the ministry of the Rev. Joseph Smith, about one year after he took the pastoral care of these congregations. During the winter season, week-day and night sermons, and meetings for social worship were frequent, the assemblies numerous and attentive, and a considerable number under deep convictions, with frequent instances of new awakenings. The summer following was remarkable for the increase of the awakened; although most labored long without relief. The few pious who were in these infant congregations were at this time earnestly engaged for additions to their number, and felt something of the pangs of travailing in birth for souls. Much of the spirit of prayer was poured out. In the latter part of this summer, the work became more glorious and comfortable; numbers of the distressed souls obtained sweet deliverance; and at the time the Lord's Supper was administered in Buffalo, in the fall of 1783, about one hundred of the subjects of this good work were admitted to communion, and many were awakened on that occasion. The awakening and hopeful conversion of sinners continued and increased through three or four years; nor was there much appearance of a decline for six or seven years after it began. Within this gracious season there were many sweet, solemn sacramental occasions. The most remarkable of these was at Cross Creek, in the spring of the year 1787. It was a very refreshing season to the pious, a time of deliverance to a number of the distressed, and of awakening to many. The Monday evening was peculiarly and awfully solemn: some hundreds were bowed down and silently weeping, and a few crying out in anguish of soul. After the solemn disunion of the assembly, most of the people remained on the ground. The scene was very remarkable: the pious were generally joyful and lively, sinners greatly alarmed, and many deeply distressed. The people, unwilling to part, did not leave the place till an hour or more in the night; when they parted with an appointment to meet there again the next morning. Thursday was indeed a solemn day. It was spent chiefly in exhortations and prayers by the Rev. Messrs. Smith, Dod, and Cornwell. The effects of this gracious visitation were very comfortable, producing a good harvest of souls. Upwards of fifty were added to the church in these congregations at the communion the next fall.

Nearly about the same time in which this gracious work began in these congregations, the divine influences were poured out upon the congregations of Chartiers and Pigeon Creek, under the ministry of the Rev. John M'Millan; many were awakened, and the pious much revived and quickened. There were a goodly number of judicious Christians in these congregations who actively stepped forward in their proper places, and were very helpful in carrying on the good work. As many attended from considerable distances with a great thirst for ordinances, it was thought expedient to have social meetings for prayer and exhortation on the Sabbath nights; they generally continued all the night; many attended, and conviction and conversion work went graciously on. Frequently the exercised could not suppress their feelings of joy or distress, but gave them vent in groans and cries. There were, also, frequently week-day and night sermons and societies in different parts of the congregations. Thus this good work went on for several years; and it is believed that many were brought savingly to close with Christ in these congregations. And it is evident, from a trial of near twenty years, that the work is real and genuine with respect to some hundreds in those two charges above stated; many of whom are now faithful leaders, zealous and active Christians, and pillars in the Church of Christ.

In the same time, whilst this gracious work was going on in those places, the Lord also poured out his spirit on several other neighboring congregations; particularly Bethel and Lebanon, under the ministry of the Rev. John Clarke; Ten-mile, under the ministry of the Rev. Thaddeus Dod, and King's creek and Mill creek, then vacant congregations. In all of these places the power of God was graciously displayed, and many souls gathered in, who have since given evidence in their lives and conversation, that the work with them was a reality and of divine original.

We are able to state, from particular acquaintance and frequent conversation with some hundreds of those who were exercised, during this happy season of gracious visitation in all the above places, that in general their distress arose from a deep sense of the contrariety of their hearts and lives with the law of God, and the awful wages of sin which they saw they were in imminent danger of receiving, of their utter indisposition to turn to God, to love his law, or to embrace Jesus Christ, by reason of the hardness of their hearts, blindness of their minds and enmity against God. The peace and consolations of those who obtained relief, did not arise from a view of either their hearts or lives being less offensive to God, or from their having done anything recommending or entitling them to divine notice or favor, nor merely from a persuasion of God's having pardoned their sins; but from a scriptural discovery of the plan of salvation, by free sovereign grace, through the obedience, sufferings and death of

Jesus Christ, the God-man; which they viewed as suitable to their perishing condition, and to every valuable purpose; and they found their wills gained over to the cordial choice of this plan, and that their souls became delighted with the character and holy law of God."

The writer or compiler of this instructive narrative proceeds to tell of the abundant effusions of divine influence, during the years 1795 and 1798, and thence onward, till he comes to the great and widely extended revival of 1802 and 1803. But as these periods are since the times of the Old Redstone Presbytery, and our object is merely to give some account of what the Lord did for our old ministers then, we will quote no further. Though the preceding account refers exclusively to the charges of Messrs. Smith, Dod, M'Millan, and Clarke, being intended to relate merely what had taken place in the then bounds of the Presbytery of Ohio — he might, if his range had been more extended, have given some very pleasing accounts of a similar work in the charges of Messrs. Power, Dunlap, and Finley.

Thus the Lord comforted his people, and owned the labors of these men. Was not this one of the "lights" indeed, amidst all their shadows? and more than compensated them for many trials and sorrows? There are many, we trust among the living ministry, who would be willing to exchange circumstances with these old ministers, could they possess their "joy in the Lord," and witness such "days of the right hand of the Most High."

Among the minor circumstances of comfort, it may also be mentioned, that most of the members of the old Presbytery had the satisfaction of seeing their children all safely in the fold of Christ. Most of them had large families; the daughters of many of them became ministers' wives. Some of their sons entered the ministry; as a general case, also, they had excellent wives, that in every way were help-meets indeed Their salaries, though often not very punctually paid, especially during the early part of their ministry, were really

18

larger, considering the times and circumstances of the people, than ministers now generally receive. We think this can be proved beyond all question, and it ought to be rung in the ears of all our churches in our day. Mr. Smith's salary was £150; Mr. M'Millan's was about the same; Mr. Power's, Mr. Dunlap's, and Mr. Finley's, from £120 to £130. Now, when we take into consideration the cheapness of living, the low price of lands, and of all articles of clothing, and table consumption, except salt, these salaries were better to them than $600 now, to any of our ministers living in villages or in the country. Most of these ministers were able to purchase, and eventually to pay for good farms. And they did so with no fear that their people, finding them thus committed to a permanent settlement, would, on that account, be more tardy in paying their stipends. Now-a-days, it is, in many cases, rash for a minister to buy and improve even a house and garden.

The plain, frugal habits of the times did not impose upon the ministers then, the necessity of anything further than the cheapest furniture and the plainest style of living. Most of them assisted in much of the work that was done on their farms. With but one or two exceptions, they owned colored servants, both male and female, who were carefully instructed and kindly treated; most of these servants were members of the church. This statement may surprise some readers, and if they are abolitionists, will be rather an unwelcome piece of information; but it was truly so. At least six of the early ministers, and almost all their elders, were slaveholders. We never heard that their consciences were disturbed on the subject. They provided well for their servants; and those born after 1780, were, in due time, entitled to the benefit of the Act passed that year by the Legislature of Pennsylvania "for the gradual abolition of slavery." So far as we know, they all cordially responded to the sentiments of the noble preamble of that Act — drawn up by the Hon. George Bryan, afterwards one of the Judges of the Supreme Court, and also one of the Commissioners on the part of Pennsylvania to settle the boundary line between Pennsylvania and Virginia.*

* The following is that famous Preamble, well worth reading:

"When we contemplate our abhorrence of that condition to which the arms and tyranny of Great Britain were exerted to reduce us: when we look back on the variety of dangers to which we have been exposed, and how miraculously our wants, in many instances, have been supplied, and our deliverances wrought, when even hope and human fortitude have become unequal to the conflict, we are unavoidably led to a serious and grateful sense of the manifold blessings which we have undeservedly received from the hand of that Being from whom every good and perfect gift cometh. Impressed with these ideas, we conceive that it is our duty, and we rejoice that it is in our power, to extend a portion of that freedom to others which hath been extended to us; and release from that state of thraldom to which we ourselves were tyrannically doomed, and from which we have now every prospect of being delivered." (This was two years before the close of the revolutionary war.) "It is not for us to enquire why, in the creation of mankind, the inhabitants of the several parts of the earth were distinguished by a difference in feature or complexion. It is sufficient to know that all are the work of the Almighty hand. We find in the distribution of the human species, that the most fertile as well as the most barren parts of the earth are inhabited by men of complexions different from ours and from each other: from whence we may reasonably, as well as religiously infer, that He who placed them in their various situations, hath extended equally his care and protection to all, and that it becometh not us to counteract his mercies. We esteem it a peculiar blessing granted to us, that we are enabled this day to add one more step to universal civilization, by removing, as much as possible, the sorrows of those who have lived in undeserved bondage, and from which, by the authority of the king of Great Britain, no effectual legal relief could be obtained. Weaned by a long course of experience from those narrow prejudices and partialities we had imbibed, we find our hearts enlarged with kindness and benevolence towards men of all conditions and nations; and we conceive ourselves, at this particular period, extraordinarily called upon by the blessings which we have received, to manifest the sincerity of our profession, and to give a substantial proof of our gratitude: and whereas the condition of those persons denominated negro and mulatto slaves, has been attended with circumstances which not only deprived them of the common blessings that they were by nature entitled to, but has cast them into the deepest afflictions, by an unnatural separation and sale of husband and wife from each other and from their children;

We would further state that three of these ministers were at the meeting of the Synod of New York and Philadelphia, in 1788, which adopted the following (see printed Records, p. 540,): "The Synod of New York and Philadelphia, do highly approve of the general principles in favor of universal liberty that prevail in America, and the interest which many of the states have taken in promoting the abolition of slavery; yet inasmuch as men introduced from a servile state to a participation of all the privileges of civil society, without a proper education, and without previous habits of industry, may be, in many respects, dangerous to the community—therefore they earnestly recommend that masters, wherever they find servants disposed to make a just improvement of the privilege, would give them a peculium, or grant them sufficient time, and sufficient means of procuring their own liberty at a moderate rate; that thereby they may be brought into society with those habits of industry, that may render them useful citizens; and finally, they recommend it to all their people to use the most prudent measures, consistent with the interests, and the state of civil society, in the countries where they live, to promote eventually the final abolition of slavery in America."

We believe our fathers generally held the sentiments expressed by the Synod, as well as those in the Preamble to the Assembly's Act.

Another thing which cheered these fathers of Western Presbyterianism, after a few years of trial and toil, was, that

---

an injury, the greatness of which can only be conceived by supposing that we were in the same unhappy case. In justice, therefore, to persons so unhappily circumstanced, and who, having no prospect before them whereon they may rest their sorrows and their hopes, have no reasonable inducement to render their service to society, which they otherwise might; and also in grateful commemoration of our own happy deliverance from the state of unconditional submission to which we were doomed by the tyranny of Britain;—Be it, and it is hereby enacted," &c.—See Laws of Pennsylvania, Vol. I., p. 870.

it was their privilege to introduce into the ministry a noble set of young ministers of their own training, possessed of a like spirit with themselves. Of themselves, there were only four at first. Soon three more were added, coming from the same region they had left. For four or five years there was no addition, from within or from without. After that, were licensed, first Messrs. James Hughes, and John Brice—then James M'Gready, and Joseph Patterson. Then Robert Marshall, then J. M'Pherrin and Samuel Porter. Then George Hill and William Swan — then Thomas Marquis and David Smith, and Boyd Mercer—twelve men, all during the last five years of the Old Presbytery. In this respect, the first seven ministers who had waited long and suffered much anxiety, in view of the growing vacancies and destitutions, were now "reaping in joy." Their new recruits had not received a Princeton education; but they were a noble set of young men. As Doddridge justly remarks, "the course of education which they gave their pupils was indeed not extensive; but the piety of those who entered into the ministry more than made up the deficiency." It is true, they were called to surrender two of these younger fellow-laborers, M'Gready and Marshall, who soon went forth to do a glorious work in Kentucky. Under the ministry of the first of these, began that wonderful revival that extended to Tennessee and Virginia and North Carolina; and at length into all Western Pennsylvania and part of Ohio.* This may suffice for the "lights" of our picture.

We had thought of mentioning another source of relief and comfort. As in their revival labors, and sometimes in their efforts to introduce a New Testament Psalmody—many were grievously offended and forsook them; such persons did not generally go back into the world, or turn Unitarians or Universalists—for such communions of error did not exist in the West — but they almost uniformly betook themselves into

* See Davidson's Ecclesiastical History of Kentucky.

colder latitudes of Presbyterianism, where revivals and Psalmody would not disturb them, and yet where there was much soundness in the faith and at least a dead orthodoxy. This was better for them and for their children. And the piety and evangelical spirit of many of those churches are, in our day, greatly improved. Now we ought not to underrate this source of relief to our fathers. In New England it was otherwise. One of the consequences of their early and even present revivals has been that they were almost certain to be followed by organizations of Universalism and Unitarianism. Not so in the days of our fathers.

A BIOGRAPHICAL SKETCH

OF THE

REV. JAMES FINLEY.

NINETY years ago, the country between the Laurel Hill, where it was crossed by the road first made for General Forbes' army, and the Monongahela, was an almost unbroken forest. To the eye of the traveller, descending the mountain, there would appear, at remote points, indications of the hand of civilized man, by the deadened timber, and occasionally by the rising of smoke. Two such travellers—one a short, ruddy man, in black clothes, apparently about forty years of age; the other considerably older and stouter—might be seen, at that time, wending their way down the mountain. They would look wearied and jaded—for they had now travelled near 200 miles, and had slept on the bare ground the last two or three nights. For no human habitation had they seen since they entered, some 70 miles back, the great Appalachian chain of mountains. They are near the end of their journey now, and have felt the thrilling power of the landscape, stretching, in all directions, far towards the west, without a single mountain to intercept the range of their vision. But they have some 15 or 20 miles yet to travel before the sunset; and they have no time to stop long, and indulge themselves in a rapturous gaze. They must get, perhaps, to within 8 or 10 miles of Fort Burd (Brownsville) that night, if possible. The elder and stouter man is an old Chester

County farmer and fuller of cloth, by the name of Tanner; and he has come out to see "the lands," and select, possibly, a future home for his family and himself. The other fat, nervous, red-faced little man in black, is the Rev. James Finley, the first minister of the gospel, if we except chaplains of armies, who has ever set foot on Western soil.

He, too, designs to keep an eye upon good tracts of land, as suitable homes for his half dozen of promising boys, the oldest of whom is, perhaps, a stout lad of twelve years of age. But far higher and nobler views, if they have not already a place in the thoughts of that father, are soon to take controlling possession of his mind, and to give a new direction to his whole future life. He has already been preaching the gospel for more than fourteen years, with great acceptance and success. He has heard, perhaps, from some of his people, who have already preceded him, touching accounts of the moral wastes, and yet of the rising prospects of this western Canaan. He is, in the divine purpose, soon to be one of the noble pioneers of the gospel, in the frontier settlements; here to live and toil, and weep and rejoice, through the last twelve years of his pilgrimage; and then to hear from his Master the welcome discharge, "well done, good and faithful servant." His noble brother, the Rev. Dr. Samuel Finley, has not, at this time, (1765,) much more than another year to live, and then to go down into the very floods of Jordan, with the joy of salvation in his heart, and the song of victory on his lips.* But James, ten years younger, after many tossings and trials, through many years to come, will be found laboring as a faithful pastor, at last, in this very field that, for the first time, opened, that morning in June, on his wondering view.

But who was he? The Rev. James Finley was born in the County of Armagh, in the province of Ulster, Ireland, Fe-

* For an account of his triumphant death, see Dr. Mason's Christian's Magazine.

bruary, 1725. To that part of the Old World, the American Presbyterian Church is indebted for the first man whose name heads the lists of her ministers, the immortal Francis M'Kemie. Finley, like M'Kemie, and a host of others, was the son of eminently pious parents, of Scottish descent. With them he crossed the ocean, when he had attained the age of nine years. His education was obtained under the direction of the Rev. Samuel Blair, who was himself an Irishman, but educated at the celebrated "Log College." He was a burning and a shining light—a star of the first magnitude.

When Mr. Smith settled at Fagg's Manor, he took charge, also, of a Classical School. In this institution was James Finley trained to a very accurate scholarship in the languages and sciences. It was the school in which, under the Rev. John Blair, in after years, were educated John M'Millan and James Power. The subject of this paper was, most probably, at this school, when the great revival under Mr. Smith's ministry began, in 1740, and continued a number of years. Of this remarkable work of grace we have an account in Dr. Alexander's "Log College."

Whether Mr. Finley, who could not have been more than 15 years of age at that time, was a subject of this revival, we have not heard. It was no doubt of great advantage to him, however, through all his subsequent life, thus early to have been in the midst of so glorious a work. When we have heard ministers who have been, perhaps, some years in the ministry, confess that they had never witnessed an extensive revival, we could not but feel that it was a serious disadvantage to them. But Mr. Finley enjoyed another peculiar privilege. About this time he travelled in company with Mr. Whitefield for more than two hundred miles, with no other view than to enjoy the benefit of his society and his preaching.

After being licensed, it is supposed, by the New Castle Presbytery, he was by them ordained in 1752, and installed pastor of East Nottingham, now called the Rock. This was six years before the union of the Synods of New York and Philadelphia, which took place in 1758. His elder brother, Samuel Finley, was still the pastor of Nottingham, across the Maryland line, but adjacent to his own charge. These brothers labored in adjoining charges for nine years together; for Dr. Finley was not called to the presidency of Princeton College till 1761.

About eight years after the settlement of James in this place, his pastoral charge was enlarged, perhaps for the purpose of securing a more competent support for a growing family, by uniting Elk with East Nottingham. Here he labored faithfully and successfully till called to another, and perhaps far more important station in the Master's vineyard. In 1777, he had asked his Presbytery to dismiss him; but the opposition of his people, enforced by the presence and tears of several of the congregation who attended the meeting, induced him to acquiesce at that time in the unanimons decision of the Presbytery to refuse his request. Five years afterwards, upon the death of an aged mother-in-law, he conceived that the strongest tie of his family to East Nottingham was broken, and that his way was now clear to renew his application for a dissolution of his pastoral relation. But his Presbytery, in view of the earnest remonstrance which his affectionate people made against his request, again felt constrained to yield to their wishes. His mind, however, was made up; and greatly as this strong proof of attachment given to him by his people, perhaps many of them his spiritual children, must have affected him, and wrung his heart with anguish, he knew that mere sensibilities and tender social affections were not to be his guide as to his duty in this case. He appealed to his Synod, and they dismissed him by their own act. And they, at least by plain implication, directed his Presbytery to dismiss him to the Presbytery of Redstone. This was at a meeting of the Synod of New York and Philadelphia, May 17th, 1782. "The Synod proceeded to consider Mr. Finley's appeal from the judgment of the New

Castle Presbytery. The parties were fully heard, and the Synod, having deliberated on the matter, are of opinion that the pastoral relation between Mr. Finley and his congregation ought to be dissolved, and they do accordingly dissolve it." His dismission to the Presbytery of Redstone was not finally granted until April 26th, 1785.

Before this period, Mr. Finley visited Western Pennsylvania — was at the meeting of the Redstone Presbytery at Pidgeon Creek, March 12th, 1783 — and during that year he removed to the West with his family.* He was at Chartiers, October 19th, 1784, when this minute is found: "The Rev. Mr. James Finley, having been regularly dismissed from his former charge, and accepted a call from the two societies in the forks of Youghiogheny with the approbation of this Presbytery, yet being present and invited, sits as a correspondent." At this meeting, also, he was appointed to supply at various places: by which it appears that he was regarded by the Presbytery as entering regularly upon the duties of his ministry among them. On January 25th, 1785, when the Presbytery met at Rehoboth, he was still invited to sit as a correspondent, and had various supplies assigned to him.

Not until June 21st, 1785, is he actually present with his regular dismission from the Newcastle Presbytery, when it is recorded that, "he having accepted a call in our bounds, applies to be admitted as a member of this Presbytery; and, upon producing sufficient testimonials, and a dismission from that Presbytery, is accordingly received, and takes his seat as a member with us." And this is all we find in the minutes in the case. In truth, he had informally, and with the consent of Presbytery, no doubt, become a pastor of Rehoboth and Roundhill; and so he continued, without any further

* About this time he was appointed an agent for some service, not mentioned, by the Supreme Executive Council of the State, to be performed in Western Pennsylvania. His subsequent report to the Council was satisfactory.—See "Col. Records," Vol. XIII., p. 481.

action of Presbytery. As Dr. Hill expressed it, "we were not very strict in observing church rules in those days."

Previous to his dismission from East Nottingham, he had made several visits to the western country. The first one we have already noticed. Between that time and his request to be dismissed from his pastoral charge, he was thrice across the mountains: first, in 1767, and next, in 1771; when he came, by appointment of the Synod of New York and Philadelphia, to spend two months as a missionary in the West. Of this we have spoken in another place. Again, in 1772, he came over the mountains, bringing with him his son Ebenezer, then a lad of fourteen years of age. Him he placed on a farm he had purchased in Fayette County, in the bounds of Dunlap's Creek congregation.

This son, about three or four years after, had a perilous adventure with the Indians at Fort Wallace. This place is supposed to have been in or near the bounds of Salem Congregation, not far from the Kiskeminetas. Young Finley had gone from Dunlap's Creek on a short tour of militia duty to this then frontier settlement, in place of Samuel Finley, who then lived with him, though not a relative. While this young man was in the fort, tidings were brought by a man on horseback, in breathless haste, that Indians had made their appearance at a little distance; that he had left two men and a woman on foot trying to make their way to the fort; and that, unless immediately rescued or protected, they would be lost. Some eighteen or twenty men, and, along with them, young Finley, started immediately for their rescue. About a mile and a half from the fort, they came unexpectedly upon a considerable force of savages. They were, for a while, in the midst of them. A sharp fire began immediately, and a zig-zag, running fight took place. Our people making their way back towards the fort, numbers of them were shot down or tomahawked. Finley's gun would not "go off." He stopped for a moment to pick his flint, and fell behind. An Indian was seen levelling his gun at him, but was fortunately shot down just at the moment. Being fleet of foot, he soon was abreast with one of his companions; and, in passing round the root of a tree, by a quick motion of his elbow against his companion's shoulder, succeeded in passing him, when, the next moment, this comrade sunk under the stroke of a tomahawk. A Mr. Moor, seeing Finley's imminent danger from a bridge on which he stood, stopped, and by his well-directed fire, again protected him, and enabled him to pass the bridge. At last, after several doublings and turnings, the Indians being sometimes both in the rear and ahead of him, he reached the fort in safety. But the most extraordinary part of this matter remains to be told. Mr. Finley, the father, then at home, east of the mountains, three hundred miles off, had, as he thought, one day, a strange and unaccountable impression that his son was in imminent danger of some kind, but no distinct conception of its nature or cause. He betook himself to intense and agonizing prayer for his son; continued in this exercise for some time; felt at length relieved and comforted, as though the danger was past. It was altogether to himself an extraordinary thing; such as he had never before experienced. He made a note of the time. A few weeks afterwards, he received from his son, upon his return to his father's, an account of his narrow escape from death. The time precisely corresponded with the time of Mr. Finley's strange experience. This is the substance of the statement we have received. Its accuracy, in its most essential features, may be fully relied on. What shall we say of it? Mr. Finley was a man of most scrupulous veracity. We leave the simple statement of the case to the reflections of the reader.

It is said that during the period that intervened from 1765—the time of his first visit to the West—to 1783, the time of his removal, as many as thirty-four families, consisting chiefly of young married persons connected with his congregation, emigrated to Western Pennsylvania, and settled within an area, the extreme boundaries of which were not more than forty miles from each other.

There was one thing somewhat remarkable in the orderings of Divine Providence in this case. These men had wished and fully intended to settle in a cluster, and thus to be near each other with their families. They came out, however, successively, as their convenience allowed, to purchase or enter lands. They were completely thwarted in their plans. No such opportunity of getting near each other was afforded; one was obliged to get a piece of land in Laurel Hill Congregation; another, in Pigeon creek; another, in Chartiers; another in Buffalo or Cross creek, and so on. Thus they became scattered through almost all these young, weak churches, and became the very bone and sinew of them all. They were amongst the choicest and most efficient men, by their eminent piety, and by their generous efforts and contributions in sustaining all our first ministers. Some of them, years afterwards, as they would meet as elders at Presbytery, could not but advert, in conversation with one another, to this remarkable feature in their history. "There is that scattereth abroad and yet increaseth." No wonder Mr. Finley had a peculiarly strong hold on the affections of all his Western brethren.

"The settlement of several of his children in Western Pennsylvania, and the removal of so many of his congregation to that region, excited in Mr. Finley a strong desire to take up his abode with them. He foresaw that all his children would probably remove thither, and he deemed it important that he should be with them. He believed, moreover, that his own usefulness, and the spiritual interests of his family, would be promoted by such a step. He had become familiar with the country, having visited it every second year, from the time of his son's settlement there, until that of his own removal thither. Hence he was led to think it his duty to remove to the West; and not because he felt any dissatisfaction with the people of his charge, or because they did not afford him an adequate and comfortable support." *

While he still resided in East Nottingham, we find, from the Records of the Synod of New York and Philadelphia, (p. 502,) that he dissented from the judgment of the Synod, in a case that bears an exact resemblance in its main features, to the celebrated M'Queen case, that was disposed of by the General Assembly, a few years ago, much in the same way. Mr. Finley's dissent, entered on the records at large, will be found to express the views and sentiments entertained by the commissioners from the Synod of Pittsburg, in the M'Queen case — and will show that Mr. Finley was a conscientious, firm, and fearless man, in thus proclaiming, in the face of the Synod, his own convictions on the subject.

He was a man of eminent piety, and a devoted, excellent pastor. He was much among the people of his charge, visiting and teaching from house to house. He thus rendered himself highly acceptable and useful, and the people of his congregation were strongly attached to him. Of this, his former charge gave strong evidence by their resistance to his removal.

There is one interesting fact that remains to be recorded. Of the 34 families above referred to, who had emigrated from his former charge, 22 of their heads became ruling elders in different churches, at their first organization in Western Pennsylvania. Among these were Judge Allison, Judge M'Dowel, and James Bradford, of Chartiers; Henry Graham, Robert Barr, and James and Samuel Fleming, of Cross creek; John Wright, Robert Moore, and John Powers, of Rehobath; John Allen and Samuel Finley, of Laurel Hill, &c. Of his own sons, Ebenezer was an elder of Dunlap's creek; and Joseph, Michael, and William have long held the same office in Rehobath. Joseph and William still survive, waiting, at a very advanced age, their call to follow departed friends, who

* Appendix to Life of Macurdy.

now inherit the promises. Mr. Finley himself was called home, January 6th, 1795. His last words were exhortations to his children to attend, above all, to the interests of their souls that "were of infinite worth." This expression was the last that passed his lips.*

His attention to the catechetical instruction of the youth of his congregation was remarkable. In his own family, he was no less careful. He had a considerable number of colored people. Their children he sent to the same school with his own. They were alike examined, sabbath evenings, on the subject of the sermons and discourses which they had heard, and were required to recite the shorter catechism along with his own children. All his colored people were uniformly required to attend family worship. In his Will, he took special care to provide for them their future homes and support. He left, also, a small bequest to Jefferson College, for assisting poor and pious youth preparing for the ministry.

Dr. Alexander, in his "Log Cabin," states that "he was reckoned to be eminently pious, and continued laboriously to preach the gospel until an advanced period of life. His latter years were spent in the western part of Pennsylvania, where he died a few years before the close of the last century. The writer remembers to have seen him at a meeting of the Synod of Virginia, in 1789. He was one of the pioneers, who, amidst many hardships and privations, carried the gospel to the settlers round about Pittsburg, and was the companion and coadjutor of such men as M'Millan, Joseph Smith, Power,

* This concern for the spiritual welfare of his children, which he displayed with his dying breath, was illustrated through his whole life by another circumstance of touching interest: it was his custom to devote a special day, along with his wife, to fasting and prayer; some short time after the birth of each of his children, with reference to its conversion and salvation. This, we believe, was the practice with several of our early ministers and their wives. It was the practice also of Mr. Finley's parents, as will be seen in some notices of the Rev. Dr. Samuel Finley, in the Missionary Magazine, Vol. I., p. 336.

Patterson, Dod, Dunlap," &c. "Precious in the sight of the Lord is the death of his saints.'

Note.—In a previous note we have referred to Mr. Finley's appointment by the Supreme Executive Council of the State, in 1783. The following extract from the "Colonial Records," vol. 13th, pp. 481 and 617, will explain this matter:

"Philadelphia, January 16th, 1783.—A letter from John M'Dowell, Esq., of the 3d instant, acquainting the Council that the Rev. Mr. Finley will undertake a journey to the Western frontiers, on the business which Council had requested him to communicate to that gentleman. Ordered that the Secretary write to the Honorable John M'Dowell, and inform him that Council approve of the Rev. Mr. Finley as a very proper person for the said business, and that Council wish to see him before he sets out."

Then, vol. 13th, p. 617:

"Philadelphia, July 1st, 1783.—A letter from the Rev. James Finley, stating his proceedings, under the direction of Council, in the Western Counties of this State, was received, and the Secretary directed to express the approbation of the Board."

There will also be found, in "Colonial Records," vol. 15th, p. 472, the following passage, which, probably, refers to the subject of the foregoing Memoir:

"June 14th, 1788.—A letter from James Finley, of Westmoreland County, requesting Council to accept his resignation of the offices of Justices of the Peace and of the Court of Common Pleas, of the said County, was read; whereupon it was resolved, that the said resignation be accepted."

We have never heard that Mr. Finley acted as Associate Judge of Westmoreland County. But the office might have been tendered to him. One of our ministers, the Rev. Boyd Mercer, was, for many years, an Associate Judge of Washington County.

CHAPTER IX.

THE VIEWS AND PRACTICE OF OUR FATHERS ON PSALMODY.

It may be satisfactory to some of our readers to know what were the principles held, and the practice adopted, during the period of the old Presbytery, on the subject of Psalmody. It has been often said, that Presbyterians of the present day are a very degenerate race on this subject, and have apostatized from the principles held by our early fathers and founders of the western church. What were their views on this subject? As nothing on the subject of Psalmody is recorded in their minutes, can we otherwise ascertain what they believed, and how they felt, on this subject? We certainly think we can. Let it be remembered, then, that they were all members of the Synod of New York and Philadelphia; and, from the period of their ordination, were generally in attendance on its sessions till they removed to the West—and afterwards, most of them in turns. Now, what were the views entertained and expressed by the Synod, and of course by themselves, so far as we can now know? We find no dissent, no protest from any of them, at least, and have a right to infer their acquiescence, if not their cordial concurrence. About eighteen years before the organization of the Presbytery of Redstone, the Synod of New York and Philadelphia, in 1763, recorded the following minute:

"A query was brought in, in these words—'As sundry members and congregations within the bounds of our Synod, judge it most for their edification to sing Dr. Watts' imitation of David's Psalms, does the Synod so far approve said imitation of David's Psalms, as to allow such ministers and their congregations the liberty of using them?' As a great number of this body have never particularly considered Dr. Watts' imitation, they are not prepared to give a full answer to the question; yet, as it is well approved by many of this body, the Synod have no objection to the use of said imitation by such ministers and congregations as incline to use it, until the matter of Psalmody be further considered. And it is recommended to the members of this body to be prepared to give their sentiments respecting this subject at our next meeting."

Now, Mr. Clark and Mr. Finley were members present at that Synod—the two oldest of those who afterwards removed to Western Pennsylvania—and, indeed, the only ones then ordained. But let us go to the next meeting of Synod in 1764.

Here we find this record, (p. 338, Rec.): "The question respecting Psalmody came to be considered; and after much discourse on the subject, the Synod do judge that they are not at present prepared to give a final answer thereto, and that it is most for the edification of the church to defer it to the next Synod. In the meantime, we do confirm the agreement of the last Synod, and allow those congregations who find it most expedient to continue in the use of Dr. Watts' imitation till the matter be further considered and determined."

At the next meeting of Synod, in 1765, we find the following record: "After some consideration of the query concerning the use of Dr. Watts' imitation of the Psalms, the Synod judged it best, in present circumstances, only to declare that they look on the inspired Psalms in Scripture to be proper matter to be sung in divine worship, according to their original design and the practice of Christian churches, yet will not forbid those to use the imitation of them, whose judgment and inclination leads them to do so."

Here are the views of the Synod for three successive years, at that early period. Then eight entire years pass before they say anything further on the subject. The next minute is in 1773. "An appeal was brought in by several members of the second Presbyterian congregation in this city, from a judgment of the first Philadelphia Presbytery, confirming the judgment of the session of the second Presbyterian church, with respect to the introduction of Dr. Watts' imitation of the Psalms into public worship; and, as the moderator was a member of the Presbytery from whose judgment they appealed, he left the chair, and Mr. Joseph Treat took his place. The case was stated, the minutes of the Presbytery read, and the parties fully heard, and withdrew. The Synod, after considering the matter, declare that with respect to the judgment of the Presbytery, although it appears to be drawn up with great caution and tenderness, yet they do not think it proper finally to judge and decide upon it at present, but appoint Dr. Witherspoon, Dr. Rodgers, Mr. Strain, and Mr. M'Whorter, a committee to converse with the parties in the congregation who differ about Psalmody, and report to the Synod to-morrow afternoon."—(P. 447.)

Accordingly we have their report, the whole of which we need not give, but only what is relevant to the point of our enquiry, which is as follows, (p. 449): "As there is not now time to consider fully the different versions of the Psalms in question, and there are minutes of the Synod formerly which countenance congregations in determining this matter according to their own choice, they cannot make any order to forbid the practice now begun. Which, being considered, was approved, and the Synod on this occasion think proper earnestly to recommend to both parties peace and harmony, and to forbear all harsh expressions and sentiments, and, in particular, that neither of them intimate that either of the versions in question is unfit to be sung in Christian worship."

We pass over twelve years more, till 1785, when all the old seven members of the Redstone Presbytery are now also members of the Synod of New York and Philadelphia. At their sessions, that year, "A motion was made in the following terms, viz: Whereas the nearest uniformity that is practicable in the external modes of Divine Worship is to be desired, and the using different books of psalmody is matter of offence, not only to Presbyterians of different denominations, but also to many congregations under our care; it is queried if the Synod might not choose out, and order some of their number to take the assistance of all the versions in our power, and compose for us a version more suitable to our circumstances and tastes than we yet have;" which having been read and seconded, after some consideration thereon, the question was put whether to appoint a committee or to defer, and was carried by a small majority to appoint. Whereupon Dr. Allison, Dr. Davidson, Dr. Ewing, Mr. Blair, and Mr. Jones were appointed a committee for that purpose, who are to make report of their diligence herein at our next meeting." The following year this committee reported "that they had paid attention to the affair, but had not yet completed it." (p. 522.) Next year (1787), "The Synod did allow, and do hereby allow that Dr. Watts' imitation of David's Psalms, as revised by Mr. Barlow, be sung in the churches and families under their care." At the same meeting the Synod adopted the following—"The Synod have allowed the use of the imitation of the Psalms of David for many years, to such congregations as chose them, and still allow of the same; but they are far from disapproving of Rouse's version, commonly called the Old Psalms, in those who were in the use of them and chose them, but are of opinion that either may be used by the churches, as each congregation may judge most for their peace and edification; and therefore highly disapprove of public, severe, and unchristian censures being passed upon either of the systems of psalmody, and recommend it to all ministers in those parts of the church, to be more tender and charitable on these heads." This was their language, in reference to the Presbytery of Abingdon, where troubles at that time existed. We believe it very precisely expresses the views of the members of the Old Presbytery of Redstone. At that meeting,

Messrs. Finley, M'Millan, Power, and Barr, of this Presbytery, were present, and we have no doubt voted for its adoption. In the next, and last year of the meeting of that old Synod (in 1788), we find nothing on their minutes. But it was then that all the parts of our old Confession of Faith were finally considered, adopted and ratified. And in the Directory for worship which they then approved and adopted, the first sentence of Chapter IV., (of singing of Psalms,) is, "It is the duty of Christians to praise God, by singing psalms or hymns, publicly in the church, and also privately in the family." Now this Directory, the Presbytery of Redstone did virtually if not explicitly, approve and adopt. From the review which we have now given of the action of the Synod of New York and Philadelphia, through a period of twenty-five years, can there be any doubt about the views of our fathers on the subject of Psalmody? But what was their practice? In their own families, we believe, they used Watts' Psalms and Hymns generally. But in their congregations, they wisely acted in conformity with the sentiments last quoted from the records of the Synod. Where the way was clear, and not likely to distract or divide the people, Watts' version and hymns were introduced. When it was otherwise, Rouse's version continued in use. Perhaps in a majority of cases, for the sake of peace, this was the case, till some time after that old Presbytery ceased to exist. In some places, a compromise was adopted. They would begin with an old psalm, and conclude with a psalm from Watts' version, or with a hymn. This was a favorite method in several of the churches. But though Dr. Power used Watts in his family, he yielded to the preferences of his people in the use of Rouse in public worship. The lines were "given out" by a precentor, or clerk as he was called. Dr. Power's clerk used to give out one line at a time, and always, in so doing, sounded the last syllable on a dead level with the first note of that part of the tune, prolonging the sound a little, so as to slide gracefully and imperceptibly into the singing. To a stranger, the effect was rather ludicrous. But he was considered a great master of his business, especially by the older people. But we trust they have all gone where they sing the song of Moses and the Lamb.

In Mr. Dod's congregation on Ten-mile, a New Testament psalmody was always used. These emigrants from New Jersey had been accustomed to sing no other in their native state. Mr. Dod was often congratulated by his brethren, especially by Mr. Smith, on account of his release from any trouble on that score. It seems probable that though in Buffalo and Cross creek, Rouse's version was used, either wholly, or in part, on the Sabbath day—Watts' Psalms and Hymns were used at their prayer meeting. For there is a tradition that at one of these meetings, Mr. Porter was greatly troubled upon hearing them sing with great animation —"Let those refuse to sing who never knew our God," &c., and was constrained to join with them in that service; remarking afterwards, that when he heard those words, he said to himself, "If my conscience won't let me sing, I'll wring its neck."

Though we hope that our church will "stand fast in the liberty, wherewith Christ has set them free," and will always in their singing, as in their prayers and preaching, confess that "Jesus is the Christ"—an essential element of Christian faith—we would, nevertheless, be glad that our Board of Publication would not only publish the Old Version, as we believe they have done, but an edition of our Assembly's Book of Psalms and Hymns with a larger variety of the old psalms; either separately or mingled with the others.

It ought not to be forgotten or overlooked, that the introduction of a New Testament Psalmody, the necessary exercise of church discipline, and the faithful, and searching, and scorching preaching of our early ministers were the three causes, sometimes separate, and sometimes combined—of driving many from the pale of our communion and of strengthening other branches of the Presbyterian family. The

Covenanters, Seceders, and Associate Reformed, received considerable recruits from our ranks in this way—especially the two latter. However they may "squirm" under the statement, and question its truth, it is capable of perfect demonstration! But we mean nothing unkind in the statement. In earlier times great deadness and formality prevailed in some of their churches, but not greater, perhaps, than is now found in some Presbyterian churches. Even gross clerical irregularities were tolerated. Some of these bodies violently opposed the revivals of religion which at different times prevailed in the Presbyterian churches. They were all ready to receive, with open arms, those who found revival scenes too warm for their consciences.

That there has been a great improvement in vital piety in all these churches, we firmly believe. No longer now would an elder lead off the dance in a social party. A half-intoxicated minister would not now be suffered to preach. It was better for our renegades, at least for their families, that they should get into these churches—than into Unitarian or Universalist societies. In this respect, we had the advantage of our New England churches.

A BIOGRAPHICAL SKETCH

OF THE

REV. JOHN CLARK.

WHEN we advert to the times of the founders and fathers of our Western Zion, and endeavor, in imagination, to look in upon them, when met together to consult about the interests of the church, we are apt to fancy we see a group of venerable gray-haired men sitting together, and engaged in their Presbyterial business. We are mistaken. Five of them are just in the early prime of manhood. Yet two of them begin to wear the marks of age. One of them, however, being of a fresh, ruddy complexion, does not appear to be over forty-five, though he is near, if not quite, sixty years of age. This is Mr. Finley. But there is another older than he, wearing a large white wig—the only wigged clergyman we ever had.* He has come out to the West, in his sixty-fourth year, to spend his old age amidst the hardships and trying scenes, for which the vigor of youth would be better adapted. But he has fourteen years yet to live, and they are not to be spent in "otio cum dignitate," but with the harness on, and in arduous labors in his Master's service, to the very verge of life. Such a man claims a respectful notice.

* This peruke, or big white wig, excited some prejudice against Mr Clark. The Rev. Dr. Wylie will be reminded of his feelings in the case, when he reads in the Life of Dr. Alexander, p. 97, how Dr. Green's wig, in 1791, excited the prejudices of the then youthful Alexander.

The Rev. John Clark was born in the year 1718, and the place of his nativity, though not certainly known, is supposed to be somewhere in the State of New Jersey. The place of his first labors was in the Forks of Delaware. In a brief history of the Churches of Allentown and Tehicken, it is said, that, on the 13th of October, 1762, he was installed as the second pastor of those Churches. It is farther said, that he graduated at Nassau Hall, Princeton, in the year 1759, and was taken under the care of the Presbytery of New Brunswick, November 30th, 1759. And when licensed by them, on the 9th of May, 1760, was sent to supply the Churches of Tehicken, Allentown and Upper Mount Bethel. It is worthy of notice, that the time which elapsed between his graduation and licensure, if the history be correct, was very short; and, in view of it, we would be led to suppose that he either must have prosecuted his theological studies, to some extent, prior to his graduation, or that the necessities of the Church must have been very urgent, to warrant so short a course of preparatory study."

It is possible that the true solution of the matter is, that it was done by the New Brunswick Presbytery, which, though now in good standing in the Synod of New York and Philadelphia, had been long chargeable with such irregularities, and at an earlier period had, for these and other alleged offences, been excluded from the Synod. This was prior to the disruption of the Synod, in 1745. It is not unlikely they still continued somewhat lax, in their notions and practice, on this subject.

"In the following October, a call from these Churches was presented to him; and he took the matter into serious consideration. No further mention is made of this call; but it is stated that the Presbytery, believing that it would be of great service to the Church, and the interests of religion, ordained him as an evangelist, at Bethlehem, New Jersey, April 29th, 1761, and directed him to supply the Churches of Oxford, New Jersey, and Smithfield, on the Forks of the Delaware, in Pennsylvania. On the 28th of May following, he was dismissed from the Presbytery of New Brunswick, and joined the Presbytery of Philadelphia on the 12th of August, 1761. At that time he received a call to the Forks, but did not accept it until the next meeting of Presbytery, on the 17th of November following. At this time opposition to his settlement was made, and the dissatisfied party was heard at the bar of the Presbytery. The special ground of objection is not stated, and we are left in the dark, or to idle conjecture, as to its nature. The commissioners were then asked if they could support him without the aid of the dissentient party, and their reply was in the affirmative. Whereupon liberty was granted them to prosecute their call, and Mr. Clark was installed October 13th, 1762, over the two congregations of the Forks, with a salary of £80 per annum, and the use of a parsonage.

"After some time troubles occurred, which were brought before the Presbytery October 22d, 1766, and the advice given, that the matter be dropped. Here, again, the special grounds of grievance are not stated, further than a general charge of misrepresentation. It seems probable that some leaven of dissatisfaction had been working in the breasts of some during the whole period of his labors there."

Perhaps it may be traced to his earlier theological training, and his inadequate preparation. For however successfully a minister may eventually repair such deficiencies, they are apt to bring him into trouble during the younger part of his ministry.

"Mr. Clark then gave reasons why he wished to be released from the pastoral care of Upper Mount Bethel, inasmuch as eighteen persons were found united against him in the general charge already mentioned. The Presbytery pronounced the paper disorderly, and refused to release him. In the following April, some of the signers of this paper renewed their charge against him, and asked Presbytery to have Mr. Clark tried at their bar. The Presbytery refused their request on the ground that no sufficient reason appeared for such a course. But to heal, if possible, the difficulties, the Rev. Mr. Beatty and Mr. Ramsay were sent as a committee to bring the parties together, and promote peace. Of the success of this committee in the matter referred to them, we know nothing. It has been related, by a late writer, as an historical incident, that the only Indian massacres of which there is any tradition, occurred in that congregation during the time that Mr. Clark was pastor. It may be remarked, that a writer in the Presbyterian of July, 1847, states, 'Of the Rev. John Clark, no tradition now exists in the settlement—a very few aged persons remain who were baptized in infancy by Mr. Clark.'

"On account of bodily weakness, Mr. Clark resigned the pastoral charge of these churches Nov. 3d, 1767, and went, soon after, to labor, as he was able, within the bounds of the Presbytery of Newcastle. On the 27th of December, 1769, he was called to be the pastor of Bethel Church, in Upper Node Forest, Baltimore County. Here he remained a few years. But transition seems to have been his lot; for in 1775, the pastoral relation was again dissolved. He remained at Bethel as a stated supply till 1781, when he removed to the West. In this year he became a supply, and, shortly after, the pastor, of the United Congregations of Bethel and Lebanon, at that time under the care of the Presbytery of Redstone. Of the amount of support promised him, the character of his ministrations, his acceptability to the people, and success in his work, in these congregations, we have comparatively but little information. It is generally known, to those advanced in life, that at the era of his settlement here he was past the meridian of life, and of very feeble health; but in appearance, grave, sedate, and venerable; and as a preacher, solemn and impressive. He died July 13th, 1797. What has been called the 'Whiskey Insurrection,' occurred, in part, in the bounds of his congregations; and when the attack was about to be made on General Neville's house by five hundred of the insurgents, he, as a man of God, besought them to desist, but in vain."

Mr. Findley, in his "History of the Insurrection," giving an account of the meeting held at Couche's Fort, in the Mingo Creek settlement, states (page 85), "While they were deliberating what was best to be done, the Rev. Mr. Clark, a venerable and very old clergyman, expostulated with them on the impropriety of the enterprise, and used his utmost endeavours to dissuade them from it." Again the same historian, in a conference held with the President on the part of David Redick and himself, who were sent for this purpose, states (page 182), "We mentioned, as another ground of our confidence, the industry of the clergy in promoting submission to the laws, and stated several instances of it," &c. There can be no doubt he alludes in part, though he does not expressly mention it, to the course pursued by Mr. Clark. There was an extensive revival of religion, under his ministry, in the year 1787, of which some notice is taken in the "Western Missionary Magazine," for September, 1803.* The foregoing account of Mr. Clark, the Nestor of the Presbytery of Redstone, is taken mainly from a sermon preached in Bethel Church by the Reverend George Marshall, the present pastor, and afterwards published.

The following brief account of the only remaining one of those seven men who, for a number of years, composed the clerical members of the Old Redstone Presbytery, is taken from Dr. Elliot's Appendix to the "Life of Macurdy:"

"The Rev. James Dunlap, D.D., was a native of Chester County, Pennsylvania, and was graduated at the College of New Jersey in 1773. He studied divinity with the Rev.

* It is said that the singing in Mr. Clark's meetings was unusually good; owing, greatly, to the uncommon vocal powers of a pious colored woman belonging to Mr. C. Her voice, which was very sweet and melodious, could be heard above the voices of all the congregation. He had also a colored man, Dave, whose bass alone was sufficient for a large congregation.

James Finley, of East Nottingham, and was licensed to preach the gospel by the Presbytery of Donegal, some time between 1776 and 1781. (Printed Records, p. 491.) He was ordained, *sine titulo*, by the Presbytery of Newcastle, August 21st, 1781, at Fagg's Manor, and shortly afterwards removed to Western Pennsylvania, where he became a member of the Presbytery of Redstone, and settled in the congregations of Laurel Hill and Dunlap's Creek; of which he was installed the pastor, October 15th, 1782." This statement is probably founded on the following minute in the Records of the Presbytery at Dunlap's Creek, October 25th, 1782: "The Rev. James Dunlap, formerly a member of the Newcastle Presbytery, having accepted a call in our bounds, now applies to be admitted as a member of this Presbytery; and upon producing sufficient testimonials, and a dismission from that Presbytery, is accordingly received, and takes his seat as a member of this." As to his installation, there is no account of it whatever, either then or afterwards. This was the case as to all the others. A formal installation in the congregation, and a charge to the people, were matters of a much later date. "The connection with the latter congregation was dissolved April 22d, 1789; and with the former, June 29th, 1803; when he was dismissed to connect himself with the Presbytery of Ohio. It was in this year (1803), that he became the President of Jefferson College, Canonsburg; which station he held until 1811. During that period (A. D. 1807), the Board of Trustees conferred on him the degree of D.D. In connection with his labors in the college, he preached to the congregation of Miller's Run, and finally resigned his charge of it, on account of growing infirmities and inability to discharge to them the duties of a pastor. In October, 1813, he again became a member of the Presbytery of Redstone, having removed within their bounds; and in October, 1816, was dismissed to connect himself with the Presbytery of Philadelphia. About the same time, he removed to Abingdon, near Philadelphia, where his son, the

Rev. William Dunlap, resided, and where he died, November 22d, 1818, in the seventy-fifth year of his age. He is represented to have been a very pious man, and a fine scholar.* He was especially distinguished for his accurate attainments in classical literature." He seemed to have the classics completely in his memory; for he could hear long recitations in Virgil, Homer, &c., without a book in his hand, and then thoroughly drill the reciting class; asking all the questions as to words, sentences, &c., while walking to and fro, with his hands behind his back—his usual position on such occasions. "His eldest daughter was married to the Rev. Stephen Boyer, of the Presbytery of Newcastle."

This is, indeed, rather a meagre account of this excellent man, who was so long associated with his brethren in the Redstone Presbytery, and shared with them largely in their trials and conflicts; and who for many years presided over Jefferson College, and aided in training a vast number of valuable men in all the various walks of professional life. But our want of materials for minuter details must plead our apology.

* Soon after his settlement in Dunlap's Creek, at the close of the forenoon service, one Sabbath, after announcing a second service, with the usual intermission, and after pronouncing the benediction, he withdrew, and, in a state of despondency and dejection, retired, unobserved, to his own house, some half-mile or more off; whither some of the elders traced him, and, with much persuasion, succeeded in bringing him back; when he preached with considerable liberty.

As to his eminent scholarship, tradition relates that a very difficult passage in one of the Latin or Greek classics had passed round among some half-dozen or more of American colleges, without meeting with any one who could satisfactorily explain it, or render it into our language, when Dr. Dunlap took it up, and very promptly disposed of it to the entire satisfaction of all who were capable of judging in the matter.

CHAPTER X.

EARLY TROUBLES OF OUR MINISTERS AND PEOPLE, ABOUT THE STATE BOUNDARIES.

The controversy between Pennsylvania and Virginia, about their boundary line had, indeed, commenced as early as 1752. But it did not assume a threatening aspect, till during the few years immediately previous to the American Revolution. Virginia relied upon a charter granted by James the First, which was broad enough in its terms to cover nearly one half of this continent — although the company to which it was made, had been dissolved by a judgment on a writ of Quo Warranto, and although the lands had reverted to the crown. Pennsylvania, or rather the Penns, claimed under a charter from Charles the Second, in 1681, which assigns the Delaware river as the eastern boundary, and then says, "said lands to extend westward five degrees in longitude, to be computed from the said eastern bounds." Under this charter, the Penns contended that Pennsylvania extended several miles west of Fort Pitt; while on the other hand, it was contended that Virginia embraced not only Pittsburg, but all the country east of it, to the Laurel Hill. As the period of the Revolution approached, the dispute became more violent. Lord Dunmore, governor of Virginia, would listen to no terms of compromise, though the commissioners of Pennsylvania even offered to make the Monongahela the boundary line. Fort Pitt, and almost the entire country now embraced by Alleghany, Westmoreland, Green, and Fayette counties, were under the control of Virginia officers, civil and military. Colonel Connolly, a man thoroughly devoted to Lord Dunmore and his views, then ruled it with a high hand at Fort Pitt. In a letter from Æneas Mackay to Governor Penn, written at this time, we find this strong and emphatic language: "The deplorable state of affairs in this part of your government is truly distressing. We are robbed, insulted, and dragooned by Connolly and his militia, in this place and its environs." So far was this matter carried, that a party of armed men under command of Connolly, went to Hanna's-town, and released two prisoners, confined in the jail under execution; and a few months after, another party repeated the act, releasing three prisoners. Three of the magistrates also of Pennsylvania were arrested and held in custody for performing the duties of their office. The continued collisions and disorders at Pittsburg and throughout Western Pennsylvania, could not fail to attract the attention of all the patriotic citizens of the two states—and on the 25th of July, 1775, the delegates in Congress, including among others, Thomas Jefferson, Patrick Henry, and Benjamin Franklin, united in a circular, urging the people in the disputed region, to mutual forbearance. In that circular was the following language: "We recommend it to you, that all bodies of armed men, kept up by either party, be dismissed; and that all those on either side, who are in confinement, or on bail, for taking part in the contest, be discharged." As there were no armed men maintained by the Pennsylvanians, the expression "either party" was probably only used to avoid any invidious distinction.

The war of the Revolution for a considerable period suspended the excitement and the dispute, and though a military officer, Captain John Neville, came out with a small force and occupied Fort Pitt under the authority of the government of Virginia—he appears to have been a prudent man and soon allayed the jealousies which his presence at first excited. It seems to have been gradually understood on both sides, that it was wiser for them to defer, till a more auspicious period, the settlement of the boundary line, and to unite all their zeal and energies in the common cause of their country, to whose interests they were alike devoted. It would not be easy indeed to determine which party were the warmest whigs, or which expended most, in sufferings and blood, for the cause of American Independence. That cause once secured, it was their interest and their desire, that all further trouble about disputed territory, and conflicting jurisdictions should be brought to a peaceful issue. Under the kinder feelings, produced by united resistance to Great Britain, movements were made as early as 1779, to bring the question to an amicable settlement. For this purpose, George Bryan, the Rev. Dr. John Ewing, and David Rittenhouse on the part of Pennsylvania; and Dr. James Madison, late Bishop of the Protestant Episcopal church in Virginia, and Robert Andrews, on the part of Virginia, were appointed commissioners to agree upon a boundary. These gentlemen met at Baltimore, on the 31st of August, 1779, and entered into a preliminary agreement to run the southern boundary, from the river Delaware along Mason and Dixon's line—the old line between Pennsylvania and Maryland—five degrees west; and thence by a meridian line from the extremity of this line (Mason and Dixon's, extended), to the northern limit of the state—to be the western boundary of Pennsylvanian forever. The legislatures of the two states concurred in this; and nothing was left but the actual drawing of the line—which was done in 1784, by the commissioners. Thus forever was settled this long dispute, giving to Pennsylvania what perhaps few of the people interested expected, not only Pittsburg and its environs and all Alleghany and Westmoreland counties—but all Washington, Fayette, and Green counties. It seems a pity now, that what is called the Panhandle of Virginia, including at least Hancock and Brook counties, could not have been included. But this was out of the questiom. The Virginians, no doubt, thought they had much the hardest of the bargain, as it was.

But while this contest lasted, it contributed much to distract our people, and to turn away their minds from their spiritual interests. Yet we cannot doubt that one indirect advantage flowed from this conflict for the West, between the two States. They both contributed more cheerfully to aid in protecting it against the French and Indians, and afterwards against the British. We doubt whether either of the governments would have done as much for this country, had the line been early settled. Again, it brought out two streams of emigration from these States, and filled up the country much sooner with a thriving population, and promoted, more rapidly, the progress of converting the western wilderness into thriving farms, and, at length, into happy homes. "Per damna, per caedes, ab ipso, ducit opes, animumque ferro."—*Horace.*

CHAPTER XI.

OTHER EVANGELICAL BODIES IN THE WEST.

THE historical sketch we have attempted, of the early efforts of our Church to spread the gospel through what, at length, became the field of the Redstone Presbytery, has not been given with a view of making an impression, that Presbyterians monopolized this work of faith and labor of love.

The Seceders early began their efforts to organize Churches in Washington County, and to supply them with the stated ministrations of the gospel. At a very early period, a distinguished minister of that denomination, Mr. Henderson, was settled near Canonsburg.* The Rev. John Anderson, of

* "The Rev. Matthew Henderson was the first minister of the Associate Church settled west of the Allegheny mountains, where he was settled a number of years previous to the Union of 1782."

"A strong current of emigration had already set in from the Eastern to the Western parts of Pennsylvania. Many who understood and were attached to the principles of the Associate Church, were amoug the emi-

King's Creek, who had received his theological training, in part, from the celebrated John Brown, of Haddington, was one of their first ministers. We have not access to any work, however, that would enable us to extend this notice of that respectable branch of the Presbyterian family, in their first efforts among the frontier settlers.

The Baptists were early in the field, also, and labored with diligence and zeal, and great success, especially in what is now Fayette County. The Redstone Association, Mr. Benedict, their historian, supposes, was organized in 1776.

"One of the oldest Churches was gathered in 1770, under the ministry of Elder John Sutton. It was, at first, called Great Bethel—now Uniontown, in the County of Fayette. This Church was the mother of many others which arose around it. Mr. Sutton was a native of New Jersey, and was one of five brothers who were Baptist preachers. Two of them removed to this country with him. He settled in the Redstone country when it was in a wilderness state, and was long a laborious and much respected preacher, throughout an extensive circle of Churches, which were planted, either wholly or in part, by his means. The time of his death is not known, but it is believed to have been not far from 1800.

"Cotemporary with this evangelical servant of God was the pious and successful John Corbley, who was made to drink deeply of the cup of affliction, (by the massacre of his wife by the savages, on a Sabbath morning, as they were going on foot to the place of worship—of which see a thrilling account in Day's Hist. Coll. of Penn.*) This distinguished man was a native of England, where he was born in 1733—came to this country in very early life—paid for his passage by four years' service in Pennsylvania—became a Baptist preacher in

---

grants. These carried their profession with them, and wherever they settled, they generally formed the beginning of a congregation. These congregations were rapidly multiplied in the Western part of Pennsylvania."—*Miller's "Sketches and Sermons," p.* 80.

* See, also, our Sketch of the Life of Mr. Dod.

Virginia, where he suffered maltreatment and imprisonment, in the times of persecution in the Old Dominion—settled in Western Pennsylvania, in 1768, and became the coadjutor of Sutton, and others, in planting tho first Churches of our order in that region.

"For half a century, or more, the Old Redstone Association was regarded as a very important institution in the whole Baptist connection, and embraced the talent and enterprize of our Society, in this great field of labor."—*Benedict's Hist. of Bap.*

We have no means of ascertaining at what time and where the Methodists began their itinerating labors; but have reason to believe it was not much, if at all, before the beginning of the present century, or at least, till after the period of the Old Redstone Presbytery.

RECORDS OF THE PRESBYTERY OF REDSTONE.

In placing before the reader the minutes of the Presbytery during its earlier history, we hope that we will not merely gratify curiosity, but furnish additional materials for a monument to the honor and praise of our fathers. Our original plan was to publish these Records entire, and we had carefully twice transcribed them for this purpose — employing a system of abbreviations, in order to condense the whole into a reasonable space. But we have since concluded to drop out of our transcript all those portions of the Records that are only used as necessary forms in such cases; as, for instance — "Presbytery adjourned to meet to-morrow morning at 9 o'clock — concluded with prayer." "Presbytery met according to adjournment — ordered to read the minutes of the last meeting," &c., &c. We have also drawn our pen across all statements about congregational settlements — and about supplies — about leave of absence — reasons sustained for late attendance — or non-attendance, or non-compliance with appointments, &c. These, especially the first two items, form a considerable mass of the minutes. We have also, after a few of the earlier meetings of the Presbytery, deemed it unnecessary to give the names of the ministers and elders present, and of the absentees. With these exceptions, and with some abbreviated forms of expression respecting candidates and their exercises for trial, we have given the entire minutes. To many it may seem that we should have gone further, and left out much more. But we cannot doubt that, to many others, much satisfaction will be afforded by the perusal of such portions of the Records as may appear of little intrinsic value. They will sometimes serve to illustrate the times to which they belong, and, in some cases, will prove abundantly suggestive. We have spent much time and pains in preparing the notes, which we hope will be found to contain some agreeable variety, if not information. The Biographical Sketches, which form a part of these notes, will give a novel character to this part of our work; and should this feature of the "Records" meet with acceptance, it is not improbable that a Work of a similar character, bringing down this kind of Ecclesiastical history more nearly to our times, will be attempted. There are materials at hand for a continuation of this part of our Work. Indeed, we apprehend that some disappointment will arise from the absence, in this Work, of any account of several of our old churches, and of many fathers and brethren whose memory will long be cherished in the West. We have meant no invidious distinction by their exclusion, and can only plead that the plan of our volume did not seem to open a door for their admission.

In the records now published, after striking out as above described, we have thought it unnecessary to notice the successive days of each meeting of the Presbytery. The reader will, of course, understand that even the brief statements of their transactions, as now condensed, often belong to successive days.

Lith. of P.S. Duval & Co. Phila.

SACRAMENTAL SCENE IN A WESTERN FOREST.

RECORDS

OF THE

PRESBYTERY OF REDSTONE.

FROM ITS ORGANIZATION, SEPTEMBER 19TH, 1781, TILL ITS DIVISION, OCTOBER 18TH, 1793.

"AT a meeting of the Synod of New York and Philadelphia, held on the 16th of May, 1781, the Rev. Messrs. Joseph Smith, John M'Millan, James Power, and Thaddeus Dod, having requested to be erected into a separate Presbytery, to be known by the name of the Presbytery of Redstone,(1)

(1) REDSTONE.—This name was given to the Presbytery by the Synod, at the suggestion, no doubt, of the ministers who sought this organization; not because the term, in its stricter sense, denoted either the region of country where the first churches were organized, or the most central part of the Pesbytery—for that was farther west,—but because the expression "Redstone Settlement," then, and for many years afterwards, was employed to denote most of the country, whether claimed by Pennsylvania or Virginia, which lay west of the mountains. It derived its origin from the name of a creek which enters the Monongahela below Brownsville. This place was long known by the name of "Redstone Old Fort."

"The hills around abounded with bituminous coal; and along the water-courses, where the earth had been washed off, the coal was left exposed. The inflammability of that mineral must have been known to the inhabitants at that early period; for, where those exposures happened, fire had been communicated, and an ignition of the coal taken place: and probably continued to burn until the compactness, and so-the Synod grant their request, and appoint their first meeting to be held at Laurel Hill, the third Wednesday of September next, at 11 o'clock, A. M."

FIRST MEETING.

Wednesday, Sept. 19th, 1781.(2)—The Presbytery, according to appointment of the Rev. Synod of New York and Philadelphia, met at Pigeon Creek,(3) as the circumstances

---

lidity of the body, and want of air, caused its extinguishment. These fires, in their course, came in contact with the surrounding earth and stone, and gave them a *red* appearance; indeed, so completely burned were they, that when pulverised, they have been substituted in painting for Spanish brown. Many of the *Red Banks* are now visible; the most prominent one, perhaps, is that near the junction of a creek with the Monongahela river, a short distance below the fortification, and which bears the name of *Redstone*—doubtless from the *red* appearance of the bank near its mouth."—Am. Pioneer, Vol. II., p. 55.

Our State geologist, in his third Annual Report on the Geological Survey of the State of Pennsylania, p. 97, gives a different account of the origin of the ignition of coal banks. "In many places," says he, "the coal of the roofs has been precipitated by a slipping of the hillside upon the lower part of the seam, in which case the latter has often taken fire from the heat evolved by the chemical decomposition. This has occurred particularly at the mouth of Redstone Creek, in Fayette County, where the overlaying slate has been baked and *reddened* by the combustion."

(2) The first meeting of the Redstone Presbytery was just one month before the surrender of Cornwallis at Yorktown. This important event, which was soon followed by a treaty of peace with Great Britain, and the final establishment of the independence of the United States, did not, as might have been expected, bring immediate peace and quiet to the western borders—as will appear from the minutes of the Presbytery presently.

(3) PIGEON CREEK.—This congregation, one of the oldest in Washington County, in union with Chartiers, gave a call to the Rev. John M'Millan, at a meeting of the Donegal Presbytery, April 23d, 1776, at which time he was ordained with a view to his settlement among them as their pastor—though he was never formally installed. Whether this congregation was organised previous to this time is uncertain. Dr. M'Millan, in his journal, speaks of his ordaining elders, baptizing chil-

of some of the members, by reason of the incursions of the savages, rendered it impracticable for them to attend at Laurel Hill. Ubi post preces sederunt, the Rev. Messrs. John M'Millan, James Power, and Thaddeus Dod. Elders—John Neil, Demas Lindley, and Patrick Scott. Absent—the Rev. Joseph Smith. The Presbytery was opened by Mr. Dod, with a sermon from Job xlii. 56. The Presbytery then proceeded to the choice of Moderator and Clerk; whereupon, Mr. M'Millan was chosen Moderator, and Mr. Power Clerk, for the ensuing year. Application was made in behalf of Muddy Creek and the South Fork of Ten Mile, in conjunction, for supplies; and also for liberty to apply to the Presbytery of Donegal. Adjourned to meet to-morrow morning. Concluded with prayer.

---

dren, &c., among them, soon after he was ordained; but not expressly of his organizing the church. As he received "a call" from the two churches, they must have been previously organized, unless the term "call" be taken in a looser sense.

In this church, which then covered a very wide field, were, from the first, some eminently pious people who had emigrated from Nottingham, Chester County; and here the Spirit of God was remarkably poured out several times during Dr. M'Millan's ministry among them, which continued till near the close of the last century. For a short time, the Rev. Boyd Mercer labored among them. He was succeeded by the Rev. Andrew Gwin, who was ordained and installed pastor of Pigeon Creek and Pike Run in 1800; he continued their pastor till October 7th, 1819. For some subsequent years, the Rev. Andrew Wylie, D. D., acted as stated supply; but the precise times when this relation began and ended are not known. On April 17th, 1832, the Rev. Wm. C. Anderson, D. D., was installed pastor of this church. Upon his resignation after a few years (July 15th, 1836,) he was succeeded by the Rev. E. S. Graham, who continued the pastor until his death in 1844. He was succeeded by the Rev. James Sloan, the present pastor, December, 1844. Number of communicants in 1854—370. This congregation has enjoyed many revivals of religion, and is still one of the strongest and most flourishing churches in our connection. It has passed through many severe trials from its earliest days. The old Presbytery of Redstone met here oftener than anywhere else; and here, by the remarkable orderings of Divine Providence, they held their *first meeting*.

Thursday, Sept. 20th.—The Presbytery met, according to adjournment. Ubi post preces sederunt qui supra, except Mr. Neil. Ordered, that the minutes of the last session be now read. The appointment for supplies deferred till our next meeting. Adjourned to meet at Mount Pleasant the first Wednesday of November, at 12 o'clock. Concluded with prayer.

MOUNT PLEASANT, Wednesday, the 7th of November, 1781.—A sufficient number of members not attending to form a Presbytery — by those who did meet, agreed to appoint a meeting at Sewickly, on the second Tuesday of April next.

SEWICKLY, Friday, 9th of April, 1782. (4) — A sufficient

---

(4) The years 1781 and 1782, were years of great trial and hardship to our fathers on account of the inroads of the Indians. "The summer of 1782," says a writer quoted in Day's Historical collections, p. 683, "was a sorrowful one to the frontier inhabitants. The blood of many a family had sprinkled their own fields." About a month before the second unavailing attempt to hold a meeting of Presbytery at Sewickly, occurred the dreadful and diabolical massacre of the Christian Indians at the Moravian settlement on the Muskingum. "Here, while peaceably gathering their corn, without any provocation, and without the least resistance, more than ninety of these unoffending creatures were barbarously and deliberately murdered; not by hostile Indians, but by more than savage white men, under the command of Colonel Williamson." — History of Western Pennsylvania, p. 204. One writer has stated a circumstance, which, if true, explains, but does not justify, the outrageous conduct of our people at the Moravian towns. Articles of clothing, known to have belonged to white females murdered by the savages, were found in possession of these Moravian Indians; and, though they protested their innocence of any participation in the murder, and attempted to explain how they became possessed of these clothes, it was altogether unavailing; and the authority of the officers to exercise any control over our men was completely set aside; and, as if a spark had been thrown on gunpowder, indiscriminate murder was the consequence. This dreadful occurrence raised to a fearful pitch of exasperation the hostile spirit of the savages. Then, in two months, followed Crawford's expedition, signal defeat, and terrible death. "The massacre of the Moravian Indians was the prelude to other scenes of blood and attending calamities. Immediately after the return of the expedition to the Moravian villages, another campaign was planned,

number of members not attending, by reason of the incursions of the savages, to form a Presbytery, those who did meet, agreed to appoint a meeting at Dunlap's Creek the third Tuesday of October.

SECOND MEETING.

DUNLAP'S CREEK,(5) October 25th, 1782.—The Presbytery met, according to adjournment. Ubi, post preces, sederunt, the Rev. Messrs. Joseph Smith, John M'Millan, and James

---

and the command given to Colonels Williamson and Crawford. These officers, with their men, penetrated the Indian country to the wilds of Sandusky; where they were met, and utterly defeated, by an Indian force composed of the warriors of the 'Six Nations.' Well do I remember when the dreadful news reached the neighborhood where I resided, near Washington, Pennsylvania. And to illustrate the effects, let me mention that three widows, all residing within two miles of where I then was, and thirteen children, lost their protectors. This may afford evidence of the wide-spread desolation. It was a fearful hour of tears, distraction, and momentary despair. Few families but had to mourn a relative."—William Darby, Esq., in Nat. Int., 1851. Then, in the course of that summer, Hanna's Town was burnt. Frightful murders were committed all round the frontier. No wonder the Presbytery could not meet. The outskirts of every congregation in the Presbytery, unless it might be Chartiers and Dunlap's Creek, were in immediate danger during all this time. We might, perhaps, also have excepted the Forks of Youghiogheny. This Mesopotamian region, from the junction of the Youghiogheny and Monongahela to the Laurel Hill, was remarkably exempt from the Indian raids. The savages coming in on the settlements, either from the Ohio or the Allegheny River, scarcely ever reached those rivers; and if they sometimes did, as in the case of the Muddy Creek settlement, they are not known to have crossed them. Here were two abortive attempts to hold a meeting of Presbytery, occasioning more than an entire year from the first till the second meeting. Truly, the walls of our Zion were built in troublesome times!

(5) Dunlap's Creek.—This congregation embraced, within its early indefinite limits, the real original "Redstone Settlement." Some Presbyterian emigrants, both from Eastern Pennsylvania, and from Virginia, settled within its bounds nearly, if not quite as early, as 1760. When the settlement was visited by Mr. Finley in 1765, he found a few of such families. The missionaries sent out by the Synod of New York and

Power. Absent, the Rev. Thaddeus Dod, (6) Elders James Edgar, (7) John M'Dowell, and Moses Latta. The Presby-

---

Philadelphia probably visited them. Messrs. Power and M'Millan, in their first visits to the West in 1774–5 and 6, were also among them, and preached to them. Perhaps about this time the church was organized. Dr. Power moved out, with his family, and settled here in the fall of 1776, and supplied them for some time, though he did not assume the pastoral relation. Their first pastor was the Rev. James Dunlap, D.D., who entered upon his labors among them in 1781, and was installed their pastor October 15th, 1782. This connection was dissolved April 22d, 1789. They were supplied for a short time by the Presbytery, until, in 1791, the Rev. Jacob Jennings settled among them, and, in the following year, accepted a call from them, and remained their pastor till June, 1811; when, on account of increased infirmities, he asked and obtained a dismission. He continued, however, to preach occasionally till his death, February 17th, 1813. The Rev. William Johnston became their next pastor, in connection with Brownsville, and continued in this relation with Dunlap's Creek till December 3d, 1839, and with Brownsville till his death, December 31st, 1841. The Rev. Samuel Wilson, D.D., received and accepted a call from Dunlap's Creek early in 1840, and was installed their pastor November 17th, 1840. This congregation, once a very large and flourishing church, has been much weakened and reduced by emigration, the inroads of the Cumberlands, and the organization of the Brownsville church, within the limits of its original boundary. It has been for some years, however, fast recovering from a state of almost complete prostration, and bids fair to reach again its pristine vigor and prosperity. Some refreshing seasons of divine grace have been enjoyed by them in later years, reminding them of days of which their fathers told them. The number of communicants — in connection with M'Clellandtown — last reported, 201.

(6) Mr Dod was absent. Perhaps his congregation was both in deep distress and great dismay at that time. For a company from his congregation had been with Colonel Crawford in his disastrous expedition, and only a portion of them ever returned. — Hist. West. Pa., p. 209. There was no part of the country more exposed to the savages than the settlements on Ten-Mile.

(7) James Edgar. — "Judge Edgar was born in York County, Pennsylvania, in the congregation of Slate Ridge, November 15th, 1744. He for the first time sat down at the Lord's table in the church of Deer Creek, about 14 miles from his father's house, on the 14th of September, 1760, when he was 16 years old. His father's family emigrated to

tery was opened with a sermon from Prov. viii. 4, by Mr. Smith. The Presbytery proceeded to the choice of a moderator and clerk for the ensuing year. Whereupon Mr. Power

North Carolina; but he was never there, except on a visit to his relations. He removed from York County to Western Pennsylvania in the fall of 1779." — Letter of the Rev. Dr. Stockton.

Judge Brackenridge, in his "Incidents of the Western Insurrection," where he proceeds to give an account of the great Brownsville meeting, says, "I proposed that we should get James Edgar, a member of the Committee of Twelve, to begin. He was an associate judge of the Court of Washington, and a kind of Rabbi in the Presbyterian churches in the western country. He had been a presbyter or elder from his youth; had been a member of committees in the early period of the American Revolution, and of legislative assemblies, executive and censorial councils, or deliberative conventions, ever since. His head was prematurely hoary with prayers and fastings, and religious exercises; his face thin and puritanical, like the figures of the old republicans in the long parliament in England. He was a man of sense, and not destitute of eloquence. It was agreed that he should open the way for us. It was proposed to him, but he appeared reluctant; I know not on what principle. It was imposed, therefore, on Gallatin. Edgar followed me with great earnestness, and with the solemnity of an evening sermon, in a discourse of great length." Dr. Carnahan, in his Lecture on the Whiskey Insurrection says, "This truly great and good man, little known beyond the precincts of Washington County, had removed to Western Pennsylvania, at an early period. He had a good English education; had improved his mind by reading and reflection; so that, in theological and political knowledge, he was superior to many professional men. He had as clear a head, and as pure a heart, as ever falls to the lot of mortals; and he possessed an eloquence which, although not polished, was convincing and persuasive. Yet he lived in retirement on his farm, except when the voice of his neighbors called him forth to serve the church or the state. He was a ruling elder in the Presbyterian church, and one of the associate Judges of Washington County, &c." — "I recollect to have heard him at Buffalo on Monday, after a sacramental occasion, address a congregation of at least two thousand people, on the subject of the Insurrection, with a clearness of argument, and a solemnity of manner, and a tenderness of Christian eloquence, which reached the understanding and penetrated the heart of every hearer. The consequence was, that very few in his neighborhood were concerned in the lawless riots."

Such was one of the men that the Rev. Joseph Smith was greatly was chosen moderator, and Mr. M'Millan clerk. Ordered, that the minutes of the last meeting of Presbytery be now read. Mr. Smith's reasons for not attending our last meeting are sustained. The Rev. James Dunlap, formerly a member of the Newcastle Presbytery, having accepted a call in our bounds, now applies to be admitted as a member of this Presbytery; and upon producing sufficient testimonials, and a dismission from that Presbytery, is accordingly received, and takes his seat as a member of this. His elder is Robert Adams. Adjourned to meet to-morrow morning at nine o'clock. Concluded with prayer.

Wednesday, the 16th.—The Presbytery met, according to adjournment. Ubi post preces, sederunt qui supra. Ordered that the minutes of the last session be now read. A supplication for supplies, from Tyrone congregation, was brought in and read. An application was made in behalf of Muddy Creek, for supplies. Mr. Smith appointed to supply, &c. [Here follows a list of appointments for supplies, to the several members. There was one appointment at Ohio Court-House.(8)] Upon motion being made, the Presbytery unanimously agreed that they would, in no case whatever, marry any persons by license, but would adhere to the rules laid down in the Westminster Directory.(9) Application

---

instrumental in training for the church, for his country, and for heaven. He was nine times a member of the old Presbytery.

(8) Ohio Court-House.—This place was some miles west of the present town of Washington, and was a seat of justice under the government of Virginia—as all Washington County, together with Fayette and Greene, and a large portion of Allegheny and Westmoreland Counties, were claimed by that State, and considered a part of Augusta County, Virginia. It is probable that not more than two or three families resided there, or in the immediate vicinity. This is the first and last appointment for a supply at that place. (See Note on Short Creek.)

(9) The following passage in the old Westminster Directory, respecting marriage, is, no doubt, referred to:

"Before the solemnizing of marriage between any persons, their purpose of marriage shall be published by the minister three several Sabbath-days, in the congregation, at the place or places of their most usual

being made by the united congregation of the Forks of Youghiogheny, for liberty to present a call to the Rev. James Finley, a member of the Presbytery of New Castle—the Presbytery grant their request, and order the clerk to furnish them with a copy of this minute.

John Matson appeared before Presbytery and exhibited the following charges against the Rev. James Dunlap. 1. That Mr. Dunlap charged him with coming to his house to take the advantage of, and wrangle with him. 2. That Mr. Dunlap accused him with unchristian conduct towards him. 3. That Mr. Dunlap denied him ordination as a ruling elder; and, 4, For not letting the reasons why he did so be known to the congregation. Mr. Dunlap acknowledges that he did say that Mr. Matson treated him in an unchristian manner, and gives as the reason why he said so, that though he had made some concessions, and acknowledged that he had been too rash with respect to the baptising of a certain Audley Rea's child, with which Mr. Matson declared himself satisfied, yet he still continued to mention that piece of inadvertence to others; in such a manner as had a tendency to hurt his character as a gospel minister. In support of which Mr. Dunlap produces the following witnesses: Caleb Wingate being called upon to declare the truth, says that Mr. Matson told him that Mr. Norris informed Mr. Dunlap of Audley Rea's drinking

---

and constant abode respectively. And of this publication the minister who is to join them in marriage shall have sufficient testimony, before he proceeds to solemnize the marriage. Before that publication of such their marriage, (if the parties be under age,) the consent of the parents, or others under whose power they are, (in case the parents are dead,) is to be made known to the church officers of that congregation—to be recorded."

We know not whether, in the times of our fathers, a publication of a purpose of marriage was usually made for three successive Sabbaths. But once sufficed, we know, at a somewhat later period; and this custom continued for a number of years, though now altogether laid aside, in our branch of the Presbyterian Church. It is said to be still observed in the Secession and Covenanting bodies—the latter rigidly adhering to the old rule of publishing for three successive Sabbaths.

and swearing, previous to his baptising his child; and that he spoke in such a manner as showed him to be still dissatisfied, after acknowledgments made, with which he professed himself satisfied; and expressed himself in such a manner as had a tendency to hurt Mr. Dunlap's usefulness as a minister of the gospel. Isaac Sterritt, being solemnly called upon to declare the truth, says, that at a raising at Mr. Tate's, Mr. Matson said that Mr. Dunlap baptised Audley Rea's child, and would not baptise others in like circumstances. He said also that Mr. Dunlap had confessed his fault and afterwards denied it; that Mr. Norris had informed him of Mr. Audley Rea's character. That Mr. Norris had made it appear at another time that he had informed him; and that Mr. Dunlap had nothing to say in his own defence. Mr. Matson acknowledges that he told Mr. Wingate and Mr. Sterrit these things which they have declared, and gives this as his reason for so doing, viz: That he heard Mr. Dunlap saying, that he looked upon it that he had done no wrong in baptising Audley Rea's child, after he had made the forementioned concession. The Presbytery, after fully hearing both parties, with respect to the first charge, do judge that Mr. Dunlap had sufficient grounds for saying what he did, inasmuch of John Matson coming to Mr. Dunlap's, in company with some others, joined with them in wrangling with, and treating him in a very unbecoming and disorderly manner. With respect to the second charge, the Presbytery judge that Mr. Dunlap was treated in an unchristian manner by John Matson; and at the same time could have wished that Mr. Dunlap had been more cautious in the admission of Audley Rea. With respect to the two last charges, the Presbytery judge that Mr. Dunlap had sufficient occasion for not ordaining Mr. Matson, inasmuch as it had been made to appear before them that objections had been laid against him, by a member of the congregation; and that he was justifiable in not publishing the reasons to the congregation. Upon the whole, the Presbytery cannot but highly disapprove of Mr. Matson's conduct, especially at Mr. Dunlap's house; and do judge that he submit to an admonition from the Moderator. To this judgment the parties submitted, and Mr. Matson was accordingly admonished by the Moderator. Adjourned to meet at Pigeon creek, the second Tuesday of March next, at 12 o'clock. Concluded with prayer.

THIRD MEETING.

PIGEON CREEK, Tuesday, 11th of March, 1783.—The Presbytery met according to adjournment. Ubi post preces sederunt, the Rev. Messrs. Joseph Smith, &c. The Presbytery was opened by Mr. Dunlap, from John iii., 3.

The Rev. James Finley, a member of the Presbytery of New Castle, being present and invited, sits as a correspondent. The Rev. John Clark, formerly a member of New Castle Presbytery, now makes application to be admitted as a member of this. Upon his producing sufficient testimonials and his dismission from that Presbytery, he is accordingly received and takes his place as a member of this. The Presbytery find that the members have punctually fulfilled their appointments, except Mr. Dunlap, in one instance, whose reasons for the omission are sustained.

Upon motion, resolved, that magistrates belonging to our community, marrying any person in a way contrary to the prescriptions of the law respecting marriages, and all persons belonging to us, obtaining marriage either by magistrates or ministers contrary to the law, shall be esteemed censurable by the church. (10) Ordered that this, and the minute of the

(10) The law respecting marriages, (see "Laws of Pennsylvania," Vol. I., p. 21. Purdon's Digest, p. 568,) required "that all marriages not forbidden by the law of God be encouraged; but the parents or guardians shall, if conveniently they can, be first consulted with, and the party's clearness of all engagements, signified by a certificate from some credible person where they have lived, or do live, produced to such religious society to which they relate, or to some justice of the peace of the county, where the parties do reside or dwell, one month before

last meeting of Presbytery, respecting marriage, be read by the members in their congregations and in the vacancies under our care.

As the Synod of New York and Philadelphia, taking into consideration the evil consequences of congregations suffering arrearages to be long unsettled between them and their ministers, did enjoin it upon them to produce a settlement every year to their respective Presbyteries: (11) therefore,

---

solemnization thereof; the which said publication, before it be so affixed as aforesaid, shall be brought before one or more justices of the peace in the respective counties to which they respectively belong; which justice shall subscribe the said publication, witnessing the time of such declaration and date of said publication, so to be affirmed as aforesaid. And that all marriages shall be solemnized by taking each other for husband and wife, before twelve sufficient witnesses; and the certificate of their marriage under the hands of the parties and witnesses, at least twelve, and one of them a justice of the peace, shall be brought to the register of the county where they are married, and registered in his office, &c. Provided that this law shall not extend to any who shall marry or be married, in the religious society to which they belong, so as notice shall be given by either of the parties to the parents, masters, mistresses, or guardians, one full month, at least, before any such marriage be solemnized." But that "no license or dispensation shall hinder or obstruct the force or operation of this act, in respect of notice to be given to parents, masters, mistresses, or guardians, as aforesaid."

(11) In the course thus early adopted, so wise and salutary—of requiring churches to report annual settlements, they refer to the authority of the Synod of New York and Philadelphia, as sanctioning and requiring this measure. It appears that so long ago as 1765, a number of elders and gentlemen, having met in Philadelphia, had deliberated upon several important measures necessary for the interests of the churches, touching matters and points that could more properly be taken up by them than by the ministers. The result was, that they laid their suggestions in the form of a petition, before the Synod. It was laid over till the following year. (Printed Records, 350.) At the next meeting, in 1766, this Address was committed to a large committee, to prepare, by the next day, an overture on the subject. (p. 356.) The result was the adoption of the following: "The Synod taking into their serious consideration several matters, suggested to them in an address and representation from a number of lay-elders, and others of

in obedience to this act of Synod, this Presbytery does require their several members, with their respective congregations, to produce such settlements to us at our next meeting; and that the congregations be required to answer such questions put to them respecting the diligence and care of their respective pastors. Adjourned to meet at Mount Pleasant, on the third Tuesday of October next. Concluded with prayer.

FOURTH MEETING.

MOUNT PLEASANT (12), Tuesday, Oct. 21st, 1783.—

---

the Presbyterian denomination, occasionally assembled at Philadelphia, do, after mature deliberation, look upon said affairs to be of much importance and deserving the strictest regard as very useful and salutary measures, whereby many pernicious evils may be prevented and various great advantages procured," &c.; then recommend their adoption by the Presbyteries and congregations, &c.: "and that all proper pains be taken by each Presbytery to have said measures put in execution, viz.: 1st. That in every congregation a committee be appointed, who shall, twice in every year, collect the minister's stipend, and lay his receipts before the Presbytery preceding the Synod; and at the same time that the ministers give an account of their diligence in visiting and catechising their people." Then follow seven other matters, recommended, &c. The above shows the origin of that wise measure, still pursued in our Presbyteries — that it was not a measure which began with the ministers, but with the people. (Printed Records, p. 358.)

(12) MOUNT PLEASANT.—This is one of the oldest churches in the West. It is near two miles from a village of the same name in Westmoreland County; but which gave the name to the other, we cannot tell. The church is perhaps older than the town, and was probably organized as early as 1776, when Dr. Power removed to the western country. It was supplied by him from that period till the Spring of 1779, when he became the pastor of the united congregations of Mount Pleasant and Sewickly. On the 22d of August, 1787, he was dismissed from Sewickly, and continued the pastor of Mount Pleasant till April 15th, 1817, when, from age and infirmity, he resigned this charge. It continued vacant till April 18th, 1821, when the Rev. A. O. Patterson, D. D., was ordained and installed pastor of the united congregations of Sewickly and Mount Pleasant. This relation continued till October 8th, 1834.

The Presbytery met according to adjournment. Ubi post preces sederunt, the Rev. Messrs. Joseph Smith, &c. The Presbytery was opened with a sermon on Isaiah lxiii. 1, by Mr. Smith. A supplication for supplies from Unity congregation, also for liberty to apply to Donegal Presbytery for supplies, was brought in and read. The Presbytery proceeded to make out supplies. The Presbytery find that the members present have fulfilled their appointments, except Mr. Power, whose reasons are sustained. Mr. Smith, agreeably to the requisitions of Presbytery at their last meeting, produces a settlement with the congregation of Cross Creek, whereby it appears that there will be due to him from said congregation, against the 1st of December next, the just and full sum of £113 *5s 3d.* Upon inquiry, it was found that settlements have not been made by congregations with their respective pastors, according to the requirement made at our last meeting, except between Mr. Smith and Cross Creek; it

---

Soon after, the Rev. S. Montgomery became its pastor, April, 1836. On May 19th, 1840, the congregation was unhappily divided, a part adhering to the New School division. In this weakened and crippled state of the congregation, it formed a connection with Greensburg. The Rev. James J. Brownson became their pastor November 25th, 1841, and was dismissed in January, 1849. In 1849, these congregations united in a call to the Rev. Wm. D. Moore, who became their pastor soon after. In October, 1851, Mr. Moore resigned the pastoral charge of Mount Pleasant. On the 14th of April, 1852, the Rev. Wm. W. M'Lain received and accepted a call from them, and was installed their pastor soon after, in 1852.

This church shared largely in the early revivals of the West; and though, towards the close of Dr. Power's ministry among them, the church was almost threatened with extinction, principally on account of emigration, it again greatly revived and prospered during the ministry of Dr. Patterson. Could the breach which exists among them be healed, and could they all come together again with one heart and one mind, the times of which our fathers have told us might yet return to that church, so intimately associated with the early history of Redstone Presbytery, and having so many precious ties with the church in glory. The number of communicants in 1854—89.

is therefore enjoined upon them to have such settlements made, and to produce them at our next meeting. Upon inquiry, it was found that the congregations were satisfied with the care and diligence of their respective pastors.

A reference was brought in from the session of Mount Pleasant, respecting a complaint of George Latimer against Deborah Ross, which is as follows: That Deborah Ross has falsely reported that she left her house sundry times for fear of him. The Presbytery, after duly considering said complaint, and hearing all that the parties had to offer, do judge that said complaint is without any just foundation; inasmuch as it appears that George Latimer stands convicted of immodest behavior towards Deborah Ross, for which he ought to submit to an admonition before the session; and that for removing the scandal, his compliance be made known to the congregation. To which judgment, George Latimer refuses to submit.

Robert Hall appeared before Presbytery, and exhibited the following complaint against the session of Mount Pleasant congregation, viz.: "To the Moderator and remanent members of Redstone Presbytery, now sitting at Mount Pleasant meeting-house. The complaint and application of Robert Hall humbly showeth, that whereas I, your complainant, upon application to the Rev. Mr. Power for a continuation of the common privileges of a regular church member, have been refused the same; and afterwards to several members of the session, but was still kept back; upon which I made application to the Rev. Moderator and other members of session in writing: but was still denied, without even satisfying me with anything that appeared like reason for my being so refused. I, therefore, your complainant, do lay the case before your wisdoms, that you may judge whether I am justly debarred from privileges or not; as I do apprehend that I neither said nor did anything that might be a bar in my way, in that respect. Therefore, upon examining into the case, your wisdoms will be able to judge whether I have cause of complaint or not: unto whose judgment I do humbly appeal.—Robert Hall." The Presbytery, after hearing the parties, do judge, that though Mr. Hall had ground of uneasiness, inasmuch as he was really a sufferer, yet Mr. Power was not to be blamed, as it was entirely through the fault of the congregation that he failed in performing his contract. Therefore, though the Presbytery could have wished that Mr. Hall had not expressed himself so rashly, in some instances, yet everything considered, we are of opinion that he may be admitted to church privileges without making any particular concessions. Upon new light being offered, the Presbytery further judge that Mr. Hall profess his sorrow for using some expressions reflecting upon Mr. Power's character. To this judgment, Mr. Hall refuses to submit. Adjourned to meet at Buffalo, the second Tuesday of April next. Concluded with prayer.

FIFTH MEETING.

BUFFALO, (13) Tuesday, 13th of April, 1784.—The Presbytery met according to adjournment, ubi post preces sederunt, the Rev. Messrs. John Clark, &c. The Presbytery

---

(13) BUFFALO.—It is not known when this congregation organized. It is probable it was in 1779, the year in which Cross Creek was organized. (See App. to Life of Macurdy, Marquis.) The Rev. Joseph Smith became its pastor in 1780, in connection with the latter place, and continued to labor among them till his death, which occurred April 19th, 1792. During this period of 12 years, the church was favored with an almost constant revival of religion, though, at different times, greatly harassed by the incursions of the savages. After Mr. Smith's death, the congregation was supplied, for a short time, by the Presbytery, till the Rev. Thomas Marquis, June 13th, 1794, becoming pastor of Cross Creek, acted as a stated supply for Buffalo, until this church gave a call to the Rev. John Anderson, who was installed their pastor March 9th, 1802. There is some reason to believe, however, that Dr. Anderson acted as stated supply from the spring of 1800. He ministered to this people with much fidelity and success, till June 18th, 1833, when, on account of declining health, and at his own request, the pastoral relation was dissolved. He was succeeded by the Rev. John Eagleson, its present

was opened by Mr. Dod, with a sermon from John, ix, 35. The Stated Clerk being absent, Mr. Dod was chosen Clerk pro tem.

The Presbytery proceeded to appoint supplies to such places as have made application, and amongst others, Pittsburg. (14)

---

pastor, December 23d, 1834. The number of communicants reported in 1854 was 274. This church has witnessed and enjoyed some of the most remarkable effusions of the Holy Spirit that have ever been experienced in our Western country. It was here that the ever memorable meeting, called "the great Buffalo Sacrament," took place, commencing on the 13th of November, 1802. Many brought their wagons, provisions and tents from a considerable distance. Fifteen ministers were present. About 960 persons sat down to the Lord's table on the Sabbath. Many hundreds of persons, of both sexes, and all ages, were brought under deep conviction of their sins. Multitudes, it is believed, were hopefully converted to God. The meeting was continued till Tuesday evening. It was the most remarkable scene that had ever before, or has ever since, been witnessed by either ministers or people who were then present. This church has given some of the best materials for the formation or strengthening of new churches through the West, and has furnished several eminent ministers of the gospel.

(14) PITTSBURG.—The first notice of this place. It appears that Mr Smith was the first member of the Presbytery sent to preach the gospel there, on the fourth Sabbath of August, 1784. The Rev. Messrs. Beatty and Duffield had been there in 1766, during their missionary tour, in pursuance of an appointment by the Synod of New York and Philadelphia, and found the people living, as Mr. Beatty states in his Journal, "in some kind of a town." Mr. Arthur Lee, a distinguished Virginian, visited that place a few months after this visit of Mr. Smitt, and gave this account of the place: "Pittsburg is inhabited almost entirely by Scots and Irish, who live in paltry log-houses, and are as dirty as in the north of Ireland, or even Scotland. [We fear that, like Dr. Samuel Johnson, Lee hated the Scotch.] There is a great deal of small trade carried on, the goods being brought, at the vast expense of 45 shillings per cwt., from Philadelphia and Baltimore. They take, in the shops, money, wheat, flour and skins. There are, in the town, four attorneys, two doctors, and *not a priest of any persuasion, nor church, nor chapel;* so that they are likely to be damned without the benefit of clergy. The river encroaches fast upon the town, and to such a degree, that a gentleman told me that the Allegheny had, within 30 years of his memory,

The Presbytery proceeded to inquire with regard to the several congregations' settlements with their respective ministers. Mr. Clark produced accounts, whereby it appears that there was due to him, on the 1st of September last, from the Eastern division of Peters' Creek congregation (Lebanon), the just and full sum of £40 3s. 9½d.—and from the Western division (Bethel), on the 1st of October last, £18 14s. 9½d. Mr. M'Millan produced accounts, whereby it appears that there was due to him, from Chartiers congregation, of his last year's stipend, on the 1st of February last, the just and full sum of £42 7s. 6d.; and from Pigeon's Creek congregation, £40 17s. 3d. of the last year's stipend, which became due November 1st, 1783. The three preceding years remain unsettled in both congregations. Mr. Smith produced a settlement between him and the congregation of Buffalo, whereby it appears that there was due to him, from said congrega-

---

carried away 100 yards. *The place, I believe, will never be very considerable.*" (Hist. of Pitts. p. 186.) When Washington was there, 31 years before, the ground was then covered with a dense forest. When he was there again, in 1770, Pittsburg then contained 20 houses, and perhaps 120 inhabitants. Virginia then claimed it, and all the country thence to the Laurel Hill. When Mr. Smith first carried the gospel there, as the messenger of the Redstone Presbytery, it is probable the number of inhabitants did not exceed 400. For, two years afterwards, Judge H. H. Brackenridge, writing of the place, in the first number of the Pittsburg Gazette, published in 1786, says, "This town consists, at present, of about 100 dwelling-houses." "Could Arthur Lee," says the historian of Pittsburg, "now revisit this point, he would probably be surprised to see the change already produced there; and would not be very much gratified by the comparison of Pittsburg with Richmond." The country across the Allegheny river, opposite Pittsburg, when Mr. Smith was there, was still owned by the Indians. The present site of Allegheny city was then even without an Indian wigwam, and was the occasional resort of the Pittsburg boys in pursuit of rabbits, opossums, &c. There are now six Presbyterian churches here, numbering more, perhaps, than 1300 communicants; and numerous Methodist, Baptist and other churches. Sketches of the history of the Presbyterian churches of Pittsburg may be given hereafter.

tion, on the 1st of December last, the just and full sum of £39 2*s*. 2*d*.

Henry Taylor brought in an appeal from the judgment of the session of Chartiers congregation, with respect to his having and encouraging a *promiscuous dance* at his house. The Presbytery, after hearing both parties, upon mature deliberation, considering the smallness of the number present, [at the meeting of Presbytery,] and the importance of the case, defer the decision of it to the next meeting of the Presbytery. Adjourned to meet at Chartiers, 3d Tuesday of October next. Concluded with prayer.

SIXTH MEETING.

CHARTIERS, (15) October 19th, 1784.—The Presbytery met according to adjournment, ubi post preces sederunt, the Rev. Messrs. John M'Millan, &c. The Rev. James Finley

(15) CHARTIERS.—It has been supposed that this church was organized by Dr. M'Millan, soon after he was ordained, in 1776. There is, however, some reason to suppose that, as in the case of Pigeon Creek, it was organized some years earlier—possibly by some missionary sent out by the Synod of New York and Philadelphia. Dr. M'Millan became its first pastor, in the year above mentioned, though he had visited it and labored some time there during the previous year. He continued the pastor of Chartiers till dismissed April 21st, 1830, having long before been dismissed from Pigeon Creek, which was originally a part of his charge. This was an eventful year in the history of Chartiers.

Towards the beginning of that year, or near the close of the previous year, Centre church was organized, taking off a considerable wing of old Chartiers. Then, in the fall, Canonsburg church was also organized, cutting into the very vitals of the mother church. So that, whereas they had reported, up to this year, 304 members, we find them in their next report reduced to 70. (See printed Records of Synod of Pittsburg.)

The Rev. Samuel F. Leake was installed pastor of Chartiers, July 12th, 1831, and was dismissed June 21st, 1843. He was succeeded by the Rev. A. A. Brown, D.D., September 3d, 1844, who continued till January 11th, 1848. He was succeeded by the Rev. Robert White, September 6th, 1848, who died December 14th, 1848. The Rev Joseph R.

having been regularly dismissed from his former charge, and accepted a call from the two Societies in the Forks of Youghiogheny, with the approbation of this Presbytery, although he has not yet received a dismission from New Castle Presbytery, yet being present and invited, sits as a correspondent. The Presbytery was opened with a sermon on Romans vii. 9, by Mr. Finley.

Ordered that Mr. M'Millan and his congregations produce a settlement for all past time, at our next spring's meeting, and that they no longer defer it; also, that this minute be read to the congregations.

Henry Taylor being necessarily absent, the consideration of his appeal is deferred till our next meeting.

The Presbytery being informed that 160 Bibles, purchased by the Synod for the use of the poor within the bounds of

---

Wilson, June 20th, 1849, became their pastor, and continued till January 15th, 1851. On October 16th, 1852, the Rev. William Ewing, their present pastor, received a call, and was ordained and installed January 14th, 1852. The number of communicants reported in 1853 was 139.

This church, one of the oldest in the West, for half a century enjoyed the faithful labors of Dr. M'Millan, and under his ministry was favored with many happy seasons of revival. Its graveyard contains his mortal remains, together with those of his wife and two sons-in-law—the Rev. John Watson and the Rev. William Morehead. On the tomb-stone of Dr. M'Millan are these words, arranged, not as here given, but in the usual manner in such cases:

"Erected in memory of the Rev. John M'Millan, D.D., an able divine, a preacher of the first order. His distinguished talents, his active benevolence, his private virtue, his exalted piety, the skill and ability which he displayed in instructing and training young men for the gospel ministry, his indefatigable zeal in promoting his Master's cause, and the best interests of his fellow-men, have raised a monument to his fame far more imperishable than the stone which bears this inscription. He was the leading founder of Jefferson College. The Chartiers Presbyterian congregation, in which he labored for more than half a century, owes its origin to the blessing of God on his instrumentality. He died November 16th, 1853, enjoying the undoubted hope of a blissful eternity, in the 82d year of his age, and the 60th year of his ministry."

this Presbytery, were brought out by Dr. Ewing,(16) and left at several places, order that those in Mr. Power's hands,

---

(16) DR. EWING was out—along with the celebrated American astronomer, David Rittenhouse, Bishop Madison, of Virginia, and the other Commissioners of the two States—running the line between the States of Pennsylvania and Virginia, in the summer and fall of 1784. Here is a curious illustration of the manner in which cotemporary secular history verifies and illustrates the minutes of the Presbytery. It is remarkable, that two of the most eminent clergymen of their respective churches—the Presbyterian and the Episcopal—were employed in this specific business of settling the long-disputed boundary line between the two States. This difficulty had brought the Western people, at one time, almost to the verge of civil war among themselves. And yet, though they were also involved in hostilities with the Indian tribes, when the United States began their Revolutionary struggle, there was but one common feeling among both parties on that subject. They held two great meetings, on the 16th of May, 1775, only four weeks after the battle of Lexington—the Virginia party mainly, not exclusively, at Pittsburg, calling it a meeting of the inhabitants of that part of Augusta County, west side of Laurel Hill—the Pennsylvania party at Hanna's-town; both adopting, unanimously, strong Whig resolutions, in consonance with the patriotic feeling of the land. They all struggled together in that cause. But as soon as it was gained, they fell to quarreling again, about whether they were Pennsylvanians or Virginians, almost worse than ever. And now these ministers of peace, with others, had come out to fix and determine finally the boundary line! And one of them came, bringing with him 160 Bibles for the use of the Presbytery, to supply their poor and destitute people with the bread of life!

The Synod of New York and Philadelphia had, at their session of 1783, "taken into consideration the situation of many people under their care, who, through the indigence of their circumstances, are not able to purchase Bibles, and are in danger of perishing for lack of knowledge.

"Ordered, that every member of this body shall use his utmost influence in the congregation under his inspection, and in the vacancies contiguous to them, to raise contributions for the purchasing of Bibles, to be distributed among such poor persons; and that Doctors Sproat and Ewing, and Mr. Duffield, be a committee to receive such contributions, to purchase Bibles therewith, and send them to the several members of the Synod, who, in conjunction with their respective sessions, shall distribute them." (Printed Records, p. 500.)

viz., 43, be distributed by him and Mr. Finley in the best manner they can—that Col. M'Clane be instructed to send the greater part of those in his hands to Mr. M'Millan—and that Mr. Dod make inquiry concerning those in Col. M'Leary's hands. Adjourned to meet at the Upper meeting-house in the Forks, the 4th Tuesday of January next. Concluded with prayer.

SEVENTH MEETING.

January 25th, 1785.—The Presbytery met, according to adjournment, at the Upper meeting-house in the Forks, (17)

And now we find, from the minutes of the Redstone Presbytery, that Dr. Ewing (pastor of the First Presbyterian church in Philadelphia,) did not forget to bring the Bibles along with him, leaving them at different places on his route.

(17) Upper Meeting-house, or Rehoboth, and Lower Meeting-house, or Roundhill. — These, it is believed, are among the oldest congregations of our denomination west of the Allegheny mountains. The Rev. James Finley visited this part of the country about the year 1772, and preached the gospel to a few scattered whites, who were living contiguous to the Indians. From this time, or till 1783, he occasionally visited this region, and by his preaching and Christian conversation, watered the seed which had been sown. On one of these visits, probably about the year 1778, he gathered the scattered sheep of Christ's flock into regularly organized churches. Rehoboth, or Upper Meeting-house, as it was first called, is in Westmoreland County, about nine miles from Roundhill, or the Lower Meeting-house, which is in Allegheny County. At that time they were indeed like sheep in the midst of wolves. For the inhabitants were much annoyed by savage Indians; and on the opposite side of the Monongahela river some fell victims to their barbarity.

In the year 1784, Mr. Finley having taken his dismission from the New Castle Presbytery, took the pastoral charge of these congregations. After his death, which took place January 6th, 1795, these churches remained vacant two years or more, when the Rev. David Smith was installed over them. During the last year of his ministry among them, the Spirit of God was shed down upon these churches in a very remarkable manner; and the Word preached seemed to be attended with a power that astonished the people, numbers falling down to the earth,

[Rehoboth,] ubi post preces sederunt, the Rev. Messrs. John Clark, &c.

The Rev. James Finley, a member of the New Castle Presbytery, being present and invited, sits as a correspondent. The Presbytery was opened with a sermon from John, v. 40, by Mr. Clark.

The Presbytery, understanding that Unity Congregation is in considerable arrearages to Mr. Power, and also that they expect shortly to be supplied with a stated pastor, do therefore order Mr. Finley to write to the sessions of that congre-

---

and others crying out with distress, on account of their sins. At that memorable period, while in the full vigor of life, and in the midst of his usefulness, he was removed by death, August 24th, 1803. He was succeeded by the Rev. William Wylie, D.D., in 1805. At that time there were, in these churches, about 130 communicants. Dr. Wylie continued their pastor till the spring of 1817, when, at his own request, he was dismissed. In the following June the Rev. Robert Johnston became their pastor. His ministry and labors among them continued in Roundhill till October, 1831, and in Rehoboth till December, 1832. The congregations remained vacant till July, 1833, when they were supplied by the Rev. N. H. Gillett, who was installed their pastor in December, 1834. He continued the pastor of the united congregations till 1841, when he was dismissed, at his own request, from Roundhill, Rehoboth giving him a call for the whole of his services. He remained as the pastor of Rehoboth until 1848, when he was dismissed, at his own request. In 1849, their present pastor, the Rev. James R. Hughes, receiving from them a call, settled among them, and was installed their pastor.

In the mean time, Roundhill gave a call to the Rev. William Eaton, in 1841, who became and continued their pastor till 1844, when, at his request, he was dismissed. In 1845, the Rev. A. Calhoon was ordained and installed their pastor. He was removed by death in the spring of 1848. The congregation of Roundhill then remained vacant until the spring of 1851, (though supplied by licentiates, Messrs. Edgar, Fulton and Hamilton,) when the Rev. Joseph Smith, their present pastor, receiving from them a call, settled among them, and was installed in June following. The congregation of Roundhill have recently built a large and commodious house of worship in Elizabethtown, and worship there and in their former house alternately. The number of communicants in Rehoboth, in 1854, is 160—in Roundhill, 140.

gation, and inform them that a settlement with Mr. Power must be produced at our meeting, in order to prevent disagreeable consequences, and that Mr. Power and his congregations produce a settlement for all past time, at our next spring meeting; and that this order be made known to the congregations. Adjourned to meet at the Lower Meeting-house, on the third Tuesday of April next. Concluded with prayer.

EIGHTH MEETING.

Tuesday, April 19th, 1785.—The Presbytery met according to adjournment, at the Lower Meeting-house, (17) in the Forks. Ubi post preces sederunt, the Rev. Messrs. John M'Millan, &c. The Presbytery was opened with a sermon from Matthew ix., 12, by Mr. Power.

Mr. M'Millan produces a settlement, whereby it appears that the balance due to him from the congregation of Chartiers is £107 16*s* 4*d*, which became due the 1st of February, 1785. And from the congregation at Pigeon Creek, £91 9*s* 3*d*, which became due November 1st, 1784. Mr. Power's reasons for not fulfilling his appointments at Fort Pitt and Long Run, are sustained. Mr. Power produces settlements between him and his congregations, whereby it appears, that the balance due from the congregation of Mount Pleasant, by the 1st of May next, is £90 15*s* 7*d*—and from the congregation of Sewickly, by the 1st of May next, £84 1*s* 0*d*. Upon inquiry it was found that the congregations are satisfied with the diligence and care of their respective pastors. Adjourned to meet at Pigeon Creek, on the third Tuesday of June next. Concluded with prayer.

NINTH MEETING.

PIGEON CREEK, Tuesday, 21st of June, 1785.—The Presbytery met according to adjournment. Ubi post preces sederunt, the Rev. Messrs. John Clark, &c.

The Rev. James Finley, (18) formerly a member of New

---

(18) The Synod of New York and Philadelphia had, on the 17th of May, 1782, by their own act, dissolved the pastoral relation between

Castle Presbytery, having accepted a call within our bounds, now applies to be admitted a member of this Presbytery. And upon producing sufficient testimonials, and a dismission from that Presbytery, is accordingly received, and takes his seat as a member of this. His elder is John Gaston.

Henry Taylor being come, the Presbytery proceeded to hear the reasons of his appeal. The Presbytery having heard what each party had to say, and maturely deliberating on the whole, conclude that though Henry denies that the charge against him was proved, or that he had ever confessed that he had done what he was charged with; and although the session, through inadvertency, we suppose, neglected to set down his acknowledgment to Mr. M'Millan, which we have now heard, viz: That he said Taylor had directed and assisted the company in going through a reel in dancing, which he supposed they had gone wrong in; yet we think that the evidence of John Riddle, now offered to us by Mr. Taylor, viz: that Mr. Taylor, at the request of the company, had allowed them an hour to recreate themselves in dancing; together with the testimony of some members of the Presbytery who had heard him acknowledge the same at a former meeting, gives us sufficient reason to conclude that he did give such a relation to Mr. M'Millan, and did countenance and approve promiscuous dancing; which was greatly aggravated in him by the circumstances mentioned in the minutes of the session, and some other things in the congregation did carry the ap-

---

Mr. Finley and East Nottingham—and though they did not, as stated in the "Appendix to the Life of Macurdy," direct the Presbytery to dismiss him, yet as their act in dissolving the pastoral relation must have been mainly, if not solely, on the ground of his having received a call to the West, and of his desire to accept it, the Presbytery were virtually directed to dismiss him. Yet they do not report his dismission till May 19th, 1785. (See Records, p. 507.) Why this good man was treated in this manner does not appear. The Presbytery of Redstone seems to have received him informally, and to have permitted him to enter upon his full pastoral work, well understanding, no doubt, that it was not his fault that he had not, long before, received his dismission.

pearance of being done in contempt. Therefore, as promiscuous dancing is condemned by the body of the godly and judicious in all ages, as well as by our own standards, and is generally attended with bad effects, we cannot think that the sessions were too rigorous in their judgment; and, therefore, with them, must conclude that Mr. Taylor, in order to admission to church privileges, ought to acknowledge his fault before this Presbytery, or before the session of the congregation to which he belongs, and be admonished to be more circumspect for the future; and that this his acknowledgment should be signified to the congregation by Mr. M'Millan. Finally, as Mr. Taylor declares that he did not act in the above affair out of contempt, we think this declaration ought to be received as candid and true. From this judgment, Mr. Taylor reserves a liberty of appealing to Synod, if, upon deliberation, he shall think proper. If he does appeal, the clerk is ordered to furnish him with a copy of the above judgment, upon his producing the reasons of his appeal.

The Presbytery, finding that many difficulties arise from marriages celebrated by Mr. Hughy, (19) and such persons who have no authority, either civil or ecclesiastical, for so doing, do therefore judge that such marriages be discountenanced, and people cautioned against them as unlawful.

The Presbytery, taking into consideration the unspeakable goodness of God, in planting his church, in this, not long since an howling wilderness, the habitation of savages; in accompanying his ordinances with the Almighty influences of his Holy Spirit (20); and considering also the great danger

---

(19) Mr. Hughy. The Presbytery of Donegal reported to the Synod of New York and Philadelphia, May 19th, 1773, that they received the Rev. Mr. Huey from the Presbytery of Derry, in Ireland—and in May 18th, 1774, that they had suspended the Rev. Mr. Hughey since the last meeting of Synod. (See printed Records, pp. 437 and 451.) This is probably the same man, though the name is spelt differently in each case; and his general character, a little like his name, somewhat slippery.

(20) This clause refers to some gracious seasons enjoyed by some of

we are in of provoking God to withdraw those gracious influences—and that multitudes are still careless and hardening under the means; do therefore think it their incumbent duty to appoint a day of fasting and prayer, to be observed in their respective congregations, to implore a more plentiful outpouring of divine influences upon the church in general, and upon his infant church in this land in particular, and at the same time to acknowledge with gratitude the many mercies, both special and common, conferred upon us. We do therefore appoint the first Thursday of September, to be observed for the above purposes. Adjourned to meet at Peter's creek on the third Tuesday of October next. Concluded with prayer.

TENTH MEETING.

PETERS' CREEK, Oct. 18th, 1785.—The Presbytery met according to adjournment. Ubi post preces sederunt, the Rev. Messrs. John Clark, &c. The Presbytery was opened with a sermon on Phil. i. 28, by Mr. M'Millan.

The Rev. James Grier, member of the Presbytery of Philadelphia, being present, and invited, sits as a correspondent.

Messrs. M'Allister and John Hopkins, having represented to Presbytery that Mr. Barr, a member of New Castle Presbytery, during his preaching in these parts, appeared to neglect the measures ordinarily taken, in the admissions of persons to baptism, and in the administration of that ordinance; and having desired to know whether we did approve of such measures, viz.: the omitting the confession of faith in baptism,

---

the churches shortly before that time, June, 1785. In the Western Missionary Magazine, Vol. II., p. 289, is the following passage, that may in part serve to illustrate this clause. "At the time the Lord's supper was administered at Buffalo, in the fall of 1783, about one hundred of the subjects of this good work were admitted to communion; and many were awakened on that solemn occasion. The awakening and hopeful conversion of sinners continued and increased through three or four years; nor was there much appearance of a decline for six or seven years after it began."

as in the case of one Meek; and baptizing privately, when it might have been done publicly, as in the case of one Gilkeson; and baptizing four persons, without proper inquiry into their moral character, as in the foregoing instances and some others; the Presbytery are fully satisfied that the measures they have observed are just and necessary; and agree that further inquiry be made into the supposed irregular conduct of Mr. Barr.(21)

Mr. Clark, Mr. Smith, and Mr. M'Millan, are appointed as a committee to examine and receive, if the way be clear, and make appointments for such ministers and candidates as may come into our bounds before the next meeting of Presbytery. Mr. Finley is appointed to preach in Mr. Dunlap's congregation as soon as convenient, and use his best endeavors to promote a settlement between him and his people, for the relief of Mr. Dunlap in his present difficult circumstances.

---

(21) We see how our fathers disapproved of any laxity in the administration of the seals of the covenant, and in the exercise of discipline. Had they connived at the beginnings of a looser system, whereunto might the evil have grown? The report of some irregularities, in regard to the administration of baptism, reaching their ears, they not only express their decided views on the subject, but adopt another wise precaution, before they adjourn—the appointment of a committee of three, Messrs. Clark, Smith, and M'Millan, to stand, as it were, at the gates of the city, and examine ministers and candidates from other Presbyteries and foreign bodies, and "make appointments for them."

There is something rather unpromising about the alleged conduct of Mr. Barr. The Synod had given his Presbytery (New Castle,) leave to ordain him, *sine titulo*, "in order that he may travel through the various churches of the *Southern* States," only a few months before. (Print. Rec., p. 511.) But here we find him in the *West*, and likely to give trouble; we shall hear more of him after awhile. The Presbytery of New Brunswick, on the 19th of May, 1785, reported him as a licensed candidate from the Presbytery of Derry, in Ireland. (Rec., p. 507.) Ireland was a fountain that then, and for many years after, sent forth streams both sweet and bitter. If Dr. M'Millan got, as a friend and brother to cheer him all his life, a *Ralston*—he also got a *Birch* to plague him,—*both from Ireland!*

Adjourned to meet at Pigeon Creek the third Tuesday in December next. Concluded with prayer.

ELEVENTH MEETING.

PIGEON CREEK, Dec. 20th, 1785.—The Presbytery met according to adjournment. Ubi post preces sederunt, the Rev. Messrs. James Finley, &c. The Presbytery was opened by Mr. Addison, a candidate from Scotland, with a sermon from Romans v. 10. The committee appointed to examine such ministers and candidates as may come into our bounds is continued.

Mr. Alexander Addison, a candidate from the Presbytery of Aberlowe, in Scotland, having produced a copy of his licensure, and a certificate of his good deportment from said Presbytery, and having also applied to this Presbytery to be taken under our care, the Presbytery proceeded to make some inquiries of him, in order to their having clearness for said purpose; but, after conversing with him at some length, did not obtain the satisfaction desired; and, therefore, cannot agree to receive him as a candidate under their care, without some limitation: yet, as some things appear very agreeable in Mr. Addison, they are not without hopes of obtaining such satisfaction, and therefore permit him to preach in our bounds until the next meeting of Presbytery. Application was made from the town of Washington for the stated labors of Mr. Addison until our next meeting, and also for a member to moderate in drawing up a call for him. The Presbytery agree that Mr. Addison's labors be allowed statedly, until our next meeting, to the town of Washington; but as the moderating, in drawing up a call, does not consist with a minute of Synod on this subject, we cannot at present make the appointment.(22)

---

(22) We have not been able to find the "minute of Synod" referred to; but it is of no consequence. The cautious and guarded manner in which the Presbytery acted in this case, was, no doubt, intended to

Mr. Barr, a member of the Presbytery of New Castle, being present, informed us that a call had been drawn up for him by the united congregations of Pittsburg and Pittstownship, under the inspection of Mr. Finley; and that upon this call being presented to him, he declared his acceptance thereof, upon condition that this Presbytery approve thereof. We do approve thereof, provided Mr. Barr becomes a member of this Presbytery. Adjourned to meet at the Upper meeting-house, in the forks of Youghiogheny, the third Tuesday of April next. Concluded with prayer.

TWELFTH MEETING.

REHOBOTH, Tuesday, April 18th, 1786. Presbytery met according to adjournment. Ubi post preces sederunt, the Rev. Messrs. James Finley, &c. The Presbytery was opened with a sermon on Ps. lxxi. 16, by Mr. M'Millan. The committee for examining such ministers and candidates as may come into our bounds, continued.

Upon inquiry, found the congregations satisfied with the diligence and care of their respective pastors.

The Presbytery having formerly urged this congregation (Unity,) to settle with Mr. Power for the time of his laboring among them, and as they have given no notice of their compliance, the Presbytery deem it improper to appoint them supplies, until they have given satisfaction with regard to such settlement. A supplication for supplies from Wheeling brought in and read.

Upon a new application of the town of Washington, the Presbytery agree that Mr. Addison continue to preach until the meeting of Synod.(23)

---

avoid giving offence to the people of Washington, and to deal tenderly with Mr. Addison.

(23) Mr. Addison, after some time, gave up preaching, and turned his attention to the Law — became a member of the Washington bar, and rose to distinction as a lawyer. He afterwards became a Judge of the Court, and acted in this capacity during the latter part of his life—

The Presbytery being sufficiently informed that the congregation of Sewickly are divided in their sentiments respecting the place of public worship — that one party has determined to build at a place remote from the place first agreed upon, the other determined not to join with them; by which, Mr. Power is quite embarrassed, and refers to the Presbytery to judge what his future conduct should be. The Presbytery, after considering the matter, resolved that unless said congregation do alter their proceedings, Mr. Power cannot continue with them as formerly; and that, therefore, he call them together, and inform them thereof. The Presbytery do also judge that unless they agree to join together, the union between him and them should continue no longer than until the 1st of May next; but that he after that should be at liberty to accept of an offer from any other quarter.

Henry Taylor appeared before Presbytery, and signified that, upon due deliberation, he was earnestly desirous that the jar between him and the Presbytery, respecting a judgment concerning his conduct on a certain occasion, be removed, and to live in love and concord with that branch of the church where he resides: and therefore professes that he is sorry that, by his conduct, he has given offence to the church; and that he will conscientiously guard against the like conduct for the future, and is willing to submit to an admonition before the Presbytery. The Presbytery agree to accept of his acknowledgment and promise, and that the Moderator do admonish him accordingly, and that this judg-

---

residing in Pittsburg till his death. He took an active part in the affairs of the first Presbyterian church, and was its efficient friend and supporter.

"Alexander Addison was president of the courts in the four counties; and I venture to say that a more intelligent, learned, upright, and fearless judge was not to be found in the State."—Dr. Carnahan's "Western Insurrection."

"His charge to the Grand Jury, September 1st, 1794, during the Insurrection, is a noble monument of his talents and worth."—See Haz. Reg., Vol. XII., p. 241.

ment be read before the congregation of Chartiers. To this judgment, Mr. Taylor submitted, and was admonished accordingly. Adjourned to meet at Pigeon Creek the third Tuesday of August next. Concluded with prayer.

THIRTEENTH MEETING.

PIGEON CREEK, Tuesday, Aug. 15th, 1786.—The Presbytery met according to adjournment. Ubi post preces sederunt, the Rev. Messrs. James Finley, &c. The Presbytery was opened with a sermon from 2 Cor. xi. 9, by Mr. Hugh Morrison, a candidate from the Presbytery of Roote, in Ireland.

Mr. Smith reported settlement with Cross Creek—has nothing to demand from them, save what became due from December last.

Mr. Power reports that he called the congregation of Sewickly together, according to the order of Presbytery, and notified them of the judgment of Presbytery: that the heads of the congregation, after consultation being had, informed him that they determined to continue in union, and had fixed upon a spot of ground for erecting a house of worship, and that, in the mean time, they desired him to preach at the old meeting-house; that therefore he yet continued with them as usual. A supplication for supplies brought in and read. Supplies granted to George's Creek and Three Ridges by Mr. Dod.

The Presbytery, upon deliberation, find it is not in their power to make any appointments on the Sabbath for Unity and Salem congregations, as all the members have already as many appointments as they can fulfil before our fall meeting. Mr. Finley, however, is appointed to preach at Unity on a week-day as soon as convenient, and endeavor to have a settlement made between them and Mr. Power. Their supplication for liberty to present a call to Mr. Hugh Morrison, Jr., the Presbytery conceive cannot be granted, as they are entire strangers to the gentleman, and know not whether ever he was regularly licensed to preach the gospel; he having never called upon the committee, nor shown his credentials to any member of the Presbytery. The Presbytery conceive that the supplication of Mingo Creek, Horse-Shoe Bottom, and Pike Run congregations, for a man to preside in drawing up a call for Mr. H. Morrison, Jr., cannot be granted for the reasons assigned above. Mr. Hugh Morrison, Sen., a candidate from the Presbytery of Roote, in Ireland, applied to be taken under the care of this Presbytery; but the Presbytery did not see their way clear to admit him.

G. Latimer applied to Presbytery, requesting a rehearing of the affair between him and Deborah Ross. The Presbytery agree that he have liberty to offer whatever new light he thinks may be of use to him upon the subject; and if it shall appear that he affords new light, that then they will reconsider the affair. The Presbytery appoint Messrs. Alexander M'Clure, Æneas M'Allister, James Moor, George Shields, John Fulton, and William Beard, elders, to meet at John Man's, near Long Run, with Mr. M'Millan, who, with them, is appointed to hear and determine in an affair between a certain John Hamilton and Sarah Reyburn, on Tuesday week; and that a copy of this minute be sent to said Sarah, who is ordered to attend, as well as said Hamilton, with what evidence they have. Messrs. John Brice (24) and James Hughes

(24) "The Rev. John Brice was a native of Hartford County, Maryland. He removed with the family to Western Pennsylvania, and received his education chiefly under the direction of the Rev. Joseph Smith. He studied theology partly under Mr. Smith, and partly under Mr. Dod. He and James Hughes were students together at Mr. Smith's, and were licensed together, April 15th, 1788, by the Presbytery of Redstone. By the same Presbytery he was ordained and installed pastor of the congregations Three Ridges and Forks of Wheeling, April 22d, 1790. When the Presbytery of Ohio was formed in 1793, he was one of its original members. In the above-named congregations, he labored until about the year 1807, when, on account of ill-health, the pastoral relation between him and them was dissolved. He still continued, however, to preach the gospel in Green County, Pennsylvania, and in the

(25) appeared before Presbytery, and offered themselves to be taken on trials in order to their being licensed to preach the gospel. The Presbytery proceeded to converse with them

---

adjacent parts of Virginia, as often as health would permit, until the 18th of April, 1810, when he was dismissed to connect himself with the Presbytery of Lancaster. He died the next year, August 26th, 1811, aged fifty-one years. He was a man of nervous temperament, subject, occasionally, to great despondency of mind, but of deep piety. His labors were attended with a divine blessing, and many rich fruits of his ministry have appeared, since his decease, both in his former charge and in the country adjacent. The late Rev. John Brice M'Coy, of the Presbytery of Washington, who died at Wheeling October 18th, 1841, was his grandson."—Append. Life of Macurdy.

"The Rev. Mr. Brice married one of the sisters of James and John Kerr, both sons-in-law of the Rev. Dr. Power, and was called to Wheeling, where he became pastor of two congregations—one at West Alexander, and the other at the Forks of Wheeling, near Sheppard's. In the summer of 1792, I think it was, I was living on Wheeling, when John Kerr and his sister died on the same day. Mrs. Brice died on Sabbath-day, whilst her husband was two or more miles distant, administering the sacrament I was boarding in the family of a James Martin, whose wife attended Mrs. Brice in her last moments. At that time Mrs. Martin had an infant at home; and therefore, after paying the last duties to the departed, returned, and told her husband, a young woman residing in the family, and myself, that Mrs. Brice was dead; and that nearly her last words were 'My brother John will die to-day! and this night we'll meet in heaven!' We did not hear from John Kerr, who really died the same day, until the ensuing Friday; and who, we were told, made, in his last moments, a similar declaration. The circumstances which I have here related were strange; but they are stated as they occurred."—William Darby, Esq.

Mr. John Kerr's residence was on Pigeon Creek, twenty-five miles from the residence of his sister!

(25) "The Rev. James Hughes was a native of York County, Pennsylvania. His father, Rowland Hughes, emigrated from England. His parents were both esteemed for their consistent religious character; especially his mother, who was eminently pious. About the year 1780, he removed, with his mother and family, to Washington County; his father having died about a year before. His education, so far as we have been able to learn anything respecting it, was prosecuted under the direction of the Rev. Joseph Smith, of Upper Buffalo, in that county; with whom it is also probable that he studied theology." ["James

REVD. JAMES HUGHS,

First Preacher of the Gospel licensed in the West, and first President of Miami University.

P. S. Duval & Co. Steam lith. press Phila.

on their experimental acquaintance with religion, and proposed to them several cases of conscience, and having obtained satisfaction on these points, agreed to take them on trials. The

Hughes, while with that critic, Mr. Dod, acquired, or rather in him was developed, a taste for the accuracies and intricacies of science, which he still improved until he became the president of a state university." —Letter of Rev. J. Lindley."] "He was licensed to preach the gospel April 15th, 1788, by the Presbytery of Redstone. His labors appear to have been very acceptable to the churches, as three several calls were presented to him: one from the united congregations of Short Creek and Lower Buffalo; one from Donegal, Fairfield, and Wheatfield; and one from New Providence and the South Fork of Ten-Mile. The first of these calls he accepted, and was ordained by the same Presbytery, and installed the pastor of Short Creek and Lower Buffalo on the 21st of April, 1790."—Pres. Ad. 1845, and App. to Life of Macurdy.

The following extract from "Fragment of Recollections," written by Charles Hammond, Esq., of Cincinnati, a man of distinguished eminence and worth, and published by him in the Cincinnati Gazette in 1838, is worthy of an insertion here. We do not know to which of Mr. Hughes's churches Mr. Hammond refers, but it is not material:—

"In the month of June, 1788, an arrangement was completed for organizing a religious congregation many miles in advance of any existing congregation. Preparation was made in the depth of the forest. A rough wooden erection was constructed as a pulpit, and felled timber was arranged as seats. Thursday was the day of the week selected for the first meeting; and the sun never shone on a more genial day in the month of June. For miles around the whole population was collected together. The minister came to make his trial sermon, a young licentiate, with his young wife in company. In the tract of country I have described, the Presbyterian clergy were the religious pioneers — John M'Millan and Joseph Smith. Young men studied divinity in the private establishments of those pioneers. More than this, they acquired all the elements of such education as they possessed in these same family establishments. From these beginnings the college at Canonsburg arose. The founders were the clergymen I have named, and their few friends and associates.

"The minister who presented himself to make his trial sermon on that day was the pupil and son-in-law of the Rev. Joseph Smith.

"The Rev. James Hughes has since been well known as a faithful and unpretending preacher of the gospel in the Presbyterian church. In its infancy this church was sadly divided upon the vexed question of Psalmody. For this it was rooted out from its first locality, furnished

Presbytery examined them on the Latin and Greek languages, and metaphysics. — Sustained.

Presbytery examined Messrs. Brice and Hughes on logic

---

by a zealous member. A stranger of the Episcopal church bestowed its abiding-spot in the immediate vicinity.

"In these congregations he labored upwards of 24 years with very encouraging success. During that period, a number of revivals occurred under his ministry, and many precious souls were born into the kingdom of Christ. On the 29th of June, 1814, he resigned his pastoral charge, and was dismissed by the Presbytery of Ohio, to which he then belonged, and of which he was an original member, to join the Presbytery of Miami. About the same time he removed to Urbana, Ohio; where, for three years, he acted as a stated supply and missionary. In the month of June, 1818, he was chosen Principal of what is now the Miami University. This office he accepted and held to the time of his death; which occurred May 22d, 1821, at Oxford, Butler County, Ohio, in the 56th year of his age. He died firmly resting on the atoning blood of that Saviour whom he had so long and so faithfully preached. "At every time, through his sickness, when he could converse, he expressed his unwavering confidence in the atonement of Christ; and that overcoming faith cheered him in his dying hours. With the utmost composure, tranquillity, and resignation, he languished and died. He expressed great anxiety for the prosperity of Sion, for which he had been so long zealously engaged. He died as he lived. He was always, through life, aloof from the world, and escaped all contentions about worldly affairs. He was an affectionate husband and father, ruling his house according to the testimony of the Lord."—"Mr. Hughes was an early and decided friend of missions. He was an active member of the Board of Trustees of the Western Missionary Society for a number of years, and, as appears from their records, was a very constant attendant on their meetings. Besides other missionary tours in destitute settlements, he performed two journeys, at least, as a missionary to the Indian tribes on the Sandusky River."

Mr. Hughes's Journal while on his missionary tour among the Wyandots, published in the Miss. Mag., Vol. I. p. 401–6, is one of the most interesting and instructive we ever read. He was eminently successful in this work. Nothing but time and opportunity were wanting to have made him another Brainerd.

"The Rev. Smiley Hughes, who died shortly after he was licensed, and the Rev. Thomas E. Hughes, deceased, were his brothers. He had two sons who entered the ministry, viz.: the Rev. Joseph S. Hughes, and

and moral philosophy, and Mr. Hughes on mathematics and natural philosophy — all sustained. Presbytery assigned to Mr. Hughes an Exegesis — "An sit originale peccatum?" Mr. Brice, ditto —"An mortuorum resurrectio erit?" — both at next spring meeting. Adjourned to meet at Dunlap's Creek the third Tuesday in October. Concluded with prayer.

FOURTEENTH MEETING.

DUNLAP'S CREEK, 17th Oct., 1786.—Presbytery met according to adjournment. Ubi post preces sederunt, the Rev. Messrs. J. Finley, &c. Presbytery opened with a sermon on Hosea ii. 1, 2, by Mr. Dod. Mr. Finley reports that he had fulfilled his appointment at Unity, and a plan adopted for settling with Mr. Power. The committee sent to Long Run report they had come to a judgment in the affair; that Mr. Hamilton appealed, but is not now present to sustain it.

The Presbytery being informed that Mr. Hugh Morrison, Sen., has misrepresented the conduct of this Presbytery relative to him, Mr. Clark and Mr. M'Millan are appointed, when they preach at Monteur's Run and Potato Garden, to set that matter in a proper point of light, and warn the people against encouraging him. George Latimer now come—and it appearing that some new light may be obtained respecting his affair, the Presbytery agree to hear, and determine the same at their next meeting.

A reference from the sessions of Dunlap's creek, respecting a certain Armstrong Porter—brought in, and the minutes of the session relative thereto read: by which it appears that said Armstrong Porter has been guilty of profane swearing—the evidence of which he does not deny—and also that he absents himself from public worship, which he acknowledges; but his reasons do not appear sufficient. Upon the whole,

---

the Rev. Thomas E. Hughes, of the Presbytery of Oxford. The Rev. David S. Anderson, who is also a member of the Presbytery of Oxford, is his nephew."—Pres. Ad. 1845, and App. to Life of Macurdy.

the Presbytery judge that the said Armstrong Porter submit to a rebuke from the Moderator of the session, and promise reformation and a more circumspect walk in future and that a copy of this minute be referred to the congregation upon which he may be admitted to privileges in case the session have nothing further against him. Mr. Porter does not see fit to submit to the aforesaid judgment. Adjourned to meet at Sewickly on the first Tuesday of December. Concluded with prayer.

The meeting at Sewickly being prevented by the extremity of the season, the members who did attend, appointed to meet at the stated time, at Roundhill.

FIFTEENTH MEETING.

ROUNDHILL, April 17th, 1787.—Presbytery met according to adjournment. Ubi post preces sederunt, Rev. Messrs. James Finley, &c. Presbytery opened with a sermon from Matthew x., 32, 33, by Mr. Waite Cornwell, (26) a licensed candidate from an association of Connecticut. The Rev. Samuel Barr, having accepted a call within our bounds —was received from the New Castle Presbytery.

An application from Sewickly, requesting one-fourth part of Mr. Power's time. Mr. Cornwell, willing to tarry some time in these parts and under the direction of the Presbytery, and they being fully satisfied of his being regularly licensed,

---

(26) Waite Cornwell. The librarian of Yale College, from whom, through the Rev. Dr. Sprague, information about Mr. Cornwell was sought, states: "By the class catalogue, I find that the Rev. Waite Cornwell came to the college from Middletown, and was graduated in 1782. In Dr. David C. Field's Centennial Address, or rather in a note appended to it, it is stated that Waite Cornwell preached occasionally, but never had charge of a parish—moved, late in life, to some part of the state of Ohio, where he died, in March, 1816. I find nothing more concerning him." The Rev. Dr. Lindley states that he assisted Mr. Dod, during a revival at Lindley's Fort, in 1787. His health was feeble, which probably led to his travelling, and prevented his settling as a pastor.

and of his good moral character, from his testimonials, took him under their direction.

Mr. Finley, having made application in behalf of Unity Congregation for supplies — Mr. Barr appointed to inform them by writing, "That the Presbytery are surprised that the settlement with Mr. Power is deferred so long; and that they cannot consistently expect any supplies until such settlement is made." Presbytery find that members had fulfilled their appointments generally. When otherwise, reasons sustained.

The supplies from the south part of Sewickly congregation being taken under consideration, it is thought proper that the Rev. Mr. Clark, Messrs. A. Mitchell, and A. M'Clure be appointed to attend at the usual place of meeting in Sewickly congregation, on the first Tuesday of June next, in order to take the minds of the people in both parts of the congregation respecting their continuing as a united body. And if they do not agree to remain united, to see that a fair settlement be made with Mr. Power, in order to prepare the way for a dismission at our next meeting, by their representatives, duly prepared to give such light as may be necessary in order to a final issue of the matter.

John Hamilton appeared before Presbytery, and desired that a new committee be appointed to reconsider his affair. The Presbytery being of opinion that Mr. Hamilton has not given them sufficient reason to expect any new light on the affair, cannot agree to grant his request, and consequently do confirm the judgment of the committee.

George Latimer and Deborah Ross being present, the Presbytery proceeded to consider their affair. The Presbytery, after maturely deliberating upon it, and examining all the witnesses that were produced on either side, cannot but testify their abhorrence of such conduct as is mentioned in D. Ross's solemn declaration; and had there been no obscurity thrown on her evidence by the seeming, (though perhaps not ill-designed) variations in her conduct and evidence, we would have been very clear in asserting that the censure in the former judgment was low, but as Mrs. Ross's evidence is rendered, in part, somewhat dubious, although there is too much ground to suspect immodest conduct in Mr. Latimer, yet we cannot, with sufficient clearness, fix such a positive censure upon him—but think there is ground for: and we do hereby admonish him to be more cautious and watchful in time to come: and as this affair is become public, do order this judgment to be read to the congregation of which he has been a member, on the Sabbath day. To this judgment the parties submitted.

Upon inquiry, congregations are satisfied with the diligence and care of their pastors.

Mr. Clark represents that the congregation of Lebanon has not taken effectual measures to discharge their dues to him; and that he apprehends it will be necessary to notify said congregation that such application will be made, and call upon them to attend, by their representatives, duly prepared to do what is necessary in the affair. Mr. M'Clure is appointed to notify the congregation thereof.

Messrs. Joseph Patterson and James M'Gready, having offered themselves to be taken on trial, in order to their being licensed to preach the gospel, the Presbytery proceeded to examine them on their experimental acquaintance with religion, cases of conscience, logic, and moral philosophy, and Mr. M'Gready on Latin and Greek,—all sustained, as parts of trial.

Messrs. Brice and Hughes—their Exegeses sustained. Mr. Brice appointed to prepare a discourse on John vi. 29; Mr. Hughes, on Rom. iii. 28, by next meeting. Mr. Patterson, an Exegesis, "Whether miracles are an evidence of a divine mission, and what miracles do prove such mission?" by next meeting. Mr. M'Gready, "An sit concursus Dei cum omnibus hominum actionibus?" by next meeting. Presbytery proceeded to read and consider the plan of government and discipline proposed by the committee of the Synod of New York and Philadelphia, and find many things which should be altered, and many omitted, which, we apprehend, ought to be in a draught of church discipline. Adjourned to meet at Lebanon the third Tuesday in August. Concluded with prayer.

SIXTEENTH MEETING.

LEBANON, (27) Aug. 21st, 1787. (28) — Presbytery met, &c. Opened with a sermon by Mr. Dod from Psalms cx. 3. Mr. Barr reports — fulfilled, (his writing to Unity congrega-

---

(27) LEBANON.—This church was probably organized by the Rev. Dr. M'Millan in 1778 or 1779. Its first pastor was the Rev. John Clark, it being then united with Bethel in 1781 or 1782. Mr. Clark was received into the Presbytery of Redstone, at Pigeon Creek, March 12th, 1783, (see Minutes,) but appears to have entered informally upon his pastoral labors, in his united charge of Bethel and Lebanon, some time before. They were then called the eastern and western divisions of Peters' Creek congregation. The pastoral relation between Mr. Clark and Lebanon was dissolved April 17th, 1788. It appears to have continued vacant, and been supplied occasionally by the Presbytery, till June 28th, 1797, when it united again with Bethel, under the pastoral care of the Rev. Wm. Woods. It became vacant again in 1820; Bethel taking the whole of Mr. W.'s pastoral labors thenceforward. It subsequently had as its pastors, the Rev. T. Baird, (for many years the editor of the Christian Herald,) the Rev. S. Henderson, (now of Beaver Presbytery,) the Rev. W. G. Johnston—dismissed, June 21st, 1843—recalled, August 31st, 1843—again dismissed, April 15th, 1845; the Rev. J. M'Conoughy —settled, January 30th, 1846—dismissed, September 5th, 1848; and the Rev. O. H. Miller, the present pastor — settled, second Thursday in February, 1849. Number of communicants reported in 1854—140.

(28) 1787.—During this year, the Constitution of the United States was adopted, and our country commenced a new career of prosperity. It was during this year, also, that the "Ordinance for the government of the North-Western Territory" was passed, which resulted in immense benefit, not only to the country embraced by the Territory, but to western Pennsylvania and Virginia, by eventually securing complete relief from Indian troubles, and opening the way for rapid emigration from western Pennsylvania, over the Ohio river, and thus carrying Presbyterianism over the boundless West. This was, therefore, the *Annus mirabilis* for our forefathers; but their troubles from border warfare did not entirely cease till *six years* afterwards.

tion.) The committee appointed to meet at Sewickly—reported, fulfilled — and that after all their endeavors, found but little ground to expect a union; and that upon this, they urged them to be speedy, and use their utmost endeavors to settle their arrearages to Mr. Power, and report the same to this Presbytery.

Mr. Power reports that the judgment in the case of G. Latimer and D. Ross was read publicly, according to order.

Mr. Robert Hall having offered some reason to expect new light upon an affair between him and the session of Mount Pleasant, Presbytery agreed to grant them a new hearing at their meeting next Spring; and ordered Mr. Power to grant citations for witnesses when he saw it necessary, or was applied to for that purpose.

The affair of Mr. Clark and Lebanon congregation deferred till next meeting.

The affair of Sewickly congregation and Mr. Power being maturely considered, the Presbytery, after all the light they could obtain, found it necessary that the pastoral relation between him and them should be dissolved, and it is hereby dissolved. The Presbytery also enjoin it upon said congregation, that they take effectual measures to settle and pay off their arrearages to Mr. Power, and report the same at the next meeting of Presbytery. Mr. Power is appointed to read this minute publicly to the congregation.

Messrs. Finley, Power, and Dunlap are appointed as a committee to examine and appoint such ministers and candidates as may come into our bounds until October, 1788.

Messrs. Brice and Hughes — their discourses — sustained.* Mr. B. had appointed to him a Presbyterial exercise on Heb. xi. 27, and Mr. H. on Rom. viii. 3, by next meeting.

Mr. Patterson — his Exegesis — sustained.* A homily appointed to him on Gal. iii. 24, by next meeting.

---

* These and similar abbreviated forms of expression, in these cases, will henceforward be employed.

John Brice, Joseph Patterson, and James M'Gready, examined on Natural Philosophy, and James Hughes with them on Theology, at some length — all sustained. Adjourned to meet at Pigeon Creek the third Tuesday in October. Concluded with prayer.

SEVENTEENTH MEETING.

PIGEON CREEK, Oct. 16th, 1787.—Presbytery met, &c. Opened with a sermon from Micah vi. 8, by Mr. Smith.

The affair of Mr. Clark and Lebanon congregation deferred till next meeting, as no commissioner appears from that congregation. The Presbytery recommend to that congregation to do all in their power to discharge their arrearages to Mr. Clark, and appear at our next meeting, duly prepared to have the affair finally issued.

No report from Sewickly congregation.

Mr. M'Gready read his Exegesis, which was sustained. A homily appointed him on Rom. iii. 31, by next meeting.

Messrs. Brice and Hughes — their Presbyterial exercises— sustained. A lecture appointed to Mr. Hughes on Hebrews xii. 22–29; and to Mr. Brice, on John iii. 1–9, by next meeting.

Mr. Patterson — his homily — sustained. A Presbyterial exercise on Genesis iii. 15, appointed him, by next meeting. Adjourned to meet at Bethel, the second Tuesday in December. Concluded with prayer.

EIGHTEENTH MEETING.

BETHEL, (29) Tuesday, Dec. 11th, 1787.—Presbytery

(29) Bethel.—This church, in Snowden township, Allegheny County, is one of the oldest of our western churches. In the latter part of 1778, or early in 1779, the Rev. Dr. M'Millan first preached the gospel within its bounds; and, probably, about that time organized the church. The Rev. John Clark became its pastor about the year 1781. It was then united with Lebanon, under his pastoral care. Its bounds were at first quite extensive. Several Presbyterian churches have since been formed

met, &c. Opened with a lecture from John iii. 1–9, by Mr. J. Brice.

Mr. Patterson — his Presbyterial exercise—sustained. A lecture on John xv. 1–8, assigned to him by next meeting.

Mr. M'Gready — his homily — sustained. A Presbyterial exercise on Heb. ii. 9–16, assigned him by next meeting.

Messrs. Brice, Hughes, Patterson, and M'Gready examined on systematic theology — sustained. Messrs. Brice and Hughes—lectures—sustained. A popular sermon on Phillippians ii. 12, latter clause, assigned to Mr. Brice — and on Psalms lxxxix. 16, to Mr. Hughes — by next meeting. The Presbytery finding that the affair between Mr. Clark and Lebanon congregation is in a fair way to be settled, defer any further procedure therein till our next meeting. Adjourned to meet at Mount Pleasant, third Tuesday of April. Concluded with prayer.

---

within its original limits: Bethany, (now under the pastoral care of the Rev. Dr. Jeffery,) Pisgah, Centre, and Concord. Its first elders were James Dinsmore, James Brice, and James Kirkpatrick. Mr. Clark continued its pastor till his death, July 13th, 1797. But a short time before his death, the Rev. Wm. Woods, a native of Lancaster County, and a graduate of Dickinson College—having received his theological training partly from the Rev. Dr. R. Smith, of Pequea, and partly from the Rev. Dr. Witherspoon — after spending some time as a missionary licentiate, accepted a call from this church, in union with Lebanon, and was ordained and installed their pastor, June 28th, 1797. His pastoral relation was dissolved in 1831, and he died Oct. 17th, 1834. He was succeeded by the Rev. George Marshall, the present pastor, in 1832. It is now a sole pastoral charge, and had been so some time before Mr. Woods ceased to be its pastor. Though it has been a mother of churches, it still retains its strength and vigor—numbering about 176 members. It has enjoyed many seasons of refreshing visitations of the Holy Spirit. The first was in 1787, under the ministry of the Rev. John Clark. It shared largely in the blessed influence of the widely extended revivals of 1803–4, and has had some cheering seasons of divine power and grace since that period. It has also, by emigration, made many valuable contributions to western churches. Not only private members, but many elders and ministers, born and reared in its bounds, are to be found in the wide West.

NINETEENTH MEETING.

MOUNT PLEASANT, (30) Tuesday, April 15th, 1788.—Presbytery met, &c. Presbytery was opened by a sermon on

(30) A few days before this meeting of the Presbytery in Dr. Power's church, an event of some notoriety had occurred in the bounds of his Sewickly charge. A large number of emigrants from New England had come out, the previous fall, and had spent some time in the neighborhood of what is now West Newton, then called Simeralls' Ferry. Late in the fall they launched their boat, which they called the "May-flower," and set off for their future home, down the Youghiogheny, and Monongahela, and the Ohio, and formed their settlement at Marietta. Dr. Hildreth, of Marietta, gives the following account of their starting their boat from Robstown, or West Newton:

"After laying in a stock of provisions, they pushed out merrily into the 'Yoh,' as it was familiarly called by all the borderers of that region, and floated rapidly along, sometimes grazing on the shallows, and at other times grounding on the sand-bars. By dint of rowing and pushing, they made out to get on, especially after falling into the larger current of the Monongahela, and reached Pittsburg on Sunday evening. They were now at the junction of those two noble streams, the Allegheny and the Monongahela, and saw the waters of the charming Ohio, the object of all their toils, and were, apparently, at the end of their journey. Near the point of land where the Ohio takes its name, they landed their uncouth and unwieldy water-craft, making it fast to a stake on the bank. It was late in the afternoon — and the men went up into the town, to purchase some articles needed to make the families comfortable on their downward voyage. Pittsburg then contained 4 or 500 inhabitants, several stores; and a small garrison of troops was kept in old Fort Pitt. To our travellers, who had lately seen nothing but trees and rocks, with here and there a solitary hut, it seemed to be quite a large town. The houses were chiefly built of logs; but, now and then, one had assumed the appearance of neatness and comfort."

Such was the beginning of that new emigration which filled the great territory with a civilized population, that has converted the wilderness into a garden, and made the valleys to bloom as a rose. Some of these emigrants had tarried behind, and lodged with Mr. Power's people through the winter, and were just gone when this Presbytery met at Mount Pleasant. One tradition is, that another emigrating party, arriving to join their friends at Simerall's Ferry, did not get on "in time for the boat," and remained, along with some who had been left of the

Philippians ii. 12, by Mr. Brice. Messrs. Brice and Hughes —sermons—sustained.

The Commissioners appeared from Unity congregation, and report that they have discharged the greater part of what was due from them to Mr. Power, and that they will use their utmost endeavors to have the whole discharged as soon as possible. The Presbytery do therefore agree to appoint them supplies. "The Presbytery having received," &c., (see Formula for the Government of the Church, Chapter 14, Section 8,) Messrs. John Brice and James Hughes were licensed to preach the gospel. Messrs. Patterson and M'Gready—lectures—sustained.

Mr. Hamilton having made application for advice respecting a difference subsisting between him and George Glenn, the Presbytery appoint the representatives of Donegal congregation to endeavor to settle said difference, which, if they cannot effect, the Presbytery order the parties to appear before Mr. Power's session, at such time as it may be convenient for said session to attend upon them.

John Coleman (31) having left his wife in Ireland, and mar-

---

first party, to take care of their beasts through the winter, and take the land route in the spring. These New England folks introduced the new tunes—especially the *fugueing music*, as it was called, among our Scotch-Irish people — that winter. Two or three of them were good singing-masters: one of them, M'Knight, went up, in his vocation, as far as Dunlap's Creek. The good old "*twelve tunes of David*," as they were considered by some, were all that were known previously. The introduction of these tunes, in some of the churches, raised quite a breeze. In one instance, when the Clerk opened, with full blast, on one of them, some one of the old people struck in upon one of their old favorites, and made such sad confusion, that Col. Cooke, who was present, rose, and seconding the remarks of his distressed pastor, gave the people a severe rebuke and sharp lecture, which completely humbled and subdued them.

(31) The case of John Coleman would have occasioned some difficulty had it been brought to an issue. But, as it will appear in the sequel, it was deferred until one of their members, Mr. Power, along with the session of Salem, should take further testimony, and report. This is

ried another in this country, his former wife being yet alive, makes application to this Presbytery to be restored to church privileges; alleging that, by the laws of God and man, he was free from her, as by her conduct, in his absence, she had violated her marriage covenant in a very essential part, of which he had sufficient information before his second marriage — which he proposes to support by evidence. (Three witnesses — Alexander Hunter, Barbara Hunter and Robert Reyburn — were brought forward, and, on oath, deposed many things very unfavorable to the character of the first wife; and as Mr. Coleman proposed to adduce other witnesses, Mr. Power was appointed, together with the session of Salem, to take their evidence, and report the same at the next meeting of Presbytery, in the fall.)

The Presbytery, according to the order of our last August meeting, proceeded to consider the affair of Mr. Hall and the session of Mount Pleasant; and after fully hearing both parties, do judge that, though Mr. Hall was disappointed in his expectations, and might thereby be a sufferer, yet we do not think that Mr. Power was to blame, nor that Mr. Hall had any just reasons for using some expressions reflecting on Mr. Power's character; and we further judge, that, before he be restored to distinguishing privileges, he acknowledge his rashness in using such expressions, and that he be admonished by

---

the last we hear of it. Yet the man, by his witnesses, before Presbytery, had made out a strong case of conjugal infidelity, before he married his second wife. It appears that, three years before, (1785,) the Synod of New York and Philadelphia were much divided, in their sentiments, on this subject. The following question had been referred to them, by the Donegal Presbytery, for their decision, viz.:

"Whether, on full proof of adultery by one party, the Presbytery has a right to declare the marriage so void, as that the innocent party may marry again, without being liable to church censure? And after some time spent in debating the case, it was moved and agreed that each member should speak to the question, in the order of the roll. After which the vote was taken, and the question carried in the affirmative, by a *small* majority." (Printed Records, pp. 509–10.)

the Moderator. To this judgment Mr. Hall submitted, and was admonished accordingly.

The Presbytery finding that there are no good grounds to expect that the affair between Mr. Clark and the Lebanon congregation will be comfortably settled, do therefore judge that the pastoral relation between him and that congregation ought to be dissolved, and is hereby dissolved; and enjoin them to produce a settlement with Mr. Clark, at our next meeting; and Mr. Clark is hereby appointed to preach in that congregation on a week-day, and Mr. Shields to read this minute.

Ordered, that those who have not produced settlements bring them in at our next meeting.

A reference being brought from Lebanon congregation, respecting a certain John Barret, the consideration whereof was deferred till this meeting; but he not attending, the Presbytery further defer it until our next meeting, and cite him to attend.

A popular sermon, 1 John v. 4, assigned to Mr. Patterson; on Romans v. 20, to Mr. M'Gready — by our next meeting. Adjourned to meet at Chartiers, second Tuesday of August. Concluded with prayer.

TWENTIETH MEETING.

CHARTIERS, Tuesday, August 12th, 1788.—Presbytery met according to adjournment, &c. The Presbytery opened with a sermon from I. John v. 4, by Mr. Patterson; Mr. M'Gready, also, a sermon on Romans v. 20 — both of which sustained.

Mr. Power informs Presbytery that the affair between William Hamilton and John Glen is settled. Mr. Clark fulfilled his appointment at Lebanon—no settlement yet obtained. "The Presbytery having received," &c., Messrs. Joseph Patterson and James M'Gready,(32) &c., (see Formula for the Government of the Church, Chapter 14, Section 8,) they were licensed to preach the gospel. Application being made to this Presbytery for their judgment in the following case, viz., "Whether ministers ought, in the administration of baptism, to require of parents to promise to perform certain duties, or only to recommend the performance of them?" The Presbytery are unanimously of opinion, that it is the duty of ministers not only to recommend, but to require of parents a solemn promise that they will, through grace, conscientiously perform certain duties which are usually mentioned on such occasions. (33) Adjourned to meet at Rehoboth, third Tuesday of October. Concluded with prayer.

(32) BIOGRAPHICAL SKETCH OF JAMES M'GREADY. — The name of M'Gready is connected with revivals. He was blest in being instrumental of a revival of religion, in his early

---

(33) This *unanimous expression* of the views of the Presbytery shows how much they dissented from the more lax views and practice too prevalent in some parts of our church, at the present day. The New School brethren often, now-a-days, assert that the old fathers of our Western church leaned, in their sympathies, to the New-side party of a still earlier period; and that as they (the New School) claim to be the descendants of the New-side party of former times, they have a stronger claim of kindred to the founders of the Western church than we have. The claim is absurd. Our fathers possessed some of the best qualities of both the old parties—the revival spirit of the New-side, and the strict rules of discipline of the Old-side. How little like the sentiments or language of the above minute is the following, from the Records of the New-side Synod of New York!

"Previously to the administration of baptism, the minister shall inquire into the parents' knowledge of the great and fundamental doctrines of the gospel, and the regularity of their life; and being satisfied, so as to admit them, shall, in public, point out the special duties of the parents, and particularly that they teach their children the doctrines and precepts of Christianity contained in the Scriptures of the Old and New Testament, and comprised in the Westminster Confession of Faith and Catechisms, which, therefore, they shall *recommend unto them.*" (See Records, p. 266.)

Our fathers were conscientiously careful in binding solemn vows upon parents, when they applied the seal of the covenant to their children.

ministry, in North Carolina, the salutary effects of which are felt to this day in churches, in different States, enjoying the labors of faithful men who then came into the visible church of Christ, on a profession of faith. Subsequently he was honored of God to be the first agent that moved successfully in breaking up the deep sleep that weighed down the Christian public; and was personally active in the commencement of that revival which began, in 1800, in Kentucky, and soon was felt in Tennessee, Ohio and Western Pennsylvania—in 1802, on to 1804, and was enjoyed in parts of North Carolina, South Carolina and Virginia. The fruits of this revival remain to this day, and will be felt, in their remote consequences, forever, in these United States, and wherever else the gospel has been preached, by those who may be considered the fruits, more or less direct, of this great display of the divine Spirit upon the hearts of men.

Who was M'Gready? His parents were of the Scotch-Irish race; but whether they emigrated from Ireland, or were born in Pennsylvania, is not now known. When he was quite young, they removed to Carolina, and settled in Guilford County. Here James passed part of his boyhood, and part of his youth, in such labor as persons of no very extensive property were, in those years, accustomed to in Carolina.

The sedateness of the youth, and his punctuality in religious duties, united to a desire for religious improvement, so pleased an uncle of his, who was on a visit to his father's, that he conceived the idea of having James educated for the ministry, and prevailed on his parents to consent to his taking their son with him to Pennsylvania, to secure an education in preparation for his preaching the gospel. His uncle believed him to be religious; he thought so himself. In speaking of these, his early days and impressions, Mr. M'Gready used to say that he never omitted prayer from the time he was seven years old; and having been preserved from outbreaking sins, from profane swearing, from intoxication, and from Sabbath-breaking and other excesses, he had begun to think that he was sanctified from his birth. He was placed with Dr. M'Millan, and obtained employment for a season as an assistant on the farm—a temporary arrangement, no doubt, until he could regularly begin his studies. He was seized with a dangerous illness — the small-pox — and lay some time so low that little hope was entertained of his life. But at length he slowly recovered. How far his self-righteous Pharisaism was shaken by this affliction, is not known. On the first Sabbath that he was able to attend public worship, he was present, somewhere in the Mingo Creek Settlement, where Dr. M'Millan had appointed an administration of the Lord's Supper on that day. The Rev. Joseph Smith, of Buffalo, assisted. Mr. Smith's sermon was made instrumental in the conversion of James M'Gready. He ever afterwards spoke of him as his spiritual father. This statement, which we have from a living witness, and which seems to have been unknown to Drs. Foote and Davidson, is confirmed by an interesting fact related on the testimony of Mr. George Anderson, of St. Clairsville, by Dr. Elliott, in his Sketch of the late Dr. John Anderson, of Upper Buffalo, appended to his "Life of Macurdy:"—

"He, (Dr. A.,) was first awakened to a serious concern about his eternal interests under the preaching of the Rev. James M'Gready, who himself had been converted through the instrumentality of the Rev. Joseph Smith, pastor of the church of Upper Buffalo. These facts, taken in connexion with Dr. Anderson's settlement in that church, are sufficiently curious, as illustrating the providence of God in the whole matter. Mr. M'Gready is sent from Carolina to be taught the way of salvation by Mr. Smith. He is then sent back to Carolina to be the instrument of Dr. Anderson's conversion; and then Dr. Anderson is sent to Western Pennsylvania to be the pastor of the flock which Mr. Smith had gathered at Upper Buffalo. Truly God moves in a mysterious way."

Mr. Smith, in the course of that fall (1785), opened a

school to prepare young men for the gospel ministry; and Mr. M'Gready immediately repaired to that school, and after pursuing his studies there for some time, returned to a similar school that was then begun under the care of Dr. M'Millan. Here he hastened through his literary and theological studies, and was licensed by the Presbytery of Redstone, as we have seen above, August 13th, 1788. Numerous "supplies" were assigned to him till the fall meeting of Presbytery. At that meeting, October 22d, as will be seen, he obtained leave to travel to Carolina during the ensuing winter. Mr. M'Millan was appointed to furnish him with suitable credentials. More than two years afterwards, the Presbytery, at their sessions held at Dunlap's Creek, April 20th, 1791, record the following minute: "Mr. James M'Gready, being detained by sickness in the bounds of the Orange Presbytery, applied, by letter, for a dismission to that Presbytery. The Presbytery ordered the clerk to send him a dismission and a letter of advice on the occasion." He was about 30 years of age when licensed. On his way back to Carolina, he passed through the places in Virginia which had been visited by the revival that spread so far and wide under the ministrations of J. B. Smith and William Graham, in 1788 and 1789. He made some stay in Prince Edward, at Hampden, Sydney College, then under the care of Dr. Smith, that eminently successful minister of Christ. With his heart warmed by what he heard and saw, he reached Guilford, prepared to bear a testimony to men in favor of divine truth in its spiritual application. Religion was at this time at a low ebb in most of the Carolina churches. Spiritual apathy and formality had crept over the majority of professors. Many practices and customs, at variance with a healthful state of religion, were countenanced. Among other things of a very objectionable nature, which had become prevalent, was the habit of distributing spirituous liquors at funerals. Provisions of some kind were set out. To preserve the appearance of religion, some one — an officer of the church, if present —

was called upon to open the scene of eating and drinking by asking a blessing on the refreshments prepared. Mr. M'Gready attended such a funeral soon after his return to Guilford, and was called upon to ask a blessing. "No," he replied, "I will not be guilty of insulting God by asking a blessing upon what I know to be wrong!" The startling effect of this remark may be imagined. The attention of the neighborhood was turned to him. He commenced preaching along Haw River, and in various other places in Guilford. His first sermons were directed against the formality and deadness of church members. Under his searching addresses, they felt themselves unworthy to be acknowledged as members of Christ's visible kingdom, and abhorred themselves in dust and ashes. He excelled in public prayer. Often the congregation was in tears under the influence of his devotions. In his delivery he was solemn, and sometimes very animated from the commencement. Wherever he preached the excitement was great. An extensive revival of religion prevailed through Orange, and some of the adjoining counties, mainly the result of the divine blessing on the labors of M'Gready.

In 1796, he removed to Kentucky and settled in Logan County. He had three congregations—Muddy, Red, and Gasper Rivers. In the two latter, began that mighty revival which spread so far and wide through all the West in 1800, 1801, 1802, 1803, and 1804. Mr. M'Gready was one of the sons of Thunder, both in manner and matter; and an uncompromising reprover of sin in every shape. It was not long till the effect of his impassioned preaching was visible. During the summer of 1797 and '98, there was considerable solicitude evinced in the above-named congregations. But it soon subsided. The summer of 1799 witnessed a renewal of the excitement, which grew and deepened until it reached its height, in 1800 and 1801. In the words of M'Gready, "it exceeded every thing his eyes had ever beheld on earth, and to which all that had preceded it was but an introduction—as a few drops before a mighty rain." We cannot here attempt the narrative. Suffice it to say, that this distinguished servant of God, with some occasional irregularities, which he lived to correct, pursued his bright and useful career for many years; and was instrumental, directly or indirectly, in the conversion of many souls, most of whom are now rejoicing before the throne. Towards the close of his career he removed to the town of Henderson, on the Ohio River, where he spent the remainder of his days, and died in 1817.

The above sketch we have collected from various sources—principally from Dr. Foote's "Sketches of North Carolina," and Dr. Davidson's "History of the Presbyterian Church in Kentucky;" works which we cannot too warmly recommend to the reader as replete with interest upon this and many other subjects. If Mr. Smith, of Buffalo, and Dr. M'Millan and the Old Presbytery of Redstone, had done nothing more than train such a man as M'Gready, they had not lived in vain.

TWENTY-FIRST MEETING.

REHOBOTH, Tuesday, October 21st, 1788.—Presbytery met, according to adjournment. Ubi, post preces, sederunt, the Rev. Messrs., &c. The Presbytery was opened with a sermon from Jer. x. 25, by Mr. Dunlap. Ordered, that the act of Synod respecting the settlement of litigious suits in the congregations under their care be published and recommended, both by the ministers of Presbytery, and the probationers under their care.

Messrs. Finley, Power, and Dunlap, were appointed a committee to examine and appoint such ministers and candidates as may come into our bounds.

An appeal from the judgment of the session of Bethel congregation was brought in by Hugh Sterling and read; together with all the papers relative thereto. The Presbytery having maturely considered the matter, and also having enquired of the moderator of the session, and of Mr. Clark, who was present at the time, respecting the manner in which Mr. Tidball submitted to the judgment of the session; and found that both agreed that Mr. Tidball declared that he did not remember his denying his promise to give the order; but if he did, it must have been in a passion, and without due consideration, and was a deviation from the truth in words, though not in design; and that the submission was not therefore absolute but conditional. The Presbytery maturely deliberating on the whole, do unanimously conclude that the sessions are defective in their minutes, and ought to have been more cautious in their judgment respecting Mr. Tidball. In other respects, we see no reason to alter their judgment with regard to Hugh Sterling. The Presbytery order that Mr. Clark read this judgment, together with the judgment of sessions in the congregation of Bethel.

Mr. Dunlap having applied for a dismission from the congregation of Dunlap's creek, the Presbytery order that the congregation be notified thereof, and attend at our next Spring's meeting, to show reasons, if any they have, why Mr. Dunlap's request should not be granted.

The Presbytery, taking into their serious consideration the declension of vital religion among us, the spreading of error, the threatening aspect of Divine Providence, in respect to the seasons, and the great danger we are in of provoking God to withdraw the gracious influences of his spirit, do therefore think it their incumbent duty to appoint a day of fasting and prayer, to be observed in their respective congregations, and vacancies under their care, to implore a plentiful outpouring of Divine influences upon the churches in general, and upon this infant church in this land, in particular; and at the same time, to acknowledge with gratitude, the many mercies, both special and common, conferred upon us, and deprecate the judgments which now threaten us. The Presbytery do therefore appoint the third Thursday of November next to be observed for the above purposes.

Mr. M'Gready having obtained leave to travel to Carolina

during the ensuing winter, Mr. M'Millan is appointed to furnish him with suitable credentials. Adjourned to meet at Chartiers, on the third Wednesday of January next. Concluded with prayer.

TWENTY-SECOND MEETING.

CHARTIERS, Wednesday, January 21st, 1789. Presbytery met, &c. The Presbytery was opened with a sermon from Acts xvi., 31, by Mr. Dod.

Mr. John M'Pherrin, (34) having, at our last meeting, offered himself to be taken on trials, in order to his being licensed to preach the gospel, the Presbytery conversed with him upon his experimental acquaintance with religion, and proposed to him several cases of conscience, and having obtained satisfaction on these points, agreed to take him on trials, and appointed him an Exegesis.—"Num Christus, qua mediator, adorandus sit?" by our next meeting, and which, being now read, was sustained.

Mr. Samuel Porter, (35) having offered himself to be taken on trials, in order to his being licensed to preach the gospel—the Presbytery, having received sufficient testimonials of his good moral conduct, and of his being a regular member of the church, proceeded to converse with him upon his experimental acquaintance with religion, and proposed to him several cases of conscience; and having obtained satisfaction on these points, agreed to take him on trials.

Messrs. M'Pherrin and Porter examined on Latin and Greek languages and logic—and at some length on Divinity—all sustained.

Mr. Pherrin—a homily on Matthew v. 8,—and Presbyterial exercises on Romans iii. 25—by next meeting.

Mr. Porter—an Exegesis—"An lapsus Adami omnibus ejus posteris naturali generatione ab eo oriundis, imputatur?" by next meeting. Adjourned to meet at Pigeon creek, on the third Tuesday of April next. Concluded with prayer.

(34) BIOGRAPHICAL SKETCH OF REV. JOHN M'PHERRIN.—"The Rev. John M'Pherrin was born in York, now Adams County, November 15th, 1757. His father was a ruling elder in the church of Lower Marsh Creek, under the pastoral care of the Rev. John M'Knight, D. D. He learned the languages preparatory to his going to college, under the Rev. Robert Smith, D. D., of Piquea, and was graduated, May 7th, 1788, at Dickinson College, Carlisle, during the presidency of the Rev. Dr. Nesbit. His theological studies were prosecuted under the direction of the Rev. John Clark, pastor of Bethel, Allegheny County, Pennsylvania. He was licensed to preach the gospel, August 20th, 1789, by the Presbytery of Redstone, and ordained and installed by the same Presbytery, pastor of the united congregations of Salem and Unity, in Westmoreland County, Pennsylvania, on the 22d of September, 1791. Dr. M'Millan presided at the ordination, and Mr. James Finley gave the charge. In these united congregations he labored with great success for a number of years. But on the 25th of June, 1800, he resigned the charge at Unity—and on the 20th of April, 1803, that of Salem; and having accepted a call from the united congregations of Concord and Muddy Creek, within the bounds of the Erie Presbytery, he was dismissed to that Presbytery, October 16th, 1804, and received by it, April 9th, 1805. About the same time, he removed his family to Butler County, in which his congregations were situated. A few years afterwards, Concord and Harmony appear as his charge on the Records of the Presbytery; and still later, Butler and Concord. He is said to have been the founder of the church in the town of Butler, and was its pastor for ten or twelve years. When the Presbytery of Allegheny was erected in the fall of 1820, he was included within its limits, as one of its original members. He acted as Moderator of the Synod of Virginia, in 1799, and of the Synod of Pittsburg in 1805. He died, February 10th, 1822, in the sixty-fifth year of his age. He was a thorough Latin and Greek

scholar, and for a number of years after he was settled in the ministry, taught a class of young men, most of whom became ministers of the gospel. He also possessed a knowledge of the Hebrew language, which was a rare acquirement, in this region of country, at that time. His character is said to be well expressed in the following sentiment, inscribed on his tombstone: 'He was an able, faithful, and devoted minister of Jesus Christ.' The writer of his obituary in the Pittsburg Recorder, says, 'He was a warm, zealous, and evangelical preacher. For some years before his death, he appeared to be remarkably weaned from the world; he, indeed, lived above the world. His whole heart and soul were absorbed in the love of God; and his whole aim was to promote the interests of the Redeemer's kingdom." He was father-in-law to Walter Lowrie, Esq., Corresponding Secretary of the Board of Foreign Missions of the Presbyterian church, and grandfather to his sons, the Rev. John C. Lowrie, Assistant Secretary to the same board, and formerly a missionary to Northern India;—and the Rev. Walter M. Lowrie, deceased, a missionary in China."—*Appendix to Life of Macurdy.*

(35) Biographical Sketch of the Rev. Samuel Porter.—"The Rev. Samuel Porter was born in Ireland, on the 11th of June, 1760, of pious parents, belonging to the Reformed Presbyterian church, commonly called Covenanters, and was strictly educated in their peculiar tenets. His mother devoted him to the Lord, for the work of the ministry, from his birth; in reference to which, she called him Samuel Having no means of acquiring an education, however, he learned the business of a weaver, and was married some time before he left Ireland. He emigrated to this country in 1783, about the close of the Revolutionary war. The first winter after his arrival in the United States, he spent in the vicinity of Mercersburg, Franklin County, Pennsylvania, where a near relative of his then resided. He was extremely poor, having only eighteen pence left, after paying the expenses of

his journey. But he met with kind friends who aided him in sustaining his family. While in the neighborhood, he was induced to go and hear the Rev. Dr. John King, who was pastor of the church of Upper West Conococheague, although he had been admonished by his friend of the danger of his being corrupted by his unsound doctrine. Indeed, he himself expected to hear something very erroneous, and rather desired that it should be so, that he might have cause of reproach against the Presbyterian Church.

"The first time he heard Dr. King, he returned home disappointed, having heard nothing to which he could object. It was so on a second and a third visit to his church. He still discovered nothing to condemn, and was surprised to find him so evangelical and sound in his views. Having heard him frequently during the winter, his objections against the Presbyterian church began to give way; and he came to the conclusion that his past opposition to that church was the result of blind prejudice, rather than enlightened conviction. The next year he removed to western Pennsylvania, and settled in Washington County, where he had frequent opportunities of hearing Mr. Smith and Dr. M'Millan; and the result was that he united with the Presbyterian Church, having satisfied himself fully that her ministers preached the pure gospel, and that his usefulness and comfort would be increased by entering her communion.

"Having become acquainted with Dr. M'Millan, and other ministers of the West, he was induced, by their advice, to enter on a course of preparation for the ministry. His studies were prosecuted partly under the Rev. Joseph Smith, in company with James Hughes, John Brice, and Joseph Patterson; and partly with Dr. M'Millan, with whom he studied theology. As he was without the means of support, Dr. M'Millan kindly gave him his board and instruction, free of expense; and Alexander Wright, Esq., a benevolent Irishman, generously furnished a house and provision for his family, while he was pursuing his studies. Thus did God, in a remarkable manner, meet the wishes and answer the prayers of his pious mother, by providing ways and means to facilitate his admission to the ministry, to which she had consecrated him.

"Up to the time of his prosecuting his studies at Dr. M'Millan's, he was strenuously opposed to the use of a New Testament Psalmody in the worship of God. While there, he determined to write out and publish a thoroughly prepared exposition of his reasons against its use. In the progress of his investigations, which were accompanied at every step with prayer to God for direction, his mind underwent an entire change on the subject; and he found that the proof was against his views, and in favor of that he was laboring to subvert. The result was that he abandoned his opposition, and he became the friend and advocate of a New Testament Psalmody. His son, John Porter, of Rural Valley, from whom this information has been derived, has a distinct recollection of the time when his father first sang one of Watts' Psalms in family worship.

"Mr. Porter having made theology his study from early life, and having had a considerable stock of knowledge on various subjects before he commenced a formal course of preparation for the ministry, the Presbytery permitted him to preach as a probationer, after a shorter course of study than usual. He was licensed by the Presbytery of Redstone, Nov. 12th, 1789. At a meeting of the Presbytery, April 20, 1790, he had a call put into his hands from the united congregations of Poke Run and Congruity, one from the congregations of Dunlap's Creek and George's Creek, and one from Long Run and Sewickly. The first of these calls he accepted, and was ordained, in company with the Rev. J. M'Pherrin, Sept. 22d, 1790, and installed pastor of the congregations of Poke Run and Congruity. In these congregations he labored till April 11th, 1798, when, on account of ill health, he was released from Poke Run, though much against the wishes of the people, who remonstrated against the dissolution of the pastoral relation.

Congruity agreed to take the whole of his time, promising £120 per annum, one-half in merchantable wheat at 5*s* per bushel, and the remainder in cash. He continued the pastor of this congregation until the time of his death, which occurred on the 23d of September, 1825. Mr. Porter was held in high esteem by his brethren of the ministry, as a man of undoubted piety and vigorous talents. He was a bold, original, and independent thinker, distinguished for his controversial talent and ready wit. He appeared to particular advantage in the judicatories of the church, in which he exerted a commanding influence. He was a very acceptable speaker, had a clear, musical voice, and had great power over an audience: sometimes exciting in them the most pleasurable emotions—at others, melting them to tears."—Appendix to Life of Macurdy. See also "Porter's Sermons and Dialogues," recently published by Dr. Elliott. Either of the sermons is worth the price asked for the whole book.

We cannot withhold a passage from one of them, which will show how this polemical giant would have stood, had he lived to mingle in the scenes of 1835, '36, and '37. It is taken from his discourse on the Atonement of Christ, delivered at the opening of the Synod of Pittsburg, October 1st, 1811:—

"Rev. Fathers and Brethren:—We have been called, in the Providence of God, to the awfully responsible office of the gospel ministry, in a perilous time. A spirit of innovation, hostile to all existing systems, has gone forth into the world, and is to be found in operation within the precincts of the Christian church. For the purpose of uniting in communion professing Christians of every species and description, and thereby to render the church perfectly analogous to the ancient Babel, those religious systems in which the church of Christ has expressed the sense in which she understood the Scriptures, and which men of superior learning and piety have long considered as necessary barriers between truth and error, are attacked, *in toto*, by men in our vicinity and elsewhere, who have sagacity enough to perceive that they stand in the way of the execution of their schemes; whilst others are engaged in brandishing their javelins at doctrines contained in those confessions of faith to which they profess adherence, as systems founded on the Word of God. Human nature, in avoiding one extreme, tends to the other; and the candid and well-informed will grant, that if a bigoted attachment to human systems prevailed in some of the periods that have passed, the present tendency is to a lawless catholicism, which would fill the church and people heaven with men of the most heterogeneous and hostile principles and dispositions. The prevailing taste is so much in favor of a liberality in sentiment, which affects to look down on systems and confessions of faith as old-fashioned, musty, useless lumber, not calculated for this enlightened, refined, philosophic age, that the man who aspires to celebrity and fame must endeavor to gratify that taste. Therefore, clergymen of science, talents, and ambition, are under a strong temptation to sail with wind and tide, and acquire the character of men of enlarged, cultivated, generous minds, superior to narrow systems and vulgar faith."

"There are clerical boys, of no gigantic talents, who have scarcely passed the threshold of Christian science, or read the title-page of one-half the accessible books on divinity, until they are disposed to enlighten the world, and bless the church, by the introduction of new theological doctrines, which they have discovered in those regions of illumination and refinement which lie far beyond the hazy atmosphere of Scripture and common sense."

The Synod of Pittsburg embraced, at that time, the region afterwards occupied by the Synod of the Western Reserve, one of the exscinded Synods; and in this region, thus early, it was understood, prevailed some of those notions which Mr. Porter here so sarcastically handles. Let the reader buy the book, if he wants a real treat.

TWENTY-THIRD MEETING.

PIGEON CREEK, Tuesday, April 21st, 1789.—Presbytery met, &c. The Presbytery was opened with a sermon from Jonah i. 6. by Mr. Patterson.

Two calls for Mr. Patterson — from the united congregations of Upper Raccoon and Monteur's Run, and from Unity and Salem—were brought in and read, and put into his hands for consideration. Two calls for Mr. Brice—from united congregations of Three Ridges and Forks of Wheeling, and from the united congregations of Mill Creek and King's Creek — were brought in and read — put into his hands for consideration. Ordered to read the minutes of last fall's meeting. Mr. Clark reported that though Mr. Finley attended at Lebanon, according to appointment, no settlement was yet made with the congregation. Messrs. Brice, and Hughes, and Patterson, have fulfilled their appointments. The members present have fulfilled their appointments, except Mr. Dunlap, whose reasons were sustained.

The congregation of Dunlap's Creek appeared by their commissioners, and signified that they had no reasons to offer why Mr. Dunlap should not be dismissed; especially since he manifested an unwillingness to remain with them any longer; and although the Presbytery cannot justify his conduct in forsaking that congregation without a regular dismission, yet, as we do not think his continuance there would be for edification, we do therefore judge that the pastoral relation between him and that congregation ought to be, and it hereby is, dissolved.

Mr. Patterson gave up the call from Unity and Salem congregations, and declares his acceptance of the call from the united congregations of Upper Raccoon and Monteur's, provided that some of the difficulties now subsisting be removed before our next meeting. Messrs. Brice, Hughes, and Patterson appointed to supply, as much as they can conveniently, in those congregations from whom they have received calls, until our next meeting. The Presbytery find that the congregations are satisfied with the diligence and care of their respective pastors. Mr. Finley and Mr. Power, together with Mr. Cook and Mr. Baird, elders, are appointed to represent this Presbytery in the General Assembly. (36)

The Presbytery, having had frequent applications made to them respecting the settlement of places of worship; in order to prevent waste of time about this matter in future, the Presbytery now give it as their opinion in general, where congregations are in union with each other, their houses of worship ought not to be less than eight miles apart; and where the congregations are not in union, nor expect to be, that their places of worship ought not to be less than nine miles apart.

Application having been made by Mr. Barr for a dismission from the united congregations of Pittsburg and Pitts-township, the Presbytery order that the congregations be notified hereof, and to attend at our next meeting, to show reason, if any they have, why Mr. Barr's request should not be granted. Mr. M'Pherrin brought in and read his Homily and Presbyterial Exercise—sustained.

Mr. Porter—his Exegesis—sustained. Mr. R. Marshall, having offered himself, &c. (see foregoing form), was taken on trial, examined on Latin and Greek Languages, and Messrs. M'Pherrin and Porter along with him, on moral philosophy—all sustained. Mr. M'Pherrin to prepare a lecture on James ii. 24–26, and a popular sermon on I. John iv. 18, by next meeting. Mr. Porter to prepare a homily on I. Cor. ii. 14., and a Presbyterial Exercise on Heb. ii. 14, by next meeting. Mr. Marshall, an Exegesis, on this theme: "An constat essentia fidei, in persuasione, quod remissa nobis peccata, et nostrum Christus sit?" and a homily on Rom. iii., 20, by our next

(36) This appointment of commissioners to General Assembly, which was to meet the 3d Thursday of May, 1789 (the first General Assembly), is a new event in the history of the Redstone Presbytery. As the Presbytery consists of more than six members, they were entitled to two ministers and two elders.—See printed Rec., p. 524.

meeting. Adjourned to meet at Chartiers the 4th Monday of May next. Concluded with prayer.

TWENTY-FOURTH MEETING.

CHARTIERS, Monday, 25th May, 1789. — The Presbytery met, &c. The Presbytery was opened with a sermon from Matt. xxvi. 41, by Mr. Patterson. Mr. Patterson reported that those difficulties which subsisted between the congregations of Upper Raccoon and Monteur's are now removed; and he, having accepted their call, is now appointed to prepare a discourse on James iii. 6, at our next meeting, as a part of trial, in order to ordination. Mr. Hughes declares his acceptance of the call from the Ridges and the Forks of Wheeling: appointed to prepare a discourse on John xv. 4, to be delivered at our next fall's meeting, as parts of trials, in order to his ordination.

A number of commissioners appeared from Pittsburg, in consequence of Mr. Barr's application for a dismission; and, it appearing evident to the Presbytery that there were some difficulties which could not be settled without a meeting on the spot, the Presbytery therefore agreed to defer all further proceedings in that affair for the present, to meet at Pittsburg on the 2d Tuesday of June, and to send notice to absent members. Adjourned, to meet at Pittsburg on the 2d Tuesday of June. Concluded with prayer.

TWENTY-FIFTH MEETING.

PITTSBURG, (37) June 9th, 1789.—The Presbytery met according to adjournment. Ubi post preces sederunt, the

(37) PITTSBURG. — The period when this congregation was organised is uncertain. It appears that in 1766, the Rev. Messrs. Beatty and Duffield, who were appointed by the Synod of New York and Philadelphia to visit the frontier settlements, and also some of the Indian tribes, as missionaries, for two months, were in this place, and found "some kind of a town." They also found there the Rev. Mr. M'Lagan, chaplain to the 42d regiment. Of what denomination he was, it is not stated. These brethren preached in the fort and in the village.

Rev. Messrs. James Finley, John Clark, Joseph Smith, John M'Millan, and Samuel Barr.

The Presbytery was opened with a sermon from Philip. iii. 8,

There was then no regular congregation, and no house of worship. It is probable that some of the other missionaries appointed by the Synod visited and preached in the place; especially Mr. Power and Mr. Finley; both of whom were out preaching to the settlements some time before the beginning of the Revolutionary War; the latter of whom was appointed to labor two months in the West, and it is not likely that he failed to visit Pittsburg. Dr. M'Millan, during his first visit to the West in 1775, preached here on the 2d Sabbath of September. Whether there were any further visits, or labors of Presbyterian ministers or missionaries, during the next nine years, we cannot learn. Mr. Smith was sent to preach here on the 4th Sabbath of August, 1784. In the following year, the Rev. Samuel Barr, after laboring some short time as a supply, was recognised as the pastor by the Presbytery, without any regular installation. About this time the church was organized, and a small log house was erected for a place of worship. Mr. Barr continued the pastor till June 12th, 1789. For a number of years afterwards they were occasionally supplied by the Presbytery. In 1791, Mr. Mahon, a licentiate of the Carlisle Presbytery, preached to them for a short time—perhaps about a year, or even more. In 1793, (Oct.,) having applied for ordination, he was not able to give satisfaction to the Presbytery on the subject of his experimental acquaintance with religion; and applying immediately for his dismission back to his former Presbytery, he was dismissed, and left the place. After Mr. Mahon left, a licentiate, by the name of Semple, who afterwards became a lawyer, preached there a short time. In 1795, the Rev. Messrs. Porter and D. Smith were sent to supply one Sabbath each. Thence, till June, 1799, they appear neither to have sought nor obtained supplies from the Presbytery. At the last date, the Rev. Robert Steele, who had left Ireland precipitately, without having time to get his credentials from his Presbytery, but with testimonials from his former congregation, and letters from brethren in New York, Philadelphia, and Norfolk, was allowed to preach as a supply—till the following meeting of Synod—to the people of Pittsburg. Mr. Porter and Mr. Henderson were also sent as supplies during that year. During the year 1800, Mr. Steele, though not fully received, was allowed to act as a supply. In October, though an ordained minister, he was taken on probation, and a text was assigned him for a trial sermon by the next spring meeting. At that time (April, 1801), the Presbytery, not being satisfied with his sermon, assigned him another text for a sermon by the fall meeting. In the by Mr. M'Millan. Mr. Barr produced the following reasons why he desired to be dismissed from his pastoral relation to Pittsburg and Pittstownship, viz.: —

---

mean time, the congregation asked for Mr. Steele as a stated supply "until the Presbytery shall finally receive or reject him." In October the sermon was not sustained, and they appointed him another, to be delivered at the next spring meeting. Then (April, 1802) he was taken in and permitted to take his seat with them, rather speciali gratia, as it would appear from the minute. In the mean time, he was still acting as supply to the congregation of Pittsburg; and in the following October, (1802,) a call from this people was put into his hands by the Presbytery, and accepted by him; and thenceforward, without any further action of the Presbytery, he was recognized as the pastor. In this relation he continued till his death, which occurred March 22d, 1810. The Rev. Mr. Stockton then acted as supply for some time. The Rev. Francis Herron, D. D., expressed his intention of accepting a call from this church April 3d, 1811, being then a member of the Presbytery of Carlisle. From that Presbytery he was dismissed to join the Presbytery of Redstone, and removed to Pittsburg in the ensuing month of May. On the 18th of June he was received by the Presbytery of Redstone, and accepted the call. He continued the pastor of this church till, at his own request, in 1850, he was dismissed. During the same year, the Rev. Mr. Paxton, the present pastor, received and accepted a call, and is now laboring among them with great and encouraging success. This church, during the earlier period of its history, seemed not to be remarkable for exemplary piety. Many of them were a gay, fashionable, worldly people, conforming to the customs and manners of the times. Their financial affairs were also in the greatest embarrassment. In a very short time after Dr. Herron entered upon this arduous and trying field of labor, a new era opened upon the church. From the utmost temporal and spiritual prostration, it soon rapidly rose to a high degree of prosperity in both respects. With the consent of the leading men of the congregation, Dr. Herron bought the church and lot, when publicly sold by the sheriff to pay the debt of the congregation, and soon after he sold part of the lot for a sufficient sum to extricate the church out of all debt, conveyed the balance of the ground, with the house, back to the trustees, and, with their co-operation, and that of the citizens, soon provided means for erecting a much better house of worship, which was afterwards much enlarged. The congregation grew rapidly. The Lord poured out his Spirit on this congregation; and several times during the long-continued pastoral labors of this now ancient servant of God, many were added unto the church. It is the mother church of our body in Pittsburg. All the other five

1st, Because he supposes he may preach the gospel elsewhere with more success. 2d, Because he has not been able to exercise church discipline; having too few to support him in that branch of his duty. 3d, Because no active measures have been taken by the trustees to comply with their agreement; but, on the contrary, they have appointed him to collect his own salary for the last year; which was as much as to say he might hunt after his salary from door to door — it was none of their business. 4th, Because Robert Galbraith and John Wilkins, Esqs., elders of the church, have not supported characters becoming their office, but have indulged themselves in drinking and card-playing. Mr. Wilkins is charged with being idle with women; and Mr. Galbraith has not settled his accounts with him for stipends collected from October, 1785, to April, 1787. 5th, Because Mr. Dunning, elder, besides his not paying a strict attention to his word, has not been scrupulous in altering his neighbor's landmark; which betrays a covetous disposition, and unbecoming one who should be an example to the flock. 6th, and lastly, That since his application, he has still more reason to continue his resolution, from the industry of the above-named gentlemen, together with George Wallace, Esq., to render his labors useless, both here and elsewhere, by circulating false reports, and preventing the congregation and himself from worshipping God, in a peaceable manner, in the house of God, on the Sabbath day.

Presbyterian churches, and the churches of Allegheny City and Lawrenceville, were, more or less, formed out of it. Two of them were literally colonies from it. Its contributions in aid of our Board, of the Seminary, of weak churches, and of other benevolent objects, have been vast; but whether they have given in proportion as the Lord hath prospered them, it is not for us to determine. They will soon, it is expected, enter a new and spacious building, far exceeding, in magnificence, its predecessors. May the true glory of the latter house exceed the glory of the former houses. The Synod of Pittsburg, October 4th, 1822, detached this church, with its pastor, together with several other churches and pastors, and attached them to the Presbytery of Ohio. Number of communicants in 1854, 311.

Charges exhibited by the session and trustees of Pittsburg congregation against the Rev. Samuel Barr, in consequence of his application to Presbytery for a dismission from the Unity congregation of Pittsburg and Pittstownship, and in compliance with a notification from Presbytery to the Session and Trustees of Pittsburg congregation, to show cause, if any they have, why said Barr should not be removed from his pastoral relation to them. 1. They intend to show that Mr. Barr has not had any reason, from Pittsburg congregation, to make any such application. 2. They intend to show that Mr. Barr has not done his duty, as a clergyman, to said congregation, by absenting himself from them at sundry times, without the consent of session or congregation, or leave obtained, or his business abroad known to them. 3. They intend to show that Mr. Barr has not done his duty as a clergyman, by not visiting the families of said congregation at their houses, and in not catechising and examining them, as he ought to do. 4. They intend to show that Mr. Barr has collected a considerable sum of money in Philadelphia and New York, for the use of Pittsburg congregation, and has never rendered any account of the same, nor paid any part of it into the hands of the Trustees, or to any other person, for the use of said church. Adjourned to meet to-morrow morning, at 8 o'clock. Concluded with prayer.

Wednesday, June 10th.—Presbytery met according to adjournment. Ubi post preces sederunt qui supra. Ordered to read the minutes of the last session. Mr. Barr alleges, in support of his first reason, &c. [The whole testimony is then introduced and recorded, on both sides, which we will not here publish. This occupied the Presbytery on Wednesday and Thursday. We shall give next the finding of the court.]

Friday, June 12th.—Presbytery met according to adjournment. Ubi post preces sederunt qui supra. Ordered to read the minutes of the last session. The Presbytery, after hearing all the parties had to say, examining the witnesses that were produced on both sides, and maturely deliberating on the matter, are of opinion, that the reasons offered by Mr. Barr, why he desires a dismission from the congregations of Pittsburg and Pittstownship, are groundless; and some of them, if they had been true, did not at all exist at the time when he made the application — it appearing evident to the Presbytery, in the course of the trial, that it was his own misconduct, principally, that occasioned the people's non-attendance on his ministry: that he never had used any proper means to have discipline duly exercised, but, on the contrary, did himself countenance card-playing, and night-revelling, and did nominate and ordain persons as elders, though he knew that they did practice, and by his permission, determined to practice, some of those very things which he now brings in as charges against them. And though he has brought in some very grievous charges against particular persons, yet it does not appear that he, even in private, endeavored their reformation, by admonishing or reproving them for their misconduct; and has entirely failed in proving any of them, except that of card-playing, which was not denied. It further appears, in the course of the trial, that Mr. Barr has, in many things, behaved in a manner entirely unbecoming a minister of the gospel—in neglecting the visitation of families in the town of Pittsburg, and catechising, except a few children, on the Sabbath evenings — in one case refusing to baptise a child without money being first given, which last, however, is supported by only one witness — in publishing a piece in the Gazette, in which are some very unbecoming expressions, and one profane oath — in neglecting to consult with his session, and make use of their assistance, in the spiritual matters of the congregation — in his inconsistent procedure in the affair of baptising Gen. Gibson's child — and in neglecting to give the Trustees a proper account of the money subscribed for the use of the congregation, though there is not evidence to show that he designed any fraud thereby.

Upon the whole, the Presbytery conclude that the state of

things, in these congregations, is such, that there is no prospect of Mr. Barr's being useful among them — and that, therefore, the union between him and them ought to be, and is hereby dissolved. They do also conclude that his conduct has been very injurious to the cause of religion and virtue; and that, without an alteration, it will continue to be so: therefore, although we feel tenderly for him, we cannot see how we can justify ourselves before God, the world, or our own consciences, without declaring this as our judgment, viz.: that he ought not to exercise any part of his ministerial office until the mind of our Synod is known thereon; to whom we do defer the ultimate determination of the matter.*

---

* The Rev. Dr. Foote, in whose hands, at present, are the old Records of the Synod of Virginia, has kindly furnished us with the following statement, as the result of this matter, when it came up in the Synod:

" At the second meeting of the Synod of Virginia, which was in Lexington, Virginia, 1789, on Thursday, 22d of October, the case of Mr. Barr was brought up by the Committee of Overtures, as a reference from Redstone Presbytery, stating that the Presbytery has suspended Mr. Barr till the judgment of Synod could be known. The subject was under consideration; and papers from Mr. Barr were read, but not recorded. The Synod determined that, as Mr. Barr had introduced new matter in those papers, and referred to new witnesses, and made insinuations against the Presbytery, 'they therefore agree to refer the consideration of the whole affair, de novo, to the Rev. Messrs. James Power, Thaddeus Dod, James Dunlap, Edward Crawford, John Montgomery, Moses Hoge, and Col. Robert White, Elder, or any three of the whole number, as a Committee of Synod: and the Synod recommend it to said Committee, to be as careful as possible, with regard to the nature of the evidence which they admit upon the occasion — that no appearance of prejudice or party spirit may exist in the decision. The Committee is appointed to meet at Pittsburg, on the fourth Tuesday of November next. Mr. Barr is directed to give notice to the parties concerned, about Pittsburg, of the resolution of the Synod: and Messrs. M'Millan and Finley are directed to give notice to the parties in the bounds of Redstone Presbytery contiguous to them: and the witnesses who appeared against Mr. Barr, before the Presbytery of Redstone, are to have notice to specify the times and places of the respective charges: and Mr. Barr is to specify his charges against the members of the con-

The Presbytery cannot but testify, upon this occasion, their disapprobation of card-playing, night-revelling, and using any

---

gregation against whom he complains: this interchange of notice to be at least ten days before the meeting of the Committee of Synod.'

"At the meeting of the Synod of Virginia, in Winchester, (their third meeting,) September, 1790, on Thursday, the 30th, 'Ordered that the Committee of Synod appointed to meet at Pittsburg, the 25th of November last, now make their report. Upon which the minutes of the Committee were read, which are as follows: Pittsburg, Wednesday, November 25th, 1789.—The Committee of the Synod of Virginia having been prevented from meeting yesterday, agreeably to the appointment of Synod, because of the badness of the roads, and the inclemency of the weather, met this morning, at the house of Mr. David Waters, at 10 o'clock. Present—the Rev. Messrs. Thaddeus Dod, Edward Crawford, John Montgomery. Absent—the Rev. Messrs. James Powers, James Dunlap, Moses Hoge, and Robert White, Elder. The Committee was constituted with prayer. The Rev. Mr. Dod was chosen Chairman, and Mr. Montgomery, Clerk. Mr. Francis Hindman, a preacher of the gospel from Lewis Presbytery, occasionally present, was appointed Assistant Clerk.' Then follow about twenty pages, quarto, of charges, evidence, and doings, &c., &c., all of which was read to the Synod, and put on their record. 'The Committee then agreed to the following determination: This Committee, finding that the members who composed the Presbytery, which formerly sat on Mr. Barr's trial, did not attend, and it not appearing to the said Committee whether or not they consider themselves as having legal notice; and finding that Mr. Barr's former prosecutors did not wish to appear in any form against him in the trial, the Committee then proceeded to attend to the papers produced by Mr. Barr, duly attested, and a number of personal evidences, which tended to give light to the subject; and having compared these with the minutes of the Presbytery which sat upon his former trial, and finding matters to stand in a different view—therefore, the Committee determined that the charges exhibited by the session and Trustees of the Pittsburg congregation, against Mr. Barr, are *wholly unsupported;* and that he be considered in full and regular standing in the church.'

"The action of the Synod, on this subject, is in these words: 'The Synod accepted the report of the Committee, as now amended, and consider Mr. Barr in *regular standing* in the church.'

"That is all," says Dr. Foote; "and this short sentence immediately follows the report of the Committee, without any resolution being recorded."

expressions leading to immodest ideas, as practices very unbecoming in any professor of religion, and such as would lay a just foundation for exclusion from church privileges, in any congregation where discipline is duly exercised; and that, therefore, such of the elders of the church of Pittsburg as have appeared before us to be guilty of such things, ought to be, and are hereby admonished to abstain from such practices for the future—and be informed that, without a reformation, they ought to be further dealt with. Adjourned to meet at Laurel Hill, the third Tuesday of August. Concluded with prayer.

TWENTY-SIXTH MEETING.

LAUREL HILL, (38) Tuesday, the 18th of August, 1789. —Presbytery met according to adjournment, &c. The Presbytery was opened with a sermon from I. John iv. 18, by

---

(38) LAUREL HILL.—This church was, perhaps, organized as early as 1776, by Dr. Power, soon after his removal to the West, in that year. It appears to have been supplied, in part, by him, for a few years, in connection with some other places in Fayette and Westmoreland Counties, until, in 1779, he became the pastor of Sewickly and Mount Pleasant congregations.

This church, in connection with Dunlap's Creek, obtained the pastoral services of the Rev. James Dunlap, D.D., who was installed among them October 15th, 1782. From the latter church he was dismissed, April 22d, 1782, and remained with Laurel Hill till June 29th, 1803. The Rev. James Guthrie was ordained and installed in the congregations of Laurel Hill and Tyrone, August 17th, 1805. He remained their pastor till his death, August 24th, 1850. In June, 1850, these congregations called the Rev. Joel Stoneroad, the present pastor, who was installed co-pastor with this venerable man.

This church of Laurel Hill, one of the oldest in the West, after a period of decline for some years past, is now in a growing and prosperous state, and has recently erected a large and commodious brick house of worship, having a good parochial school in the basement. It has often been visited by refreshing showers of divine influence. Number of communicants in the two churches of Laurel Hill and Tyrone, as recently reported, 203.

Mr. M'Pherrin. Messrs. Patterson and M'Pherrin — discourses — sustained.

The Rev. Messrs. Finley, Smith, and M'Millan are appointed to transact the affair relative to Mr. Barr's suspension, at the next meeting of Synod. Messrs. Clark and Patterson appointed to supply one Sabbath each at Mr. M'Millan's pulpit, during his absence at Synod.

Mr. Finley's and Mr. Power's reasons for not attending the meeting of the General Assembly—sustained.

"The Presbytery having received sufficient testimonials," &c.—(see Formulary for the Government of the Church, chapter xiv., section 8.) Mr. M'Pherrin was licensed.

Mr. Porter's Homily and Presbyterial Exercises—sustained.

Mr. Marshal's Homily and Exegesis sustained. The ordination of Mr. Patterson—appointed at Upper Raccoon, on the second Wednesday of November. Mr. Dod—to preach the ordination sermon; Mr. Smith to preside, or in his absence—Mr. Power. Mr. Porter was appointed to prepare a lecture on Isaiah vi. 1–8, and a popular sermon on Philippians iv. 13, by our next meeting. Mr. Marshall to prepare a Presbyterial exercise on Romans viii., 16, by our next meeting.

Ordered that collections be raised from the several congregations under the care of this Presbytery, agreeably to an act of the General Assembly, and that the money collected, be brought in at our next meeting. Adjourned to meet at Upper Raccoon, on the second Tuesday of November. Concluded with prayer.

TWENTY-SEVENTH MEETING.

UPPER RACCOON, (39) Tuesday, 10th of November,

---

(39) RACCOON.—The Rev. Joseph Patterson was installed pastor of this church, in connection with Monteur's Run, November 11th, 1789. The latter charge he resigned, April 16th, 1799—but remained pastor of the former till October 16th, 1816. He was their first pastor; but the church was organized some years before. On the 27th of May, 1817,

1789.—Presbytery met, &c. Presbytery was opened by Messrs. John Brice, and James Hughes, with sermons on subjects appointed to them at the preceding meeting. The discourses of Messrs. Brice and Hughes were sustained.

Mr. M'Millan reported that Mr. Finley and himself attended Synod according to appointment; and that the affair of Mr. Barr's suspension was referred to a committee of Synod to meet at Pittsburg, on the fourth Tuesday, inst. Mr. Dunlap, by letter, informed Presbytery, at his own request the settlement with Dunlap's Creek Congregation is deferred. Mr. M'Pherrin reports his appointments fulfilled.

The Rev. Robert Finley, formerly a member of the Presbytery of South Carolina, applied to be received; and producing the requisite testimonials and a dismission—was duly received. The Presbytery, according to appointment, proceeded to the ordination of Mr. Joseph Patterson, and did by fasting and prayer, and with the imposition of hands of Presbytery, set him apart to the holy office of the gospel ministry. Mr. Dod preached upon the occasion from Acts xx., 28. Mr. M'Millan presided, and Mr. Robert Finley gave the charge. Mr. Patterson now takes his seat as a member. Mr. Marshal produced his Presbyterial exercise, which was sustained. A lecture—appointed to him on Malachi iv., 1–6, and a popular sermon on Titus ii., 14, by next meeting. The ordination of Mr. Hughes—appointed to be at Short creek, on the third Wednesday of April next—Mr.

---

the Rev. Moses Allen was installed pastor of this church. He was dismissed in 183–. In June, 1841, the Rev. Clement N. M'Kaig, their present pastor, was ordained and installed among them. Their present number of communicants (1854)—280. This church shared largely in the glorious revival of 1802. In October of that year, the Lord's supper was administered there; and the mighty power of divine grace was displayed on that occasion, in the conviction and conversion of great numbers. This church has also ministered to the formation and growth of not only other churches around, but of various churches through the West. It has always been, and is still, one of the heights of our Western Zion.

Smith to preach the ordination sermon, and Mr. J. Finley to preside and give the charge. The ordination of Mr. Brice—appointed at Three Ridges, on the fourth Thursday of April next: Mr. Dunlap is appointed to preach the ordination sermon, and Mr. M'Millan to preside and give the charge.

Agreeably to a recommendation of the Synod of Virginia, for raising contributions for the support of missionaries, the Presbytery agree to make contributions in the several congregations for that purpose, as soon as convenient, and that the report of success in the same, be brought in, at our next meeting. Mr. Porter—discourses sustained.

"The Presbytery having received sufficient testimonials," &c.—(see Formulary for the Government of the Church, chapter xiv., section 8.)—Mr. Samuel Porter was licensed. Supplies assigned him at nearly all the above mentioned places. Adjourned to meet at Short creek, on the third Tuesday of April next. Concluded with prayer.

A Biographical Sketch of the Rev. Joseph Patterson—*by the Rev. E. P. Swift, D. D.,—to which are added several illustrative anecdotes.*

The Rev. Joseph Patterson was born in the county of Down, Ireland, A. D. 1752. He was descended from an ancestry distinguished for their piety: and the exemplary and eminent godliness of his parents appears to have early impressed itself upon his youthful mind. Although there is reason to believe that he became the subject of permanent and saving impressions of religion at the early age of ten years, his conviction of sin, and his apprehension of the work and offices of Christ and the plan of salvation, were apparently marked with all the clearness and impressiveness of maturer years. Under the impulse of these deep impressions of divine truth, he, with three or four little associates, exhibited the delightful scene of a circle of children, accustomed statedly and privately to meet in a retired copse of thorns to

Your affectionate Uncle
Joseph Patterson

P. S. Duval & Co. steam lith. press, Phil.a

unite in their supplications to the Divine Redeemer for pardon and salvation: and it was when these serious and observant children began to ask him, with increasing astonishment, where he obtained those new prayers which he was accustomed to offer in their hearing, that we may trace the first openings of that Christian character, which has since, for more than half a century, been maturing and shedding its influence upon all the circles in which he moved. His first clear apprehensions of the way of salvation seem to have been derived from an affectionate explanation of it by his pious father while ploughing in the field, when he was enabled cordially to accept it, and embrace Christ, as his everlasting portion. Nor would such early beginnings of a life of faith and prayer be so rare as they are in the church, if Christian parents in like manner were in the habit of thus wisely and kindly turning the hours of active business into the seasons of mingled instruction and fervent prayer.

At the age of twenty, Mr. Patterson, having united in marriage with one whose domestic virtues, and humble, fervent piety greatly contributed to his prosperity and happiness for many years, emigrated to America, and after a short stay in Pennsylvania, established himself under the ministry of the Rev. Dr. Clarke, in the county of Saratoga, in the State of New York. He appears to have been influenced in this choice of a residence, by a desire to enjoy the instructions of this estimable man, of whose sincere godliness and useful labors he often spoke with great respect and commendation. The arrival of his parents in Pennsylvania, in 1774, led him to return to this State; and from this period until the commencement of the Revolutionary war, he was chiefly employed in the instruction of a school near Germantown. Being thus near the spot where that illustrious convention met which drew up and signed the Declaration of Independence, he was present to hear it first publicly read, and his mind largely shared in those exalted sentiments of patriotism, which then so universally consecrated the intelligence, and piety, and resources of our country, to one great effort for its deliverance. As a volunteer in this good cause, he forsook his school, and embarked in all the dangers and perils of his country's freedom; and here, amidst the varied fortunes of the Revolutionary contest, he passed some of the most interesting scenes of his long and prosperous life.

In 1777, he removed to York County, and in 1779 to Washington County, accompanied in his removal to this then new and thinly inhabited country by many valuable Christian friends, with whom he had become acquainted in the place of his last residence. These were the days, in the settlement of this western land, which "tried men's souls." Besides the moral courage demanded in removing so far from the nearest white settlements on the eastern slope of the mountains, and that by a road almost impassable, on which alone some of the staple articles of life were to come, if they ever reached these remote dwellings in the West, they were subject to the most appalling scenes of massacre and devastation from those numerous tribes of Indians who occupied the Western forests. Often were the new and thinly-scattered clusters of civilized habitations alarmed by the sudden incursions of this barbarous foe; and the patriarchal father, now deceased, in common with the sturdy, and pious, and enterprising yeomanry of that period, often took his rifle upon his shoulder, as he started through the woods of a Sabbath morning to the house of God, as a kind of necessary appendage, to defend his person by the way, and to aid in the protection of his fellow-worshippers, in the event of a preconcerted and murderous surprisal. And these desperate invaders often lurked for days around the abodes and fields of the unsuspecting settlers, and here and there, as they found it practicable, they would fall upon the unprotected cabin, rob it of its contents, massacre its inmates, and reduce it to ashes. Amidst these scenes of danger, and these exercises of trust in God, often did this worthy man, in common with others, experience those manifest interpositions and deliverances of

Providence, which recalled to their minds, with grateful emotion, the assured aspiration of the Psalmist, 'Because thou hast made the Lord which is my refuge, even the Most High, thy habitation; thou shalt not be afraid for the terror by night, for he shall give his angels charge over thee, to keep thee in all thy ways.'

"Mr. Patterson had, at a very early period of his life, felt a strong desire to devote himself to the work of the gospel ministry; but as the events of his life did not seem to open the way for the prosecution of the studies which are customary in such cases, he appears to have for some time abandoned that pleasing hope with respect to himself, and concentrated his wishes and his prayers in the object of rearing up a son, whom he might thus devote to the work of the Lord. The rapid increase of the settlements, and the great destitution among the people of the means of grace, led those honored and self-denied fathers, on whom 'came daily the care of all the churches' in the wilderness, to put in requisition every practicable means of supplying the lack of gospel instruction: and with a judiciousness and discrimination which subsequent events abundantly confirmed, they directed the attention of a few men 'of good report' in the churches, and inured to the privations of this new country, to the duty of such an immediate preparation for the sacred office as circumstances would permit. Mr. Patterson's character for religious attainments and eminent piety, at once identified him as one on whom the hopes of Zion should be fixed; and, accordingly, in a short narrative now before the writer, he modestly and briefly says, in reference to this subject: 'In the fall of the year 1785, being thirty-three years old, it was thought best, with the advice of the Presbytery of Redstone, that I should endeavor to prepare for the gospel ministry. There being no places of public education in this western country, I, with a few others, engaged in preparatory studies with the Rev. Joseph Smith, of Buffalo congregation, Washington County, Pa.' While under the tuition of this able man, of whose zeal, and fervor, and pulpit eloquence, the ancients have preserved a lively remembrance, and while engaged in his theological studies, Mr. Patterson appears to have preserved, in an eminent degree, a life of communion with God, and deep and growing concern for the spiritual welfare of his fellow-men. Among the original papers, which, we regret to say, are few, that were left by this venerable man, there is a series of letters which he wrote to Mrs. Patterson and the children, during his residence abroad, and the perusal of which cannot but produce an earnest wish that every student of theology might learn how entirely, as it were, the great and glorious topics of practical religion may absorb the mind, and interweave themselves with all the communications of private friendship, and conjugal and parental affection, while, at the same time, the mind is successfully engaged in the acquisition of academical knowledge. This term of preparation was also replete with such periods of great religious enjoyment, and with such special answers to prayer, and such Providential leadings and deliverances, as not only tended to confirm his mind in the belief of his call to the work of the ministry, but to make that ministry a richer blessing to the people of his charge.

"Having completed his studies, and sustained his trials before the Presbytery of Redstone, he was licensed to preach the gospel in August, 1788. There was a little incident connected with this event, and related to the writer by him, a short period before his death, which not only illustrates the beauties of domestic piety, but the loving-kindness of the Lord to all who wait upon him. The mind of this godly man was anxious, for some time before, not only that his trial discourse might be sustained by the Presbytery, but that his first essay at preaching the gospel might be blessed to the souls of the people in whose audience it was to be delivered. As he was about to mount his horse to repair to the Presbytery, therefore, he said to Mrs. Patterson, on taking his leave: 'According to the established order of Presbytery, I shall be called to preach my trial sermon on Thursday at 12 o'clock, and I would thank you to remember me at the throne of grace at that time.' Contrary, however, to his expectation, he was called to fulfil this customary service at the same hour on the preceding day. On entering his house on his return, Mrs. Patterson said to him: 'I think you did not deliver your trial sermon on Thursday, as you expected.' 'When did I, then?' he inquired. 'I think,' she seriously replied, 'from the impressions which were made upon my mind, that it was at 12 o'clock on Wednesday!' Such a fact needs no comment.

"In April, 1789, or about eight months after his licensure, Mr. P. received and accepted a call to take the pastoral charge of the united congregations of Raccoon and Montour's Run. He continued to serve these two congregations for about ten or twelve years, when it was found that each had become sufficiently large to require the exclusive services of a gospel minister, and he accordingly resigned the care of the latter; and from that time until bodily infirmities rendered it impossible for him longer to sustain the pastoral relation, (which occurred in the autumn of 1816, after he had been for twenty-seven years and a half pastor of Raccoon,) he continued his persevering and faithful labors among that favored people. The only record which this venerable father has left of these years of exemplary ministerial fidelity, is contained in the brief and humble memorandum which he made on demitting his solemn charge into the hands of Presbytery:—'I resigned my charge on account of bodily infirmity, after being pastor of Raccoon twenty-seven years and six months; for every day of which I need pardon through the blood of Christ.' That record, however, which his humility and self-abasement would not allow him to make, abundantly exists in the grateful remembrance of the people, in the growth and size of his congregations, and in those frequent and powerful revivals of religion with which his ministry was owned and blessed of God. That, as a pastor, he was abundant in his labors, was honored and beloved of his people, and for a long course of years dwelt as a father among his children, is a fact to which many can bear the fullest testimony.

"Besides some other bereavements of his children, Mr. Patterson was called, during his residence at Raccoon, (in 1808,) to follow his pious partner to the grave; and, deeply as his feelings must have been affected by so trying a dispensation, he was enabled, in compliance with a mutual agreement which had been entered into between them years before, in relation to the survivor, to sit at her dying pillow, and explain the nature and consequences of the believer's death, till her spirit fled. He had the satisfaction, however, amid the darkest hours of life, to enjoy the precious light of the Redeemer's presence, and to see all his children hopefully united to Christ in the bonds of the covenant, and happily settled in the relations and pursuits of life. At his second marriage, (in 1812,) which was one of much happiness to himself and his children, and of which he makes a very affectionate mention in his will, it would be unsuitable for us to say more than that his departure has left in widowhood one of kindred spirit with himself.

"Nor were his cares and efforts confined to the people of his charge. He was one of the founders, and an active officer for many years, of the Western Missionary Society; and, from numerous memoranda in his note books, it appears that he not only diligently collected funds in aid of that Society, but that he was, for some years from and after the erection of the academy at Canonsburg, (now Jefferson College,) much engaged in collecting donations, and otherwise actively promoting the interests of that flourishing institution, of which he was a trustee.

"Like other ministers of his day, 'whose praise is in all these western churches,' he often took missionary tours, for the purpose of visiting new and destitute settlements, and administering gospel ordinances to young and feeble churches. It is believed that he preached the first sermon which was ever delivered to a congregation of white people north-west of the Ohio river; and there is before us a journal of a tour of several months, as a missionary to the Shawnee Indians, on the branches of the Maumee, Ohio, in the summer of 1802, which is replete with useful information, and with interesting and surprising incidents, illustrative of the perils and privations of the enterprise, the zeal and perseverance with which it was executed, and the Brainard-like spirituality and prayerfulness of the missionary.

"That this devoted man was, during the period of his stated ministry, engaged in preaching the Word both 'in season and out of season,' at home and abroad, more abundantly than most men, is manifest from the fact that, besides exhortations and addresses delivered in numerous social meetings, he preached in this time 2572 sermons and lectures, exclusive of afternoon discourses, when they formed part of the subject discussed in the morning. It is worthy of remark, also, as appears from the list which he regularly kept of the passages on which he discoursed, that he seldom preached a second time on the same text, and when he did, it was seldom substantially the same discourse.

"When the infirmities of life required this venerable minister reluctantly to relinquish the charge of his beloved flock, he wisely resolved to leave the field of his former labors, and pass the remainder of his days in this city, where his attendance on divine ordinances would be attended with less inconvenience — where he might enjoy the society of the families of two of his surviving children — and where he might also prolong the period of his active services in the cause of Christ. Indeed, it may well be doubted whether this change did not, in fact, augment, rather than diminish, the amount of his usefulness to the church of God. This suggestion is based upon the unquestionable fact, that no man, at his time of life, could have been more actively engaged in his Master's work, than was this excellent man during the fourteen years in which he dwelt in this city, and that it is difficult to see how his qualifications for usefulness could, at his age, have been turned to better account than they actually were.

"Without, it is believed, any formal rule on the subject, Mr. P. was accustomed, when in tolerable health, and the weather favorable, to divide his time in such a way as to give to every day its appropriate share in the three following employments, viz.: 1. Reading, meditation and prayer. 2. Social religious intercourse, in which he received and conversed with his friends, and those who sought his advice and an interest in his prayers; friendly visits to the sick, bereaved and afflicted, and calls upon such of various denominations and stations in life as prized his friendship, and were cheered, quickened and instructed by his kind and parental admonitions, and his judicious and affectionate counsels. 3. Active labors in the distribution of the Holy Scriptures — in watching over the interests, and transacting a large share of the business, of Bible, Missionary, Sabbath School, Tract, and such other benevolent societies as relied upon his prompt and vigilant attention to their welfare. At some seasons of the year, almost every day of the week would find him passing along the shores of our rivers, entering hundreds of boats containing families of emigrants from various parts of the world, kindly inquiring after the temporal and spiritual welfare of these often destitute and afflicted strangers, giving them such advice as to their secular concerns as they needed, and making sure that they were supplied with a copy of the Bible. There was a familiarity, an affection, and an impressiveness in these brief communications — so benevolent, pains-taking and cordial in themselves — as often made a deep impression upon the mind: and it is believed that there are hundreds of families scattered through the vast regions of the West, who will long remember the kindness and counsels of this apostolic man, whom they never saw or knew, but when they touched for a few hours at the wharves of this city.

"Sometimes they would follow him from boat to boat, to listen to his brief and appropriate instructions — at others, they would betray a strong curiosity to know what could be his motive, in taking so much pains, at his advanced age, to ascertain whether they possessed the Bible, or wanted anything which he could supply; but, at all times, they treated him with great respect, and often expressed their obligations in the most grateful manner.

"He acted as agent for the receipt and distribution of Bibles, to a greater or less extent, for the Pittsburg, the Young Men's and Female Bible Societies of this city, and for the Philadelphia and American Bible Societies, which occasionally placed donations of the sacred volume at his disposal, as did the British and Foreign Bible Society, on one occasion, 100 Irish Testaments. During his fourteen years' residence in this city, it appears, from his entries, that he received and distributed 3920 Bibles, and 2943 Testaments, making a total of 6863 copies. When it is considered, that most of these were accompanied with his affectionate and faithful counsels and fervent prayers, we see what a noble monument to his industry and usefulness is here reared.

"Individuals and societies at a distance also were occasionally in the habit of requesting him to transact for them such items of business, pertaining to the interests of religion, as demanded the exercise of his judgment; and it was frequently truly instructive to see with what fidelity and promptness he fulfilled their wishes, and aided them in their attempts to build up the Redeemer's kingdom. He was long a very efficient and active friend of the American Tract Society, and distributed, with his own hands, many thousands of these and other useful publications.

"From a book containing the names of a large number of citizens of different denominations, engaging to meet and form a Sabbath School Society, and dated November, 1817, it would appear that the association, afterwards called the Sabbath School Union, originated in the personal exertions of this diligent and persevering servant of Christ; and, for some years after this period, he was chiefly depended upon for the collection of its necessary funds, as he was frequently found visiting and addressing those precious seminaries of youthful piety and virtue. Indeed, among no class of persons was he more highly respected, and sincerely loved, than the youths and children of our Sabbath-schools. He had a faculty of interesting and gaining the attention of children, as valuable as it is rare, and hence, they not only loved to hear him speak, and to greet him when they met him in the streets, but were often ambitious to do him some act of kindness.

"His known reputation for wisdom and prudence, and accessibility to all classes of persons, united with his deep experimental knowledge of religion, naturally led persons of various ages and stations in life to spread before him their peculiar difficulties, and solicit his judgment on questions of casuistry, and his advice on points of duty; and while he never betrayed the trust reposed in him, and entered feelingly into the trials and perplexities of his friends, and led them earnestly to a Throne of Grace, he seldom failed to leave on their minds a deep sense of the soundness of his understanding and the sincerity of his heart.

"To the ministers of the Gospel, and especially to his young brethren, preparing for, or just entering upon the work, and such as were going to labor in the new and distant fields of the West, he was eminently useful, as an intimate acquaintance with the trials, and discouragements, and temptations of the ministerial office, and a long and accurate knowledge of men and things, fitted him to point out to them their dangers, and the grounds of their encouragement, and impart to them the most valuable practical instruction. He usually saw, interested himself in, and conversed with, ministers passing through this city to their respective stations in the West; and it is believed that there are many who will remember him with gratitude and pleasure as long as they live. Thus, on the verge of eighty, and with bodily infirmities which would have entirely laid aside any man of ordinary resolution, this venerable minister of Christ was in these useful employments exhibiting a pattern of industry and of method in the despatch of business which often astonished and delighted the observer. Nor was this all. Besides a great number of addresses and exhortations delivered in public assemblies, and in more private circles of social worship, he preached one hundred and seventy sermons during his residence in this city; and almost always bore a large share of the labors attendant on the administration of the sacramental supper in our churches. Although all his public performances were highly edifying and instructive, especially to experienced Christians, (the class of persons for whom they were generally intended, and whom, as he often remarked, he seemed especially qualified and designed to benefit,) yet it was on these occasions in particular that the depth of his experimental knowledge, the lustre of his graces, and the intimacy of his communion with God, shone out in the strongest light. Every one who knew his worth, delighted to see and hear him when he rose to dispense those sacramental emblems, and address, out of the fulness of his heart, those whom he loved as dear children in the family of Christ. His addresses also, and his prayers on days of fasting, humiliation, or any special occasions, and in church judicatories, were always singularly fervent, appropriate, and impressive.

"The last discourse which he delivered was on Sabbath, the 8th of January, in the Second Presbyterian Church; and it was truly, in its matter and its manner, such a testimony for the great Master, as any gospel minister might feel happy to give, on taking his final leave of the pulpit, and ascending to his last account. The 'path of the just as a shining light' was his topic, and to unfold the duties and sins, the trials and deliverances, the hopes and fears of that path, until it terminates on Jordan's other shore, was the object of the preacher, and an object which seemed so to interest, to absorb his thoughts, and to fill his heart with such high and comprehensive views of the mysteries of redeeming grace, that he forgot the infirmities of the flesh, and with the vivacity and animation of youth, he labored, though often apparently in vain, to give utterance to those conceptions of the subject which crowded upon his mind.

"During the protracted meetings which were held in the first and second Presbyterian churches, and the seasons of sacramental communion with which they were accompanied, he attended most of the services, and took an active part in their labors. These public exercises were closed in the congregation with which he usually worshipped, on Monday, January 30, when he gave a very solemn exhortation to the people, which proved to be the last official act of his life. On Wednesday, Thursday, and Friday, he seemed as well as usual, and nothing very noticeable occurred, except that in the devotional exercises of the family, particularly on the last of these evenings, his mind seemed remarkably drawn out in prayer for his children, his grand-children, the Theological Seminary, the ministers of the gospel, and the church of God, and, last of all, for this ungodly city. It is interesting and solemn here to record the fact, that on this memorable occasion, in which, with his beloved and affectionate partner, he approached, for the last time on earth, the family altar, he dwelt with so much length and earnestness upon these topics, that when he closed, he needed her assistance to rise and resume his seat. What a sublime and enviable termination this, of the domestic devotions of sixty years! And except, also, that often during the day he was heard to hum to himself, as though enjoying a pleasing foretaste of heaven, that beautiful hymn, containing the words —

"'Soon shall I pass the gloomy vale,
Soon all my mortal powers must fail
O may my last expiring breath
His loving-kindness sing in death.'

"He had frequently expressed it as his desire and prayer, that his departure might be sudden and tranquil, and he often spoke with a degree of confidence that it would happen during his 80th year. Having spent the chief of the day in the family of his son, Rev. Robert Patterson, he returned home, and retired as usual on Friday night. About one o'clock, on Saturday morning, he awoke unwell, and arose, expressing the hope that he should feel better by so doing. Soon after, however, he said to Mrs. Patterson, with great composure: 'I am dying — call in the doctor, and my son Joseph'—these gentlemen occupying the dwellings immediately adjoining his own. Aware, it would seem, of the rapidity of his decline, and anxious once more to see his son, Joseph Patterson, Esq., he asked, 'Is Joseph coming?' On being answered in the affirmative, he simply added: 'The time is come—Lord help;' closed his eyes, and, without a struggle, sank into the sleep of death — completely realizing, in his decease, all his fond anticipations respecting it. Though long expected, his departure produced a deep sensation among all classes of the community, and the grave and solemn air of the vast assemblage which followed his remains to the tomb, testified their sympathy and great sense of his worth.

"In casting a retrospective glance at the prominent traits of character in the venerable subject of the preceding narrative, and presenting a true and faithful delineation of what he was, we find a large number of estimable qualities, all moulded and formed by the influence of an early and eminent piety, rather than the unusual and prominent development of any one attribute.

"Without the benefit of a collegiate education, without the aids of family or fortune, and without a direct opening to the ministry until somewhat advanced in life, he was enabled by the force of his own moral energy and perseverance to arrive to a degree of respectability and veneration in society, of usefulness to the cause of Christ, and of maturity and lustre of Christian character, which few men under such circumstances ever obtain.

"On inquiring into the causes which led to these results, we find them (under God,) to consist in the union of a sound, active, practical judgment, and a heart early and very deeply imbued with the graces of the Holy Spirit, with habits of great industry, and untiring perseverance.

"1. The life of this venerable minister of Christ illustrates the benefits of early piety, and piety of a clear and decided stamp. His moral energies, his trains of thought, his mental powers, the affections of his heart, and the aims and purposes of his life, were at the very opening of life, influenced, and vitally influenced, by the forming, and invigorating and sanctifying power of gospel grace; and hence his Christian character at eighty, as he stood on the verge of life, like the awe-inspiring river just entering the ocean, is broad and deep, and has enriched and fertilized many a land in its course, because it took its rise at a distance, and has traversed immense districts, making every part to contribute something to augment its volume, and to multiply its treasures. His course was early taken—and his onward march was steady to the last. In the extent of the empire of grace over him, he was truly one of thousands: and the extent to which his words, and example, and prayers, in their entire moral energy, have affected the minds of hundreds and thousands of the living and the dead, during the long course of his godly life, must have been great indeed. This early beginning, and beginning well, involves a measure of physical, and intellectual, and religious training, without which such eminency in grace and usefulness can hardly be expected to exist. The tall, majestic oak, that overtops the wide cluster of the forest, indicates as truly the upward course of its early shoot, as the antiquity of its beginning and the appropriateness of the soil on which it grows.

"2. Mr. Patterson was eminently a practical man. He undertook nothing without due consideration; but as he had an accurate practical judgment, and was resolute and persevering in what he undertook, so his expectations of ultimate success were sanguine. The same principle that led him to prefer practical to speculative knowledge—action to mere theory, and which led him to exactness and punctuality in small money matters, in keeping his promises and observing his appointments, also led him to say and do whatever he intended, just as the occasion presented. Hence he had a word in season for every event that occurred, and to meet the character and situation of every friend he met in the street—if the busy, driving merchant, he would say, 'Well, I suppose it would be a great inconvenience to you to die to-day'—if the afflicted Christian he would say, 'The children of God must travel the tribulation road to heaven,'—and if the smiling little child, he would say, 'Do not forget how dearly Christ loves pious, obedient, and praying children;' and then pass on, producing no interruption in the engagements of others, and steadily prosecuting his own. This trait of character also made him an interesting and instructive associate, an engaging preacher of the gospel, and a wise counsellor. It furnished him with brief, appropriate and striking proverbial remarks, which arrested the attention and fastened indelibly in the memory. His practical wisdom and stirring activity enabled him, while laboring with becoming industry as a Christian pastor, so to manage his temporal affairs as to provide amply for the maintenance of his family, the education of his children, and the liberal exercise of hospitality and charity; and to make all his pursuits subservient to the increase of his knowledge and the vigor of his piety.

"3. The life of this patriarchal father in our Israel, affords a very remarkable exhibition of the effects of a clear and comprehensive view of the covenant of grace, as it regulates and influences the life and conduct of true believers. He regarded the promises of God, made in and through Christ, to the church, and every genuine disciple, not as mere verbal declarations, but glorious pledges of the divine favor, to be received and trusted in implicitly, and he looked upon the believing sinner in the day of its ratification with him, through faith, as brought into a state that would affect his duty, his safety and happiness in every situation in life. Thus he became a most attentive observer of Providence, and relied upon its general results with as much confidence, as on the continued laws of nature. Hence, he became pre-eminently among us, a man of prayer. By this I do not mean simply that he prayed much, but that he prayed so as to be heard and answered. His views of the covenant led him not only to draw near to God — to exercise the privilege of laying every matter before Him, but it led him to expect, for Christ's sake, answers of peace, and tidings of joy from heaven ; and while there certainly was nothing credulous in his character, his private history is replete with striking and remarkable instances of direct and unequivocal answers to prayer.

"He looked upon the Providence of God as a development of the pledges of the covenant, so far as the church and every believer in Jesus is concerned; and hence all its events instructed him, and its smallest incidents attracted his notice. The frequent striking connection between the course and turns of Providence and his own prayers, not only confirmed his faith in Christianity, but gave a constant and gracious impulse to all his religious feelings and efforts. That 'the eyes of the Lord are upon the righteous, and his ears open to their cry,' are facts, of both of which his own experience served to afford peculiar attestations. Thus, when in the army, and while the troops were sheltered in a kind of temporary shed made of rough boards, he was engaged in prayer in his own apartment, when the rifle of a neighboring soldier accidentally went off so as to shiver and break its force on a board just in the direction and near the person of the kneeling suppliant. At another time, the loss of an article of great value to him, because given in answer to prayer, led him so to address the Throne of Grace as to arrive at a satisfactory persuasion that it would be regained, though such a result at the time seemed nearly impossible. A train of apparently mere accidental circumstances, most striking in themselves, realized his expectations, and filled him with gratitude and astonishment. Many affecting instances of a similar kind might be enumerated. One of the most common and familiar themes of his conversation was, that the whole scheme of Divine Providence is one most wise, and just, and benevolent and perfect work, of which every trying event in the believer's life is a necessary part. In a letter written to a beloved daughter, then in deep affliction, after dwelling with great force and beauty upon this thought, he concludes by saying, 'Do you remember the dear, pious Mrs. B. of Carolina, who, when her two only sons were murdered, said, 'The pattern of my chequered web would not have been complete without these two red stripes. This I shall see when it is out of the loom.' So it is with all the stripes in your chequered web, my dear child. You will not tell me when it is out that it was an ill-chosen pattern. It is just as good and as handsome now as it will be then, could you but see it as plain.' The Redeemer was thus to his mind constantly in view, as the Surety, the Guide, and sovereign Lord of all his people; and he held his life and all his comforts and all his possessions as not his own; and he recommended it to his friends, often to renew this gift and consecration of all things to Christ. This sentiment he carried with him to the very end of his journey. In the introductory part of his last will and testament, he has this impressive sentence: 'I have not my soul and body to dispose of—they have with my most cheerful and resolute determination been dedicated to the Lord Jesus Christ, more than sixty-four years, and he has already taken a tender, faithful, gracious care of them, and will at last dispose of them to the glory of God the Father, Son and Holy Ghost, the only living and true God. All my dear relatives I do solemnly dedicate to Him, to be ruled, governed and saved from sin and wrath by his wisdom, power, righteousness and saving grace—and it is at the peril of each of them who neglect to confirm this dedication.' The same feeling, that believers were Christ's and Christ their's, induced him, whose prayers were in general any thing but sameness or formality, to conclude his supplications often with the petition, 'Undertake for us, O Lord Jesus, in all the concerns of thy glory'—

thus recognizing, as it existed in his own mind, the principle that he is the great undertaker and perfect surety of all his ransomed ones. So after preaching in reference to the word spoken, he would say, 'Lord accept what is thine and pardon what is ours.'

"The character of Mr. Patterson's religion, and the warmth and vigor of his social feelings, were such as to make gratitude, contentment, cheerfulness, and affection, among the most noticeable of his Christian virtues. His private letters to Mrs. P., and his missionary journals, are full of expressions of obligation to God, and satisfaction and delight at the thought that the Lord Jesus was doing with him and his just as he pleased. He took great pleasure in social intercourse; and his easy, polished manners, his great accessibility, and his inexhaustible fund of striking observations and useful anecdotes, made him a most agreeable companion to almost every description of persons. To the strength of the social principle of our nature, which he possessed in a large measure, and which made the kindness, and tenderness, and sympathy, which it was his lot to experience, in union with strong religious affections, to produce so much tranquillity and cheerfulness, may be ascribed, in part at least, his great longevity, and the unimpaired vigor of most of his faculties. Like the peaceful surface of the lake, when the evening rays of a summer sun repose upon its quiet bosom, his mind was resting in sweet tranquillity on the covenant of God, and in the enjoyment of the cheering beams of the Sun of righteousness; and no external event could destroy its composure, because he felt and acted on the principle, that the whole plan of Providence, and every part of it, was, as he frequently said, infinitely desirable. As his was not a religion of sudden impulses, but of calm, deep, and uniform steadiness of action and of feeling, so there was nothing in it gloomy, forbidding, or unkind. The uniform smile of friendship which abode upon his countenance—the solemn air with which he reproved sin, even in his dearest friends—and the kind and cordial greeting with which he met those he loved, were all the sincere and simple utterances of a heart that knew no disguise, and suppressed no generous emotion. As he seemed uniformly to possess an assured evidence of his union to Christ, and as, wherever he went, he saw those who respected and loved him, it was no labor, but his element, to glorify his Redeemer, by promoting the welfare of mankind. Thus, deriving enjoyment from all his engagements—blessed in all his domestic relations, and keeping himself acquainted with the state of the world, to be cheered by the prospects of Zion, he appeared, for years past, to move among us as the happiest person in society. One reason for this doubtless was, that he was accustomed through life to gather the materials of gratitude and praise from a constant reference to the blessings he enjoyed.

"Thus, when on his tour among the Indians, he writes in his journal: 'I now felt myself beyond the verge of the Christian world, the precious privileges of which appeared great beyond all calculation. I would not have been without this salutary, solemn opportunity, for all the difficulties of my journey, and all the disagreeable prospects before me.' On meeting with some white persons who had been early taken off by the Indians, and, banished from the Christian world, had become heathens, he exclaims: 'O, why was not this the lot of *my* children, who were brought up on a dangerous frontier! While others were taken within a few miles, they were left. Bless the Lord, O my soul!' His letters also abound much in exhortations to his friends, not to indulge in desponding fears and mistrusts of Providence, but consider more what they already have — what they deserve, and learn to think well of Christ, and freely trust him for what they need. Here was the secret of his contentment and his happiness; and how much does the Lord of grace and providence delight to honor such a spirit of meek and affectionate acquiescence in all his dispensations.

"5. The instructive character of this departed man of God, illustrates the importance of a strict and conscientious attention to all the duties of religion, as they bear upon the powerful influence of example. When men are esteemed and venerated for their general uprightness, their smallest omissions, as well as their errors, do injury. While, in the present instance, no man's example could have been looked upon with more universal respect—none, in its main features, could have been expected to be more exactly and truly drawn. During upwards of twelve years, in which the writer has intimately observed his 'manner of life,' in respect to the Sabbath and the sanctuary, he has often been surprised at the uniformity and constancy, at all seasons and in all weathers, with which this aged father in Israel has occupied his seat in the house of God — the manifest glow of holy feeling with which he came, and the simplicity and affection with which he heard 'the Word,' from the lips of his younger and less experienced brethren.

"To behold one who, if any, might have made his own domestic meditations to have supplied the place of the ablest preaching, on the verge of fourscore years, thus statedly coming up to the house of prayer, when hundreds of the young and healthful would consider an unpleasant day, or a slight indisposition, as a sufficient excuse for neglect, was truly instructive.

"It was delightful to see, also, when he listened to the ministrations of strangers, and particularly young men, and saw in the spirit, fervor, and evangelical character of their performances what he approved, with what affection he would greet them, and interest himself in their welfare, and with a judicious precaution, simply say, by way of encouragement, 'I am willing to license you to be a preacher of the glorious gospel of Christ.' When he saw defects in matter, or faults in manner, which he was apprehensive might be injurious, he would be seen kindly taking his young brother aside, to mention them in private; and it was always done in a way to secure increased respect and affection for him. As in his attention to public worship, so in all other things, he was a strict observer of the Sabbath, and all the Sabbath; rising earlier on that than other days, and truly making it a season of rest and refreshing from the presence of the Lord. When meetings for social prayer were held at the rising of the sun, on these and other days, he was among the earliest to resort to these places of supplication.

We might also speak of his exemplary character in all the relations of husband, father, friend, and pastor — of his singular conscientiousness—his Christian hospitality at home, in which he greatly excelled, and his habitually profitable conversation abroad—of his soundness in the faith—his conscientious adherence to the standards of the Presbyterian Church — his deep-felt interest in the affairs of the church, and the intense feeling with which he looked forward from the borders of the tomb upon the promised spread and coming glory of Messiah's kingdom on earth — but time will not allow us to dwell upon these and other subjects which belong to the character and history of this eminent disciple of Christ. S."

The following anecdotes, some of which we have derived, in whole or in part, from the "Patterson Family Record," by William Ewing Dubois, Esq., and others we have gathered from various authentic sources, will serve to illustrate the character of Mr. Patterson, and will, perhaps, be read by many with interest. We would premise that the list might be enlarged to fill a volume. We select some of the best:—

"Some time after his removal to the West, he and some others made a purchase of land and paid the money. It was soon discovered that the seller was not the owner, and consequently, that the title was worthless and the money lost. How much Mr. Patterson's investment amounted to is not known, nor is it material to the story; only that it was a greater loss than he could well bear. The other purchasers had recourse to law, and advised him also to 'employ counsel.' 'I have heard in the Bible of a Wonderful Counsellor,' was the quaint reply, 'and my application shall be to him.' He thereupon made it a matter of repeated and earnest prayer; not, we presume, for a specific restitution of the money; which no intelligent Christian could do, in absolute terms, but that by some Providential interposition, this serious loss might be made up to him, or that he might be duly reconciled to it, and eventually none the worse for it. The prospect of a specific answer was small; for M'Clure, the man who obtained the money, had absconded, both from the neighborhood and from his family. But as Mr. Patterson was passing near M'Clure's house, not long after, a child, running up to him, begged him to come in. As he did so, the wife handed him the identical bag, with the identical dollars, and explained to him the strange action in such words as these: 'When my husband went away, he charged me to give this money back to you; for, said he, I am afraid the man will pray me to death if I do n't return him his money.' Thus his suit was gained; the others, it is said, never got anything."

Another incident, more minute, and therefore more to the point, we take from one of his letters. The poor student of divinity, whose course of study must have lessened his ability to provide a living, regarded with mortification the napless, worn-out hat, not fit to appear in at Presbytery. But if it was of sufficient importance to give him concern, he held that it was a fit subject for prayer; and so he writes to his absent wife as follows:—

"In retirement for special prayer yesterday, the Lord let me talk familiarly with him about many things; particularly about a hat; and he made me willing to go to Presbytery with my old one. I came away with a pleasant hope, and well pleased with all his government; and this day there was one bought for a guinea and sent to me, a present by A. S."

The distribution of the Bible along the landings of Pittsburg was of course attended with some expense; and as his own means were always moderate, he was obliged to make collections to defray the charges. In such a cause, he felt as if he had a claim upon any citizen who had a spare dollar. In one of these collecting rounds, he was met by an acquaintance. "Well, Father Patterson, what errand are you on to-day?"—"I am going to the man that keeps store over there, to get a dollar for my Bible distribution."—"Why certainly you will not go to such a man as that—an open infidel and a scoffer. You will not get a cent from him."—"Yes I will; I'll get a dollar. Come and see." They walked into the store. The old gentleman was not welcome from the first; but upon opening his request, he was treated with positive scorn. The indignant man behind the counter would give nothing for any such purpose. "Do you say you wont?"—"I say I won't."—"Well, I'll go home with my subscription-book, and lay it before the Lord, and tell him that Mr. —— absolutely refused to give anything towards the distribution of the Bible." There was a solemnity and reality in this rejoinder which seemed to frighten the man, unbeliever as he was. Opening the money-drawer, he threw out a piece, saying, with a subdued voice, "Here, take your dollar."

His prudence in his mode of reproving sin was a prominent feature. At a house-raising, a man, somewhat intoxicated and very profane, said he would inflict personal insult on old Patterson if he attempted to rebuke him. Mr. Patterson, who was not aware of his threat, took the man aside upon his giving fresh vent to his profanity, and affectionately remonstrated with him, and begged him to desist from swearing. The swearer was completely disarmed, and was melted down. He afterwards became, as Mr. Patterson testified, one of the most pious members of his congregation.

He was once saluted, as he descended from the pulpit, by a gentleman of his own name, after this manner: "Mr. Patterson, you and I must be relations; for all my ancestors by the Patterson side were naturally a religious people."—"We can't be at all related, then," said Mr. Patterson, "for my ancestors were all naturally an irreligious race."

A man who expressed to Mr. Patterson his dissatisfaction

with the view which had been given of the utter helplessness of the sinner in his unconverted state, being asked if he thought he could get religion whenever he pleased, expressed no doubt of it. Upon which, Mr. Patterson, after endeavoring to show him his dreadful guilt in neglecting or deferring that all-important matter, begged him, as a special favor, that he would set about the matter at once in his own way. He promised he would. Not long after, he came to Mr. Patterson in great distress and despondency, related the result of his promised efforts, and expressed the conviction that it was all over with him; that he was absolutely lost, and that he was now satisfied his case was hopeless. Mr. Patterson told him that he anticipated just such a result of his own efforts to get religion, and proceeded to lay open to the self-despairing sinner God's plan of saving sinners, and was instrumental in leading him to the footstool of sovereign grace. He soon became a joyful believer, and thenceforward a devoted, consistent professor of religion.

On Friday, before he died, he took the final sitting for his portrait. The artist had been expressing his purpose to visit the celebrated Sully, the great American painter, with a view to receive instructions for his own improvement. As Mr. Patterson rose from the chair, after looking for a while at his own picture, he turned to the artist, and taking him by the hand, he said to him, with great solemnity and affection, "I can recommend to you another great painter. Do you get the Holy Ghost to draw the image of Christ upon your heart, and it will last for ever. And he will charge you nothing for it!" The painter, who was of infidel sentiments, probably despised the counsel, and might soon have forgotten it, but from his hearing, a few days after, to his great surprise, of Mr. Patterson's death. He then related this remark of Mr. Patterson. He subsequently abandoned his infidel sentiments, and made a profession of religion.

A pious man, overtaking Mr. Patterson on his way to the church, when they were both compelled, from the icy state of the sidewalks, to take the middle of the street, asked Mr. Patterson to explain the passage "The path of the just is as the shining light," &c.; perhaps suggested by the state of their walking. Mr. Patterson proceeded to give his views, which occupied him till they reached the door of the church. He was only a hearer himself that day; but he was requested to preach the following Sabbath, probably in the absence of the pastor. And he did preach, and from those words above stated, to the great satisfaction of his friend and many others. It was his last sermon—but a few weeks before he died. And he himself was a bright illustration of the truth of the text!

TWENTY-EIGHTH MEETING.

SHORT CREEK, (40) Tuesday, April 20th, 1790.—Presbytery met, &c. The Presbytery was opened with the lecture

(40) SHORT CREEK.—This congregation, which received its name from the creek which passed through a part of its territory, extended originally, like all the early churches, over a considerable space of country. It seems to have been gathered some years before, and was early one of the places to which supplies were sent. It was partly included in the wide, indefinite field of Mr. Smith's labors. In the bounds of this congregation the seat of justice was fixed, in 1776—at Black's Cabin, on the waters of Short Creek. On Monday, January 16th, 1777, the first Court for the County of Ohio was held at this place. "There is every reason to believe that this was the first civil Court held in the Valley of the Mississippi." On the 7th day of April, the Court ordered a court-house and jail to be erected. The first attorneys admitted to practice in the Court were Philip Pendleton and George Brent, on the 2d of November, 1778. Mr. Pendleton was appointed Commonwealth's attorney.

West Liberty, in Ohio County, (which afterwards became the name of the congregation,) was incorporated November 29th, 1786. The Order Book of Ohio County Court contains the following entry, under date of June 6th, 1780:

"Ordered, that the ordinary keepers in this County sell at the following rates—for half pint of whiskey, \$6; breakfast or supper, \$4; dinner, \$6, lodging, with clean sheets, \$3; one horse to lay over night, \$3; one gallon of corn, \$5; one gallon of oats, \$4; half pint of whiskey, with sugar, \$8; a quart of beer, \$4. October 2d, 1780, the Court and sermon of Mr. Marshall — previously assigned — which were sustained. Three calls to Mr. Samuel Porter — from Dunlap's Creek and George's Creek, and from Poke Run and Congruity, and from Long Run and Sewickly — all put into his hands for consideration.

Mr. M'Pherrin declared his acceptance of the call, from Unity and Salem congregations; and Mr. Porter also, from Poke Run and Congruity — returning the other calls — upon which the Committee from those congregations applied for supplies. A call for Mr. R. Finley — from Mill's Creek and King's Creek — ordered to be forwarded to him, and his answer required as soon as possible. Mr. James Hughes ordained. Presbytery "did, by fasting and prayer, and with the imposition of hands, set him apart to the holy office of the gospel ministry." Mr. Smith preached on the occasion, on John iv. 36; and Mr. M'Millan presided, and gave the charge. Mr. Hughes now takes his seat as a member.

Mr. Barr appeared before Presbytery, and produced an attested copy of the judgment of the Committee of Synod, whereby it appears that he is restored to the exercise of his ministerial office, and made an application for a dismission from this Presbytery, in order to join that of New Castle. The Presbytery, after deliberating on the matter, cannot see their way clear for giving him a dismission at this time. 1. Because they are not yet satisfied that all the charges which were proved against him, before this Presbytery, have been disproved. 2. Because there is a complaint lodged against

---

increased the price of *strong beer* to $6 per quart. March 6th, 1781, dinners rated at $20, and breakfast and supper at $15. June 4th, 1781, whiskey was ordered to be sold at $8 50 per pint. All this was, of course, in continental money.—*American Pioneer*, vol. 2, p. 378.

The Rev. James Hughes, their first pastor, labored here with great usefulness and success, till June 29th, 1814. The congregation remained vacant till 1828, when the Rev. William Wylie became stated supply. The Rev. J. W. M'Kenna, December 9th, 1829, was ordained and installed the pastor. The Rev. N. Shotwell is the present pastor. Communicants, 70.

him for disorderly conduct, by three of the Sessions of Pittsburg congregation, which has not yet been examined into. 3. Because we have good reason to believe that he continued to preach while under suspension, and before the Committee reversed the judgment.

John Barret asked for a reconsideration of his case, at next meeting, (a reference formerly brought in, from Session of Pittsburg congregation, in which he is concerned.) It was granted, and Mr. Clark ordered to furnish him with such papers as he shall think necessary for the trial and citation of witnesses.

Mr. Porter to prepare a discourse on Ephesians vi. 17; and Mr. M'Pherrin, on Psalms lxxi. 16 — by our next meeting, preparatory to ordination. Adjourned to meet at Three Ridges, at 1 o'clock P. M. Concluded with prayer.

TWENTY-EIGHTH MEETING.

THREE RIDGES, 1 o'clock, P. M.— Presbytery met, &c. The Presbytery proceeded to ordain Mr. John Brice, and "did, by fasting and prayer," &c. Mr. Dod preached, on the occasion, from Galatians vii. 10. Mr. M'Millan presided, and Mr. James Finley gave the charge. Mr. B. now takes his seat, &c.

The Presbytery find that the order of the Synod for raising contributions for the support of missionaries to vacant congregations, has been, in part, attended to, and order that those who have not complied with it, do it, and pay the money raised to Mr. M'Millan, who is appointed Treasurer, and report the same at our next meeting.

Mr. Power and John Wright to attend next General Assembly, as Commissioners from this Presbytery.

Presbytery agree that Mr. M'Pherrin and Mr. Porter be ordained—next meeting—if way clear. Mr. Dunlap to preach the ordination sermon—Mr. Dunlap to preside, and give the charge.

The Presbytery give leave to Pittsburg congregation to apply to any other Presbytery, within the bounds of our church, for supplies.

Messrs. John Hanna and George Hill (41) appeared before Presbytery, &c. (see the usual form, *ante.*) They were taken under the care of Presbytery — provided Mr. Hill give fuller satisfaction with regard to the subjects on which he has been conversed with — examined on Latin and Greek languages, and Mr. Hanna and Mr. Marshall on Hebrew—all sustained. Mr. Hill — an Exegesis — "Quid est discrimen inter fœdera gratiæ et operum?" Mr. Hanna — ditto — "In quo constat essentia fidei salvivicæ?" — both by our next meeting.

"The Presbytery having received sufficient testimonials," &c., (see form of license,) Mr. Robert Marshall was licensed.

The Presbytery finding that the congregation of Buffalo have paid but a small part of their salary to Mr. Hughes, for the last year — order that notice be given that unless they pay up this salary before next meeting, Mr. H. will be under the necessity of removing from them. Adjourned to meet on third Tuesday of September, at James M'Kee's, in Congruity congregation. Concluded with prayer.

(41) A Biographical Sketch of the Rev. George Hill. — The Rev. George Hill was born in York County, Pennsylvania, March 13th, 1764. When about nineteen years of age, he removed, with his father and family, to Fayette County, and settled within the borders of the congregation of George's Creek. His literary studies were prosecuted chiefly, if not entirely, under the direction of the Rev. James Dunlap, pastor of Laurel Hill and Dunlap's Creek congregations. It is affirmed by some aged persons yet living, that he studied theology under the Rev. Jacob Jennings, which is, probably, correct.* He entered the Presbytery of Redstone, as a can-

* It will be seen, by the minutes, that the Rev. Jacob Jennings sat as a corresponding member of Presbytery, in December, 1791, when

didate for the ministry, April 23d, 1790, and was licensed December 22d, 1791, at the church of Bethel, in Indiana County, where the Rev. Joseph W. Henderson was afterwards settled.

At the next spring meeting of the Presbytery, calls were presented for his pastoral labors from the united congregations of Fairfield, Donegal and Wheatfield, and from Mill Creek and King's Creek. The former he accepted, and was ordained and installed their pastor on the 13th of November, 1792. On the 11th of April, 1798, he resigned his charge of Wheatfield; and a new congregation, called Legonier, having been formed between Donegal and Fairfield, he continued to labor in these three last named churches until the time of his death, which took place June 9th, 1822.

Mr. Hill is reported to have been a faithful and laborious pastor, and to have exposed himself frequently to considerable danger in fulfilling his engagements on the Sabbath. Having to cross the Conemaugh, in going to one of his places of preaching, he has been known, in times of high water, to swim the river on horseback, preach in his wet clothes, recross the river, and return to his own house—a distance of ten miles—the same day. Such, however, was the vigor of his constitution, that he suffered no injury from it. He was a man of great sensibility, exceedingly modest and humble in his deportment. When duty required, however, that he should take decided ground, and appear in the defence of the truth, he showed himself to be equal to the crisis, and displayed much firmness of character, as well as acuteness of intellect.

Although, during most of his life, he had enjoyed excellent health, in his last illness he suffered much. But in this extremity, his Christian principles did not forsake him. To those around him he said, "I have learned, whatever is my Heavenly Father's will, therewith to be content." And

---

Mr. Hill was licensed; and that he (Jennings) had not been in the bounds of the Presbytery long before. The above supposition seems, therefore, to be a mistake.

almost the last words which he spoke were, "I know in whom I have believed." * The Rev. George Hill, of the Presbytery of Blairsville, is his grandson.—*Ap. Life of Macurdy*, p. 257.

TWENTY-NINTH MEETING.

Tuesday, 21st of September, 1790.—The Presbytery met at James M'Kee's, &c. Discourses—appointed Messrs. Porter and M'Pherrin — sustained.

Presbytery find their order for raising funds for missionary purposes, in part, complied with, and that the sum received is £22 14*s*. 3*d*. Ordered, that those who have not contributed, do it as soon as convenient.

Rev. David Bard, lately a member of Carlisle Presbytery, being present and invited, sits as a correspondent. The Presbytery proceeded to ordain Messrs. M'Pherrin and Porter, and "did, by fasting and prayer, and with the imposition of the hands of the Presbytery," &c. Mr. Dunlap preached, on the occasion, from Romans i. 16. Mr. M'Millan presided, and Mr. J. Finley gave the charge. Mr. M'Pherrin and Mr. Porter now take their seats as members.

The congregations of Pittsburg and Pittstownship request the Presbytery to grant them such supplies as they can, and to use their best endeavors, at the next meeting of Synod, to procure them such supplies as they shall find convenient.

Mr. Hughes is ordered, by Presbytery, to inform the congregation of Buffalo that a compliance with the order of Presbytery, respecting a settlement, will be expected by the next meeting of Presbytery. Adjourned to meet at Roundhill, third Tuesday of October. Concluded with prayer.

---

* He requested that the Rev. William Wylie, D.D., should be sent for, to preach at his funeral; and suggested that the text should be Jeremiah xlix. 11, "Leave thy fatherless children — I will preserve them alive: and let thy widows trust in me." Dr. Wylie accordingly attended and preached, and has testified to us, that it was one of the most solemn and affecting days he ever witnessed or spent.

WINCHESTER, September 30th, 1790.—The Presbytery met pro re nata. Ubi post preces sederunt, the Rev. Messrs. Joseph Smith, John M'Millan, Thaddeus Dod, Robert Finley, Joseph Patterson, John M'Pherrin, Samuel Porter, and Samuel Barr.

The Synod having accepted the report of the Committee which met at Pitsburg, whereby it appears that Mr. Barr is restored to the full exercise of his ministry — and Mr. Barr having produced sufficient evidence to clear himself of the charge of disorderly conduct, exhibited against him by some members of the Session of Pittsburg, now makes application for a dismission from this Presbytery, in order to join the Presbytery of New Castle; which was accordingly granted, and the Clerk is ordered to furnish him with suitable testimonials.

The Commissioners of Synod having represented to us that they had chosen Mr. R. Marshall as a missionary, provided the Presbytery would recommend him — the Presbytery concurred therewith, and gave him such recommendations as were necessary. Adjourned to meet at time and place before appointed. Concluded with prayer.

THIRTIETH MEETING.

ROUNDHILL, Tuesday, 19th October, 1790.—The Presbytery met, &c. The Presbytery ordered a sermon from II. Cor. vi. 2, by Mr. R. Finley.

The Presbytery continued their order to raise contributions for the support of missionaries under the care of the Synod of Virginia.

The congregation of Lower Buffalo not having complied with the requisition of Presbytery, respecting salary — the Presbytery recommended to the congregations of Short Creek and Lower Buffalo to alter their first plan, and enjoy Mr. Hughes' labors according to their strength.

The Presbytery proceeded to consider the reference respecting John Barnet, from Session of Lebanon congregation; and having read the minutes of the Session relative thereto, and heard all that was further offered by the parties, agreed to defer the final determination thereof until to-morrow.

The Presbytery proceeded to the consideration of the reference respecting John Barnet, and after mature deliberation, came to the following determination, viz.: That although the oath of Jane Miller appears to lay a ground of much suspicion of immodest conduct and language in John Barnet — yet, as there are no circumstances to corroborate her evidence, and something in the acquittance she gave, that seems, in some measure, to weaken the force thereof — we are not clear peremptorily to judge him guilty, but must refer the matter to the judgment of the great day, and in the mean time admonish him to such circumspection in his conduct, as may tend to wipe away all grounds of suspicion respecting him. Ordered, that this judgment be publicly read in the congregation of Lebanon.

The Presbytery proceeded to converse with Mr. Hill on the subjects referred to in the minutes of our last spring meeting, and received such satisfaction as induced them to take him on further trials. His Exegesis — sustained. Mr. Hanna not sufficiently prepared — to have the same subject for an Exegesis formerly assigned him, and a Homily on Romans vii. 9 — by our next meeting. Adjourned to meet at Rehoboth, last Tuesday of December. Concluded with prayer.

THIRTY-FIRST MEETING.

REHOBOTH, December 28th, 1790.— Presbytery met, &c. The Presbytery ordered a sermon from John vii. 37 — by Mr. Porter. Mr. Hanna — Exegesis and Homily — read — not determined concerning them till further examination on Divinity. Mr. Hill a Homily — sustained.

Presbytery examined Mr. Hanna, at some length, on Divinity; and after maturely deliberating on the matter, and prayer to God for direction, from all the light which they could obtain, notwithstanding they felt tenderly for Mr. Hanna, (42) and could not but entertain favorable hopes of his piety — yet, taking into consideration his natural incapacity, his small acquaintance with Divinity, after so long a time spent in study, and the small prospect of his ever taking that pains which is necessary, in order to obtain a competent acquaintance with it — the Presbytery were unanimously of opinion that it was not their duty to encourage him to proceed any further on trials, with a prospect of being licensed to preach the gospel. Adjourned to meet at Dunlap's Creek, third Tuesday of April. Concluded with prayer.

---

(42) Mr. Hanna having been thus dismissed, went to New Jersey, and united himself with the Morris County Presbytery — a small, independent body, the memory of which is principally preserved by the fact that the father of the late Rev. Dr. Ashbel Green was a leading man in that connection. Mr. Hanna was by them licensed and ordained, and is said to have labored with acceptance and usefulness among them till his death. The Morris County Presbyterians resembled, in some respects, the modern Cumberland Presbyterians — in their laxity as to the literary and theological training of their candidates for the ministry — but were not, we believe, semi-Armenians in their theology. There were several pious, zealous, and useful men among them. The Rev. Thaddeus Dod, who was personally acquainted with some of their ministers, and many of their people, was once written to by Mr. Bradford, respecting some one of their body coming out to labor in the West. Mr. Dod, no doubt deprecating the introduction of that sort of Presbyterianism into this region, wrote to his friend a statement of the character of the Western field — stating that it was new and very rough ground, and required sturdy, strong oxen to break it up; and that he doubted whether *two years' olds* would suit for the work. This seems to have put an end to any further thoughts of sending their missionaries into this quarter.

Since the above was written, we have learned, from the Rev. Dr. William Wylie, that Mr. Hanna died a most peaceful, happy death, at the house of Mr. Allen, near the Horse-shoe-bottom settlement, Washington County, being on his way out, on a visit to his brother.

THIRTY-SECOND MEETING.

DUNLAP'S CREEK, April 19th, 1791.—Presbytery met, &c.—The Presbytery ordered a sermon from II. Samuel xxiii. 5—by Mr. Power.

Supplies appointed at nearly all the places heretofore mentioned, and all the ministers two Sabbaths each—and an unusual number of communions appointed.

Messrs. Finley, Dunlap, Power and M'Pherrin, or any two of them—a committee for examining and making appointments for ministers and probationers as may come into the bounds.

Mr. James M'Gready being detained by sickness in the bounds of the Orange Presbytery, applied by letter for a dismission to that Presbytery. The Presbytery ordered the Clerk to send him a dismission, and a letter of advice upon the occasion.

The Presbytery agreed that a letter respecting the affair of Mr. M'Gready's dismission be sent to the Moderator of the Presbytery of Orange.

The Presbytery find, upon inquiry, that the several congregations are satisfied with the care and diligence of their respective pastors.

Mr. William Swan (43) "having offered himself to be taken under the care," &c., (the usual minute in such cases,) was taken on trial. Mr. Hill and Mr. Swan—examined at some length, on Divinity—sustained. Mr. Hill to prepare a Presbyterial Exercise on John xv. 5—by next meeting. Mr. Swan an Exegesis on "An gratia convertens sit irresistibilis?"—and an Homily on Romans vi. 23—by next meeting. Messrs. James Finley, John M'Millan and James Dunlap appointed Commissioners to General Assembly. Adjourned to meet at Chartiers, the last Tuesday of June. Concluded with prayer.

(43) BIOGRAPHICAL SKETCH OF THE REV. WILLIAM SWAN.—The Rev. William Swan was a native of Cumberland, now Franklin County, Pennsylvania; and was educated at Canonsburg Academy. He was licensed to preach the gospel by the Presbytery of Redstone on the same day with the Rev. George Hill, Dec. 22d, 1791. His labors were much in demand, as appears from the fact that at a meeting of his Presbytery, October 16th, 1792, he had calls presented to him from the congregations of Mingo Creek and Horseshoe Bottom, Bethel and Ebenezer, on Blacklick, Long Run and Sewickly, and King's Creek and Mill Creek. The call from Long Run and Sewickly was finally accepted at a meeting of Presbytery held on the 7th of April, 1793; and on the 16th of October following, he was ordained and installed pastor of these united congregations. Here he labored for a period of twenty-five years. In the year 1804, and for some years afterwards, his congregations were visited with special outpourings of the spirit of God during the great revival, and considerable numbers were added to the church. On the 18th of October, 1818, he asked and obtained leave to resign the pastoral charge of his congregations. But in the spring following, April 20th, 1819, he was recalled to Long Run, and having accepted the call, was installed again, during the summer, as the pastor of that church. After laboring among this people for an additional period of three years, with declining health, the pastoral relation was dissolved finally, at his request, April 17th, 1822. His health continued to decline under the slow progress of pulmonary consumption; and on the 27th of November, 1827, he fell asleep in Jesus in the 63d year of his age. His last hours were peaceful and happy. Mr. Darby states that Mr. Swan succeeded James Ross, Esq., as teacher at Dr. M'Millan's "Log Cabin."

Ap. to Life of Macurdy, p. 280.

THIRTY-THIRD MEETING.

CHARTIERS, Sunday, June 28, 1791.—Presbytery met according to adjournment. Presbytery was opened with a sermon from Jer. vi., 4, by Mr. Marshall. Commissioners to General Assembly fulfilled appointments. Mr. Swan—Exegesis—sustained.

Mr. Robert Finley, having represented to Presbytery that probably he might be under the necessity of removing to Kentucky before their next meeting, therefore requested that a member might be appointed to furnish him with suitable credentials in case it should be necessary. The Presbytery granted his request, and appointed Mr. James Finley for this purpose. Mr. Hill—Presbyterial Exercise—sustained. Mr. Swan, examined on Latin and Greek languages — sustained. Mr. Swan—Homily—sustained. Mr. Hill and Mr. Swan — examined further on Divinity—sustained. Mr. Hill—to prepare a lecture on 11th Psalms. Mr. Swan — Presbyterial Exercise on I. Peter iii. 18, and lecture on 60th Psalms—all by next meeting. Adjourned to meet at Pigeon Creek, 3d Tuesday in October. Concluded with prayer.

THIRTY-FOURTH MEETING.

PIGEON CREEK, Tuesday, Oct. 18th, 1791. — Presbytery met according to adjournment. Presbytery was opened by Messrs. Hill and Swan with discourses on subjects previously assigned to them — sustained.

Mr. M'Pherrin informed us by letter — detained by sickness. Treasurer reported that he had received from the following congregations the following contributions for the support of missionaries, viz. .—

Mr. M'Millan's congregation, £7 12*s* 6*d*; Mr. Patterson's, £4 3*s* 9*d*; Mr. M'Pherrin's, £6 8*s*; Mr. Hughes', £4 8*s* 6*d*; Mr. Clarke's, £1 7*s* 6*d*; Mr. Power's, £2 12*s*; Mr. Smith's, £17 7*s*; in all, £43 15*s* 3*d*; for the payment of which in the hands of the commissioners of Synod, he produced their receipt. Mr. J. Finley, reported his attending to the duty assigned him, as to Mr. R. Finley. Upon motion, ordered that the ministers and probationers under our care keep a particular account of the sums received at the different places where they supply, and make report at our spring and fall meetings; and that vacancies be ordered to inform Presbytery, at our next spring meeting, what places they had fallen upon for the discharge of supplies and promoting of religion among them. All the ministers were appointed to supply two Sabbaths. Their appointments were disposed over the places heretofore mentioned.

Contributions for the support of missionaries enjoined upon those delinquent—to be in next meeting. The Presbytery, after conversing upon the recommendation of Synod respecting Baptism, deferred the further consideration of it till our next spring meeting. The Presbytery, after considering a recommendation of Synod respecting the institution of seminaries of learning for the purpose of educating pious youth for the ministry, did approve thereof; which is as follows:—

"As the supplying of churches with a pious and well-qualified ministry is of acknowledged importance—overtured,—

"1st. That the Synod of Virginia undertake the patronage of a seminary of learning for the purpose of educating young men for the gospel ministry.

"2d. That they devise means for supporting or assisting young men of piety and genius in procuring an education, who may not be possessed of sufficient property for the purpose. The Synod highly approve of the proposition contained in the overture, as they are well convinced of the necessity of extending the opportunities of acquiring knowledge, and especially the knowledge of the doctrines of religion, to all who intend to preach the gospel of Jesus Christ to the world. Taking this measure, therefore, into serious consideration, the Synod recommend that there be two general institutions for learning, conducted under the patronage of this body; one to be established in Rockbridge County, Virginia, under the care of the Rev. William Graham, as the President; the other in Washington County, Pennsylvania, under the care of the Rev. John M'Millan. The principles upon which these institutions are to be conducted are as follows:—

"1st. The learned languages and usual circle of sciences

shall be taught in them to as many as may be sent there for instruction.

"2d. During the course of academical education, and from the first initiation of the students into the seminaries, a course of religious instruction shall also be entered upon, and continually adhered to during their residence there, according to the principles of our church. Books of a practical and doctrinal nature, shall be put into their hands at once. Catechetical lectures shall be established and examinations entered into, upon their progress in this kind of knowledge, from time to time. The attention to these studies shall be kept up during the whole of their academical course, and suited to the capacities and progress of the youth.

"3d. The Presbyteries of Lexington and Hanover shall be the trustees of the seminary in Rockbridge, to cherish it by their influence and pointedly to attend the examinations of the students; either in a collective capacity or by committees from their respective bodies, duly appointed. The Presbytery of Redstone shall, in like manner, superintend the seminary in Washington County.

"4th. In one or other of these institutions, it is the advice of the Synod that all the youth within our bounds, who intend to engage in the ministry of the gospel, shall be instructed.

"5th. As there are a number of pious youth in our country, who might be very serviceable in preaching the gospel, but through want of sufficient ability are unable to obtain an education, it is the intention and desire of Synod that the ministers in their respective Presbyteries shall seek out such, and that they, being examined and approved by the Presbytery, shall be placed in the respective seminaries, at the expense of the Presbytery who shall approve them.

"6th. In order to obtain the proper supplies for such indigent students the Presbyteries are exhorted to use their influence in their respective bounds with the pious and benevolent to make annual contributions for raising a fund for this purpose, this fund to be placed in the hands of treasurers appointed by the Synod, who are to return annual accounts of receipts and expenditures; and from it the youth upon the foundation, are to draw their supplies, by an order from their respective presidents. And those youth, upon their obtaining their education, at the expiration of one year, after being settled in some line of business, shall begin to refund to the treasury the expenses of their education, in such time and manner as the Presbytery may direct.

"7th. The rules of these seminaries and the mode of education therein, shall be submitted to the Presbyteries for their respective approbation."

The Presbytery, therefore, order their members to use their best endeavors to obtain contributions for the above purpose, and put them into the hands of Mr. M'Millan, who is appointed treasurer, as soon as possible; and of their diligence herein, to render an account at our next Spring meeting. (44)

---

(44) It will be found, by tracing the further history of this important movement, that the Presbytery, October 18th, 1792, "unanimously agreed to appoint Canonsburg to be the seat of that institution of learning which they are appointed by Synod to superintend." And November 14th, 1792, upon motion, it was agreed to reconsider the propriety of appointing Canonsburg, as the seat, &c., at their next Spring meeting. Then April 18th, 1793—confirmed the former minute respecting Canonsburg Academy, with this addition—"that if it should appear at a future day, most conducive to the good of the church, that another seminary of a like nature should be erected in our bounds, we will not oppose a division of the funds." These are all the notices until the Presbytery was divided. There are frequent notices in the minutes of the appointment of Committees to attend, along with the Presbytery of Ohio, upon the state of the Academy—the examination of the students of the Canonsburg Academy, down to December 26th, 1797—also recommendations to raise contributions for the Academy. Similar minutes are found in the Records of the Presbytery of Ohio at their sessions of October, 1793—April, 1794—October 1794, and so on, till April, 1797. From both Records, all further notice, either about examinations or about raising funds, disappear—and no reason whatever is given. At the meeting of the Presbytery of Redstone, April, 1798, Dr. M'Millan was present as a corresponding member; yet nothing was said or done about further contributions, or about appointing an examining

Agreeably to a recommendation of Synod, respecting the religious observation of the Lord's day—ordered that each minister of this Presbytery shall read this recommendation in their respective congregations, and engage spiritedly in complying with the same. Mr. Swan—a Presbyterial exercise—sustained.

Mr. Hill and Mr. Swan, examined upon Natural and Moral Philosophy—sustained.

---

committee. In like manner, the records of the Presbytery of Ohio are silent. Why was this? What now becomes of an institution entrusted to their superintendence, by their Synod? And up to this time, from 1793, what superintendence or control had they over it? It appears that all they were permitted to do was to attend the examinations—not to act as trustees—or to appoint or even nominate, either any of the Board, or any of the Faculty. They had no part whatever as Presbyteries, in the government or management of this Academy. They were asked however, for a few years, to urge their people to contribute to its support. And this they did at almost every successive meeting; sometimes three times a year. But after the year 1797, they drop from their minutes all further notice of this Academy at Canonsburg. Does the following extract from Dr. Brown's Life of Dr. M'Millan throw any light on this point? "In 1798, (Dr. Brown has it 1794, evidently a mistake,) there was an amendment to the constitution effecting important changes. The Trustees were no longer elected annually, but for life; and when vacancies occurred by death or otherwise, the corporate Trustees elected others to supply the vacancy." It, in other words, now became a close corporation. Though the Presbyterians of Redstone and Ohio had not previously such a superintendence as was manifestly contemplated in the action of the Synod, (when the Synod said, after appointing the Presbyteries of Lexington and Hanover Trustees of the Rockbridge Academy—that the Presbytery of Redstone, and afterwards, we suppose, of Ohio, shall, in like manner, superintend the institution in Washington County); yet up to this time, they were on the whole satisfied with the arrangement of attending, in a body, or by committees upon the examination of the students. Perhaps the proportion of Presbyterians in the board at that time, and afterwards when the Academy in 1802, was merged into Jefferson College, satisfied them that any further attention to the examinations was superfluous and unnecessary. Both Presbyteries afterwards, more than once, commended the Institution to the pecuniary aid of their people, even so late as 1806.

Mr. Hill—to prepare a popular sermon on Matthew xxviii. 20, and Mr. Swan—I. Timothy i. 15, both by our next meeting. Adjourned to meet at Bethel, on the third Tuesday of December next. Concluded with prayer.

THIRTY-FIFTH MEETING.

BETHEL, Tuesday, December 20th, 1791. Presbytery met, &c. The Presbytery opened with a sermon on the subject assigned at our last meeting—by Mr. Swan—sustained.

The Rev. Jacob Jennings, (45) of the Low Dutch Church, being present and invited, sat as a correspondent. Agreeably to order, minutes of the late meeting, except in regard to supplies, were read. Mr. Bruce's reasons—sustained. "Mr. David Smith, having offered himself to be taken," &c., (see former minutes,) taken on trials.

Mr. Hill—discourse on subject appointed—sustained. J. M. Bruce, elder, came, reasons — sustained. The Rev. Thomas Cooly, late a member of the Presbytery of Charleston, appeared before us, and produced a dismission and testimonials from said Presbytery, together with testimonials from a number of dissenting ministers in England, and desired to be received as a member with us. The Presbytery, after maturely deliberating upon the matter, could not see their way clear, to receive him upon his credentials from that Presbytery, as it is a Presbytery unknown to us, and not in subordination to the General Assembly: but proceeded to converse with him as a minister from foreign parts, agreeably to the direction of the General Synod in such cases, and obtained such satisfaction as induced them to employ him in their vacancies, until the next meeting of Synod; yet they expect that he will before the next meeting of Synod, produce some letters of recommendation from some ministers in South Carolina known to them.

Mr. David Smith — examined on learned languages and Divinity — sustained. Also Mr. Hill and Mr. Swan on Divinity—sustained.

"The Presbytery, having received sufficient testimonials," &c. (see form of license,) Messrs. Hill and Swan licensed to preach the gospel. Mr. Jennings having expressed a desire to continue some time in our bounds—was appointed to supply at Dunlap's Creek and Muddy Creek, as much as convenient, between this, and next meeting of Presbytery. Mr. Cooly—to supply at discretion, particularly in Harrison County. The third Tuesday in January next, was appointed to be observed as a day of fasting and prayer, particularly on account of the situation of our country, with respect to the savages. (46)

---

(46) After General Harmar's defeat, in 1790, the Indians began afresh their depredations on the Western frontiers. The settlers, especially those wholly unprotected, were left exposed to fall a helpless prey to the merciless savages, who exercised the most cruel tortures upon a large number of their victims. The heavy disasters that befel Harmar's army, seemed to inspire the Indians with the hope of ultimately extirpating the infant settlements on the Ohio. Victory seemed to perch upon their blood-stained banner, under which they rallied to spread destruction over the unprotected portions of the West. And now still more the disastrous defeat of the arms of the United States, in the battle of the unfortunate St. Clair, with the Indians, on the 4th of November, 1791, about a month and a half before this meeting of the Redstone Presbytery—spread anxiety and alarm amongst our people, especially towards the Ohio.

["Of those who do most impressively remember that defeat and the terror excited over the whole frontier region, by that fearful report; I am one who heard the report in its first echo. A part of the army was composed of drafted men from the Western settlements, and not a few of them perished in that sanguinary affair. I was then living with my parents in the vicinity, and five miles eastward of Washington, Pennsylvania, and then in my twentieth year."—*William Darby, Esq., in the National Intelligencer of November 8th*, 1851.]

During that year, there were numbers killed and taken prisoners, of the settlers near Pittsburg. "Several persons," says Major Craig, in a letter to General Knox, March 31st, 1791—"within a few miles of this place, have fallen victims to the revenge of those Indians who escaped on Beaver Creek."—(History of Pittsburg, 211.) A day of fasting and prayer was doubtless very proper at that time. It is remarkable how long the "Canaanite was still in the land," and permitted to be a thorn

Mr. David Smith — to prepare an Exegesis — "Quomodo miracula probant Scripturas sacras esse divinas" — and a Homily on Rom. viii. 5—by our next meeting. Adjourned to meet at Roundhill the 3d Tuesday in April. Concluded with prayer.

(45) BIOGRAPHICAL SKETCH OF THE REV. JACOB JENNINGS. —"The Rev. Jacob Jennings was born in Somerset County, New Jersey, in the year 1744. He was a descendant of one of the pilgrims who settled at Plymouth, Massachusetts. Of the place of his education we are not informed. He early studied medicine and commenced its practice in a small village, near Elizabethtown, New Jersey. After some time he removed thence to Readington township, Huntingdon County, where he continued in the practice of his profession, with considerable reputation, for many years. When he was about forty years of age, and after he had been a medical practitioner for upwards of twenty, he turned his attention to Theology and was licensed to preach the gospel. From the fact that when he first came to Western Pennsylvania, he was a member of the Synod of the Dutch Reformed Church of New York and New Jersey, the presumption is that he was licensed in that connection. He came to Pennsylvania about the year 1791; as in December of that year, he sat as a corresponding member of the Presbytery of Redstone; and was received to full membership by that body on the 17th of April, 1792. For several years previous to his arrival in Pennsylvania, he had resided in Virginia, to which State he had removed soon after his licensure. He accepted a call from the congregation of Dunlap's Creek, in Fayette County,

in the side of our people—now more than ten years after the Presbytery was organized. "A large portion of the killed were, of course, militia. Both Kentucky and Western Pennsylvania were filled with mourning. The Indians, elated with success, renewed their attacks on the frontier with increased force and ferocity. Meetings were called to devise means for defending the settlements."—*American Pioneer, Vol. II., p.* 215.

Pennsylvania, and continued pastor of said church until June, 1811, when, on account of his increased infirmities, he asked and obtained a dissolution of the pastoral relation. He died, February 17th, 1813. He was father of the Rev. Obadiah Jennings, D. D., late of Nashville, Tennessee—and of the Rev. Samuel K. Jennings, M. D., a highly respectable minister in the Metohdist Protestant Church, and for some time a Professor in the Washington Medical college, of Baltimore. Two of his grandsons also are ministers—the Rev. Samuel C. Jennings, of the Presbytery of Ohio, and the Rev. Jacob Jennings, son of the Rev. Samuel K. Jennings above mentioned—who is a minister in the same ecclesiastical connection with his father."—*Appendix to Life of Macurdy.*

THIRTY-SIXTH MEETING.

ROUNDHILL, Tuesday, April 17th, 1792.—The Presbytery met according to adjournment. Presbytery opened with a sermon from II. Cor. xii. 9, by the Rev. Thomas Cooly. The Rev. Jacob Jennings, formerly a member of the Reformed Dutch Church of New York and New Jersey, applied to be received as a member of this Presbytery; and upon producing sufficient testimonials of his regular licensure and ordination by the Synod of said church, together with other certificates of his good moral and Christian character for many years past, was accordingly received, and took his seat as a member. A call from the united congregations of Dunlap's Creek and Muddy Creek to Mr. Jennings, delivered to him for his consideration. Two calls from Fairfield, Donegal, and Wheatfield, and from Middle and King's Creeks, to Mr. Hill—delivered to him for his consideration.

The appointment respecting the fast-day has been complied with. (Supplies, by all the ministers two Sabbaths each, with few exceptions; and by Mr. Clark, four Sabbaths; by Mr. Swan, several months; all spread over the vast field of vacancies.) Mr. Jennings accepted the call from Dunlap's Creek and Muddy Creek, and appointed to supply at George's Creek and Sandy Creek.

The Presbytery found, on enquiry, that several of the members had done something considerable for the education of poor and pious youth, according to an order at our last meeting, and further order that the respective members go on to attend to this matter, and report what progress they have made therein at our next meeting.

The Presbytery, taking into their serious consideration the recommendation of Synod respecting periodical baptism, cannot see sufficient ground, from Scripture authority, for their compliance therewith.

An appeal from the judgment of Salem Session, in a matter between Elizabeth Trimble and Nancy Woodend, was brought in and read. The Presbytery, after deliberating on the matter, agreed to appoint Messrs. Finley and Power, together with John Shields and John Moor, elders, as a commission to take up the matter de novo, to meet at the house of John Taylor, on the 4th Monday of May next, at 8 o'clock. Mr. Hill declared his acceptance of the call from the united congregations of Fairfield, Donegal, and Wheatfield; and returned the call from the united congregations of Mill Creek and King's Creek.

Mr. Hill—to prepare a discourse on Prov. xiii. 31, by our next meeting, as part of trial for ordination. Upon enquiry, found that congregations were satisfied with the care and diligence of their respective pastors.

Mr. Thomas Marquis, (47) having offered himself to be taken on trials, in order to his being licensed to preach the gospel, the Presbytery having received sufficient testimonials of his having gone through a regular course of literature, of his good moral character, and of his being a regular member of the church, proceeded to converse with him upon his experimental acquaintance with religion, and proposed to him several cases of conscience; and having obtained satisfaction on these points, agreed to take him on trials.

Mr. Marquis — to prepare an Exegesis on the following theme, viz.: "An reatus peccati Adami, omnibus ejus posteris, naturali generatione ab eo oriundis, imputatur"—by our next meeting. Rev. Messrs. John M'Millan, John M'Pherrin, and Samuel Porter, were appointed commissioners to next General Assembly. Adjourned to meet at Chartiers the 4th Tuesday in June. Concluded with prayer.

(47) Biographical Sketch of the Rev. Thomas Marquis.—The Rev. Thomas Marquis was born at Opequon, near Winchester, Virginia. Having lost both his parents when a child, he was brought up in the family of a pious uncle. In the year 1775, he married, and, with a number of his friends, removed to the vicinity of Cross Creek, Washington County, Pennsylvania; which was then an almost unbroken wilderness. Shortly after their arrival, they were called to mourn the loss of a brother of Mrs. Marquis—Mr. Park—who, close to their own dwelling, was tomahawked and scalped by an Indian. For several years the hostile incursions of the Indians obliged the inhabitants to take refuge in forts. While thus assembled, through fear of the savages, God's Spirit was poured out upon them, and eight or ten persons, of which Mr. Marquis was one, were hopefully converted. The principal instrument in this work was a pious farmer, afterwards well known in Western Pennsylvania as the Rev. Joseph Patterson, of Raccoon. Thus, in the midst of their trials their hearts were made glad by these tokens of the divine presence. During this period, also, in the year 1778, they were favored by a visit from the Rev. Dr. Power, who preached to them at Fort Vance; on which occasion, Mr. and Mrs. Marquis presented their first child to God in baptism. This was the first sermon preached, and the first child baptised, in that region of country. The next year a church was organized, of which this pious couple became members. Mr. Marquis received his classical education at Canonsburg Academy, studied theology with the Rev. Dr. M'Millan, and was licensed to preach the gospel by the Presbytery of Redstone, at Dunlap's Creek, April 19th, 1793. Having received a call to

the congregation of Cross Creek, within the bounds of the Presbytery of Ohio, he became connected with that Presbytery April 23d, 1794; and, on the 13th of June following, was ordained and installed pastor of the congregation to which he had been called. In addition to his labors at Cross Creek, he acted as a stated supply one-half of the time at Upper Buffalo, until that church called the Rev. John Anderson to be their pastor, when his connection with it ceased. He continued, however, in the charge of the church of Cross Creek, until October 3d, 1826; which, from the time of his settlement as their pastor, included a period of thirty-two years. Several precious revivals occurred during his ministry, and upwards of four hundred persons were added to the church. He died peacefully and triumphantly, on September 27th, 1827, at the house of his son-in-law, the Rev. Joseph Stevenson, in Bellefontaine, Logan County, Ohio; whither he had gone on a visit to his daughter and her family. He was upwards of seventy years of age. All who knew him speak of him as an eloquent and impressive preacher. The tones of his voice were exceedingly musical. Hence he was often called "the silver-tongued Marquis." In the judicatories of the church he was esteemed a wise and judicious counsellor. Hence, when, in 1804, the General Assembly determined to appoint a committee to visit the Synod of Kentucky, and endeavor to heal the disorders which had taken place within the bounds of that Synod, he was chosen one of the number for that purpose. The manner in which the committee executed their commission will be seen by the following resolution, passed by the General Assembly at their next meeting, in 1805:—

"Resolved, that they highly approve the firm and temperate measures taken by the Synod of Kentucky and the commissioners of the Assembly that met with them; and are of opinion that the committee, besides the pecuniary indemnity assigned them, are entitled to the thanks of the Assembly for the diligence, prudence, zeal, and fidelity with which they appear to have executed their commission." He was one of the original members of the Board of Trustees of the Western Mississippi Society, and for a number of years gave his counsels and his labors to aid in carrying on its operations.*

It is not improbable that Mr. Marquis's visit to Kentucky, and his influence and efforts while there, contributed mainly to save Messrs. Marshall and M'Gready from their further wanderings into errors and divisive measures. And they were well worth saving; for they were noble, though, for a while, misguided men. It is remarkable that Mr. Marquis was received as a candidate for the ministry on the very day that his pastor and predecessor died!

"I believe," says the Rev. Jacob Lindley, "there is a mistake in Dr. Elliott's Life of Thomas Marquis. He says Marquis received his classical education at Canonsburg Academy, and studied theology with the Rev. Dr. M'Millan. The fact in his case is, he never studied the classics. I had this from his own mouth. He studied English grammar, a smattering of the Latin, and the sciences, at Dr. M'Millan's own house, where he repaired, occasionally, to take lessons, while he left his farm and family on Cross Creek, in the care of his two oldest sons, then but mere lads. He told me, when at his house, as an apology for his ignorance of the Greek Testament, that, under all his embarrassments and original ignorance, it was but three years from the time he commenced his studies with a view to the ministry, until he was licensed to preach. He also told me that much of these three years was spent with Mr. Smith, as he was more immediately in the neighborhood of his farm and family. Marquis was the most eminent pulpit orator of his day, because he seemed more deeply imbued with the spirit of Mr. Smith."

It is said that Dr. Ashbel Green, after hearing Mr. Marquis in his own pulpit, in Philadelphia, was so deeply affected by the matter and manner of the discourse, that he resolved

* Append. Life of Macurdy.

to abandon his own method, and adopt that of Marquis: with what success, we never heard.

During the great revival of 1802, '3, '4, Mr. Marquis was amongst the foremost of those who labored with great success in the work. In the space of two or three years, at that time, he was honored with an instrumentality in the salvation of souls that but few ministers ever enjoy during a long lifetime. His own pastoral charge at Cross Creek was especially favored with a mighty work of the Holy Spirit. In the 9th number of the Western Missionary Magazine, p. 329, we read as follows:—

"On the 5th of October, 1802, the day of concert prayer, the Lord appeared, by the powerful operation of the Spirit, in the congregation of Cross Creek, the charge of the Rev. Thomas Marquis. The people were solemn and attentive through the day; and in the evening, when dismissed, they appeared backward to go away. After part were gone, and many standing about the doors, one of the elders, who was in the house, went to the door and spoke a few words respecting their situation, and in a few minutes the young people were all in tears. They then joined in singing a hymn, and in prayer. By this time, some of those who had gone away returned. They went all again into the house, candles were brought, and the night was spent in prayer, conversation, and praise, until 2 o'clock in the morning. During this time many were much affected. It appeared that the power of God, like a mighty wind, filled the house. Numbers sunk down and cried out in the anguish of their souls, bitterly lamenting their misimprovement of time and abuse of mercies. They, in a very moving manner, expressed their sense of sin and guilt, the hardness of their hearts, and the justice of God in passing them by neglected in this their deep distress," &c. Then, of the following night,—"It was a night to be had in everlasting remembrance, for which, it is hoped, many will praise God eternally. At this time, some began to speak the language of Canaan with solemn, sweet serenity of mind, and in heavenly, heart-affecting accents."

THIRTY-SEVENTH MEETING.

CHARTIERS, Tuesday, June 26th, 1792. — Presbytery met according to adjournment. Presbytery opened with a sermon on John x. 14, by Mr. Patterson. The Presbytery found that the Rev. Joseph Smith was removed by death, on the 19th of April last. Mr. David Smith, having been detained from our last meeting by the sickness and death of his father, now brought in and read an Exegesis on a theme assigned — sustained. Mr. Hill, having informed Presbytery, by letter, that he could not attend our present meeting to deliver the discourse appointed him, is therefore required to attend to it at our next.

The committee appointed to meet on the Appeal from Salem Session, reported that they met accordingly, but found that they could not proceed, because the witnesses, though cited, did not attend; that, therefore, they had recommended to the parties to call the assistance of some of their elders, and endeavor to have the affair accommodated; which report was approved.

Mr. Smith brought in and read a Homily on the subject appointed him at our last winter meeting; also a Presbyterial Exercise on Heb. iv. 17; which, though not appointed him by Presbytery, as he was necessarily detained from our last meeting, and so had no part of trials given him, yet was received as though it had been appointed, and both were sustained as parts of trial.

Mr. Marquis—an Exegesis—sustained. Mr. Boyd Mercer, "having offered himself," &c., (see previous forms of minutes,) taken on trial. The Presbytery, having taken into consideration a reference from the session of Roundhill congregation, were of opinion that they had not sufficient evidence to prove that John Crawford is the father of Hannah Burney's child; and that said Burney be admitted to give satisfaction in the common mode.

Mr. Marquis and Mr. Mercer examined on Latin and Greek languages, and Mr. Smith on Hebrew—all sustained. Messrs.

M'Millan and Brice—leave of absence. Presbytery renewed their order respecting raising funds for the support of missionaries agreeably to the plan of the Synod, and ordered their members to bear or convey said collections to the Treasurer of the Commission of Synod at the next meeting of Synod. Commissioners to the General Assembly fulfilled their appointment.

Mr. Smith — to prepare a lecture on Heb. vi. 1–6. Mr. Marquis—a Homily on Rom. viii. 14. Mr. Mercer, an Exegesis on "An Decreta Dei conditionata vel absoluta sint?" The united congregations of Cross Creek and Buffalo, being left vacant by Mr. Smith's decease, made application for supplies. Adjourned to meet at Pigeon Creek the 3d Tuesday in October. Concluded with prayer.

THIRTY-EIGHTH MEETING.

PIGEON CREEK, Tuesday, October 16th, 1792. Presbytery met according to adjournment. The Presbytery opened with discourses by Messrs. Hill and Smith — subjects previously assigned—sustained.

Four calls — from Mingo Creek and Horse-shoe Bottom; from Bethel and Ebenezer; from Long Run and Sewickly; and from Mill Creek and King's Creek — for Mr. Swan! all put into his hands for his consideration. Mr. Swan returned the first two calls, and asked longer time about the others. (Supplies furnished to almost all the vacancies, by all the ministers — two Sabbaths each.) The Presbytery find that, agreeably to the order of the General Assembly, Mr. Cooley's testimonials were laid before Synod, and that the Synod, from the peculiar nature of said testimonials, suspected the authenticity of them, and therefore agreed to retain them and lay them before the General Assembly next Spring. Also, finding that Mr. Cooley has not complied with the order of Presbytery respecting letters of recommendation from ministers in South Carolina, did not see their way clear to employ him any longer until further satisfaction be obtained respecting these matters.

The Presbytery proceeded to consider a reference from the Session of Congruity congregation, respecting a certain James Christy and Rebecca Gordon. After hearing all the minutes of the Session relating to that affair, and duly deliberating thereon, Presbytery were unanimously of opinion that no credit ought to be given to the oath of Rebecca Gordon, and therefore that there is no sufficient evidence to criminate said Christy as being the father of said Gordon's child — yet, as there appeared to have been unbecoming conduct between the above-mentioned parties, Presbytery judged that neither of them ought to be received to distinguishing privileges, until Providence shall shed further light upon the matter.

The Presbytery agree to ordain Mr. G. Hill on the second Tuesday of November, at Fairfield; and appointed Mr. Porter to preach the ordination sermon, and Mr. Power to preside and give the charge.

The Treasurer reported that he had received the following contributions for the support of missionaries, viz.: from Mr. M'Pherrin, £5 2*s.*; Mr. Hughes, £3; Mr. Dunlap, £5 16*s.* 9*d.*; Mr. M'Millan, 15*s.*—in all £14 13*s.* 9*d.*—for which he produced the receipt of the Commission of Synod.

The Presbytery having received a dismission and certificate from the Commission of Synod, testifying that Mr. Robert Marshall had conducted himself in a becoming manner, while riding a missionary under their care and direction — and also a letter from Mr. M., requesting a dismission from Presbytery, to join the Presbytery of Transylvania — agree to grant his request, and recommend him as a licentiate in good standing. Ordered that the Clerk transmit a copy of this minute to Mr. Marshall. (48)

Upon inquiry, found that a number of the members had done something considerable towards raising a fund for the education of poor and pious youth, and that it is the design of all the members present to do what they can in this matter.

Mr. Marquis and Mr. Mercer — discourses — sustained.

Synod having appointed the second Thursday of November to be observed as a day of solemn fasting and prayer, to supplicate Almighty God to pour out his Holy Spirit upon our assemblies, and to revive religion in our churches—also to return God humble thanks for the divine influences he has already granted to some places in our bounds — Presbytery heartily concurred with the appointment, and enjoined it upon the churches in their bounds carefully to observe the same.

The Presbytery granted Mr. Swan's request to retain the two calls now in his hands till next meeting, and appointed him to supply those places till then.

The Presbytery unanimously agreed to appoint Canonsburg to be the seat of that institution of learning, which they are appointed by Synod to superintend; and that all the young men taken upon the fund for the support of poor and pious youths, shall be educated there.

Messrs. Smith, Marquis and Mercer examined on Moral Philosophy — and Marquis and Mercer, at some length, on Divinity — all sustained. Mr. Smith to prepare a popular sermon on John xv. 12; Mr. Marquis—a Presbyterial Exercise on Galatians iv. 45; and Mr. Mercer a Homily on Isaiah lxiv. 6 — all by next meeting. Adjourned to meet at Fairfield, second Tuesday of November. Concluded with prayer.

(48) Biographical Sketch of the Rev. Robert Marshall.— As this very eminent servant of God, after laboring near two-and-a-half years as a licentiate of the Redstone Presbytery, now withdraws to another field, and his name will appear no more on the minutes, it may be proper to give some further account of him.

"The Rev. Robert Marshall was born in County Down, Ireland, November 27th, 1760, and in the twelfth year of his age accompanied his family to western Pennsylvania. He was a wild boy; and when the Revolutionary War broke out, enlisted as a private soldier, at the age of sixteen, in opposition to the wishes of his mother. Contrary to what might have been expected from such a beginning, while in the army he never swore nor drank, although drinking and profanity were common in the camp, and liquor formed part of the rations. When not on duty, he retired to his tent, and devoted himself, like Cobbet, to the study of arithmetic and mathematics. He was in six general engagements, one of which was the hard-fought battle of Monmouth, where he narrowly escaped with his life, a bullet grazing his locks. To the end of life, military music had a stirring effect on him.

"After the War, he joined the Seceders, and was very self-righteous, but, as he afterwards believed, was a stranger to a real change of heart. It was under a searching sermon of that man of God, Dr. M'Millan, from Romans ix. 22, that he who had come to find food for criticism and cavil in a preacher of a rival denomination, felt that he was one of 'the vessels of wrath fitted for destruction.' His self-possession deserted him, his proud head dropped, and he was thrown into a state of the deepest anguish. He vainly sought some outward sign from heaven of his acceptance, and not receiving any, fell into despair. At length he became sensible of the presumption of dictating to God the evidences of conversion, and obtained a more rational hope. This hope he never afterwards lost, not even in his wildest aberrations, and towards the close of life it rose to a high degree of assurance.

"He was now about twenty-three years old — but not deterred by his age, he resolutely commenced preparation for the ministry. His academical studies were conducted under Mr. Graham, at Liberty Hall; his theological course under Dr. M'Millan, something of whose solemn manner he caught. While at Liberty Hall, he maintained an exemplary and consistent walk among a set of profane and wicked youths, and though standing alone, commanded universal respect. After being licensed by Redstone Presbytery, he returned to Virginia, and labored in the revival with great zeal and success. He was remarkable for his fidelity in visiting and conversing upon religion. In 1791, he removed, with his wife, to Kentucky, in the capacity of a missionary of the Synod; and on the 13th of June, 1793, was ordained pastor of Bethel and Blue Spring churches. He also conducted a classical school, at which many received their education, who afterwards made a very prominent figure in the world.

"In the great revival of 1800, Mr. Marshall was one of the chief leaders; and carried away by the torrent of enthusiasm that swept over Kentucky, and sincerely believing his more sober brethren to be wrong, he joined with Stone, in 1803, in fomenting the new-light schism. He afterwards saw his error, and in 1811 returned to the bosom of the church. The schismatics were, at first, called Marshallites; but, on his defection, were known by the name of Stonites. He afterwards used to say that he could not ascribe his conduct to any other cause than a strange infatuation; and for years, never mounted the pulpit without lamenting his errors, and warning the people against similar delusions.

"He took an appointment under the Assembly's Standing Committee of Missions, in 1812, and was soon after reinstated in his old charge of Bethel, where he continued till his decease, in 1833, at the advanced age of 73." — *Davidson's History of Presbyterian Church in Kentucky.*

THIRTY-NINTH MEETING.

FAIRFIELD, (49) November 14th, 1792.—Presbytery met, &c. The Presbytery proceeded to set apart Mr. George

---

(49) FAIRFIELD, now in the Presbytery of Blairsville, was early organized. After being supplied by the Presbytery for a number of years, it at length, in connection with Donegal and Wheatfield, obtained as its pastor the Rev. George Hill, who was ordained and installed among them, November 13th, 1792. He continued the pastor of this church until his death, June 7th, 1822. On the 17th of June, 1824, the Rev.

Hill to the holy office of the gospel ministry, according to our constitution. Mr. Porter preached upon the occasion, and Mr. Power presided, and gave the charge. Mr. Hill then took his seat as a member.

Upon motion, it was agreed to reconsider the propriety of appointing Canonsburg as the seat of that institution of learning, which Presbytery are appointed to superintend — at our next spring meeting.

Mr. Samuel Mahon, formerly a licentiate under the care of Carlisle Presbytery, having accepted a call in our bounds, professed a desire to be taken under the care of this Presbytery; and having produced a certificate of his good standing as a licentiate, with that body, and a regular dismission from them, was accordingly received — appointed to deliver a discourse on John vi. 44, at next meeting, and to supply at Pittsburg until that time.

Mr. Smith — his appointed discourse — sustained. Mr. Smith and Mr. Mercer—examined on Natural Philosophy—sustained. "The Presbytery having received sufficient testimonials,"&c., (see form, &c.,) Mr. David Smith was licensed to preach the gospel. (50) Mr. Marquis and Mr. Mercer — their appointed discourses—sustained. Mr. Marquis—to prepare a lecture on Ephesians v. 1–6—and a sermon on Psalms lx. 1; and Mr. Mercer—a Presbyterial Exercise on Hebrews x. 1—and a sermon on Romans v. 12–21 — all by next meeting.

Mr. Swan having requested longer time to determine respecting the calls in his hands — to supply as much as convenient in those congregations until his mind is determined.

Samuel Swan was ordained pastor of Fairfield, in connection with Ligonier and Donegal. He continued their pastor for some years, when the pastoral relation was dissolved. In 1843, the Rev. John Fleming became their pastor for two or three years. In 1847, the Rev. O. H. Miller became the pastor of Fairfield. His successor was the Rev. William Colledge, who has been succeeded by the Rev. Mr. J. W. Walker. This church, in connection with Union, reports number of communicants, in 1854—193.

Numerous supplies appointed to Mr. Smith. Adjourned to meet at Rehoboth, on third Tuesday of April. Concluded with prayer.

(50) Biographical Sketch of the Rev. David Smith. —The Rev. David Smith, the son of the Rev. Joseph Smith, inherited the prominent traits of both his parents, and by Divine grace was made to resemble them still more.

He was born, it is believed, in Wilmington, Delaware, in 1772; and was seven or eight years of age when his parents entered western Pennsylvania. Even at this early age, his father, discovering in him an unusual readiness to learn, put a Latin grammar in his hands. At about the age of sixteen, there being no academy in the west, he accompanied his father to one of the meetings of the Synod of Virginia, and was there transferred to the care of Dr. John B. Smith, then president of Hampden Sidney College. Under the ministry of that distinguished man, it is believed he was hopefully converted to God; and soon directed all his studies with a view to the gospel ministry. His close application to study had nearly broken down a constitution by no means vigorous, when by the advice of his friends and his spiritual father he took an excursion as a travelling companion with the Rev. Dr. Hill, who had been then recently licensed and appointed to itinerate for six months in the lower counties of Virginia. Dr. Hill, some years before his death, furnished the writer with the following notices respecting their journey and the subject of this notice.

"Although he had not commenced his trials for licensure, yet as he was near finishing his collegiate course, and had the ministry in view, I determined to call upon him occasionally to pray and give an exhortation at the close of my sermons —as we were not very rigidly bound to church rules and customs in those days. We set off upon our itinerations about the first of November, 1790. Among my first sermons, at an old deserted meeting-house, upon the borders of Powhatan,

I called upon him to conclude the services by exhortation and prayer. He attempted it, but was most excessively frightened; yet made out better than he thought he did. He was of a very timid and modest disposition. His fright was so great that it was many weeks before I could prevail upon him to undertake it again, except to take part in family worship. However, he did rally over it before our six months were expired. When we arrived at Colonel Gordon's we were introduced into a large company of persons, apparently gay and fashionable in their dress, and with all the stiff formality of worldly etiquette—so different from what we expected from the accounts we had received of the piety of Colonel Gordon and his family, that a very unfavorable impression was made upon both of us; so that, after we went to bed, Mr. Smith very seriously proposed that we should set off next morning and leave the place, not believing that any good could be done among a people so gay and thoughtless. But we soon became convinced, that under all this gaiety and formality, so different from what we ever saw before among professors of religion—were some of the most pious and devout Christians we ever met with. During the six or eight months we staid there, we found in his family as comfortable a home as we ever had, and a considerable and promising excitement upon religious subjects prevailed through the country." Thus was this young man trained in part for his work. We doubt whether more of this sort of schooling would be of any disadvantage in our day.

Mr. Smith returned to his college and in due time graduated. His diploma is honored with the name of a president whose memory ought to be more known and revered than it is. Dr. John B. Smith, the principal instrument of the great revival in Virginia, of 1787–89 and 1790, was one of the brightest luminaries of our church.

David Smith, on his return to his father's house, after spending the usual time there in his studies for the ministry, was licensed to preach the gospel, and in the course of the ensuing year, receiving a call to the united churches of George's Creek and the Tent, in Fayette County, was ordained and settled there. He soon after married a daughter of the Rev. Dr. Power, (his daughter Rebecca, the first child born in a minister's family west of the Allegheny mountains, in December, 1776.) Mr. Smith labored with great success in this his first field, for about four years; when he removed to the Forks of Yough, in Westmoreland County, and took charge of the congregations of Rehoboth and Roundhill, then vacant by the death of the Rev. James Finley. Here he preached till he died.

His labors were arduous and unsparing. Towards the close of his career, his talents as a preacher shone out with great power. It was commonly remarked that the mantle of his father had fallen upon him. He became also one of the editors of the Western Missionary Magazine, and was appointed by his Presbytery (of Redstone) as one of the visitants of their academy at Canonsburg. But he finished his work at a still earlier age than his father. A revival of religion had commenced in his congregations. He labored beyond his strength to meet the increased demand for his services. A new brick meeting-house (the first country brick house of worship ever built in the West) had been fitted up, in an unfinished state for the temporary reception of the crowded night meetings. Mr. Smith preached his last sermon on Friday night in the month of August, 1803, in this new house; reached home with fever and headache, and ten days after his spirit took its flight from earth. His death-bed was a scene of the triumph of faith. He received and exhorted his elders, and many of his people, as long as his strength lasted. He sent for two of the most respectable citizens of the county, who had been at variance for some time, reconciled them and made them shake hands across his dying bed. His weeping people bore his mortal remains to the grave near the Church where he preached his last sermon. On his tombstone are these words:

"Sacred to the memory of the Rev. DAVID SMITH, late pastor of the united congregations of Rehoboth and Round-hill, who departed this life August 24th, 1803, in the thirty-second year of his age. He was a sound divine, a faithful pastor and pathetic preacher. The word of God by him dispensed, will prove to many in this place a savor of life unto life, or of death unto death."

It is said that the unexpected death of this young servant of God produced a very wide-felt sensation, and was made instrumental in giving fresh impulse to that greatest of all revivals that has ever been in the West. Great expectations were entertained of his future eminence. It was at the beginning of an extensive work of grace, when he had, apparently, received himself a fresh baptism of the Holy Ghost. Most of the ministers around preached sermons to the people in reference to it. But he was immortal till his work was done. The Rev. Dr. William Wylie, his brother-in-law, succeeded him in his pastoral charge.

FORTIETH MEETING.

REHOBOTH, April 16th, 1793.—Presbytery met, &c. The Presbytery was opened by Messrs. Mahon, Marquis and Mercer, with discourses—previously appointed—sustained.

Messrs. Robert Galbraith and John Wilkins appeared before Presbytery, and proposed to produce evidence, in order to exculpate themselves from a certain crime which had been laid to their charge, and upon the account of which they had been laid under censure by the Synod,* viz.: that they had

* The following extracts—first, from the Report of the Committee of Synod in Mr. Barr's case; and next, from the action of Synod thereon—will explain this part of the Records of the Redstone Presbytery, furnished by Dr. Foote:—

"The former prosecutors or supporters of the aforesaid charges against Mr. Barr before the Presbytery of Redstone, viz.: Messrs. John Wilkins, Robert Galbraith, and George Wallace, Senior, being called upon collectively and severally, (being present,) entirely declined, and confessed themselves to be influenced by fraudulent motives, in their prosecution of Mr. Barr: and Presbytery finding that they were authorized by Synod to take evidence, and determine respecting the propriety of said censure, proceeded to hear and examine such witnesses.

The Rev. James Finley being solemnly called upon to declare the truth, saith, That being present, he does not remember to have heard either Robert Galbraith or John Wilkins express anything to the Committee of Synod met at Pittsburg, signifying their design of defrauding Mr. Barr of his salary—nor does he think that any such idea, as is expressed in the minutes of the Committee of Synod, in which said gentlemen are represented as having been influenced by a fraudulent design against Mr. Barr, was held forth by them: that he does not remember that said gentlemen were called upon, collectively or individually, to appear as prosecutors against Mr. Barr; but that the general question being put by the Com-

---

do decline, to have any hand, either collectively or severally, now to support these charges against Mr. Barr. The same gentlemen aforesaid declared before the Committee, that they would never have exhibited any charges against Mr. Barr, had they not been afraid, that if Mr. Barr left them, without blame, that some arrearages due to Mr. Barr would still continue a burden upon the congregation, or, in their own words, 'be saddled upon the congregation.' The Committee adjourned with prayer."

Upon this part of the Report of the Committee, the action of the Synod was as follows: —

"Upon a review of the conduct of Mr. Barr's accusers in Pittsburg, the Synod are of opinion, that John Wilkins, Robert Galbraith, and George Wallace, Esq., having acted in a manner unbecoming men and Christians, in the prosecution of Mr. Barr, as appears from their own confession of the motives which prevailed with them to prosecute Mr. Barr, and also in deceptions imposed by them upon the Presbytery of Redstone, should not enjoy the privileges of the church in our communion, until they testify repentance for their unworthy conduct—and receive a public rebuke for the same, before the church, by a regular minister, who shall be appointed by the Presbytery of Redstone for that purpose."

mittee, "Who will come forward and prosecute Mr. Barr?" they declared their willingness to appear before them in the same manner that they had formerly done before the Presbytery of Redstone.

William Dunning being solemnly called upon to declare the truth, saith, That being present the whole time that the Committee of Synod sat at Pittsburg, on Mr. Barr's affair, he did not hear either Mr. Galbraith or Mr. Wilkins express any design of defrauding the Rev. Samuel Barr of his salary, before said Committee: that neither of said gentlemen were present, after the first day that the Committee of Synod sat: that said gentlemen were not called upon, collectively or severally, to appear as prosecutors against Mr. Barr — but that the general question being put, "Who will come forward and prosecute Mr. Barr?" they declared their willingness to appear before them, in the same manner that they had formerly done before the Presbytery of Redstone.

The Presbytery, after fully hearing the matter, and examining the witnesses that were produced, and from the knowledge that they have of the conduct of Messrs. Galbraith and Wilkins throughout the whole of this affair — do judge that they ought not any longer to be held under censure, as it does not appear that they have been guilty of the crimes alleged against them.

Mr. Swan accepted the call to Long Run and Sewickly — their Commissioner requested, in behalf of said congregations, his ordination, as soon as convenient.

The congregation of Pittsburg having applied to Presbytery for Mr. Mahon's ordination — the Presbytery, after maturely deliberating upon the matter, and finding that our Directory requires that ordination and instalment should always go together — and Mr. Mahon having declared that he is not, as yet, clear for being installed as the pastor of that congregation — do judge, that they cannot regularly proceed to his ordination at present; but appoint him to supply at Pittsburg as usual.

Congregations satisfied with the care and diligence of their respective pastors. Mr. Swan — to prepare a discourse on Romans iii. 31 — by next meeting — as a part of trial for ordination, at which time, if the way be clear, Mr. M'Millan to preach the ordination sermon; and Mr. Patterson to preside, and give the charge.

The Presbytery proceeded to a reconsideration of the propriety of appointing Canonsburg the seat of the seminary of learning, which they are appointed to superintend; and agreed to confirm their former minute respecting Canonsburg Academy, with the following addition, viz.: that if it should appear, at a future day, most conducive to the good of the church, that another seminary of the like nature should be erected in our bounds, we will not oppose a division of the funds.

Upon inquiry it appeared that the members of Presbytery have made considerable progress in raising contributions, to be put into the fund, for the education of poor and pious youths for the gospel ministry.

Mr. Mercer — a Presbyterial Exercise — sustained. Mr. Marquis—examined on Natural Philosophy—sustained. Mr. Mercer and Mr. Marquis—examined on Divinity—sustained.

"The Presbytery having received sufficient testimonials," &c., (see form,) Messrs. Marquis and Mercer were licensed to preach the gospel, and supplies over almost the entire field assigned to them.

Agreeably to a recommendation of the General Assembly, Presbytery proceeded to consider whether it would be proper to extend the time to be spent by young men, in the study of Divinity to three years, at least, before they be taken on trials for the ministry, and unanimously agreed that it would not be proper — and at the same time declared their entire satisfaction with the constitution of our church on that head.

The Rev. Messrs. James Power, Jacob Jennings and James Hughes were appointed Commissioners to the next General Assembly.

The Presbytery agreed to request Synod, at their next meeting, to erect the Rev. John Clark, John M'Millan, Thaddeus Dod, Joseph Patterson, James Hughes and John Brice, together with the churches on the west side of the Monongahela, into a separate Presbytery, to be known by the name of the Presbytery of Ohio. Adjourned to meet at Long Run, on the third Tuesday of October. Concluded with prayer.

FORTY-FIRST MEETING.

LONG RUN, (51) October 15th, 1793.—Presbytery met, &c. The Presbytery find that the Rev. Thaddeus Dod was

---

(51) LONG RUN was organized nearly, if not quite, as early as the Presbytery of Redstone. It remained vacant, and was supplied by the Presbytery for several years, till, in 1793, it united with Sewickly in calling the Rev. William Swan to become their pastor, who was ordained and installed in that office October 16th of that year. He continued their pastor till October 18th, 1818, when he resigned this united charge — but in the following summer was again installed pastor of Long Run alone, and continued in this relation, till, at his request, it was dissolved April 17th, 1822. The church continued vacant till April 20th, 1825, when the Rev. A. M'Candless was ordained and installed pastor of Long Run and M'Keesport united. This relation continued till April 8th, 1845, when Mr. M'Candless resigned this charge. He was succeeded by the Rev. William D. Moore, who was ordained and installed pastor of Long Run in June, 1845. In September, 1849, this congregation again became vacant, when, for a short time, the Rev. Mr. Shermer became their pastor, in 1851. In the ensuing year, the Rev. John A. Mearne accepted a call, and was ordained and installed their pastor, on the 19th of October, 1852. Number of communicants reported, in 1854 — 195.

This church has seen more prosperous days, especially in 1804, and for some years afterwards, when the arm of the Lord was made bare for the salvation of multitudes. Like most of the early churches, it has been a nursery, whence not only many have been transplanted to heaven — but many, also, have gone out to strengthen new churches in the West. This is an honor which the Lord has conferred upon many of our early churches, and it ought to cheer and revive them, and "strengthen the things that are ready to die."

As this congregation was long united with SEWICKLY, we will briefly removed by death, on the 20th of May last. Presbytery was opened by Mr. William Swan — sermon from Romans iii. 31 — sustained, as part of trials for ordination.

---

sketch the history of the latter also. Sewickly is supposed to have been organized by the Rev. Dr. Power, as early as 1776. He continued the pastor, in connection with Mount Pleasant, till August 22d, 1787, when he resigned the pastoral charge of Sewickly, which continued vacant until, in union with Long Run, it became the pastoral charge of the Rev. William Swan, October 16th, 1793,* as above stated. It again became vacant October 18th, 1818. During the previous time, especially in 1804, both the churches were visited with a remarkable revival of religion, of which we have spoken above. In January, 1821, the congregation having united with Mount Pleasant, presented a call to the Rev. A. O. Patterson, D.D., who was ordained and installed at Sewickly, April 18th, 1821. Dr. Patterson was dismissed October 8th, 1834.

These churches having dissolved their connection, from a persuasion that each of them was now able to support a pastor — Sewickly, in April, 1836, gave a call to the Rev. William Annan, who was installed their pastor in June following. From the weak and debilitated state of his health, Mr. Annan was compelled to resign this pastoral charge in April, 1838. In December, 1839, the Rev. J. B. M'Kee was installed pastor, and continued till April, 1842. After a short period, the Rev. Richard Graham became the pastor, and continued till 1850. In 1852,

* The following is a copy of the subscription paper in Sewickly, for the support of Mr. Swan, and may serve as a sample of many others before and after:

"We, the subscribers, members of Sewickly congregation, do separately bind ourselves to pay, annually, the sums annexed to our names respectively, unto the Rev. William Swan, in consideration of our receiving one-half of his stated labors, during his continuance as minister of the gospel in this congregation. One-half of our subscription to be paid in cash, and the other half in produce, at the following rates, viz.: — Wheat at four shillings per bushel, rye at three shillings per bushel, and corn at two shillings and sixpence per bushel — to be delivered at such place or places, within the bounds of the congregation, as said minister, or a treasurer chosen by the people, may appoint. Witness our hands, this 17th day of August, 1792." — *Records*, p. 73.

We have seen a somewhat similar subscription paper of the congregation of Fairfield, dated March 14th, 1789, the close of which is in these words:

"Said subscription to be paid in the following manner, viz.: either in money or grain, at the following rates: — Wheat at four shillings the bushel, rye or corn at two shillings and sixpence per bushel — said sums to become due quarterly, and paid accordingly, if required, into the hands of any person or persons who shall be appointed by said congregation to receive the same. And said sums to be sued for as lawful debts, if payment neglected."

Two calls to Mr. David Smith — from George's Creek and Union, and from Buffalo — put into his hands for his consideration. Three calls to Mr. Marquis — from Cross Creek, from Ebenezer and Bethel on Blue Lick, and from Ten-mile — put into his hands for his consideration. A call to Mr. Mercer from Mingo Creek and Horse-shoe — transmitted to him through the hands of Mr. M'Millan, he being absent.

Mr. Swan was ordained. "The Presbytery did, by fasting and prayer, with the imposition of the hands of Presbytery," set him apart to the holy office of the gospel ministry. Mr. M'Millan preached on the occasion, from Isaiah lxii. 6, 7, and presided — and Mr. Finley gave the charge. Mr. S. then took his seat as a member.

Mr. Moore, a licentiate under the care of the Bristol Association of Massachusetts, being present, and expressing a desire to itinerate for some time in our bounds; upon his producing sufficient testimonials of his regular licensure and good standing in the church, the Presbytery agreed to employ him, and accordingly appointed him as supply over a large portion of their vacancies, which are mentioned. Messrs. Smith and Marquis, also — the former sent as far as Tygart's Valley, Middletown, (now Fairmount,) and Harrison County — all in Virginia.

An appeal from the judgment of the Session of Bethel was laid before Presbytery, wherein David Tidball stands convicted of incestuous conduct. The Presbytery, after hearing the testimony which was before the Session, and after maturely deliberating upon the matter, are of opinion, that, on

---

the Rev. Cyrus Riggs, the present pastor, received and accepted a call and was installed soon after.

Some years ago, the congregation of West Newton applied for and obtained a separate organization. This, though, perhaps, a wise and necessary measure, has greatly weakened Sewickly, which had already suffered much from emigration. It still struggles on, however, to sustain the ordinances of the gospel, and it is hoped will yet see more prosperous days, and the return of those gracious seasons of which their fathers have told them.

account of the apparent prejudices of the witnesses, and other concurring circumstances, the testimony was not sufficient to ground that judgment upon — and therefore agree that said judgment be set aside.

The Treasurer reported that he had received as follows—for support of Missionaries.

	£	s	d		£	s	d
From Dunlap's Creek	3	8	2	From Monteur's	2	0	0
" Muddy Creek	2	15	9	" Raccoon	2	7	0
" Bethel	2	9	6	" Unity and Salem	4	16	11
" Pigeon Creek	4	3	0	" Mount Pleasant	4	0	0
" Chartiers	3	16	3	" Laurel Hill	3	15	0

Total, £33 11*s* 7*d*.

For the payment of which to the commissioners of Synod he produced their receipt.

The Presbytery find that Mr. Cooly's credentials have been laid before the General Assembly at their last meeting, and were judged by them to be forged, and consequently that he ought not to be received as a minister in good standing with their body.

A reference from the session of Unity, respecting a charge exhibited before that session by Charles M'Right holding forth that a certain Hugh Bean had acted contrary to an oath taken by him, to abide by the verdict of men in a case referred to them by said Bean and M'Right, and also that Hugh Bean had said that Charles M'Right had acknowledged himself to be the father of Hugh Bean's daughter's child, which acknowledgment Charles M'Right denies. And having attended to the testimony produced, and taken all the light which they could obtain, are of opinion that Hugh Bean cannot be admitted to distinguishing privileges in our church, until he acknowledge his wrong in swearing to abide by the judgment of arbitrators, not knowing but that that judgment might involve him in sin, and for his not using every means in his power to fulfil the obligations of said oath.

The Presbytery are also of opinion that the testimony produced by Hugh Bean has exculpated him so far of the fact alleged against him in the latter charge, that they do not think him liable to any censure upon the account thereof. The Presbytery ordered Mr. M'Pherrin to read this judgment publicly in the congregation, upon Hugh Bean's compliance therewith. Dr. Lindley and Moses Coe — leave of absence. James Christy came before Presbytery, and requested a reconsideration of a former judgment of Presbytery whereby he looks upon himself to be aggrieved. The Presbytery agreed to reconsider said judgment at their next meeting. Mr. Mahon, having made application for ordination, and having professed a willingness to be installed as pastor of Pittsburg congregation, Presbytery proceeded, agreeably to our constitution, to converse with him upon his acquaintance with experimental religion, and proposed to him several cases of conscience; but did not receive such satisfaction as would induce them to proceed to his ordination at present. But if at any other time he shall think himself able to give further light upon these matters, Presbytery shall be ready to receive it. Mr. S. Mahon requested to be dismissed, and his request was granted. Robert Dickey having given offence to the session of Unity congregation by going to hear a certain Mr. Dun, a preacher of immoral character, and said session and Robert Dickey having different sentiments concerning the satisfaction to be given for said offence, both parties appeared before Presbytery, and submitted the whole affair to their decision. Presbytery, having heard the parties, and taken all the light which they could obtain, are of opinion that Robert Dickey acted imprudently in going to hear Mr. Dun, and that he ought to acknowledge his fault in so doing before he is admitted to the distinguishing privileges of the church. Ordered that the above judgment be read in the presence of Unity congregation, in case of Robert Dickey's compliance therewith.

Mr. Power appointed Treasurer of Redstone Presbytery. The Presbytery were informed, by Mr. John Baird, that

Mount Pleasant congregation had arranged with Mr. Power for all his time as their pastor; they promising yearly a salary of £120 from 1st of August, 1792. Mr. M'Pherrin chosen Stated Clerk. Synod having appointed the 2d Thursday in November to be a day of solemn fasting and prayer throughout their churches, to supplicate Almighty God to pour out his holy Spirit on our assemblies and revive religion in our land, Presbytery agreed to ratify the appointment of Synod, and recommend the careful observance of the day in the manner specified by Synod to all the congregations under their care.

The Presbytery agreed that the candidates under their care shall have liberty to declare their acceptance of any of the calls now in their hands before either of the Presbyteries of Ohio or Redstone; and further appoint Messrs. James Finley and James Power, or either of them, to furnish any of the candidates with a dismission, should they apply; and that Mr. Mercer shall have his appointments made out by the Presbytery of Ohio, if he thinks fit, until our next spring meeting. Presbytery, finding that the Synod, at their last meeting, did erect the Rev. Messrs. John Clark, John M'Millan, Joseph Patterson, James Hughes, and John Brice, into a separate Presbytery, to be known by the name of the Presbytery of Ohio, they are therefore dismissed from this Presbytery. Presbytery adjourned to meet at Mount Pleasant the 4th Tuesday of December next. Concluded with prayer.

Thus ended the Old Presbytery of Redstone.

APPENDIX

TO THE RECORDS.

There are some things that, perhaps, may not be without interest, which we have gathered from the Records, and which may be distinctly noticed here.

1. The ruling elders whose names appear in the minutes were from all parts of the wide bounds of the Presbytery. They were generally a noble set of men. The following is a list of their names; the figure attached denoting the number of times they represented their churches in the Presbytery:—

James Edgar, 9. Patrick Scott, 6. Patrick M'Cullough, 6. John Shields, 6. James Dinsmore, 5. Joseph Coe, 5. James Brice, 5. William M'Comb, 4. Hugh Scott, 4. John Neil, 4. Demas Lindley, 4. William Smilie, 4. John Allen, 4. Thomas Bracken, 3. Samuel Finley, 3. John Griffin, 3. John Baird, 3. Edward Cook, 2. John Power, 2. John Parker, 2. Andrew Frazer, 2. James Kirkpatrick, 2. Thomas Marquis, 2. John Cowan, 2. John M'Dowell, 2. Daniel Extell, 2. John Perry, 2. Josiah Scott, 2. William M'Farland, 2. George Shields, 2. Æneas M'Allister, 2. Jacob Cook, 2. Alexander M'Clure, 2. Samuel M'Clure, 2. James Erwin, 2. John Jack, 2. John Moore, 2. William Waddel, 2. John Gaston, William Wightman, Daniel Reeder, John Thompson, John Wright, Thomas Wilson, John Fulton, Joseph Pierce, John Johnston, John Shanon, Joseph Vance, Moses Latta, George Marquis, James Bradford, John Rob, Hugh Morton, Samuel Sorels, Robert Adams, John Hopkins, Stephen Cook, James Wilson, William Steel, James Wilkin, Robert M'Comb, Samuel Hollidy, James Ewing, John Vance, James Barr, Joseph Caldwell, William M'Candless, James Findley, William Sloan, James M'Clain, Alexander M'Candless, John Guthrie, Alexander Wright, James M'Kee, Samuel Riddel, James Pair, Thomas Hall, John Hamilton, William Gordon, John Steel, John M'Pherrin, Thomas Marshal, Alexander Baily, William Brown, Thomas Armstrong, Peter Wallace, Robert

Moore, James Allison, Joseph Thorn, John Danaughy, George M'Cullough, Joseph Price, John Travers, Daniel Henricks, each of them, 1.

2. A list of the Exegeses given by the Presbytery till 1793:—

James Hughes—An sit originale peccatum?

John Brice—An mortuorum resurrectio erit?

Joseph Patterson—Whether miracles are evidence of a divine mission; and what miracles do prove such mission?

John M'Gready—An sit concursus Dei cum omnibus Hominum actionibus?

John M'Pherrin—Num Christus, qua Mediator, adorandus sit?

Samuel Porter—An lapsus Adami, omnibus ejus posteris, naturali generatione ab eo oriundis imputatur?

Robert Marshall—An constat fidei essentia in persuasione, quod remissa nobis peccata, et nostrum Christus sit?

George Hill—Quid sit discrimen inter fœdera gratiæ et operum?

Mr. Hanna—In quo constat essentia fidei salvivica?

William Swan—An gratia convertens sit irresistibilis?

David Smith—Quomodo miracula probant Scripturas sacras esse divinas?

Thomas Marquis—An reatus peccati Adami omnibus suis posteris, naturali generatione ab eo oriundis, imputatur?

Boyd Mercer—An decreta Dei conditionata, vel absoluta sint?

3. Messrs. Hughes and Brice were licensed April 16th, 1788; M'Gready and Patterson, Aug. 13th, 1788; Mr. M'Pherrin, August 20th, 1789; Mr. Porter, November 12th, 1789; Mr. Marshall, April 23d, 1790; Messrs. Swan and Hill, December 22d, 1791; Mr. D. Smith, November 14th, 1792; Messrs. Marquis and Mercer, April 19th, 1793.

4. The following is a list of the places for which supplies were furnished. A few of them soon disappear from the minutes, either because they obtained settled pastors, or were merged into other places. Some of them do not appear till towards the close of the old Presbytery. We give them in the order of time in which they are found on the Records:—

"Rehoboth, Roundhill, Tyrone, Muddy Creek, Ohio Court-House, George's Creek, South Fork of Ten-Mile, Short Creek, Unity, Robinson's Run, Sewickly, Pittsburg, Long Run, Three Springs, Parkinson's Mill, Bullock Pens, Pike Run, Jackson's Fort, Donegal, Brush Run, Monteur's Run, Three Ridges, Turtle Creek, Mill Creek, Beaver Dam, King's Creek, Forks of Cheat, Forks of Wheeling, Potatoe Garden, Mingo Creek, Poke Run, Horse-shoe Bottom, Lower Buffalo, Fairfield, Sandy Creek, Salem, Bethel on Blacklick, Ebenezer on Blacklick, Morgantown, Crab Orchard, Raccoon, White Thorn, Washington, Dunlap's

Creek, (always written Delap's Creek,) Ebenezer on Puckety, Randolph, Patterson's Creek, Hollidy's Cove, Mouth of Raccoon, Clarksburg, Middletown, Puckety, Campbell's Tent, Stony Creek, Stonecoal Fork, Tygart's Valley." These places are found over a vast range of country. Several of them are no longer known by their old names.

5. One peculiarity in regard to the old Records is, that there is no account of Sessional Records or Statistical Reports. The truth is, that in general, no records were kept. Session-books were, with hardly an exception, not to be found. In some cases, Sessions appear to have made some minutes and taken testimony in judicial proceedings; but they have generally been lost or destroyed. And, for want of statistical Reports, it is difficult to ascertain the number of communicants in the several churches when they were organised, and for many years after.

6. The judicial cases which came before the old Presbytery appear to have been eleven in all; viz.: (1) The charges of John Matson against the Rev. James Dunlap — 2d meeting. (2) Robert Hall's complaint against session of Mount Pleasant—4th and 19th meetings. (3) Henry Taylor's appeal from session of Chartiers in respect to promiscuous dancing—5th, 9th, and 12th meetings. (4) A reference from the session of Dunlap's Creek in the case of Armstrong Porter—14th meeting. (5) The case of George Latimer and Deborah Ross; Mount Pleasant session—15th meeting. (6) The case of John Coleman—not issued —19th meeting. (7) An appeal of Hugh Stirling from session of Bethel —21st meeting. (8) Mr. Barr's case and that of the session of Pittsburg—25th meeting. (9) A reference from session of Lebanon, in the case of John Barnet—31st meeting. (10) A reference from the session of Congruity, in the case of James Christy and Rebecca Gordon—38th meeting. (11) A reference from session of Unity, in the case of Robert Dicky—41st meeting. The several judges appear to us to evince great deliberation, wisdom, and discrimination. We recommend them as models. There seems to be a parental kindness and tenderness, mingled with just severity, where it was necessary. They seem never to have forgotten that discipline is for edification, and not destruction. It was not in the summary style of our times; when the decision often is "sustained or not sustained," or "sustained in part." Great injustice may be done in this hasty way. Let us return to "the good old paths."

7. The congregations in Western Pennsylvania, it is believed, were much assisted in their efforts to erect houses of worship, by their brethren east of the mountains. It cannot now be ascertained to what extent this aid was received. The proper vouchers are, perhaps, almost

entirely lost. So little now is known on this subject, that many ignorantly suppose that our forefathers neither sought nor received such aid; and when called upon now to assist, by their contributions, the noble Church Extension enterprise of our day, close their hearts and their hands against all such appeals, by referring to the way they suppose our early settlers got along; and ask, in a tone that shows they regard the question as settling the point, "Why cannot people now do as our fathers did?" It would not be difficult to answer the question, were the facts of the case as they assume. But it turns out by a few isolated cases, that have been accidentally preserved from oblivion, that it is highly probable most of our early churches were assisted by their eastern friends in this very work.

For instance, from the Records, in the case of Mr. Barr, it is evident that he had collected a considerable sum of money in New York and Philadelphia, to aid the congregation of Pittsburg in the erection of their second house of worship.

And the following copy of a receipt, found on a blank leaf of an old skeleton of one of Mr. Smith's sermons, will show that the people of Cross Creek and Upper Buffalo received similar aid:—

"October, 17th, 1783.—Received of Mr. Smith, ten pounds, fifteen shillings, of the money which he collected in Philadelphia, for the use of erecting houses of worship in these congregations—I say, received by me. WM. SMILEY."

Is it not highly probable that all the other ministers made similar collections, to aid their people? It may be impossible now to find any similar receipt, like the above. But we have not a doubt, that if all the cases could be known, our people, in view of their own early history, would be left without all excuse—as to contributing liberally to aid our new, struggling Western churches.

These remarks are, perhaps, equally applicable to the churches east of the mountains, and in the Cumberland Valley and Valley of Virginia. And if we go back to a still earlier period, were not most of our oldest congregations in Philadelphia, New-Jersey, Delaware, and Maryland, assisted by contributions from Scotland and Ireland? This whole subject merits further investigation; and if the results would furnish fresh incentives to the liberality of our churches towards that most neglected department of religious benevolence, they would amply reward the labor of such investigation.

THE END.

www.ingramcontent.com/pod-product-compliance
Lightning Source LLC
LaVergne TN
LVHW020930110826
845150LV00004B/820

* 9 7 8 1 4 2 5 5 5 3 3 4 0 *